Measuring Ego Development

Second Edition

The LEA Series in
Personality and Clinical Psychology
Irving B. Weiner, Editor

Measuring Ego Development

Second Edition

Lê Xuân Hy
George Mason University, Fairfax, Virginia
Center for Multicultural Human Services,
Falls Church, Virginia

Jane Loevinger
Washington University, St. Louis

LEA LAWRENCE ERLBAUM ASSOCIATES, PUBLISHERS
1996   Mahwah, New Jersey

Lawrence Erlbaum Associates, Inc., Publishers
10 Industrial Avenue
Mahwah, New Jersey 07430

Cover design by Gail Silverman

Library of Congress Cataloging-in-Publication Data

Hy, Lê Xuân.
    Measuring ego development / Lê Xuân Hy, Jane Loevinger.
        p.   cm.
    Loevinger's name appears first on the earlier edition.
    ISBN 0-8058-2060-4 (c : alk. paper).
    1. Sentence Completion Test. I. Loevinger, Jane. II. Title.
BF698.8.S35H9 1996
155.2′83—dc20   96-6008
                                                        CIP

Printed in the United States of America
10 9 8 7 6 5 4 3 2 1

Contents

Foreword

Part I of this volume introduces the concept of ego development and the method proposed for its measurement; it includes instructions for implementing the method and self-training exercises for raters. Part II features an item-by-item scoring manual for the 36 items currently in use (Form 81).

The forthcoming companion volume, *Technical Foundations for Measuring Ego Development*, will give technical details, including the construction of the first edition and the methods employed in its current revision, sources of subjects, and the reliability and validation of the test, including its earlier versions.

Preface

The method for scoring sentence completions presented in this manual was originally evolved for a study of women and adolescent girls, and the first edition of the manual (1970) claimed no more. By the time it was published, however, the method had already come into use in studies of men and boys. Since then, it has been used with widely varying samples, and the test has been translated into several other languages. The wide adoption testifies to the need for such a test.

The present revision of the 1970 manual incorporates three major improvements: It is based on data from and is intended for use with both males and females; its format is easier to use, according to students; the examples cited reflect current public attitudes.

The choice of ego development as the variable to measure was not arbitrary or accidental. It is the master trait (though not what is usually called a "trait"), second only to intelligence, as a kind of "hidden hand." That is to say, no matter what a psychologist sets out to measure with a test, intelligence plays a big part in the score; next to intelligence, the variable called ego level appears to be a major determinant in measurable individual differences. There are other ways of describing it and other modes of access to it, although the manual was never seen as just another psychometric device for clinicians and researchers. Our aim in constructing the scoring manual was also to deepen knowledge of personality. Correspondingly, those who master the scoring method acquire more than just another psychometric technique; the tacit component of scoring is the same thing as knowledge of ego development. An abstract knowledge of the construct cannot duplicate the insights encoded in the scoring method.

Another volume (Loevinger, 1976) has shown some of the relations of the concept of ego development to other similar conceptions, such as Kohlberg's (1964) moralization of judgment, C. Sullivan, M. Q. Grant, and J. D. Grant's (1957) interpersonal integration, Isaac's (1956) interpersonal relatability, Perry's (1970) intellectual-ethical development, and others. In contrast to those approaches, focused primarily on single aspects, definition of ego level in terms of all of its manifestations can be viewed as a strength of the method. At the same time, it is an obstacle to the inexperienced rater or to any rater who scores by rote. The number of aspects to be kept in mind is almost impossibly large. Fortunately, most raters find themselves sufficiently attuned to the conception to discover many clues within themselves. At the same time, if intuition sufficed, our labors would have been unnecessary. Scoring without the manual is much less reliable and valid than scoring with the manual.

A surprising number of sheer clerical errors occur during scoring, even when conscientious professional psychologists are the raters. Hence we recommend working in teams of no fewer than two, at least until the technique is thoroughly familiar, and checking every step even after that. Research work should depend on the consensus of two or more raters if possible; exceptions should only be made with raters of demonstrated competence.

The test is intended for group administration. Small differences in instructions and conditions have occurred during our many studies, in some cases on purpose, and they do not seem to be important. (However, major differences in instructions are, in effect, a new and different test.) Most subjects spend about 20 or 30 minutes completing the form. An experienced rater takes about 20 minutes scoring a protocol.

To master the scoring system takes from 2 to 3 weeks of study, of course not full time, if the rater immerses him or herself in one or two items per day. We strongly recommend that anyone who wishes to use the test follow exactly the training program outlined in chapters 5 and 6 and Appendixes A and B. As early studies have shown, the scoring system can be mastered by these exercises. There have been no formal tests of persons trying to score without following the exercises, or without using the manual, and a person who does so has no right to claim to be using this method. Most raters can profit by checking some of their scoring with an experienced rater if one is available. Failing that, two people can criticize each other, which is, after all, the method originally used.

About a year's graduate work in psychology or its equivalent in technical training is a desirable prerequisite for manual users. The corresponding intellectual level is indispensable. No amount of intuition or sensibility can substitute for a disciplined knowledge, and no amount of technical training can make a first-class rater out of someone whose personal limitations bar him or her from free access to intuition and sensibility. At the same time, a highly trained clinician or a person who insists on deep interpretation of every sign may be grossly misled in this context. Sentence completions are not read for deep, hidden, or unconscious meanings. The meaning to be scored is the one that the subject recognizes as the one he or she meant.

The logic of ego theory dictates that only those with a relatively high ego level can become good raters of high level protocols. The chief access to a person's ego level is precisely that it limits what he or she can conceive and perceive; that limitation holds for raters as well as subjects. Fortunately, the manual and experience do extend a person's range. In general, groups such as professional psychologists will have people whose scores on the Sentence Completion Test (SCT) will range from the Self-aware Level through the Autonomous Level, with most of them probably at the Conscientious or Individualistic Levels. (These remarks are based on a number of small studies drawing on such subjects.) Theoretically, persons at the Self-aware Level are not first-rate raters, at least for the highest levels; however, there are no data on that point.

In summary, the personal qualifications for raters are technical training, its corresponding intellectual level, and a capacity for introspection, together with some inner freedom or access to intuition. More of one compensates for less of another in only a limited way; indeed, an overrefined conscience can be a handicap. Unfortunately, except for the technical training, which is not strictly necessary, these are qualities that one cannot judge in oneself.

ACKNOWLEDGMENTS

We thank the following research workers who have generously permitted us to use their data in constructing this revised manual: Sarah Beaton, Dorothy Billington, Howard Chandler, Michael D'Andrea, Diane Novy, David Patterson, Dane VerMerris, and George Vaillant.

—*Lê Xuân Hy*
—*Jane Loevinger*

INTRODUCTION AND
INSTRUCTIONS TO USERS

CHAPTER ONE

The Concept of Ego Development

The concept of *ego development* has roots in ancient Greek, Hebrew, and Hindu cultures.[1] Contrary to common belief, it did not originate with Freud or with later psychoanalysts. Psychoanalysis, in fact, originated in part as a rebellion against 19th-century ego psychology. Freud (1926/1959) consciously avoided using the term *ego*; he preferred words chosen from common speech to those of Latin origin, a preference that was ignored by his translators.

Once granted that the original sources were not written in English, it follows that one must look under other terms, the I (*das Ich*), the me (*le moi*), the self, and so on, to trace the relevant literature. There have been many similar or related conceptions, variously termed *moral development* (Kohlberg, 1964), *character development* (Peck & Havighurst, 1960), *interpersonal relatability* (Isaacs, 1956), *cognitive complexity* (Harvey, Hunt, & Schroder, 1961), and *interpersonal integration* (C. Sullivan et al., 1957). Many of the foregoing authors acknowledged as sources H. S. Sullivan's (1953) *Interpersonal Theory of Psychiatry* and Piaget's (1932) *Moral Judgment of the Child*. Although the definitions of the various stages and their sequence are not identical from author to author, there are many similarities, too many to be considered independent phenomena (Loevinger, 1976).

Interest in all aspects of development was stimulated at the end of the 19th century by the impact of Darwin's theory of evolution. For this and other reasons, in the early 20th century a child study movement in the United States led to the founding of child welfare institutes and incorporation of the topic of child development in texts and college curricula. The standard approaches to child development, at least in the past, tended to blur the topic of ego development. Children's growth was studied in terms of chronology, taking in order the behaviors characteristic of average and not-so-average children of each successive age.

Such atheoretical approaches have the weakness that all kinds of development are occurring together. Observation by itself will never yield a concept such as ego development nor distinguish signs of ego development from signs of intellectual development, of psychosexual development, or even of adjustment. Ego development is an abstraction, and the essence of science is that abstract ideas guide observations, and observations in turn alter abstract ideas.

A long-standing issue in the study of ego development is whether the ego is derived from and more or less explained in terms of instinctual drives, as Freud and many of his followers believed in the early years of psychoanalysis. That issue separated Freud and Adler in 1911. Adler maintained that the drives were largely subordinate to the ego and the ego strove spontaneously to develop. Freud countered that to adopt Adler's view would be to give up the hard-won gains of psychoanalytic insights, but many of his followers believed that the two views could be reconciled. Some years later, Freud returned to the topic of ego development and made major theoretical contributions whose importance is not always recognized either by psychoanalysts or by their opponents (Loevinger, 1966, 1987). At the same time, some psychoanalysts and some behaviorists found common ground in the instinct-derivative view of ego development. Although that remains a major theoretical issue, it does not bear directly on the enterprise of this book.

EGO AS FRAME OF REFERENCE

A second theoretical issue, one more closely related to the present enterprise, is whether ego development is best characterized as a gradual evolutionary process or as a set of discrete stages, with distinct jumps from one stage to the next. There are problems either way.

One of Adler's best-known concepts is "style of life," which at various times he equated with self or ego, the unity

---

[1]The topics of this chapter are discussed more fully in Loevinger (1976).

TABLE 1.1
Some Characteristics of Levels of Ego Development

Level	Code	Characteristics		
		Impulse Control	Interpersonal Mode	Conscious Preoccupations
Impulsive	E2 (I-2)	Impulsive	Egocentric, dependent	Bodily feelings
Self-Protective	E3 (Delta)	Opportunistic	Manipulative, wary	"Trouble," control
Conformist	E4 (I-3)	Respect for rules	Cooperative, loyal	Appearances, behavior
Self-Aware	E5 (I-3/4)	Exceptions allowable	Helpful, self-aware	Feelings, problems, adjustment
Conscientious	E6 (I-4)	Self-evaluated standards, self-critical	Intense, responsible	Motives, traits, achievements
Individualistic	E7 (I-4/5)	Tolerant	Mutual	Individuality, development, roles
Autonomous	E8 (I-5)	Coping with conflict	Interdependent	Self-fulfillment, psychological causation
Integrated	E9 (I-6)		Cherishing individuality	Identity

Note. The code for the previous version used I-levels and Delta; the current code uses E-levels. Adapted from Loevinger (1976, 1987).

of personality, individuality, the method of facing problems, opinion about oneself and the problems of life, and the whole attitude toward life (H. Ansbacher & R. Ansbacher, 1956, p. 174). Seemingly, according to Adler, those terms were meant to be different ways of describing a single thing or function. That is what is here called the *ego.* That view contrasts with that found in some psychoanalytic writings, where the ego is spoken of as a collection of different functions, with its "synthetic function" just one among many. Adler's view was elaborated in somewhat different style by H. S. Sullivan (1953), who preferred the term *self-system.*

The ego is remarkable for its relative stability; it changes slowly. Accounting for this stability is not always recognized as a major theoretical problem. Simply calling the ego a structure, as some psychoanalytic theorists do, and then adding that structures are, by definition, relatively stable is not a solution.

H. S. Sullivan (1953) formulated a theory of ego stability in terms of *anxiety gating*: A major purpose of the self-system is to avoid or minimize anxiety. A person tends to recognize only what is in accord with his or her already existing self-system, that is, his or her frame of reference. Discordant observations are anxiety producing, and they are consequently avoided by selective inattention. (Fingarette, 1963, preferred to say that the failure to integrate an observation into one's current frame of reference is what anxiety is, rather than the cause of an emotion called anxiety. Anxiety, to Fingarette, was meaninglessness.)

Thus, the search for coherent meanings in experience is the essence of the ego or of ego functioning, rather than just one among many ego functions. The ego maintains its stability, its identity, and its coherence by selectively gating out observations inconsistent with its current state—granting that one person's coherence is another person's gibberish. This assumption is the theoretical foundation for the use of sentence completions and other projective techniques to measure ego development. Projective techniques call on subjects to project their own frame of reference on the test material. In contrast, objective tests constrain subjects' responses within the test constructor's frame of reference.

Thus, the issue of ego stability is illuminated by Sullivan's theory of ego (self-system, he would say) coherence; the issue of how the ego develops remains, and is perhaps made even more difficult. Sullivan called on other aspects of development, including the drives, as impetus for renewed development. In psychoanalytic theory, *mastery* becomes a key term in accounting for development, although not exactly in Adler's terms (Loevinger, 1976).

If coherence is the hallmark of ego stability, then how does one identify the stable configurations? A working list of ego stages is presented in Table 1.1. This list is almost the same as the version used in the 1970 edition of this manual. However, it differs from other authors' lists of stages, but there are large overlaps. So far it has proved impossible to show by research that some configurations called *stages* are in any demonstrable way different from patterns that have been called *transitions* between stages. In some cases, what were originally seen as transitions are now labeled as stages. For methodological reasons that are detailed shortly, no quick solution to this problem seems likely.

STAGES

One of the newborn's earliest tasks is to construct for him or herself a stable world of objects. Constructing the world of objects and constructing the self are correlative. Many authors, especially many psychoanalytic theorists, refer to this period alone as ego development, but that leaves no distinctive term for the remaining stages that are the topic of our inquiry. This stage of ego formation is called the *first stage* and is acknowledged for theoretical completeness. It is beyond the scope of our work.

E2: Impulsive Stage

The lowest stage that is accessible by our methods of study is the Impulsive stage.[2] The child at this stage is a creature of physical needs and impulses, dependent on others for

---

[2]Capitals are used to denote stage names; lower case the everyday use of the corresponding term. No human characteristic arises all at once in one stage and disappears on passage to the next.

control. Deep and dependent attachment to caretakers is colored by physical needs. Other people are understood in terms of the simplest dichotomies, good and bad, clean and dirty. Good guys give to me, mean ones do not. The growing sense of self is affirmed by the word "No." There is little sense of causation. Punishment is arbitrary or retaliatory. Rules are poorly understood. Lacking the ability to conceptualize inner life, the child cannot distinguish physical from emotional malaise. This is normal behavior for the very young child; by school age, children optimally have advanced beyond it, but those who do not may be diagnosed as "impulsive personalities."

E3: Self-Protective Stage

The Self-protective stage, the first step toward control of impulses and hence of character development, occurs when the child becomes capable of delay for immediate advantage. Children at this stage appreciate rules and know it is to their advantage to play by them. They are creatures of more or less opportunistic hedonism; they lack long-term goals and ideals. They want immediate gratification and, if they can, will exploit others for their ends. Seeing interpersonal relationships as exploitative, they are themselves wary and self-protective. If they "get in trouble," it is because they were with the "wrong people." Thus, blame is understood but assigned to others, to circumstances, or sometimes to a part of themselves for which they do not feel responsible ("my eyes"). In small children passing through this stage in normal time, rituals and traditions tend to be prominent, a kind of embodiment of rules and controls. Older children and adults who remain at this stage see life as a zero-sum game; they may become hostile, opportunistic, or even psychopathic. However, most adults go beyond this stage, and probably most Self-protective persons find a place in normal society and may even be successful, given good luck, good looks, intellectual brilliance, or inherited wealth.

E4: Conformist Stage

In normal development, at school age or somewhere in the school years, the child negotiates the transition from the egocentric Self-protective stage to the group-centered Conformist stage. More psychologists and philosophers have described Conformity than any other stage. At this stage, the child identifies self with the group or its authority—be it parents, teachers, or peers. Rules are accepted just because they are the rules. This is the period of greatest cognitive simplicity: There is a right way and a wrong way, and it is the same for everyone all the time, or at least for broad classes of people described in demographic terms. What is conventional and socially approved is right. That is usually true with respect to conventional gender roles. However, a person who rigidly conforms to some unconventional gender norms is still a Conformist. Friendliness and social niceness are highly valued; disapproval is a potent sanction. The

person is preoccupied with appearance, material things, reputation, and social acceptance and belonging. Inner states are perceived in the simplest language (sad, happy, glad, angry, love, and understanding), contrasting with an almost physical version of inner life at lower levels (sick, upset, mad, excited) and a richly differentiated inner life at higher levels. People, including the self, are perceived in terms of stereotypes based on social groups rather than in terms of individual differences. The way people are and the way they ought to be are not sharply differentiated. People at this stage usually describe themselves and others of their in-group in socially acceptable terms. Interpersonal interaction is seen primarily in terms of actions, not feelings, and the prototypic action is talking.

Group pressure can presumably encourage transition from the Self-protective to the Conformist stage. But what impels the transition out of pure conformity? Possibly, the young person during the primary school and secondary school years finds him or herself a member of different groups that demand conformity to somewhat disparate standards. One woman, for example, said that her mother punished her for some infraction by forbidding her to go to mass. She feared punishment in the Hereafter, but her mother was the clear and present danger. An individual can hardly endure such a dilemma without abandoning his or her absolute faith in at least one of the competing authorities.

E5: Self-Aware Stage

By whatever means, the person at the Self-aware stage has become aware that not everyone, including his or her own self, conforms perfectly all the time to the characteristics that stereotypes seem to demand. Once "what I am" is untied from "what I ought to be," the way is open to begin examination of self. The ability to conceptualize inner life expands; interpersonal relationships are described not merely as actions but also in terms of feelings. In many people at this stage, there is an acute sense of the distinction between self and group; emotions such as self-consciousness and loneliness are described. At the same time, the person perceives that there may be alternative possibilities in many situations that for the Conformist are covered by absolute rules or statements. Qualifications and contingencies are allowed, although they still tend to be stated in broadly demographic terms rather than in terms of individual differences: For example, some activity is okay if you are an adult, or if you are a boy, rather than if you are personally qualified or have a deep desire for it. Such modification of absolute rules may apply to anything from sexual mores to a woman having a career. The Self-aware stage is still basically a version of Conformity.

E6: Conscientious Stage

Growth to the Conscientious stage is another major and mysterious shift, for, as Freud (1930/1961) pointed out, so long as sanctions for misdeeds come from outside oneself, they can be escaped, but a bad conscience is ineluctable punishment. How are people induced to make that shift? The psychoanalytic answer is by identification with others admired, loved, or even feared; the social learning answer is that in the long run a person without conscience is punished or socially disapproved. The social learning answer seems more adequate to account for growth to Conformity than to growth past that stage, and intuitively conscience seems to be less calculating than is implied by social learning theory. However, research has no clear answers.

The distinctive mark of the Conscientious stage is self-evaluated standards: I approve or disapprove of a given conduct not just because my family or my schoolmates or the authorities do, but because that is what I personally feel. Of course, most people at this level do choose to adopt conformity as an everyday rule, so the difference between this stage and the Conformist and Self-aware stages is not the behavior itself. At this stage, one is guilty not primarily, or not only, when one has broken a rule, but rather when one has hurt another person. Motives and consequences are more important than rules per se; *ought* is differentiated from *is*. Inner states and individual differences are described in vivid and differentiated terms. Long-term goals and ideals are characteristic.

The Conscientious person is reflective; self and others are described in terms of reflexive traits. The only reflexive traits that regularly appear at a lower level are self-consciousness and self-confidence. The Conscientious person is self-critical but not totally rejecting of self, as are some persons at the lowest levels (as well as depressed people of any level). The recognition of multiple possibilities in situations leads to a sense of choice; decisions are made for reasons. The person strives for goals, tries to live up to ideals, and to improve the self.

The moral imperative remains, but it is not just a matter of doing right and avoiding wrong; priorities and appropriateness are considered. Moral issues are separated from conventional rules and from esthetic standards or preferences. To make such distinctions entails greater conceptual complexity than at the Conformist level or lower. Achievement is highly valued, not only in terms of competition or social approval (which always retain some importance), but in terms of one's own standards. Work, rather than being purely onerous, is an opportunity for achievement, so long as it is not dull or boring. People at this level are more likely than those at lower levels to think beyond their own personal concerns to those of society. The conscientious character has the negative aspect that the person may feel excessive responsibility for others.

E7: Individualistic Stage

Where the Conscientious person has a vivid sense of individual differences, the person at the next stage (Individualistic) has a sense of individuality, of the personality as a whole or the style of life. There is a greater tolerance for individual differences than at earlier stages. The inner self and the outer self are often differentiated, a distinction anticipated at the Conscientious level in concern about deceptive behavior. Although a concern for the problems of dependence and independence is a recurrent one, at this stage the person distinguishes physical, financial, and emotional dependence; there is particular concern for emotional dependence. Relationships with other people, which have been becoming deeper and more intensive as the person grew from the Conformist to the Conscientious stage, are recognized as being partly antagonistic to the striving for achievement and the sometimes excessive moralism and responsibility for others at the Conscientious level.

There are other new elements at the Individualistic level, more fully developed at the Autonomous stage. These ideas include psychological causation and psychological development. Below the Conscientious stage, almost no one ever mentions spontaneously the development of personality or of traits. Another new element is a concept of people as having and being different in different roles. The prime example of role differentiation—that a modern woman is expected to serve as wife, mother, housekeeper, lover, working woman, and so on—has become such a staple topic of women's magazines that it turns up at lower levels too. It illustrates the fact that not all clichés are Conformist.

E8: Autonomous Stage

Autonomy is a need that recurs throughout life in different forms. Erikson (1950) used the term *autonomous* for the stage here designated as Self-protective. The young child, even in the Impulsive stage, asserts him or herself by demanding to "do it by self." Here the term *autonomy* is reserved for a stage at the other end of the scale. Its chief characteristic is the recognition of other people's need for autonomy. There is also some freeing of the person from the excessive striving and sense of responsibility characteristic of the Conscientious stage. Moral dichotomies are no longer typical. They are replaced by a feeling for the complexity and multifaceted character of real people and real situations. There is a deepened respect for other people and their need to find their own way and even make their own mistakes. Crucial instances are members of one's own family, particularly one's children.

Conflicts between needs and desires are recognized and often acknowledged as part of the human condition, and thus they are not totally solvable. There is a high toleration for ambiguity and recognition of paradoxes. Humor is not hostile but tends instead to be existential, touching on the droll aspects of the nature of things. The Conscientious person's striving for achievement is transmuted into a search for self-fulfillment.

E9: Integrated Stage

Only a few individuals, probably less than 1% of an urban population in the United States, for example, reach the theoretical highest point, the Integrated stage. Data at present do not suffice to describe fully this theoretical high point.

Maslow (1954) probably provides what is the best description of the self-actualizing person. Because this stage is rare in most samples and there are major differences among qualified raters both as to the description of this level and application of the description in particular cases, under most circumstances it is best combined with the Autonomous stage.

There is a temptation to see the stages of ego development as a kind of ladder to be climbed and to suppose that the people at the highest stages are the best adjusted. There are probably well-adjusted people of all stages; surely, many children are well-adjusted, and they cannot be at the highest stages. In principle, ego maturity and adjustment must be described independently in order to ascertain empirically the relation between them. Those who remain below the Conformist level at maturity may be described as maladjusted from the point of view of some pillars of society; nonetheless, they may become quite successful in life. Because acknowledgment of inner conflict is one of the clearest signs of high ego level, some of those at the highest level may appear to be or may in fact be among those who are not well adjusted. On the other hand, some persons in the Conformist to Conscientious range may also have conflicts, acknowledged or not.

The relation between adjustment and ego level depends on one's definition of terms. From one point of view, each ego level has its own appropriate mode of adjustment, but in that case, not much is added by asserting a relation of ego development to adjustment. From another point of view, there are meanings to adjustment that do permit comparison of different ego levels. Then they must be defined independently, and one could argue that the result does not do justice to the characteristic adjustment of the highest levels.

Understandably, there is special interest in the lowest and highest stages, because both have some aura of mystery. The origins of the ego are fascinating for some of the same reasons as the origins of any psychological function. The highest stages are fascinating in part because they embody so much of what each of us aspires to or believes that he or she has achieved. But to describe ego development as simply the progression from the Impulsive stage to the Autonomous or Integrated stage, implying that the developmental course is a steady progression from low to high, would be a grievous mistake. The vast majority of people would not be described that way, and the process itself would be distorted, because neither the individual differences in ego development nor the dialectics of the most populous stages would be represented. What is most observable, either in slow progression or in individual differences within a cohort, is the range from the Self-Protective to the Conformist and from the Conformist to the Conscientious stages.

METHODOLOGICAL DIFFICULTIES

Table 1.1 summarizes our current views on the substance of the successive stages. In one way or another it differs from what any of the other investigators in the field has drawn up

or would do when making a similar table. All of us deal with data, with hundreds or even thousands of cases, so why should there be such unresolved differences?

First, there is no one-to-one correspondence between any bit of behavior and its underlying disposition—in this case, ego level. No bit of behavior is or can be assumed to be more than probabilistically related to ego level.

Second, all kinds of development are occurring at the same times. There is no completely error-free method of separating one strand of development from another. A particular bit of behavior may, and in general must be assumed to, reflect more than one strand of development. Ego development is conceptually distinct from intellectual development and psychosexual development, but it is bound to be correlated with them during childhood and adolescence. There is not even a guarantee of "local independence"; that is, even for a group of constant chronological age, there may be a correlation between ego development and other strands of development. Thus, there is a confounding of variance that no amount of data will resolve into its component sources. If one depends entirely on empirical methods, one is at the mercy of confounded variance; so theory must always temper reliance on data, even more so because our data inevitably contain gaps.

Third, there is no error-free method of distinguishing probable signs of one ego level from signs of a probable correlate. To the extent that the correlates are other developmental variables, this principle is the same as the second one. Other correlates, such as socioeconomic status (SES), are not developmental. How can one be sure whether a particular kind of behavior results from low ego level or associated low economic and social level? In principle, with infinite amounts of data, one could decide; in practice, with the kinds of data available, one cannot be sure.

Fourth, no task can be guaranteed to display just what one wants to know about ego level. In a structured test, the investigator is projecting his or her own frame of reference rather than tapping the frame of reference of the subjects, which is what reveals their ego level. In unstructured tests, one cannot control what the subject will choose to reveal. Testers become very adept at interpreting minimal signs, but there is always the chance a person will conceal all or respond in a way that conceals usual ego level, in whatever sense others reveal theirs.

Fifth, every person in principle displays behavior at more than one level. Every behavior sample must be assumed to be diverse with respect to level. The basic tasks of psychometrics are to translate qualitative aspects of behavior to quantitative and to reduce diverse observations to single scores. There is no unique way to do either. Different psychometric procedures may lead to at least slightly different pictures of successive stages.

Sixth, there are intrinsic difficulties in assigning behavioral signs to any developmental level. A sign that appears at one level in tentative or embryonic version appears at higher levels in increasingly clear and elaborated versions. In sentence completions, a thought that appears at one level as a cliché appears in deeper, more convincing, and more complex versions at higher levels. A paradoxical result is that when similar responses are grouped together as a category and the most representative response is used as category title, the title response will often be the one that comes from a protocol rated a level lower.

Seventh, a behavioral sign may be discriminating in one direction only; thus, there is an intrinsic ambiguity in assigning it to any level within those to which it applies.

Eighth is the issue of base rates (Meehl & Rosen, 1955). Given a particular replicated response, what is the probability that the subject comes from a given level? If one is concerned only with the particular sample, the answer is the obvious one, the central tendency of those who give the response. But test constructors are not concerned just with the sample before them. Most samples contain few extreme cases; so this rule will ordinarily yield no signs that would receive extreme scores. The proper question is more like: Given a particular ego level, what is the probability of showing this sign? Because extreme cases are rare, most decisions about extreme ratings will be based on small numbers of cases, leaving the test constructor at the mercy of the idiosyncrasies of a few people. The same considera-

tion holds for all uncommon responses at median levels. Thus, particularly for ratings at extreme levels, theory is indispensable as a supplement to data.

Finally, consider the question about clinical insight as arbiter of the appropriate level for a given sign or response type. Clinicians rarely think of data in terms of the complex probabilities detailed earlier. They tend to think of every bit of behavior as determined by the patient's particular constellation of traits and circumstances. Responses that the ground rules of this manual (see chapter 3) call for rating, clinicians would say do not reveal ego level. Indeed, that is correct, for they are equivocal. Thus, the psychometric frame of reference is different from the clinical frame of reference. There is also a deeper reason why the clinician's intuitive perceptions may be misleading. Every developmental level builds on and transmutes the previous one. The unconscious or preconscious components of the attitudes of one level are the corresponding attitudes of earlier levels. Precisely because clinicians see the patient more deeply than any test can, they may misjudge the level of a particular sign or of a patient. Hence, clinical judgment fails as a court of last appeal, though with proper precautions it is a valuable line of evidence additional to theory and test and experimental data.

CHAPTER TWO

Manifestations of Ego Level in Sentence Completions

A single sentence completion rarely tells even the most experienced rater the exact ego level of the person who wrote the sentence. There are no precise, explicit rules for rating. Attempts have been made to computerize rating rules, but they cannot do as well as experienced raters. The link between any rule and actual ego level is too loose, too probabilistic. A complete protocol, however, can often create a vivid picture of its writer even for a relatively novice rater. But how can one convey to the beginner the principles that govern rating? This chapter attempts to answer that question.

The purposes of this chapter are to serve as an introduction to the detailed item manuals in Part II, to bring out the aspects of response that govern scoring, and to guide rating of unclassified responses. Because replicated responses are rare at E8 and nonexistent at E9, this chapter is about as helpful as the item manuals for those levels. In the process, the abstract conception of ego development is fleshed out with the words of ordinary people.

The basic strategy of the measurement is probabilistic. There are no simple, absolute, logical rules, however appealing such a prospect. There are obstacles to such rules: Topics that appear in one level for one question may appear at a higher or lower level for another question. Nor is there a guarantee that all aspects of ego development will be displayed in sentence completions at all.

Worse yet, what appear to be some characteristic ways of expressing oneself at, say, a pre-Conformist level, may in fact be artifacts of the particular individuals or groups at that level. In particular, younger subjects and subjects from lower socioeconomic class are overrepresented at the lowest ego level. Some aspects of their responses may reflect age or class rather than ego level.

The format chosen here, individual completions taken out of context, seems at first to be particularly unconvincing. One important clue to ego level is the richness of the total protocol, which cannot be displayed in terms of individual responses.

Low-level protocols tend to give the same or similar answers to several questions, whereas high-level protocols touch on a wide variety of themes. The cumulative effect of 36 completions is more convincing than any single response, but it does not permit the dissection of the aspects of the response that guide ratings; that is one purpose of this chapter.

Scoring rules are difficult to convey because ideas do not spring full-blown at one level. Rather, they tend to appear in simplified or cliché form at lower levels, and in fully realized form at the next higher levels. For many items, it turned out that category titles, expressing what was common to a group of items, were the very responses that came from lower levels. For example, the idea that women fulfill "varied roles" is typically expressed in those words at E5 or E6, whereas responses explicitly describing role differentiation are more typical of E7 or E8. That kind of variability cannot be covered adequately in explicit rules. Thus, an intuitive rater of long experience has an advantage. But even an experienced rater will have difficulty remembering which items elicit a given theme earlier, and which later. Hence, we always use the manual.

All responses listed here occurred on someone's test protocol; none are invented. (A few responses are retained from the 1970 manual.) All are quoted verbatim and, to the extent that the data can be trusted, with errors faithfully preserved. However, most or all of the originals were handwritten and many errors were indistinguishable from typists' mistakes, which have been corrected. In general, answers will have many more misspellings and less punctuation than indicated here. Erasures and crossed-out words are not indicated except where part of the stem has been crossed out.

E2: Impulsive Stage

One of the most reliable indicators of an E2 protocol is blatant and unsocialized expression of impulses, mainly hostile and sexual ones.

My mother and I—fight sometimes
   —drink
When I am with a man—want to shoot him
   —I get hot
A woman feels good when—she gets screwed
A girl has a right to—fight back
Men are lucky because—they beat on women
   —they can screw girls
A husband has a right to—screw around
   —drink and smoke
When I am with a woman—I like to fuck the shit out of her

People are sometimes talked of in terms of body parts, as if the person lacked the concept of a self.

What gets me into trouble is—my eyes.
A woman feels good when—she has a penis in her.

The world of the E2 person is dichotomized into good or bad, nice or mean, and clean or dirty. Such stereotyped thinking cannot be fully illustrated in terms of single responses; many protocols at this level give the same or almost the same completion to several stems.

A wife should—be a good lady
A good mother—is nice
For a woman a career is—nice
Being with other people—I am very mean
   —is nice if they don't do immoral things
A woman should always—keep clean
My conscience bothers me if—I am unpure
When they talked about sex, I—think it's bad

Many E2 responses are either tautological or confused. The former often repeat the stem or something almost the same. The latter are illogical, whether because the subject fails to understand the idea of the stem or just responds to a single term.

Raising a family—having children
Education—helps in school
For a woman a career is—very good work
   —be clean
My main problem is—trouble
Men are lucky because—there happy [sic]
What gets me into trouble is—school
The worst thing about being a man—abandons his family

The E2 person wants to receive money and things. The implication is passive dependence.

Women are lucky because—they get nice things
   —when they found money
A good father—should give his daughter anything she wants
If I can't get what I want—I don't want it
A man should always—make good money than women [sic]

Running away, running home, or going to one's own room are common responses, as if whatever is wrong is located in the place rather than the situation.

When they talked about sex, I—get mad and go home
When I am criticized—I like to be alone
If I can't get what I want—I run away

The most obvious of the traditional role responsibilities are recognized, but they come through as burdens.

A wife should—keep the house clean
   —stay home and watch the children
The worst thing about being a woman—having babies. If you could stop it be alright [sic]
   —is taking care of kids
A man's job—to go and work

The E2 person has a limited emotional range, with the more differentiated, abstract, or cognitively shaded emotions missing. Emotions are often reduced to physical states. Similarly, abstract ideas are reduced to concrete examples.

Being with other people—is very nice
   —gives me the creeps
When people are helpless—they feel bad
If I can't get what I want—I get mad
When a child will not join in group activities—he/she is sick
Usually she felt that sex—is good to me because I get hot
Rules are—not to sex that much or do drugs
   —to help clean up the house

Dysphoric moods and aversive and negative reactions, stated without reasons, are more frequent than at higher levels.

Sometimes she wished that—I was dead
The thing I like about myself is—not much
I am—I don't no [sic]
My father—stinks
Raising a family—is hell!

E3: Self-Protective Stage

Control is the leading issue as the child develops beyond the Impulsive level, that is, controlling and being controlled by his or her own impulses and by other people. To protect the self, the person is on guard to control the situation as well as the self. One possible outcome is a manipulative or deceptive attitude toward others, as well as a fear of being manipulated or deceived.

Raising a family—I want my family to obey me
A girl has a right to—protect herself
When a child will not join in group activities—he should be forced to
I am—very careful with whom I play with [sic]
A husband has a right to—say over his wife
The worst thing about being a woman—you are put upon
Men are lucky because—they can tell their wives what to do
Women are lucky because—they can get married and live off the men
   —they can usually get by with more things than men

The worst thing about being a man—being bugged by women
Being with other people—I will watch myself
When people are helpless—I don't like to be bothered with
  them
When I am with a man—it's none of your business
If I can't get what I want—I'll have a tantrum
  —I beg & crying works with my father
The thing I like about myself is—the way to handle boys
A woman should always—be on guard
  —stay one step ahead of a man

Although the child or older person at this stage is beginning to control impulses, the same impulses that the E2 person gives way to are evident in slightly attenuated form. Hostility takes the form of a punitive attitude and retaliation for any offense or injury.

When a child will not join in group activities—he should be
  punished
When I am criticized—I mean talk about him
What gets me into trouble is—being quick to answer back
Crime and delinquency could be halted if—you killed all the
  bastards who do it
  —people who commit crimes have that same crime committed to them
If I can't get what I want—I make sure nobody else can

Sexuality is more than just a physical state, which it seems to be at E2, but it is less social than at later levels and may even be flaunted.

What gets me into trouble is—I'm too good-looking
When they talked about sex, I—get excited
  —suggested we have it
A man feels good when—he has more than one woman
At times she worried about—me going out and having sex with
  anybody
I am—boy crazy
My main problem is—too many girls like me
  —I treat men too good & tend to get walked on
When I am with a man—I feel like kissing
  —I want his bod!
Usually he felt that sex—was the only thing in life

A characteristic of the E3 level is hostile humor; that is a discovery of the sentence completion method. The humor is not really funny, but rather sarcastic or sardonic.

Raising a family—raises your blood pressure
  —is easy on ADC
When I am criticized—I laugh because words are wind
When people are helpless—I laugh
I feel sorry—[for] the nerds of this world
  —for the sucker who is going to try to make any sense
  of this
I just can't stand people who—bug you to death to finish their
  damn survey
  —babble
  —are dweebs, dipsticks (that constitutes the majority of
  people in world)
My main problem is—this

The hedonism is simple: Work is hard and, except for the money, has no attraction. Fun is better.

Raising a family—is a lot of work
A man's job—is harder
Women are lucky because—they don't have to go out to get a
  job
A man feels good when—he has fun
A woman feels good when—she gets home from work
  —the housework is done
The worst thing about being a man—is having to make a living
For a woman a career is—lots of work

Although the emotional range is limited, it is not so narrow nor so physical as for the E2 subject.

When they talked about sex, I—felt kind of shame
A man feels good when—he is treated good
I am—a worried mom
When I am with a man—I feel nerves [sic]
When I am criticized—I get mad

A salient feature is the emphasis on right and wrong, especially as applied to people. Trouble means getting caught and is often attributed to being with the wrong people. Thus, blame is externalized. Sometimes blame is put on a part of the self, treated as if it were not something for which the person was responsible.

My conscience bothers me if—I feel that someone is watching
  me
What gets me into trouble is—being caught while doing bad
  things
  —running around with the wrong group
Being with other people—makes you feel good if your with
  the right crowd

Interpersonal relationships are spoken about, but primarily in terms of talking.

My mother and I—are like two chatter-boxes
I just can't stand people who—talk too much

There is little sense of agency; things just happen.

The worst thing about being a woman—is when trouble appears
  to happen
Usually she felt that sex—was just something happen to a
  woman
Sometimes she wished that—good things would happen
My conscience bothers me if—I happen to lie about something

Among girls and women, physical appearance is a strong preoccupation, most often in terms of a single aspect rather than the whole person.

The thing I like about myself is—my hair
  —my smile
Women are lucky because—they get to wear makeup

E4: Conformist Stage

The Conformist person is, almost by definition, the least distinctive type. Naturally, Conformists give many conventional responses; so do almost all other people, but relatively less frequently. Many of the E4 categories are close to the E3 counterparts; others are close to E5. E4 is the default rating for unratable responses, chiefly omissions. (However, whenever possible, fragmentary responses should be given a guessed rating.) But it is also the rating given to many nondiscriminating categories, that is, categories of response given by people of all levels roughly in proportion to their numbers in the sample. However, one cannot construct a portrait on such data.

Many clichés, often considered unratable in other content analysis systems, belong at this level.

> Raising a family—is a big responsibility
> A man's job—is to be the breadwinner
> What gets me into trouble is—my big mouth
> A girl has a right to—change her mind
> Rules are—made to be broken
>   —made to be followed
> I am—feeling good about myself
> My mother and I—are close
> A husband has a right to—go out with the boys

E4 responses are conceptually simple. They are often rules or absolute standards, stated without qualifications or contingencies. There are frequent sweeping generalizations containing words like *always*, *never*, or *everyone*.

> Being with other people—is good for everyone
> Education—is very important for everyone
> Women are lucky because—they can get any man
>   —they get free dinners and movies (the men always pay)
> A girl has a right to—anything she wants
> I feel sorry—for people who never listens [*sic*]
> Men are lucky because—they have all the breaks
> The worst thing about being a man—is that all the responsibilities are on you
> The worst thing about being a woman—is she has to do it all
> My mother and I—look just the same

The emphasis on right and wrong at E4 differs from that at E3. At E3, the group or the people are right or wrong; at E4, the behavior is right or wrong.

> A good mother—teaches her children about good and bad
> A woman feels good when—she does what is right
> Crime and delinquency could be halted if—older people tell children right from wrong
> A good father—tries to do the right thing

Many E4 responses reflect conventional gender-role norms. However, alternative or nontraditional gender roles are also represented at E4 today.

> A good father—makes a living for the family
> Women are lucky because—they don't have to pay for dates

> —they can be feminine and vulnerable
> A wife should—take care of her husband
>   —enjoy being one
> Men are lucky because—they can always choose the woman they want
> A husband has a right to—be head of the household
> A good mother—should not work, and stay home with her family
> When I am with a man—I like to be treated like a lady
> When I am with a woman—I try to be a gentleman
> A girl has a right to—compete in sports with boys
> For a woman a career is—a must!

The world of the E4 person is the world of social acceptability. A pleasing, friendly, socially acceptable personality is valued. Belonging makes one feel secure.

> A woman should always—be friendly and nice
> The thing I like about myself is—no one is a stranger a smile for all [*sic*]
> What gets me into trouble is—that I always try to help everybody
> Usually he felt that sex—is normal
> I am—easy to get along with
>   —a well-adjusted person
> Being with other people—makes you feel like you belong

The virtues claimed are conventional ones; the faults and troubles the E4 acknowledges are usually minor ones and occasionally backhanded compliments.

> A wife should—be faithful
> I just can't stand people who—brag
>   —lie
> At times he worried about—money
>   —grades
> My main problem is—talking too much
>   —my weight

Interpersonal relationships are often described in terms of behaviors, rather than the differentiated feelings, motives, or traits found at higher levels. Talking is prominent, as at E3, but other behaviors are also mentioned.

> A man should always—be on his best behavior
> A good mother—talks with her children
> When they talked about sex, I—sit there and just listen
>   —join right in
> My mother and I—have fun by teasing each other, and by cooking together

Descriptions of inner life are general and broad. Love is a thread running through many topics, and sympathy may be mentioned. That is an advance compared to the narrower emotional range typical of E3, but falls short of the richly elaborated emotional texture of higher levels.

> A woman feels good when—she is in love
> A wife should—love her husband
> A man feels good when—he has a good woman at his side
> My mother and I—love each other
> When people are helpless—I feel sad

Sex and love are not often mentioned together. When they are, it is as a contrast rather than as an integrated experience.

Usually she felt that sex—was less important than love
A woman should always—be true to her husband in love and sex

Physical appearance is important for women, but it is usually the appearance of the person, rather than of one part of the body, as it often is at E3.

A woman should always—be attractive
—wear dresses

Work is still seen mostly as work, not as opportunity, but it has become more like a responsibility than a burden. To the E4, the value of an activity is in the outcome; the process is only a way to get there.

Sometimes he wished that—he had already graduated from law school
A man feels good when—he accomplishes something
A woman feels good when—she succeeds in raising a happy family
—she has the housework done and the children in bed
For a woman a career is—one way to keep happy and to have a few things she wants

E5: Self-Aware Stage

The E5 level has been called at various times Self-conscious, Self-aware, and transition between Conformist and Conscientious levels. Labeling the level as Self-conscious suggested to some psychologists that it was a more maladjusted stage than others, but there is no reason to suppose so, and it seems not to be true. There is no evidence that it is more of a transition than any other level; certainly, it is not transitory. Evidence (Holt, 1980) shows that it is the modal level in urban United States. Thus, we settled on Self-aware as name, although that is only a partial description and may not be its most obvious characteristic.

The person at E5 sees multiple possibilities and alternatives in situations that the E4 person construes as simple. Sometimes the alternatives are described as flexibility.

A good mother—comes in many different packages
A man's job—can be anything
Being with other people—sometimes makes me feel good
The thing I like about myself is—that I am flexible
Women are lucky because—they can be very flexible
Rules are—made to be revised
—needed in some settings but not all

In place of the E4 tendency to classify actions into mutually exclusive categories of right and wrong, the E5 person tends to think about appropriateness: what is right for the time, place, and situation. There are contingencies, exceptions, and comparisons, though they are usually general and

not specific. More complex and differentiated contingencies and comparisons appear at E6.

Raising a family—can be difficult for a working woman
What gets me into trouble is—saying the wrong thing at the wrong time
My conscience bothers me if—I am too critical of my child or husband
When I am criticized—it depends on what it is about
Education—is important to have, but grades are overly emphasized
When I am with a woman—varies with the woman
When I am with a man—I like, I am comfortable
Rules are—good if fairly administered
Usually she felt that sex—wasn't right until you did it with the right man
Usually he felt that sex—was a topic he'd rather not discuss
A man's job—is just as easy as a woman's job
My mother and I—are more alike than my father and I are
For a woman a career is—probably no less satisfying than it is for a man

Self-consciousness is typical for some, but not all, persons at E5. However, others describe themselves as self-confident. Probably all persons at this level are more aware of themselves as people and as active agents than persons at lower levels. There is some self-criticism and sometimes discomfort in social situations, or feelings of loneliness or of being alone.

When a child will not join in group activities—he is self-conscious
When they talked about sex, I—sometimes feel awkward
—didn't feel embarrassed
Being with other people—sometimes makes me nervous
—makes my life less lonely
I feel sorry—for people who are lonely
I am—lonely but content
—immature
My main problem is—I am very shy and don't make friends easy
Sometimes she wished that—she could be a better person than she was
When I am criticized—I keep it hidden, but inside I'm hurt
My father—is hurting inside
—is stubborn
When I am with a man—I find myself not acting like me
When I am with a woman—I feel self-conscious

The emotions reported at this level are more varied than at E4 and more intimately tied to interpersonal relationships. Probably, women at E5 discuss their feelings more often than men do; that is certainly true of feelings about their appearance.

When people are helpless—they must feel very low
If I can't get what I want—I adjust
—fight for it, then I get disappointed
A good father—is one who is not afraid to show his love
A girl has a right to—express her feelings

A wife should—always try to demonstrate her love
A man feels good when—he knows he is loved
A husband has a right to—share his feelings with others
My main problem is—I worry too much about what others
    think
My father—is a very affectionate man
        —never shows he cares
Men are lucky because—we are not judged by our looks as
    much
My conscience bothers me if—I don't feel guilty when I should
A woman should always—be honest about her feelings

The person at this level is more aware of individual differences in attitudes, interests, and abilities than is the person at the E4 level. There are a few traits specially favored by those of this level. They often have connotations of moods ("stubbornness"), norms ("feminine"), or homely virtues ("honest," "respect").

When a child will not join in group activities—he may be
    interested in other things
Being with other people—can be adventurous
The thing I like about myself is—my personal habits and traits
What gets me into trouble is—selfishness
        —my stubborn persistency (in certain situations)
My conscience bothers me if—I lose my temper
I am—a very cautious person
        —very spontaneous
Sometimes he wished that—he could have been more assertive
My father—is a kind man, very intelligent too
A woman feels good when—she is given attention and respect
A good father—earns the respect of his children

The theme of opportunities becomes important, and usually refers to opportunities for achievement, described more fully at higher stages, and contrasting with desire to just finish jobs at lower levels.

Men are lucky because—they get more career opportunities
Raising a family—is challenging
Education—is very rewarding
I am—ambitious
A woman feels good when—she has accomplished something
For a woman a career is—motivating
        —a chance to move up in the world
Women are lucky because—they get the better choice of
    clothes, guy clothes are nasty

Goals, purposes, patterns, models, and expectations are another theme new at this level and more sharply defined at higher levels. Patterns often mentioned refer to gender roles; objection to gender-role stereotypes characterizes higher levels. Persons at the Conformist and pre-Conformist levels are less likely to have the time perspective implied by purposes and goals. Models and expectations require a degree of conceptual complexity and abstraction not likely at lower levels.

Education—is a must if you have high goals
At times she worried about—her children's future

I am—a person with many goals and a person set on achieving
    those goals
For a woman a career is—the most important goal in her life
The worst thing about being a man—is what's expected of you
The worst thing about being a woman—is that men expect too
    much of you
Usually she felt that sex—was a very important thing in her
    life
        —was the most important thing in a woman–man rela-
        tionship
A woman should always—behave or be a role model to children
A man should always—act like a man

The desire for independence and equality probably is present in some form at every level, but those desires are stated explicitly at the E5 level, along with a sense of choice.

I am—a very independent person
A girl has a right to—choose her own career
        —be as much an individual as males
The thing I like about myself is—I am an individual
A woman should always—stick up for her rights
A husband has a right to—be an equal partner in the family
A wife should—be her husband's equal
The worst thing about being a woman—is the inequality be-
    tween the sexes
A woman feels good when—she has accomplished the same
    thing as a man

The self-conception or ideal self at this level is that of a person responsible and fair, a person who does his or her best, who is sincere, and who above all wishes to remain his or her own self.

A wife should—try her best at whatever the task
A good mother—wants what's best for her children
I am—striving to be the best that I can
        —a person who tries to be fair to everyone
The thing I like about myself is—that I am not a phony
I just can't stand people who—are two-faced
        —unfairly criticize other people
A girl has a right to—be her own person
A husband has a right to—be true to himself
A woman should always—be true to what she feels inside
        —respect herself
A man should always—be comfortable with himself
        —be honorable
My conscience bothers me if—I am not completely honest and
    straightforward

Ordinary remarks about health, religion, God, and death are most often classed at this level, unless they include clear signs of other levels.

The thing I like about myself is—I love G-d
Crime and delinquency could be halted if—God was the head
    of every home
I just can't stand people who—make a "show" of their religion
I am—a child of God
A good mother—will train her children in accordance with the
    Bible

My father—is a loving & Godly man
If I can't get what I want—God has a better idea
My conscience bothers me if—I don't pray often enough
At times he worried about—getting ill
At times she worried about—if she would live or die
My main problem is—my biological clock is ticking
    —my cholesterol

The punitive attitude of the E3 person, that becomes a law-and-order attitude at the E4 level, is largely replaced at E5 by a wish to supply guidance and a supportive environment for the miscreant and others.

Crime and delinquency could be halted if—parents were more conscientious in raising and educating their children
    —society would be more interested in youth
When people are helpless—they need guidance
A good father—gives his children guidance through life
A wife should—support her husband (not financially)

The morality is one of helpfulness to others, altruism, and some concern for larger social issues, but mostly in general terms.

A woman feels good when—she has done something good for others
A man feels good when—he makes a woman happy
    —his children have accomplished their goals
A woman should always—make sure her children are taken well care of [sic]
The thing I like about myself is—I am a real friend
    —my moral character
A man's job—is to care for those who can't
A good father—never compromises his duties
My conscience bothers me if—I am unkind
    —I turned down a request to help someone
I feel sorry—when I unintentionally hurt someone's feelings
    —for our destructive society
At times she worried about—the planet
Sometimes she wished that—she could do more for her family
    —the world was a better place

E6: Conscientious Stage

People at E6 have true conceptual complexity, perceiving complexity and also displaying complex thinking, in contrast to the conceptual simplicity of E4 and lower levels and to recognition of multiplicity at E5. Although there is ordinarily a correlation between intelligence and conceptual complexity, such simple words as *but* or *if* are often the markers, so the correlation with intelligence is not an artifact or built into the definition of the higher levels. (Many of the following responses illustrate several facets of the E6 personality, and most also illustrate complexity.)

Raising a family—is wonderful but sometimes stressful
Being with other people—can be great if you're comfortable with them
My mother and I—have some different views but are still very close

When I am criticized—I get mad but still appreciate it
A good father—earns and sees the love of his children—not just their respect
    —doesn't come with instructions
When they talked about sex, I—was embarrassed but interested
Rules are—a necessary evil
My father—is a good father, but wasn't always a good husband
    —tries to relate to other people, but often finds it difficult
A man should always—be honest, fair, and considerate of others

The E6 response will often combine alternatives that are opposites or somewhat contradictory, each of which would by itself be rated at E4 or E5. These contradictions and contrasts are not as global, as stereotyped, or as evaluative as those of lower levels, which are typically good–bad, clean–dirty, or right–wrong. Above the E6 level, even these differentiated polarities decrease.

When I am criticized—I find it hard to react objectively and not emotionally
Being with other people—can be thrilling or miserable
A good father—will earn his children's respect, not demand it
A wife should—be loving and understanding but should stick to her guns!!
Rules are—good in principle, often bad in practice
I am—productive, but feeling burnt out
A good mother—must balance firmness and understanding
My father—is a very loving man but irresponsible
Usually she felt that sex—was scary but exciting!
A woman should always—be strong but retain femininity
A man should always—be firm yet considerate

Absolute statements and rules are often replaced by comparisons and contingent statements, less global than the corresponding ones at E5. Where a sentence stem appears to call for an absolute statement, the person may object to the stem or state refusal to answer, as opposed to simply omitting it.

Being with other people—can be great if you're comfortable with them
My mother and I—get along when we are honest with our feelings
A good father—is as important as a good mother
When I am with a man—who loves me, I feel feminine
    —I am generally more open & honest with my feelings
For a woman a career is—important, but no more important than being a mother
A girl has a right to—be on equal terms with a boy
When they talked about sex, I—in what way?
Women are lucky because—I don't like this assumption
A wife should—not let anyone "should" on her
Men are lucky because—(meaningless for me)
I just can't stand people who—there are people I can't stand, but I am not sure that I can categorize them into groups
The worst thing about being a man—? What's so bad about being a man—or a woman

Because they see many possibilities in situations and alternative courses of action, the E6 subjects see life as presenting choices and decisions. They are not just pawns of fate but are origins of their own destiny. They may even have excessive feelings of control.

What gets me into trouble is—my indecision
Men are lucky because—they make the rules
    —they control their own destiny
At times he worried about—making the right decision
My main problem is—indecisiveness (I think)

The E6 subjects have a strong sense of responsibility and duties. When they feel guilt, it is more likely to be over consequences of actions than over breaking rules per se, as those at E4 and E5 do. Along with responsibility goes a sense of rights, justice, and fairness.

Raising a family—requires dedication and responsibility
A man's job—should only be one form of his support for his family
What gets me into trouble is—my irresponsibility
When people are helpless—I would like to help them but I am lazy
Women are lucky because—they can normally escape the pressure of career building
I just can't stand people who—break promises
The worst thing about being a man—are the pressures brought about by unemployment
    —is having to make all the decisions in a relationship
A good mother—loves, cares for, and takes on a great responsibility in raising her children
Sometimes he wished that—he hadn't undertaken the book
    —he was a better father
My conscience bothers me if—I ignore an obligation
The worst thing about being a woman—is being the default parent

Self-evaluated standards, particularly moral ones, characterize the E6 level. Justice is a widely held value. The E6s are sensitive to proportions and priorities.

A woman should always—follow her conscience and her dreams
The thing I like about myself is—my integrity
    —that I try to be fair and impartial to all people
When I am criticized—I am offended if it is unjust and not constructive
My mother and I—differ in politics, values, and conviction
I feel sorry—when I see someone being taken advantage of
    —that the world is often unfair, violent, etc.
A man feels good when—he does what is correct and does not just conform
Rules are—valid only when they are just
I just can't stand people who—deceive themselves and others
    —are not sincere
A good mother—instills values in her children
My conscience bothers me if—I go against what I believe in to conform with others
    —I am not true to myself
For a woman a career is—an option but not priority to family
Education—is high on my priority list
A wife should—understand and forgive trivial faults

Some E6 subjects disclaim or decry materialism. A few embrace open-mindedness, but that is most characteristic of the E7 level.

I feel sorry—for narrow-minded people
Crime and delinquency could be halted if—society was fairer, less materially minded
I just can't stand people who—are totally materialistic
    —are prejudiced
I am—the only person I know who doesn't need "everything"
My main problem is—this corrupt world we live in
Sometimes he wished that—there were no prejudice

They have long-term goals and ideals, ideas that appear only in the most general form at E5 and are virtually absent below that level. They distinguish means from ends and are concerned in a general way with purpose in life.

Raising a family—is a long, probably never-ending process
A man's job—is to pursue his ambitions to the furthest extent (like a woman's)
The thing I like about myself is—my strong will and determination
A girl has a right to—expect her goals to be fulfilled
I feel sorry—for people when they feel they have no future
A woman feels good when—accomplishes her professional & personal goals
At times she worried about—living up to her ideal of what she should be
I am—finally setting my life in order as of from today
My main problem is—deciding what to devote my life to

The achievement motive is at its height at the E6 level; the people strive to accomplish things. As a corollary to the striving for achievement, wasting time, disorganization, and procrastination are problems.

A woman should always—reach for the stars
A man feels good when—he has done something constructive
A woman feels good when—she creates something original
Men are lucky because—they have so many diverse opportunities to make a living
The worst thing about being a woman—is that it is a man's world and we won't get the opportunities that men get
Being with other people—teaches me different ideals
Education—is very important for future goals & achievements
Sometimes she wished that—her job was more challenging
    —she would have gone to college
For a woman a career is—very important. Gives her a sense of accomplishment
What gets me into trouble is—my waste of time
    —taking on more than I can handle
I feel sorry—when I should of done something, but procrastinated
At times she worried about—meeting deadlines
Sometimes he wished that—there was more time to each day

People at E6 strive to improve themselves. As a corollary, they criticize themselves. Being honest with themselves becomes as important as being honest with others.

A man should always—try as hard as he can to become a better person for himself and family

My main problem is—not keeping up the standards of my family and myself

The thing I like about myself is—my ability to change for the better
    —that I can see my own faults
    —that I am honest with myself

The person at E6 has a richly differentiated inner life. Experiences are savored and appreciated. Where the E5 and E4 people talk about feelings, the E6 people often have more differentiated terms such as trust, respect, needs, sensitivity, and emotional support.

My mother and I—support each other

When people are helpless—my heart reaches out to them

Women are lucky because—they share a unique quality that men don't, "compassion"
    —they are more open about their emotions
    —they can feel the movement of a child in their womb

A man feels good when—he knows that he can always trust somebody

Men are lucky because—they don't seem to have as much guilt as women

I just can't stand people who—are shallow

The worst thing about being a man—is that you can't express sensitivity

When I am with a man—the whole world seems just a little brighter
    —I get on the reserve side, a little afraid at times too

My father—is a very angry and confused man

There is clear awareness of problems of impulse and control. The E6 person is aware of self, reflects on him or herself, and describes self and others in terms of reflexive traits. Self-respect is as characteristic as self-criticism. Virtues may become faults.

When I am criticized—I react in a hostile way, although I try to curb this tendency
    —I lose my self-confidence

I feel sorry—when I lose my temper with my child
    —for people who can't accept themselves for who they are

My main problem is—that I am too impulsive and controlling
    —my bad temper, I think about things after I have done them
    —self-doubt

Sometimes she wished that—she'd be more disciplined

Usually he felt that sex—controlled him, rather than vice versa

What gets me into trouble is—I am too critical of myself

A girl has a right to—love herself & respect herself

A man's job—is very important to his self-concept

The thing I like about myself is—my self-determination

What gets me into trouble is—telling it like it is
    —hasty decisions
    —when I fail to discipline my desires

When people are helpless—when they don't believe in themselves

A wife should—always maintain her self-esteem

A man feels good when—he is proud of himself

A woman feels good when—she has self-respect and high self-esteem

Crime and delinquency could be halted if—people respected their own worth and that of others

When I am with a man—I am aware of being a woman

My father—is too much of a perfectionist

I am—overly conscientious

A woman should always—care about herself also and not just her family

A man should always—seek self-love and acceptance

Where people at E4 and E5 report conventional emotions, people at E6 report emotional nuances. When parents are idealized at E6, there is a more emotional tone than in idealization at the E4 level. This person has individual interests and values what is interesting, thus he or she may complain about uninteresting obligations; this contrasts with pre-Conformists, who seem to complain about the sheer effort.

When a child will not join in group activities—he or she feels detached
    —find a toy that he may be interested in and play with him until he joins in

Being with other people—makes life interesting

The thing I like about myself is—my empathy for others

When people are helpless—their defenses are down

Women are lucky because—they are free in choosing their aims in life

I am—an avid reader

The worst thing about being a man—one can get tied down eight to five

The worst thing about being a woman—is the drudgery of housekeeping
    —is having your heart broken by insensitive males

For a woman a career is—an escape from the tediousness of being a housewife

My father—is a renaissance man
    —is a beautiful soul, I love him

People at E6 have a vivid sense of individual differences in long-term dispositions. Their descriptions of people sound more realistic because they are more complex than similar descriptions at lower levels. They recognize the inevitability of human imperfections.

A man's job—should be chosen carefully to suit the man

I am—still basically shy and reserved, a private person

My main problem is—I can't get close to people

A good mother—treats her children as individuals
    —is not necessarily a super-mom

A good father—is mine—faults & all!

Relationships with other people are invested with more affect than most similar relationships with others at lower levels. Ideas such as mutuality, companionship, and sympathy may be mentioned.

A man's job—is to be a good partner
Being with other people—helps one to appreciate others
My mother and I—have difficulty sharing feelings
  —had a close relationship with many difficulties
A good father—shares responsibilities with a good mother
A wife should—be a complete marriage partner in all ways
I feel sorry—for those who can't feel sympathy, compassion,
  love, kindness, & empathy
A man feels good when—he knows his wife is his partner and
  not his obstacle
A woman feels good when—she is in love with a man that
  equally loves her
Sometimes she wished that—her family had been warmer

The ability to see matters from the other person's perspective is a connecting link between the deeper interpersonal relationships of the E6 subject and the more mature conscience.

When people are helpless—we should try and help them in a
  way not to offend them
At times she worried about—other people's opinion too much
  —whether or not people really liked her
My main problem is—my lack of empathy
A husband has a right to—know his wife's goals or ambitions
A good mother—is sensitive to her children's needs
A woman should always—love and respect her mate for what
  he is

At lower levels, interpersonal relationships seem almost to be reduced to behavior, particularly talking; at E6, people think in terms of communication and expression, in particular, expressing ideas, feelings, and abilities.

Being with other people—creates a good flow of ideas
My mother and I—talk on the surface often
  —are learning to communicate better with each other
What gets me into trouble is—that I tend to hide my feelings
Women are lucky because—they are able to express themselves
A good father—is a man who opens up to his children
A girl has a right to—be expressive yet with a quiet spirit
A wife should—talk freely with her husband and should listen
A husband has a right to—express his most personal feelings
  to his wife
  —honest communication
A good mother—is someone who communicates with her children
When I am with a woman—I tend to communicate easier than
  with a man
Usually she felt that sex—was an expression of love
For a woman a career is—a way to express herself

Behavior reveals intentions and motives to those at E6, and it has consequences. To that extent, psychological causality is understood. At E5, those ideas are anticipated by saying that behavior has reasons. Changes over time are recognized, but mostly described as growing or growing up. More complex versions of psychological causality and psychological development occur at E7.

When I am criticized—I analyze the critic's motive
My conscience bothers me if—I have hurt someone with a
  joke, or unintentionally
Women are lucky because—they are more likely to stay home
  and watch their kids grow day by day
A good father—helps one to become whatever his ability allows
A girl has a right to—grow and develop at her own pace
I am—growing—I hope
A good mother—can let go
  —is one who lets her child grow—emotionally as well
  as developmentally
My father—won't let me grow up
  —has learned to let me make my own decisions
If I can't get what I want—I pout for a little while, then go
  back to normal
For a woman a career is—a growing experience
A woman should always—try to grow beyond what she is
Education—is vital to a child's development
  —life's carte blanche
My mother and I—have grown closer over the years

At E6, behavior is seen in terms of patterns. Abilities and traits are patterns, but so also are expectations, roles, and social mores. General references to roles are found at this level. References to roles at lower levels tend to be clichés; at higher levels, they are more explicit and less stereotyped. Gender roles are particularly important to many people. More people object to what they see as society's assigned gender role than in past years, but this is even more characteristic and detailed at E7.

Women are lucky because—they aren't expected to have a
  career
  —it is more acceptable for them to show weakness than
  for men
  —they can choose whether to liberate or not
A good father—is a model
My father—is a hard worker and a good example
A girl has a right to—decide her own lifestyle
A man feels good when—he thinks he's being manly
At times he worried about—his masculinity
A wife should—avoid feeling like a "wife"
The worst thing about being a woman—is being judged for
  your looks
  —the many "hats" you must wear
  —is the old "sex role" that goes along with it

At E6, the person distinguishes appearances from underlying feelings and is concerned about pretense and hypocrisy. The physical aspect of the person is contrasted with the mental or spiritual. At lower levels, the latter distinction is rarely made spontaneously; at higher levels, their integration and mutual interdependence may be mentioned.

My father—was the best person I ever knew. He never pretended to be anyone other than himself
  —lives in a fantasy world
Education—outside the classroom is as important as inside
When they talked about sex, I—pretended not to hear
  —was embarrassed but tried not to show it

I feel sorry—for people who are physically and/or mentally disabled

Rules are—often not as rigid as they may first appear

If I can't get what I want—I get furious on the inside but pretend I don't care

Usually he felt that sex—fell into 2 categories: physical, and meaningful and romantic

My conscience bothers me if—I am dishonest to my parents, friends, myself

A good father—provides good financial & strong emotional support for his children

The E6 subject puts things in a broad social and temporal context. The concerns of people at lower levels for appearance, sex, money, social approval, and so on, are not absent but are integrated into a larger social or personal context.

The thing I like about myself is—desire to help humanity

Education—is important for everyone, but standards are falling everywhere
    —is the great equalizer

Rules are—man-made power symbols

Crime and delinquency could be halted if—we lived in small, homogeneous societies

Men are lucky because—they have history and momentum on their side

I am—upset with the structure of false democracy

The worst thing about being a woman—is that there are many social stigmas attached to the way a woman must behave

For a woman a career is—difficult in a male-oriented and—dominated society

E7: Individualistic Stage

At the E7 level and higher most responses are unique, but not all unique responses are rated that high. Although the exact wording is rarely replicated, categorical features can be noted. Most of the following responses illustrate points in addition to the one cited. Unless an exception is made explicit, characteristics of E7 protocols are also characteristic of E8 protocols.

The E7 subject has complex conceptions more often than persons of lower levels. A frequent type of complexity, and an appreciable proportion of the responses rated E7, consists of combinations of popular or replicated responses rated singly at lower levels, with at least one aspect rated at E6. Thus, they embrace in a single thought ideas that persons at lower levels commit themselves to as alternatives.

Raising a family—is a source of great pleasure, lasts too short a time, and is unpredictable

When I am criticized—I try to listen, don't like it sometimes & try to evaluate it fairly

A man's job—is a challenge, a vise of pressure, the source of stability, and too much

The thing I like about myself is—my values, personality, ability to get along well w/ others

My mother and I—are best friends, but my mom is closed-minded, I finally come to realize

When they talked about sex, I—frequently thought it was crude, or was bored, but sometimes found it stimulating

The E7 person is likely to reconcile ideas that could be considered as polar, incompatible opposites.

My conscience bothers me if—I either intentionally or unintentionally hurt someone

Being with other people—is fun if it is balanced with alone time or time with my wife

A man's job—is his job; tackle it as a job; don't try to make it your hobby. It's more pleasurable that way

The thing I like about myself is—that I consider myself to be both a good mixer and also reasonably self-sufficient

Women are lucky because—we can be independent and still be nurtured by men

A man feels good when—he has been strong and gentle at the same time

A woman feels good when—she knows she is being feminine and intelligent at the same time

My father—was a loving, caring, religious, ethical disciplinarian

Rules are—often overly picky and not flexible enough, but necessary to provide order

Men are lucky because—women still let them believe they are the stronger sex

Distinctions are drawn that are not so obvious to persons of lower levels. Thoughts may be distinguished from feelings, process from outcome. Emotional dependence is distinguished from physical and financial dependence.

I am—emotionally independent and physically dependent
    —[age], happy w/ my life, strong willed, soft hearted, and an only child

My father—was more supportive intellectually than emotionally

A good father—is one who loves his child from the heart and teaches from the mind

A man feels good when—he is physically fit and mentally stretched

Education—continues throughout life

Interpersonal relationships are cherished, their value partly supplanting the value for ability and achievement at E6. Relationships are seen as continuing or changing over time.

My mother and I—were becoming more tolerant of each other when she died
    —have always disagreed until I had my child. Now I seek her advice and help

A wife should—keep the passion in the relationship

I just can't stand people who—are insensitive to other people's feelings

I am—a whole person because I love people (family) and they love me

A good mother—loves and "lets go" without losing the relationship

A good father—finally learns his job when it is too late to use the expertise

My father—was dictatorial and often unfair but our relationship has changed to more mutual respect

When I am with a woman—I now try to develop an entire relationship, not one just based on sex

There is greater complexity in conception of interpersonal interaction. The E6 person talks of communicating and expressing ideas and feelings; those thoughts are deepened and made more complex at E7.

Being with other people—can be great if you share similar ideals
—depends on the type of people, mutual interest, and my state of mind
The thing I like about myself is—I tend to listen to others' problems and allow them to find a solution
I feel sorry—lack of communication destroys a relationship
A husband has a right to—openly clarify the feelings of himself & his wife about all things
The worst thing about being a man—not letting women know you prefer to be one
When I am with a woman—mold my conversation and habits to the mood of the individual
—I feel that I should be receptive to her feelings and thoughts.
Sometimes she wished that—we would understand her viewpoint more
My father—is too busy being a "good guy" to be involved with me

Vague statements about reasons and problems at E5 and statements about growth at E6 become statements about psychological causality at E7.

Being with other people—is rewarding and forces me to grow & change faster
—is often a defense against being alone with oneself
The thing I like about myself is—my honesty with myself and my perception of my motives
A good father—teaches his children how to be good fathers
When they talked about sex, I—learned something about their attitudes towards humanity
My main problem is—emotional immaturity due to growing up in a dysfunctional family

Emotions are reported in greater depth, often in original or humorous or touching statements.

Raising a family—is a real joy, especially for me, for I almost gave up hope of having a child
Being with other people—is one of the most fulfilling yet exhausting activities for me
When people are helpless—it scares me & it makes me feel sorry for them. I feel guilty
When they talked about sex, I—get really embarrassed; at first I'm squeamish, but I calm down after a while
I feel sorry—that I didn't learn to appreciate my parents before I did
My main problem is—I get too intense about my goals
The worst thing about being a man—is being justifiably envied by those who are not
Sometimes he wished that—he could throw off all the "masculine covers" and just be himself
—he had had a childhood, and that he had learned to play

Sometimes she wished that—she'd married a prince, instead of a frog
When I am with a man—I enjoy being playful
When I am with a woman—I tend to either "clam up" or put on an act, I never act myself

The sense of individuality that characterizes the E7 person is anticipated at E6 or even lower levels by use of the word *individual* or *individuality*. Use of the word alone does not suffice for rating at this level. Individuality merges with identity at E8 and E9.

When a child will not join in group activities—he is probably marching to a different drummer
A wife should—be loving, loyal, but should always have a mind of her own
Men are lucky because—they are able to maintain their individuality
A woman feels good when—she is taken as an individual and not type-cast
—she knows who she is and what she wants
A husband has a right to—express his individuality within the relationship
The worst thing about being a man—is being stereotyped as a man & not just be a person
When I am with a woman—I am myself and let her know it
Sometimes she wished that—people would expect less of her, and just let her be herself
For a woman a career is—another identity, another part of a multifaceted self
A woman should always—try to stay in touch with herself—her dreams, needs, wants
—maintain her own code of morals—a sense of individuality
A good mother—values a child as an independent person

Many E7 responses present vivid and personal versions of ideas that appear as simple remarks or clichés on E6 protocols; examples are self-fulfillment, varied roles, and the joy of life.

Being with other people—and being myself, as opposed to wife and mother, is enjoyable
A man's job—in a cliché version was and is to support a family
—should coincide as closely as possible to his interests and abilities
The thing I like about myself is—my joie de vivre
Education—should be a broadening, creative experience
Women are lucky because—our culture allows them to be more real
A girl has a right to—do anything "only boys do"
A woman feels good when—you treat her as an equal and not "as a woman"
A husband has a right to—whatever a person has a right to
Rules are—necessary, but so are exceptions
—important in helping me not get bogged down in petty decisions
The worst thing about being a woman—is being left alone with all the roles of mother, widow, adult daughters
My father—is alive but his role as a father is deceased
When I can't get what I want—I make impossibles possible

Usually she felt that sex—was a wonderful thing—beautiful and mysterious

In contrast to lower levels and to responses of women in the 1970s, questioning and criticism of the stereotyped prescriptions for gender roles is frequent at E7.

The worst thing about being a man—is the stereotypic macho-stoic expectations
A woman should always—be true to herself, not what society tells her she should be
A man should always—be compassionate, considerate, and just a person instead of a "macho stud"

The E7 person will often be aware of conflicting or contrasting emotions. Conflict tends to be within the self, instead of between one's own needs and society's requirements, as is sometimes the case with E5 and E6 subjects. However, the full force of psychic conflict is felt at the E8 level.

When I am criticized—I become angry, afraid, and then try to deny or distort
What gets me into trouble is—worrying and anxiety about the future or past faults
Men are lucky because—they don't have the conflict of raising kids with their work
My conscience bothers me if—I do something I feel is wrong & not if someone else feels it's wrong

The E7 person distinguishes appearance from reality, deepening the distinction made by the E6 person between inner feelings and outward appearances. At E7, the person is more specific about attempts to cope with reality and to be objective.

What gets me into trouble is—setting unrealistic goals
Education—is what you buy, though learning be what you seek
When people are helpless—it is usually their perception, not reality
I just can't stand people who—won't make any effort to adapt
My main problem is—worrying needlessly
—I still think of myself as 15
A man should always—be aware of how fallible he is
At times she worried about—imaginary illnesses
—appearances, but now she's worried about life & death

Where the E6 person has a clear understanding of individual differences and often objects to prejudice, the E7 person may achieve true toleration of others and embrace the conception of tolerance. Being nonjudgmental is sometimes mentioned.

The thing I like about myself is—that I am learning not to impose my views on others
A good father—is one who listens without making a judgment
When they talked about sex, I—listened and gave my personal values without judging
I feel sorry—for people who are limited in thinking, i. e., right, wrong, good, bad
I just can't stand people who—are narrow-minded & rigid
—judge others harshly

A husband has a right to—be a person. Nobody is guaranteed any rights in a relationship
A good mother—is loving, patient, & non-judgmental

Similar to toleration is a kind of relativism, objecting to the implied absolutism of the stem rather than completing the sentence. These responses are more explicit than the rejections of the stem at E6.

Usually he felt that sex—is too complex a subject to deal with in one sentence
A woman should always—too absolute
A man should always—nothing—I don't like the word "should"
Rules are—made to be broken. (This may be a cliché, but it's true)
The thing I like about myself is—sorry, I don't think of myself in such terms

Persons at E7 and E8 are more likely than subjects at lower levels to reveal a broad view of life as a whole.

Raising a family—is a life-long commitment
A man's job—is to figure out what he wants from himself & life and try for it
A girl has a right to—excel, strive, be herself, & become a positive thinking woman
At times he worried about—what he was doing w/ his life
At times she worried about—no life of her own and lost opportunities
At times he worried about—the whole reason for being
At times she wished that—she could change her entire lifestyle
At times he wished that—life were not so complicated
Education—is a lifelong process
For a woman a career is—a great opportunity to round out her life and enhance her as a total person

A characteristic part of the broad view of life is seeking a balance of needs, wishes, and obligations.

A wife should—find the right balance between her desires & those of her husband
What gets me into trouble is—my priorities. Balancing family, friends, and boyfriend

Despite the rule against letting a single word or phrase determine the rating, sentence completions that include "even though" or some similar phrase (although, even when, even if) are remarkably characteristic of the E7 level. The closest we have come to describing this usage is "transcending reluctance," but it is not obvious why that translates to ego level.

When I am criticized—I am annoyed, even when I know it is justified
—my feelings are hurt, even though I know they probably shouldn't be
A good father—should listen to his children, even when they don't make any sense
A wife should—support her husband (not materially) at all times—even when she doesn't agree with him

E8: Autonomous Stage

Test protocols rated E8 display a richness and variety of topics; that feature cannot be illustrated in the present format. Also, to be rated E8 there should be at least three different E8 themes or kinds of E8 responses, but that rule is unlikely to conflict with automatic application of ogive rules.

Where the E6 person might see irreconcilable choices, the E8 person construes conflicting alternatives as aspects of many-faceted life situations. He or she has a high toleration for ambiguity.

> When a child will not join in group activities—it is "good" or "bad" depending both on the nature of the child and on that of the group
> Raising a family—is a full-time job, sometimes frustrating but others so rewarding that the frustrations are forgotten
> My father—is a man of great intellect but who is quite terrified of his own fears and vulnerabilities
> When people are helpless—they frequently first become depressed and later become angry

The E8 subject compares or collates three or more possibilities or aspects of a situation, such as appearances, actions, and feelings. Such composite responses must have at least one facet from E6 or E7 to be rated E8. At E8, the three terms usually represent more sharply differentiated points of view than for similar responses at E7. This type of response is probably the most frequent sign of E8; that is an empirical discovery of the SCT method.

> The thing I like about myself is—my integrity, optimism, and patience
> A girl has a right to—be a person no matter what age, sex, or beliefs she has [sic]
> A wife should—feel free to be a woman as well as to enjoy life and her job
> Rules are—there to guide and direct but not to suppress &/or oppress people
> Crime and delinquency could be halted if—all people's psychological, social and economic needs were met
> My main problem is—identifying w/ the failures of my parents, accepting my family, especially my mother, as well as what I have in common with her
> My father—is a very conservative man, who loves us but didn't grow with us
> My conscience bothers me if—I hold back my feelings, tell a lie, or don't live up to my expectations

The E7 person begins to recognize inner conflict, but the E8 person feels its full force. The E8 person strives to cope with it, to find a means of transcending it, or to reconcile him or herself to it.

> What gets me into trouble is—attempting or wanting to control things I can't or shouldn't control
> —I analyze people and life when I ought to live it
> I feel sorry—that my anxieties often make me so difficult to live with
> I am—a child inside a man's body

> —confident in the way I look, but scared to death of everything else
> The worst thing about being a woman—is balancing vanity and meaningful work
> Sometimes he wished that—he could be a tree & free himself from all his mental turmoil
> Sometimes she wished that—she could stop worrying for just a little while and just have some hedonistic pleasure
> My conscience bothers me if—I do something that my inner guide says not to do & I do it anyway
> —I nag my husband or have selfish motives for what I do

Social stereotypes are distinguished from realistic views of people. People at this level aspire to be realistic, objective, and unprejudiced.

> A man's job—a destructive cliché
> A good father—has gone past the role restrictions that modern society imposes on many fathers
> The worst thing about being a man—is the rigid, tight-lipped role one is forced into, in our society
> The worst thing about being a woman—is being classified as nothing more than an object to reproduce and act like a servant
> A good mother—is not always perfect and it is better if she does not pretend to be
> My father—is the hero I've always admired but sadly realized his human inadequacies
> I feel sorry—for the person who is blinded by hate or ignorance
> Crime and delinquency could be halted if—I can't finish this statement. Humanity is too variable and complex to think this generality could be true
> A woman should always—try to respect others and not be judgmental
> A man should always—be honest, open, and receptive to constructive criticism

One could construe the E7 person as striving to attain or maintain individuality in connection with the problem of emotional dependence. At the E8 level, people cherish individuality and uniqueness in self and others.

> A man's job—is the construction of personally meaningful world
> A good father—encourages his children to become whatever they want to become
> A wife should—retain her identity
> A woman feels good when—she can be a full person, doing and being what she wants

Striving for self-realization and self-fulfillment partly supplants achievement motive per se and merges with enjoyment of life. When work is onerous, it is not because it involves effort, or because it ties a person down, but because it is dull or stultifying.

> Education—is the development of the entire man, physical, mental, and spiritual
> —means a lot to me—I'll stagnate if I never do anything creative

A man should always—try to be reasonably creative. Creativity is a major human need

A girl has a right to—grow and explore her own development and direction

Men are lucky because—they can do what they want more; women seem so trapped into dull & petty roles
—we can generally get away from the tedium and the racket by going to work, and feel good about our value

At times she worried about—losing her dreams and ideals and falling prey to daily "ruts" and monotony

I am—a devoted person on the path to reaching my real potential

A wife should—be fulfilled with her life, doing whatever is required to achieve that fulfillment

Like the E7 person, the E8 cherishes relationships with other people, but the E8 person expresses this in a more complex way or in context of other ideas.

Being with other people—especially those I care about is one of the things I treasure most in life
—makes me enjoy life more, for there is nothing better than to see someone else's smile

My main problem is—I'm afraid to get close enough to let someone hurt me

A husband has the right to—the support (physical, emotional, spiritual) of his wife

When I am with a woman—I enjoy interacting with her, giving and receiving attention

At E8, people express their respect for other people's need for autonomy. The problem of identity appears only in general or cliché form; full appreciation of identity as a problem is present at E9.

When a child will not join in group activities—it may mean he has an inner strength and sees a different world

Raising a family—involves a great deal of give and take and understanding of every member's ideals and morals

My mother and I—love each other enough to respect each other's private life

When people are helpless—they need help. The tricky parts of this equation are offering appropriate help and accepting it

A good father—knows the balance between growth, freedom and control
—raises his children for their own sake

A wife should—(I could wish but I cannot prescribe)

I just can't stand people who—exercise power over others by manipulating them

A good mother—allows her children to develop according to their own potential

For a woman a career is—a way of developing an independent identity

At E8, there is a clear conception of roles and problems associated with different or conflicting roles.

When I am with a man—if I know him I feel comfortable. If I don't, uneasy (depending on whether the situation is personal or social)

When I am criticized—I am too inclined to accept it from superiors and resent it from equals (or wife)

Men are lucky because—in our society career goals and sex roles are not that far apart

At E8, people see themselves in an interpersonal context, and they see the complexity and circularity of social interaction. Thus, there is a more complex version of psychological causality than at E7. Psychological development is often noted.

Raising a family—has been a learning experience, a challenge and my favorite activity in life

A man's job—may be rewarding but cannot provide him with all the opportunities for personal development

My mother and I—have grown up together and come to terms with our different views in life

When they talked about sex, I—wondered why: bragging? complaining? trying to impress? lack of self-confidence? attention getting?

The thing I like about myself is—my personality, my drive towards mastery, my gifts at growing into my potential

I just can't stand people who—don't want to grow, mature, and expand their personalities

I am—a woman who came late accepting herself as a woman

Usually she felt that sex—was a way to identify who she was

Usually he felt that sex—was simply and naturally a good way to know himself and others

Concern is expressed for people, oneself or others, living up to expectations of self or others.

What gets me into trouble is—my ability to become impatient with myself and others when we don't meet my expectations

At times she worried about—living up to the image of her older brothers and sisters

The worst thing about being a man—is that you can easily come to expect too much of yourself and others

My conscience bothers me if—and that is very often, I don't live anywhere up to my expectations of myself

At E8, emotions are differentiated and vividly conveyed. They range from joy to poignancy to deep sorrow or regret. Sensual experiences come through vividly.

My mother and I—get along very well, but I am slightly jealous of her and (I think) vice versa

Women are lucky because—women know how to express true feelings to one another without guilt or shame

I feel sorry—for those who are walking and living but are really dead in hope, dreams, etc.

Men are lucky because—they have fewer negative feelings than women (such as fear and envy)

When I am with a woman—that's a charming and beautiful woman, I find it a life-enhancing experience

When I am with a man—who loves me, my whole heart and soul feel involved—there's no such feeling like it

A man feels good when—he can "let his kid out," and just horse around without exposure to ridicule or criticism

Sex is seen in context of mutuality, as an aspect of a relationship to another person.

> A woman feels good when—her sex life goes well, and when in all respects she and her husband are "sympatico"
> Usually she felt that sex—helped to make a stronger bond in her relationship
> Usually he felt that sex—was of secondary importance in marriage to a solid friendship and tolerant understanding

E8 subjects display spontaneity, genuineness, and intensity. They often have a light touch, fantasy, and a sensitivity to life's paradoxes, sometimes shown in a nonhostile existential humor.

> I feel sorry—[for people] who lose their potential for life through a frantic search to find themselves
> Rules are—rules and I dislike them but usually try to maintain them and am always making new ones to live by
> —to provide structure within which freedom abides
> At times she worried about—the future so much she forgot to enjoy the present
> My main problem is—that I make important things trivial and trivial things too important—problem w/ perspective
> —a combination of feeling inadequate with arrogance
> The worst thing about being a man—is often the best thing about being a man, women!
> The worst thing about being a woman—is the awesome responsibility of children. (It is also the best)
> Sometimes she wished that—she had things she would not be happy with if she had them

Concern for broad social perspectives or issues may be expressed. Men and women are part of a common humanity. Such ideas are expressed in a more original, subtler, or more elaborated form than at E6 or E7.

> Education—is important not only to absorb material but improve our place in society and society itself
> At times she worried about—money, health, the state of the world, and whether her son needed new shoes right now
> Sometimes she wished that—there were not so many tight, closed-in minds in the world

E9: Integrated Stage

Ego development has been postulated to have a higher stage than Autonomous, which we have called Integrated. Cases that can be thus classified are so rare that for practical purposes, this rating can be eliminated. The theoretical interest remains high, however. What follows includes responses gleaned over a period of many years from thousands of test protocols. Obviously, these responses come from well-educated people with excellent verbal skills. Some of the responses are poetic; but are poets the most mature people in any ordinary sense? Clinicians who have used the test have observed that many of the persons who have tested E8 and E9 have been people in psychotherapy. Thus, one cannot on current evidence rule out the possibility that the distinctions at the highest levels, E7 through E9, partly reflect some variable or variables other than ego level—whether intellectual or educational qualifications, emotional maladjustment, or experience in psychotherapy.

Another caveat is that our experience with ratings made by the most conscientious users of the test do not accord with our judgment of the ratings at E8 or E9. Some researchers, possibly identifying with or sympathizing with their subjects, overestimate them; others rate according to easily classified portions of the response, usually coming first, and neglect the unique additional clause, thus underestimating the level.

Characteristics of E8 responses that are prominent at E9, usually in combination, are existential humor and a feeling for paradox, respect for others' autonomy, search for self-fulfillment, value for justice and idealism, opposition to prejudice, coping with inner conflict, reconciliation of role conflicts, appreciation of sex in context of mutuality, and reconciliation to one's destiny. Some form of conceptual complexity is always present, whether in terms of conflict, contradiction, alternative construction of situations, or subtler complexities (such as the idea of potential for development or of intolerance of prejudice). Responses at this level are often vivid, touching, or poetic. Many unite the specific and the general, and concern for inner life (presented as differentiated self-perceptions) and outer life (usually relationships with others). Generally, responses combine two or more thoughts that would separately be rated E8.

> When a child will not join in group activities—he's probably missing an element in development that would make adult relationships easier—but someone has to carry the burdens of independent thought and behavior
> Raising a family—can break your heart and be wonderful too. One sometimes learns almost too late to accept and love and not try to change
> The thing I like about myself is—that I can let my "child" out; that I don't waste time "judging" the individuals I meet; and that I think independently and creatively
> —my concern to be honest with myself, a claim that may itself be a delusion
> When people are helpless—they particularly need our compassion but may well find precisely this the greatest burden of their helplessness
> —they need others' help to grow and become more self-sufficient, if there is potential for development. Lacking potential they need protection
> Usually he felt that sex—had been removed from its relation to love and to life, & used as a medium to promote sales, & he felt deeply resentful of it & its contribution to dehumanization of people
> —was both mysteriously exciting in itself, yet more significant because of its context and for what it expressed (or failed to express) than as an immediate experience
> I feel sorry—for the disadvantaged and particularly the negro to the point I am outraged and intolerant of prejudiced people
> The worst thing about being a woman—cannot be generalized, as one woman makes an asset of the same situation decried by another
> For a woman a career is—a matter of choice with respect to her assessment of herself in terms of the world in which she lives

The one new category at E9 is the search for identity. Clichés about "who I am" or being oneself do not qualify, only responses that on other grounds would be classed at least as E8. The problem of identity appears in terms of reconciliation of roles, striving for autonomy, individuality, and self-fulfillment, and recognizing other people's need for theirs. (In the 1970 manual there were other responses similar to one quoted here, indicating that women should search for identity in order to make their husbands happy. There are no recent examples of that sentiment.)

> When a child will not join in group activities—it may be because he feels no identity with the group, is too self-conscious, or has no real interest in the activity
>
> Raising a family—is a fulfillment, including the fascination of seeing new spirits find themselves
>
> A good father—accepts the individuality and the limitations of his children, recognizes that they too have problems, and manages to be sympathetic at a distance
>
> A good mother—is kind, consistent, tender, sensitive, and *always* aware a child is master of its own soul
>
> The worst thing about being a woman—is accepting your position as a woman and an individual, but once found ceases to be the worst and becomes the best

> A wife should—try to make some sense for herself out of the strange dual role the modern world has placed her in . . . so that she is free to make her husband happy
>
> My mother and I—get along, but I need to get away to develop myself. I praise her because she is a woman, *and* a person. I am a person but not yet a woman

Many E8 responses and almost all E9 responses are fairly long. In most cases, the response begins with a remark classified at a lower level, then adds an original remark not easily fit into any replicated category. One should guard against automatically giving a high rating for long responses (as a computerized system almost certainly would). The most convincing E9 protocols have three or four E9 ratings and more than enough E8 ratings to qualify as an E8 total protocol rating (TPR). Usually, they also have a few short answers with ratings of E5 or lower. Protocols with a very large number of long responses, even if they are mostly rated E8 or E9, are not comparable with those on which the manual is based. They may have been written to display that their authors know the "right" answers, or to teach lessons to whoever reads the test. In any case, they appear to be addressed to a different directive than simply completing sentences.

CHAPTER THREE

Getting Started
Using the SCT

ADMINISTERING THE SCT

The instructions printed on the test form are to "Complete the following sentences."

The optimal way to administer the SCT is in a situation where the test administrator, whether researcher or clinician, is present. In doing research, that often means group testing. Many people have given it on a mail-out–mail-back basis. There is always the danger with the mail-out method that the intended subject says, "Honey, how do I answer this?" That is less likely when a test administrator is standing there and can quietly and gently ask the subject to just do it by him or herself.

In group administration one could say: "Now I would like you to fill out this sentence completion form. You see that these are incomplete sentences. Please finish each one. Notice that there are two pages; please make sure you have finished both." If subjects request further information, the rule is to make a noncommittal, nonsuggestive answer. Examples are: Finish the sentence any way you wish. There are no right or wrong answers. In answer to the question, "Who is 'she' or 'he'?" "it can mean anyone; just think of anyone you wish."

Minor variations in wording have proved to be inconsequential. On the other hand, instructions urging subjects to show their best selves, particularly when they include hints as to the kind of responses researchers are looking for, make it a different test or an experimental form.

CURRENT FORMS OF THE WASHINGTON UNIVERSITY SENTENCE COMPLETION TEST (SCT) FOR MEASURING EGO DEVELOPMENT

This scoring manual is intended for Form 81 for Women and Form 81 for Men. The best items from previous versions of the SCT were assembled by Lawrence D. Cohn (1991)

using data from previous versions for men and women (Loevinger, 1985). The test forms for men and women differ slightly, mostly by an occasional pronoun. However, there is only one scoring manual for each of the 36 items. Although the sexes sometimes give slightly different answers to items, there were no proven instances where, depending on whether it was given by a man or a woman, a given response should have been given a different score. Therefore, the manual itself is unisex. This topic is left for later research.

Short Forms

The best, most reliable results are obtained if the full 36-item form is used. However, the two pages (Items 1–18 and Items 19–36) are usable as alternate, matched short forms.

PREPARING WRITTEN RESPONSES FOR SCORING AND RESEARCH

The following words used in our work have attached meanings that may not seem obvious:

Stem: The part of the sentence that is given to the subject (S) to complete.
Protocol: The test as completed by S.
Item: The individual parts of the test, used interchangeably with stem.
Response: The completion S adds to the stem, whether it completes a sentence, does not complete a sentence, or is several sentences.
Item response list (IRL): A group of responses all to the same item, usually from a single sample or study.

Total protocol rating (TPR): The score assigned to a protocol or to S on the basis of the entire test as opposed to ratings of items.

Roster: A list of Ss in a single sample or a single study. In either case, appropriate demographic information (such as source, age, gender, etc.) is included in the list. At the conclusion of the study, TPR is usually added.

Coding: Substituting a code number for each S's name. Coding has a twofold purpose: to protect the privacy of S and to protect the raters from information about S that might influence ratings. Subjects should be assured that their privacy will be protected, although it is hard to imagine how any response could be used against a person, but people will probably be more spontaneous if they are sure of privacy.

Each response should be typed exactly as S gave it, preserving errors of spelling, grammar, and punctuation, which is extraordinarily difficult for most typists. The task made more difficult because peculiarities of handwriting are not relevant and must be distinguished from actual misspellings. There is one exception to the previous rule. Any part of the response that reveals identifying data on the S must be deleted, usually substituting [deleted] for the part omitted. For example, "I am afraid of fifth-grade work next year" could be typed, "I am afraid of [grade deleted] work next year." The deletion is necessary because grade level betrays age. It is particularly important to delete information that tells something about S relevant to the hypothesis being tested, such as whether S is in the experimental or control group (when that is relevant).

SENTENCE COMPLETION TEST FOR MEN (Form 81)   Date_____

Name_____ Age_____ Marital Status_____ Education_____

Instructions: Complete the following sentences.

1. When a child will not join in group activities

2. Raising a family

3. When I am criticized

4. A man's job

5. Being with other people

6. The thing I like about myself is

7. My mother and I

8. What gets me into trouble is

9. Education

10. When people are helpless

11. Women are lucky because

12. A good father

13. A girl has a right to

14. When they talked about sex, I

15. A wife should

16. I feel sorry

17. A man feels good when

18. Rules are

SCT for men (Form 81)-2

Name_____

Instructions: Complete the following sentences.

19. Crime and delinquency could be halted if

20. Men are lucky because

21. I just can't stand people who

22. At times he worried about

23. I am

24. A woman feels good when

25. My main problem is

26. A husband has a right to

27. The worst thing about being a man

28. A good mother

29. When I am with a woman

30. Sometimes he wished that

31. My father

32. If I can't get what I want

33. Usually he felt that sex

34. For a woman a career is

35. My conscience bothers me if

36. A man should always

SENTENCE COMPLETION TEST FOR WOMEN (Form 81)   Date_____

Name_____ Age_____ Marital Status_____ Education_____

Instructions: Complete the following sentences.

1. When a child will not join in group activities

2. Raising a family

3. When I am criticized

4. A man's job

5. Being with other people

6. The thing I like about myself is

7. My mother and I

8. What gets me into trouble is

9. Education

10. When people are helpless

11. Women are lucky because

12. A good father

13. A girl has a right to

14. When they talked about sex, I

15. A wife should

16. I feel sorry

17. A man feels good when

18. Rules are

SCT for women (Form 81)-2

Name_____

Instructions: Complete the following sentences.

19. Crime and delinquency could be halted if

20. Men are lucky because

21. I just can't stand people who

22. At times she worried about

23. I am

24. A woman feels good when

25. My main problem is

26. A husband has a right to

27. The worst thing about being a woman

28. A good mother

29. When I am with a man

30. Sometimes she wished that

31. My father

32. If I can't get what I want

33. Usually she felt that sex

34. For a woman a career is

35. My conscience bothers me if

36. A woman should always

CHAPTER FOUR

Instructions to Raters:
Item Rating

This manual is intended to be self-teaching. Experiments in which new raters were given only written materials showed that by faithfully following the prescribed exercises, they attained about the same proficiency as most experienced raters. About 2 or 3 weeks, working a couple of hours a day, may be required for basic mastery. After that, individual differences seem to outweigh experience in determining rating skill. All of our raters have been reasonably intelligent and intellectually sophisticated. We have not tested the limits of personal qualities necessary for effective use of the manual. There is no reason to believe that the manual can be used effectively without following a training program substantially like the one described here. Informal observation of persons who tried to bypass the training or who used descriptions of ego levels rather than the manual revealed that they were almost never correct in their ratings.

Because many users will be clinicians, one point must be stressed. The method begins with a psychometric rather than a clinical approach or attitude. Every response first should be rated out of context, that is, without reference to the remainder of its protocol. That is compatible with taking a more clinical attitude in deciding the final total protocol rating (TPR; chapter 5).

The self-training program has been worked out carefully and is meant to lead to successively deeper levels of understanding of ego development and its manifestations in sentence completions. This understanding is an indispensable tacit component. All of the exercises in Appendix A should be completed and checked with our scoring before beginning those in Appendix B. All of the protocols in Appendix B should be rated and then the ratings should be checked against ours before rating other clinical or research materials. Otherwise, the ratings most likely will contain excessive errors; moreover, the rater might fixate incorrect interpretations of method. These precautions are doubly important where the method is extended to groups of people or to sentence stems other than the kinds used here, because the tacit component is more important in such cases.

The training program outlined here concerns the substance of the concept; however, sheer clerical mistakes are the most serious source of error. Errors of judgment about ego level tend to be small, whereas clerical mistakes can result in errors of any size and are therefore doubly important. Although the rule is difficult to enforce, every step should be checked to ensure trustworthy results; moreover, it may be almost futile if there is no system for keeping track of what has been checked.

SELF-TRAINING EXERCISES

The first step in learning to rate for ego level is to master the concept of ego development as presented in chapters 1 and 2. Rapid scanning of a few item manuals (volume 2) may also help.

The second step is to learn to rate each of the 36 items; that step should be followed even if the rater intends to work with a form that contains some different stems. Knowledge of ego development is dispersed throughout the item manuals, and there is substantial transfer to new items.

Raters find it necessary to immerse themselves thoroughly in an item to master it, so (at least at first) it is hard to work on more than a couple of items a day. (That does not mean it will take half a day per item.) Detailed knowledge of this chapter is required in conjunction with beginning to rate items.

Before working on an item, its manual should be read, noting introductory comments, themes, examples of what is included in each theme at different levels, and category titles at each level. A category in general includes responses with very similar content; however, particularly at higher levels, the common element in several responses that makes them a category may not be the obvious content. Responses listed as examples of a category show the range of content included; they are not exhaustive, and most of the obvious examples are not included.

Example:

"At times she worried about—her impulsive behavior." The only place in the manual for Item 22 where this response can be placed is "Personality traits or inner states" (E6, Category e, henceforth, E6e), although the other examples are different.

The aim of rating is to determine the ego level, regardless of the content of the response. The same content occurs at several levels, sometimes at all levels. The hard distinctions are between responses concerning similar content at adjacent levels. Themes refer to some broad similarity of content or style that cuts across levels. Many category titles are followed by cross-references to specific categories at other levels that need to be distinguished from them. (There are no cross-references to categories at the same E-level.)

After becoming familiar with the manual for a stem, the responses to that stem in Appendix A should be rated, recording E-level and category. Procedures for rating responses are given in the next section. All responses for one item should be rated before checking the ratings against ours; where the ratings differ, the rater should try to understand our reasoning. Sometimes responses can be classed in one of several categories at a given level. Such differences are not considered errors.

The third step in the self-training program is to learn to rate total protocols. The procedure for going from the distribution of 36 item ratings to a TPR is described in the next chapter. Practice protocols are given in Appendix B. The rater should first record the rating of each response of a protocol, using the same out-of-context procedure as in the previous exercise. That is, all responses to a given item are rated at one time. (This procedure is recommended for all research projects using the SCT and, where possible, even in clinical usage.)

The protocols in these exercises are all real protocols gleaned from real research projects. Therefore, unlike the exercises in Appendix A, they will have some responses that are particularly hard to rate. These protocols were not chosen as being difficult, on the contrary; real people give some idiosyncratic responses. By this time, the rater should be rating some responses by reading category titles only. Of the remaining ones, some are easily decided by reading the examples in three or four germane categories. There will always be some that require more thought. High-level protocols, because they contain more original responses, take longer to rate. Only after rating the total protocol should the rater check his or her item ratings against ours. Probably, it would be best to rate the first 10 protocols, then check, and then do the final 10.

The most common error among beginning raters is to be swayed too much by topic or content of the response. Vir-

tually any topic can be discussed at any level, but persons at different levels will discuss it in different ways. Themes, which cut across levels, call attention to this problem. Cross-references after category titles must be consulted regularly until the manual is thoroughly familiar and thereafter for difficult discriminations.

Popular categories of response are denoted by asterisks. A single asterisk denotes a category given by at least 2% of a large, diverse sample. Two asterisks denote a category given by at least 5% of a large, diverse sample.

PROCEDURE FOR RATING SINGLE RESPONSES

The ground rules are as follows: Rate every response. Rate the response as a whole. Rate on the level of meanings, that is, what the person meant to say. Deep-level inferences about what the person meant are not appropriate; the response is taken at face value. Snap judgments should not be made, but lengthy rumination does not improve ratings.

In matching a response to the scoring manual, there are essentially four possibilities: The response may fit one category (Rule 1). It may combine parts corresponding to two or more categories (Rules 2 and 3). It may be meaningful but fit no particular category (Rule 4). Or, it may be omitted or too fragmentary to be meaningful (Rule 5). The rules should be applied in that sequence.

Rule 1. Match the completion with one of the listed category titles

Completions may be simple or compound. Most responses will be simple, presenting just one idea, and should be rated following Rule 1, or, failing that, Rule 4. A compound response mentions more than one idea, although it may not be a compound sentence. The elements may be reiterations of the same ideas: "sad and unhappy"; clichés: "love, honor, and obey"; contrasting ideas: "both boring and worthwhile"; or different aspects of a situation: "look, act, and feel," for example. Many categories and many examples within categories present compound responses of one of those types, so most responses can be rated following Rule 1. Rules 2 and 3 cover compound responses not explicitly listed in the manual.

Before deciding that a category is appropriate, inspect the examples given, remembering that obvious examples are omitted. If there are cross-references, check them.

Examples:

Simple responses:

"The thing I like about myself is—my naturally curly hair." This response fits the category "my looks" (E3, category a, henceforth E3a).

"A woman should always—watch her weight." This response fits the category "look her best, as attractive as possible" (E5c) better than "be neat, well-groomed, attractive" (E4b), because the E4 version is more passive, and this response, like the E5 version, implies active participation.

Compound responses:

1. Pseudo-compounds, clichés. "A woman feels good when—she is dressed neat and clean." By the dictionary "neat" and "clean" are different ideas, but this phrase is a single banality in common speech. (Another is "love and understanding.") Such responses are usually rated E4. In this case, the response fits the category "Concern with appearance of self or house" (E4g).

2. Pseudo-compounds, repetitions. "My main problem is—I am sometimes too shy and self-conscious." "Shy" and "self-conscious" are similar thoughts, both rated in the category "I'm too shy, self-conscious" (E5j), as is this response.

"A good mother—is one that is loving, caring, & understanding," classed at E4j, "loves, understands her children." This response can be seen both as a cliché and as repetitious.

3. True compounds. True compounds contain two or more contrasting ideas or alternative aspects of a situation. "Being with other people—can be stimulating & boring." This fits the category "Contrasting reactions" (E7c).

"Raising a family—may be hectic, but never dull." This fits the category "is difficult but rewarding [one at E5]" (E6a). Although they do not appear in the manual, "hectic" and "never dull" each would best be rated E5. When rating true compounds, check to see if there is a category providing for a similar combination of ideas. If not, follow Rules 2 or 3.

"A good father—is fun, tolerant, and understanding." Fun occurs in a response at E4 unclassified, tolerant is like open-minded at E6b, understanding is at E5p. The response is classed E7a, "Three diverse ideas or qualities (one E6)."

Rule 2: Where the combination of two or more elements in a compound response generates a more complex level of conception, rate the response one step higher than the highest element

Contrasting two ideas or two aspects of a situation is a frequent way of showing conceptual complexity, which is an important clue to ego level. Two contrasting E4 responses may generate an E5 response, but that is infrequent. More often, two contrasting E5 responses generate an E6 response, two or three E6 ideas generate an E7 response, and three contrasting ideas, at least one at E7, generate an E8 response. This rule does not apply below E4.

Although it is not a fixed rule, where there are two clauses in a response, the second clause is usually the higher one and determines the rating. A special case, not noted in the 1970 manual, concerns responses where the second clause negates, withdraws, or contradicts the first one. Often the first remark will be a popular one. In such cases, the second remark should govern the rating.

Examples:

"Rules are—made to be broken. (I don't really believe this—too good to pass up)" fits the category "Comment on the stem" (E7d), not the category "made to be broken" (E4i).

"Usually he felt that sex—is the most important aspect of life. I don't feel that way." This response fits the category "Evaluation of others' opinions" (E7e), but only the second clause shows that it concerns the opinion of others as well as the self.

Rule 3: Where the combination of ideas in a compound response does not generate a higher level of conceptual complexity, rate in the less frequent category or rate in the higher category

These two considerations usually agree. If the higher category is over E4, it is always used. Where one category is at E4 and the other is lower, the category at E4 will often be popular or more frequent, and the lower rating should be given. In case of doubt, rate up. Where both elements come from the same level, for research and training purposes the response is assigned to the less frequent category, but the rating is not affected.

Examples:

"I feel sorry—for people who are lonely and helpless." Helpless would be rated at E4e, which is a popular category, and lonely at E5f; the response is rated E5f.

"A woman should always—try to keep herself neat, 'on the ball,' and thoughtful of others." By itself, "neat" would be rated E4b, but the addition of "try to keep herself . . ." raises it to "look her best, as attractive as possible" (E5c). The other two ideas could be rated in "have outside interests; help others" (E5i), but they are not repetitious. The entire response falls in "Three different traits, one E5" (E6p); it resembles other examples in that category.

"What gets me into trouble is—people and my mouth." People falls in E2c, "my mouth" is E4a, a very popular category. The response is rated E2c. This is the rare case where the higher category is not chosen.

"When a child will not join in group activities—they are either shy or prefer not to." "Shy" is classed E4a, "prefer not to" falls in category E4c. E4a is a very popular category, so the rating is E4c.

"A good mother—sets limits, controls and directs." This is a pseudo-compound response. The closest category for each element is "doesn't spoil her children; is strict" (E5i). Therefore, the response is so classified.

Rule 4: In the case of a meaningful response, where there is no appropriate category and Rules 2 and 3 do not apply, use the general theory to arrive at a rating

Unusual responses without special theoretical interest have been omitted from the manuals, partly because there is no way to verify our own ratings, partly because they offer no guidance for future raters, who will be faced with different unusual responses. The rater should first look to see whether any materials in the item manual are similar to the response.

If not, the rater should go back to chapter 2, general characteristics at different ego levels, for hints. Only when that offers no help should the rater resort to the basic concept (chapter 1). The more latitude the method gives the rater, the greater the danger that personal biases will enter.

Examples:

"When they talked about sex, I—looked away." There is no clearly appropriate category. However, "covered my ears" is an example of the category "didn't listen" (E4c). E4 unclassified is the rating.

"Being with other people—is not nice." This response does not fall in any category. The most similar category is its negative, "is nice, OK" (E2a). It is therefore rated E2, unclassified.

Rule 5: Where the response is omitted or is too fragmentary to be meaningful, it is rated E4 by default

Most grammatically incomplete sentences are ratable. Many raters overuse this rule for responses difficult to rate. Usually the rater should make an informed guess; that is one way that descriptions of the stages have evolved. It is often useful to keep track of which E4 ratings represent outright omissions or unratable fragments.

Examples:

"My father—was a governor emlope." This (real) response is interpreted as a badly misspelled version of "was a government employee," and following Rule 1, is rated in "Occupations" (E4l).

"When they talked about sex, I—mean girl." Possible interpretations of this response are that those talking about sex are mean (bad), that she herself becomes mean (bad, mad) in this situation, or that to this person sex means girls (female sex). All are compatible with a rating of E2, unclassified.

"The worst thing about being a woman—is being the default parent." In a sample contributed to our manual construction study, someone had rated this E4, Rule 5. The fact that it is a coherent sentence makes that prima facie an inappropriate rating. Clearly, the rater was not computer literate. It is now rated in "Burden of responsibilities (specified)" (E6d).

Some responses rated E4, Rule 5, are:

"When people are helpless—sometimes"
"Raising a family—church"
"Women are lucky because—they."

RECORDING THE RATINGS

For many uses of this manual, E-level is what matters, not the categories. When learning to rate, however, recording categories is valuable so that raters can compare notes with each other and with our ratings for the exercises. Optimally,

there are at least two raters in research using the manual so that recording the categories will remain useful.

Examples:

The following four responses have been given to the stem, "Education—"

1. is essential
2. is not
3. is necessary to maintain our democracy
4. is developed through contact with others

These responses are scored:

1. E4a
2. Rule 5
3. E6j
4. E6, UC

The notations mean:

1. Response is scored in category *a* at the E4 level.
2. The response is too fragmentary to rate. However, in figuring the TPR, the default rating will be E4.
3. Response is scored in category *j* at the E6 level.
4. No appropriate category could be found. Using Rule 4, the rater hypothesized that the thinking is equivalent to that of persons at the E6 level.

SOURCES OF BIAS

There are three broad classes of bias: aspects of the response or traits of the subject that are more obvious than the clues for ego level, aspects of the response or the subject that are as inferential as ego level, and characteristics of the raters.

Errors of spelling and grammar are more obvious than ego level. They are more likely to occur on protocols rated low in ego level than protocols rated high, with a great deal of overlap, but they reflect intelligence, education, and SES more directly than ego level. The fact that all those variables are correlated does not prove that ego level is an artifact of the others. There is no reason to suppose that children or retarded adults can attain the highest levels considering that most intelligent adults do not reach that point.

At times we have been tempted to reason: "Because this woman obviously comes from a low social class, to achieve this amount of insight represents a greater achievement than for someone from a more favorable environment. Therefore, let us give her the benefit of the doubt and raise the rating." At other times, there has been a temptation to reason: "This aspect of the response is more indicative of low social status than of low ego level. However, as they are correlated, chances are we will be right if we rate it low in ego level." These two lines of reasoning cancel each other out. The only solution is to avoid as far as possible assigning any weight to intelligence, social status, errors in spelling and grammar, or use of plain or fancy words.

Number of words is correlated with ego level for a straightforward reason, because on the average it takes more words to express complex thoughts and relations than simple ones. That is not a spurious correlation. The correlation becomes spurious if responses are rated higher because they have more words, regardless of content. Rigorous use of the manual is some protection against this bias. We rate neither up or down according to the number of words. That rule holds without reservation for rating a single item. For a total protocol where most or all of the responses are very wordy, one could infer that the long responses consistently favored higher ratings, and therefore possibly one should shade the TPR downward, particularly if it is borderline. But, there are no data bearing on this point.

Certain words that we use to describe high-level responses—*role conceptualization, interpersonal relationships, sense of identity, self-fulfillment*—are part of the patois of the helping professions. Some subjects used in manual construction samples have been drawn from such groups. These terms have also come through to readers of magazines, especially those aimed at women. In scoring, one should look not just for the use of the words, but also for evidence of the idea behind the words. The words by themselves may stand out as clichés, often scored E5.

Responses scored at the highest level have little of the professional patois, but they are often touching and poetic, humorous or sad. In the samples used for manual construction, no group of subjects had special literary training or talent. There are occasional signs of literary merit at various levels (outnumbered by signs of marginal literacy), and many high-level responses with no special literary quality. Whatever correlation may exist between high ego level and literary merit need not be spurious. A rich inner life is an aspect of high ego level, and that such a rich inner life would also serve as an ingredient (although neither necessary nor sufficient) of literary talent is not surprising. The literary quality per se is not the basis for scoring.

Similar considerations hold for age. The manual is not intended for ages previous to adolescence. According to our experience, it is satisfactory down to about 12 years, and on occasion we have used it down to age 9. (Other tests, such as Selman, 1980, are appropriate for younger children.) Various studies have shown consistent and appreciable increases in ego level during adolescence, and little or no increase beyond about 20 years. In any case, age-contingent scoring is explicitly excluded. That rule corresponds to an implicit rule for intelligence tests. Mental age rises during adolescence, but that does not mean more lenient scoring standards are adopted for younger ages. If the decision to score a response right or wrong depended on the respondent's age, there would be no clear way to demonstrate age changes. Consequently, we decided never to rate ego level according to whether it came from someone of a certain age, or, on similar considerations, of a particular marital or parental status. Accordingly, the manual should be used that way.

Two aspects of the response, somewhat more inferential than the foregoing sources of bias, are arbitrarily excluded from consideration in rating: the question of the truth of the response and signs of pathology. Whatever the relevance of those issues to ego level, the manual has been constructed by ignoring them and should be used that way.

We could not check the truth or reasonableness of assertions where it might have been an issue, for instance, "My main problem is—I'm too fat." So truth or reasonableness is excluded as a consideration, even where the rater feels able to make a good guess. By way of justification, there are always different ways of expressing the issue, for example, "too fat" could be restated in terms of lack of self-control, and there are always other issues the person could have discussed instead of weight. Moreover, there are 35 other items to reveal the person's characteristic level of thinking; the occurrence of a few E4 responses does not preclude any other rating for the TPR. In discouraging consideration of the factual status of a response, we are discouraging risky inferences that might introduce more error than information into the ratings. The rule must not be pushed to absurdity, however. The person who responded "I am—a secret spy for the Russians" expects the rater to know that she is joking. Such information can be used.

We try, so far as possible, not to have our rating influenced by signs of pathology. Hospitalized schizophrenics sometimes produce SCT protocols indistinguishable from those of normals. No protocols from such cases have been used in constructing either the present manual or the 1970 manual. Pathology may influence responses in either direction. Pathological responses could easily be unique, and thus confused with the unique responses characteristic of high ego levels. But it could also happen that pathology would lead to eruption of impulsive responses that belie the person's characteristic ego level.

Similar problems arise in relation to people in psychotherapy. The level of verbal exchange in psychotherapy is too close to that of the SCT not to have a possible effect, which might be either a spurious rise or spurious decline. Direct quotation of wise sayings and admonitions of the therapist might lead to too high a rating. On the other hand, therapy encourages and works by uncovering the kind of hostile, sexual, self-interested motives whose suppression or control marks some stages of ego growth. Although therapy works to breach inhibitions in speech and thought, it does not ordinarily lead to a corresponding regression in behavior. Thus, the long-sought instrument to evaluate the effects of psychotherapy is, for the foregoing and other reasons, not to be found in the present scoring manual.

A final group of biases refers to characteristics of the rater rather than of the subject. One's own problems, not necessarily neurotic ones, tend to be overestimated. If money is a major problem, then one wants to attribute realistic coping to complaints about money. If religion is a major interest, one wants to see high ego level in religious professions; an antireligious rater may be similarly loath to rate religious answers as high as they deserve. An overweight person will be touched by persons whose problem is weight, one struggling with reconciling childrearing and marriage with career may see high-level implications in that conflict, and so on. Neurotic problems are even more insidious, because one does not always admit to having them. Reliance on the manual is a substantial protection against such biases. In the early stages of the work a corresponding protection was obtained by working in groups with relentless mutual criticism. In later stages, empirical feedback performed this function. Any user of the test who substitutes his or her own judgment for that of the manual opens the way to this serious bias. The manual surely contains mistakes, but they are most likely in rare categories, not those concerned with life's universal problems.

A final bias is the end-of-the-rainbow effect. Anyone working with the scoring system for a while begins to feel that high is good and longs to believe that the achievement of high ego level will be crowned with peace and contentment. Responses expressing those feelings and self-satisfaction do occasionally occur at high levels. But, when descriptions of those responses were built into a subsequent tentative scoring manual, the raters invariably, and probably justifiably, included mostly responses from E4, E5, and E6

protocols. The absence of self-criticism at E4 is probably more conducive to expressions of contentment than at high levels. One could argue that the mark of the highest levels is not the solution of one's problems but openness to more problems and often more poignant ones.

A question similar to that of rater bias asks to what extent the ego level of the rater limits his or her ability as a rater. Given a choice, we would prefer to limit use of the manual to persons at the E6 level or higher, with above-average intelligence, and preferably with some graduate training in psychology. That is not practically enforceable. Can a person at the E6 level learn to rate accurately at higher levels? The SCT method is based on selective perception of facts in accord with one's own level. However, there is a difference between what one perceives and produces spontaneously in a free-response situation and what one can deal with adequately when the material is presented to one. Thus, in principle, people can learn to score at a somewhat higher level than their own. Our experience with many raters, few if any of us having claim to higher than an E6 or E7 level of personal development, is that we learn to rate consistently and validly beyond our own levels. As an informal impression, persons below the E6 level have trouble discriminating responses in the E7 to E9 range, in part because most such responses are unique and at best fit categories loosely.

Deriving Total
Protocol Ratings

THE SCORING ALGORITHM

Given a rating for each of 36 items, an algorithm is needed to translate that distribution into a rating for the whole protocol (TPR). Prior to the 1970 edition of this scoring manual, there were few explicit discussions of choice of algorithm for arriving at a total score from a distribution of item scores.

The most obvious and frequently used psychometric model takes either the sum or the mean of the item ratings as the TPR. Where the number of items is fixed, as in the present case (36), the mean is in effect equivalent to the sum of item ratings. In that model, every item is given equal weight in determining TPR. This model meets the problem of reliability by averaging, and, with sufficient items, is almost perfectly correlated with the first factor score in an unrotated principle components factor analysis. There is, however, an intuitive objection to it. Suppose one were trying to decide whether a given protocol belonged at the Conscientious (E6) or Autonomous (E8) stage. Normally, one would expect an appreciable number of responses to come from lower levels on such a protocol. Whether those responses are at the E2, E3, or E4 level is not germane intuitively. The Item Sum algorithm would award a higher rating to the subject with Conformist (E4) answers than to the subject with a mixture of Conformist and Impulsive (E2) and Self-protective (E3) responses. A clinician might see the variety of themes and access to different developmental levels as itself an indication of high ego level. Hence, the presence of a few low responses on a protocol with distinctive high responses may enhance the impression of high ego level.

Some researchers working with projective tests of developmental sequences similar to ego development have thought of them as similar to an ability that the subject may or may not exercise to its maximum extent. In psychometric terms, that means the most characteristic level for the person is the highest level displayed.

Another algorithm takes as TPR the mode of the distribution of item ratings, implying that the level most characteristic for the person is the level where he or she most frequently operates.

The conception of ego level as being the level of core functioning does not readily translate into any of those scoring algorithms.

We began by using the total configuration of the distribution of item ratings in assigning TPRs, guided by intuitive rules for what kinds of distributions indicated what ego levels. This model has the advantage over the other models of retaining more information, and it is more like a clinician's diagnostic thinking, because it uses the configuration of responses. It has the disadvantages of being subjective and hard to codify. If there are K discriminable levels, there are roughly K^2 parameters. To retain the advantages of this method with no more than $K-1$ parameters, we arrived at the *ogive* rules (Table 5.1). The version presented here has been slightly amended over the years to reflect accumulated experience, using as criterion, matching the collective judgments of the most experienced raters.

All of the algorithms treat the separate items as interchangeable. From a rigorously psychometric view, a preferable model would assign a separate regression weight to each item, or to each scored level of each item, or at the extreme to each category of each item. However, that would entail an impossibly large number of parameters, and it is doubtful that it would improve on the Item Sum score.

There is a major practical objection to the Item Sum score. Many users of the SCT over the years have felt free to renumber the stages of the scale and used their own code numbers in getting the Item Sum. The original patchwork of I-level numbers, Delta, and transitional stages apparently invited that. Our new E-level code has the advantage that its numbers are usable as a computational code for Item Sum scores (see Table 1.1).

TABLE 5.1
Automatic Ogive and Item Sum Rules to Assign TPR for 36-Item and 18-Item Forms

Code	Name	Item Sum	Automatic Ogive*§	Explanations of Ogive*†
			For 36-Item Forms	
E9	Integrated	235 up	No more than 34 ratings at E8^	2 or more E9^
E8	Autonomous	217–234	No more than 31 ratings at E7	5 or more E8 or higher
E7	Individualistic	201–216	No more than 30 ratings at E6	6 or more E7 or higher
E6	Conscientious	181–200	No more than 24 ratings at E5	12 or more E6 or higher
E5	Self-aware	163–180	No more than 20 ratings at E4	16 or more E5 or higher
E2	Impulsive	72–132	At least 5 ratings at E2	5 or more E2
E3	Self-protective	133–145	At least 6 ratings at E3	6 or more E3 or lower
E4	Conformist	146–162	Other cases	Other cases
			For 18-Item Forms	
E9	Integrated	119 up	No more than 17 ratings at E8^	1 or more E9^
E8	Autonomous	109–118	No more than 16 ratings at E7	2 or more E8 or higher
E7	Individualistic	101–108	No more than 15 ratings at E6	3 or more E7 or higher
E6	Conscientious	91–100	No more than 12 ratings at E5	6 or more E6 or higher
E5	Self-aware	82–90	No more than 9 ratings at E4	9 or more E5 or higher
E2	Impulsive	36–67	At least 3 ratings at E2	3 or more E2
E3	Self-protective	68–75	At least 3 ratings at E3	3 or more E3 or lower
E4	Conformist	76–81	Other cases	Other cases

*Apply ogive rule in the order given, from E9 to E4.
§Automatic ogive for 36-item forms appeared in Loevinger and Wessler (1970, p. 129).
†The explanations of ogive should yield identical results to the Automatic ogive.
^To receive an E9 rating by ogive rule, the E8 ogive criterion must also be met.

Rating a Total Protocol

In rating a total protocol the following steps should be taken in the order given:

1. Rate each completion according to its own item manual without regard to context, and record the rating. This should be considered a test-scoring task and should be as objective as possible.
2. Read the whole protocol through, trying to form an impression of what kind of person could have written it. Jot down this impressionistic E-level for the person.
3. Make a frequency distribution of your item ratings and then a cumulative frequency distribution (ogive).
4. Determine what TPR would be assigned using the ogive rules of Table 5.1.
5. Where the ogive TPR coincides with the impressionisitic E-level, record this value as the TPR and go on to the next case.
6. Where there is a discrepancy between the ogive and the impressionistic TPRs, it is necessary to take a more analytic attitude, and there is a further series of steps to take.
7. Check preceding steps. (Clerical errors are frequent.)
8. Look at the item rating distribution. To some extent, the higher the ratings are above E4, the more heavily they should be weighted. For example, if there is a marginal number of ratings at E6 or above, and if some of those are at E7 or E8, the protocol should probably be called E6. We formerly had a set of "borderline rules," but research has shown that they led to more errors than improvement in TPRs.
9. Evaluate the nonpsychometric signs, that is, indications that do not affect the item distribution.

Important Nonpsychometric Signs

9a. Repetition of words or phrases in three or more separate responses tends to be a low indicator, usually E4 or lower.

9b. Repetition of an idea or thought (such as responsibility or love), even if in varying language, may indicate a neurotic or realistic preoccupation. Several mentions of responsibility serve as a less useful indicator of E6 than mentioning responsibility plus differentiated inner feelings plus complex responses. High levels are more strongly indicated when there are varied high-level indicators. Richness and originality of the total protocol is a high-level indicator, although for originality we do not have any hard-and-fast rules for distinguishing signs of pathology or signs of unusual intelligence and intellectual productivity from signs of high ego level.

9c. Whereas, in general, repetition is a low indicator, there may be E4 and E6 (or even higher) level persons who have a neurotic or perhaps a realistic preoccupation with a particular low-level theme like drinking or interpersonal exploitation. Therefore, E2 and E3 ratings are also more secure if there are varied low indicators.

9d. Closeness to theory is also taken into account in evaluating the evidential worth of a particular response.

Some special considerations apply to rating total protocols that are not entirely conveyed by the rules for rating items. Herewith we try to make those rules explicit.

Characteristics of Total Protocols at Different Levels

E9: Integrated. Most samples will contain no E9 subjects. For most purposes, it is best to group E8 and E9 TPRs together, particularly when using 18-item forms, because a single item rating becomes unduly important, and item ratings at that level are unreliable. The following considerations are helpful when it is desired to retain distinctions at the highest levels. When about half the item ratings are over E6, the person is a candidate for an E9 rating. In addition, we look for responses that integrate innerlife and outer concerns, present and future, immediate and long-term concerns, personal and social, trivial and important, and particularly responses that include several of the foregoing. To be rated E9, the protocol must also satisfy the requirements for an E8 TPR.

E8: Autonomous. A TPR of E8 is never given unless there are at least three different types of E8 response or three different E8 themes. Typical E8 themes are coping with inner conflict, role conceptualization beyond the banal "wife and mother" level, complex psychological causation, psychological development, self-fulfillment, and conceptual complexity, (e.g., comparison of three different aspects of situations, three methods of coping, or three possible causes). Conceptual complexity can also be shown in the complexity of interpersonal relationships envisaged, such as the relationship between two persons affecting a third person (perhaps their child).

E2: Impulsive. In addition to responses rated E2, one typically finds several of the following features on E2 protocols: brief answers throughout, often with some omissions; flat affect, almost to the point of being inappropriate; alternatively or in combination with flat affect, evidence of unsocialized impulsivity (drinking, getting mad, blatant sexuality), with some answers actually sounding impulsive; repetitive answers; little concern with interpersonal relationships except as people serve as source of supplies; dichotomization of the world into the nice, clean, good-to-me category versus nasty, dirty, mean-to-me category. We try to distinguish an E2 type of illogical response ("Men are lucky because—they are happy) from language barrier due to foreign birth or semi-illiteracy, for example, "If I can't get what I want—I would get a three bathroom house," apparently misreading "can't" as "can." Language barrier is not a clue to E-level.

E3: Self-Protective. Whereas the E2 may be unable to compose an original germane response to each item, some E3 subjects just refuse to do so. They may omit some items, but they are more likely to give hostile evasions. Some such responses are scored E4, because they also occur at other levels, but where they set the tone of the whole protocol, they weigh strongly for an E3 rating. Where the tone of the protocol is permeated by themes such as exploitation, domination, and obedience, it is probably E3, even though individual responses are mostly E4, and E4 themes, such as love, are also present. References to appearance, formerly considered an E4 theme, occur on lower levels for some items often enough that for some items they are given an E3 rating. E2 responses are not uncommon on E3 protocols, nor are few of E5 and even E6 responses. However, a single clearly formulated reference to long-term values and ideals contraindicates a TPR of E4 and still more any rating below E4.

In distinguishing an E2 from an E3 protocol, we consider general haplessness (more likely at E2) and beginning sensitivity to social requirements (more likely at E3). Although the E3 person may be as selfish and self-centered as the E2 person, he or she will disguise hostility in the form of hostile humor, in deference to social norms.

Some categories of response characterize protocols below E4 but do not distinguish E2 from E3 protocols. Usually, they are assigned to the E3 level as a compromise. Partly for this reason, a large number of E3 ratings may weigh more in favor of an E2 TPR than an E3 one. According to the ogive rules, an E2 rating should be ruled out before E3 is considered.

Practice Exercises
for Item Rating

EXAMPLES FOR RATING FOR ITEM 1:
WHEN A CHILD WON'T JOIN IN GROUP ACTIVITIES—

1. he should be punished
2. it's sad—but don't force him
3. I would be somewhat concerned
4. it's too bad, but there is usually not much you can do about it except wait
5. he may have a good reason
6. I seek a way to interest the child
7. he is sullen
8. he could be shy, frightened, self-centered
9. it usually means that he is not friendly
10. he is probably too shy and introspective
11. he may not be feeling well
12. they are sick
13. don't worry about it
14. , it may be the child's imperfect nature which is at fault—but it may also be that the group is not worth joining
15. he is in some difficulty
16. the child will not know what is going on in society or in the world
17. ask him what he would like
18. let him play by himself
19. he may be doing more worthwhile things on his own
20. , it should be given some extra attention, and be shown that group activities can be a lot of fun

Scoring Key for Item 1[1]

1 3d*	6 5o*	11 4e*	16 5v*
2 4g*	7 3b	12 2b	17 6l
3 5n	8 7d*	13 4i*	18 5s
4 7a	9 4c*	14 8a*	19 7c
5 6b	10 5h	15 4b*	20 6m

---

[1]An asterisk (*) indicates that an explanatory note is appended.

Notes[2]

1. The difference between 3d and 3e represents two types of category headings. "Punish" in 3d, following a dash, is a direct quotation from the completions. "Punishments" in 3e, not following a dash, is a description.
2. "Don't force him" is 4g; "it's sad" is probably E4, somewhat similar to 4j. This is a true compound, but does not really increase conceptual complexity, so it is kept at E4.
6. Category 5o finds way to interest the child; 7b finds the child's interest first.
8. These three ideas are quite different from one another.
9. The response is similar to the second example in 4c.
11. More tentative than 2b.
13. "Don't worry" is 4i, and "worry" is 5n. These two responses have the same "form" but different content. Content can, though not always, make a difference in E-level.
14. Similar to the first example, and more elaborate than 7e.
15. The "difficulty" might be psychological (5d) but that was not explicit so cannot be presumed.
16. In the first edition, this category was at I-4, which is equivalent to E6.

EXAMPLES FOR RATING FOR ITEM 2: RAISING A FAMILY—

1. is a great pleasure
2. is a great joy, and blessing from God
3. is hell
4. is full of responsibility
5. costs money
6. requires patience, hard work and a lot of love
7. is not easy but it's a joy
8. can be a wonderful challenge
9. is tough
10. is often a dream of mine
11. is hard for a teen
12. would be nice in the future
13. is a harder task for only one parent
14. is difficult, heart-rending, requires great sacrifices—and is totally and joyfully rewarding
15. is the greatest thing anyone could do
16. takes lots of energy and commitment
17. is something I've never done
18. gives you the opportunity for growth and development
19. is one of my greatest fears
20. is the key human activity

Scoring Key for Item 2

1 4c*	6 6l	11 3c	16 7a
2 6f*	7 5d	12 4e	17 4k
3 2b*	8 6a	13 5h*	18 7b
4 4a*	9 3b	14 8c	19 6k
5 4h	10 5f	15 6b	20 7c

Notes

1. It can be argued as 5b.
2. Great joy is 4c, "blessing" is 6f. The combination does not increase complexity. Following Rule 3, the response is rated at the higher of the two, 6f. According to Rule 3, when a combination of ideas in a

---

[2]There are some elementary explanations with the first three items to help beginners.

compound does not generate a higher level of conceptual complexity, rate in the less frequent category or rate in the higher category.
3. Vague and impulsive exclamation.
4. Though "responsibility" is often higher (around E6), it is a common E4 response to this stem. Thus, using the manual is better than using theory alone.
13. The "single parent" response implies a recognition of the two-parent cooperation, which 3c does not show and 6g is more explicit about.

EXAMPLES FOR RATING FOR ITEM 3:
WHEN I AM CRITICIZED—

1. I don't listen
2. I come back and criticize the criticizer
3. I try to look at myself through another person's eyes
4. I try to evaluate the criticism with a view toward improvement
5. I take it the best I can
6. I fight back with my opinion
7. I tell everybody to fuck off
8. I try to use it in a creative way to improve myself
9. I let it roll off me
10. I am sad at first and then I grow from the criticism
11. I just normally keep my hurt to myself
12. I often get annoyed
13. I either take it to heart or "blow it off"
14. I will look at myself to see what is being criticized
15. I become more defensive than I would like to
16. I am hurt, angry, embarrassed, grateful
17. I may be amused, annoyed, angered or hurt
18. I listen and try to think it out
19. I feel sad
20. I want to know what I'm criticized for and why

Scoring Key for Item 3

1 4a	6 5b	11 5c	16 7d*
2 3a	7 3b	12 4c	17 6n*
3 8a	8 5a*	13 6n*	18 4f*
4 6i	9 4d*	14 5k	19 5e
5 4e	10 6l	15 7a	20 4g

Notes

8. "Use it in a creative way" may mean changing the meaning, the situation, the feeling for the sake of self-improvement. That argument may raise it as high as E8, or somewhere between E5 and E8 because the idea was not spelled out in full.
9. Or 5i if the response is understood as trying to refrain from emotional response and take time to let the criticism pass by. However, this extrapolates a bit much.
13. Take it to heart is 6b, with "blow it off" is a combination, but not more complex and also fits at 6n. Because 6b is a common category, the response is rated at 6n (Rule 3). The rule is more important when the two categories are at different E-levels.
16. Hurt and "angry" are 5e; "embarrassed" is 5g; and "grateful" reflects an acceptance somewhat similar to 6m.
17. Though this is a multiple compound as in the previous example, none of the components is at E6 to qualify for the overall rating of 7d.
18. This is kind of a pseudo-compound, and similar to the last example in 4f.

EXAMPLES FOR RATING FOR ITEM 4:
A MAN'S JOB—

1. is to take care of his family financially
2. is stereotypically to be the family breadwinner
3. is work that is too heavy for a woman
4. isn't much different from a woman's
5. is not as important as his family
6. can be both a major source of satisfaction as well as a major source of irritation.
7. is working with cars
8. is what he goes to each day
9. should be interesting and fun
10. should keep him busy and happy
11. takes too much of his time
12. is very hard to do
13. is to work to his best capability
14. is only partly his vocation, and he should devote effort to being a husband, father, and well-read citizen
15. is to share life with whomever he has made a commitment to
16. is to do the best he can with what he has
17. cannot be specified
18. is to survive and to be himself, to make some contribution to the survival of man on earth
19. should lead somewhere and give personal satisfaction
20. is never finished

Scoring Key for Item 4

1 4h	6 7g	11 5e	16 7e
2 7a	7 3a	12 2a	17 5c
3 3c	8 4e	13 6j*	18 8b*
4 5b	9 6f	14 7f	19 6h
5 5o	10 5g*	15 6m	20 4i

Notes

10. In this compound "happy" is 5g, a common category, so the rating relies more on the other term, "busy," which is also about E5.
13. 6j refers to doing his best for job or for others, whereas 7e implies self-fulfillment
18. This response shows global concern without losing individuality.

EXAMPLES FOR RATING FOR ITEM 5:
BEING WITH OTHER PEOPLE—

1. is a need of mine
2. makes me more outgoing
3. makes me happy if I am in an outgoing mood
4. is ok
5. can be tremendously restorative, but one needs privacy, too
6. is groovy
7. is good; its where the sharing of ideas and experiences takes place
8. makes one feel good and not alone
9. makes me feel accepted and at the same time on the outside
10. is scary
11. can be intimidating
12. makes no difference to me
13. facilitates social exchange and social interactions

14. can get pretty dull
15. is fun when I know the other people
16. is a requirement for humanity
17. makes me happy sometimes and upset at other times
18. is something I enjoy immensely
19. is hard to do at times
20. is a fulfilling experience

Scoring Key for Item 5

1 5a	6 4a	11 5e	16 5c
2 4f	7 8a	12 5o	17 6d
3 6c	8 51	13 6j	18 4b*
4 2a	9 7c	14 5f	19 5g
5 7a	10 3a	15 4c	20 6a

Notes

18. There is no comparison or condition expressed. Unconditional approval is conformist.

EXAMPLES FOR RATING FOR ITEM 6:
THE THING I LIKE ABOUT MYSELF IS—

1. I'm fun to be with
2. hard to describe
3. I don't know anything
4. I'm smart
5. that I'm me!
6. that I do not feel pressured to act or think like others
7. I like to do things for others
8. that I don't take drugs
9. that I can depend on my self
10. my love for Jehovah
11. my nose
12. I am very candid
13. that I am dependable
14. that I am always striving to be my best
15. my ability to listen and not be judgemental
16. I am sensitive and sociable
17. that I'm open minded. I like to do new things cause they are unpredictable.
18. my soft and caring heart
19. my strong sense of myself and my listening capabilities
20. that I always try to keep an open mind about things and think positively

Scoring Key for Item 6

1 4d	6 7b	11 3a	16 6a
2 5q	7 5b	12 5f	17 7f*
3 2c*	8 2a	13 4i	18 5a
4 4g	9 6k*	14 6d	19 7j*
5 3d	10 5o	15 7c	20 6b

Notes

3. Self-rejection is often found at E2; 5q implies uncertainty and is aware of alternatives.

9. 5k expresses self-confidence and 6k, self-reliance or independence, but some responses could be read either way.
17. "New things" and "unpredictable" refers to adaptation and resilience.
19. "Listening" is popular at 6a, but here is contrasted with a "sense of myself," showing identity concern.

EXAMPLES FOR RATING FOR ITEM 7:
MY MOTHER AND I—

1. aren't as close as my father & I
2. just had a nice telephone conversation
3. are much more alike than I had realized
4. look very much alike
5. are both neurotic
6. like to go fishing
7. don't love each other
8. sometimes argue
9. don't get along in our personal lives—only in business
10. are always together just like best friends
11. are working to develop a relationship as friends
12. get along very well now, but when I was growing up we didn't
13. are from two different worlds—we never speak the same language
14. were seemingly very good friends but she knew nothing about me
15. were much closer when I moved out of the house at 17 years old
16. get along beautiful
17. are very close, since she has moved away 4 years ago I feel a void in my life
18. I do not remember my mother
19. have a strange relationship
20. do not get along as well as most mothers and daughters, but our love for each other is deep

Scoring Key for Item 7

1 5c	6 2a	11 7b	16 4g
2 3a	7 4i*	12 6k	17 6h
3 7e	8 5i	13 6c	18 4e
4 4b	9 8a	14 7a	19 6o
5 6d	10 5g	15 6m	20 8c*

Notes

7. Or 4f. Though categories (such as f, i) should be recorded, disagreement at the same level (here both E4) is not important.
20. Or 8U. First clause is 5i, second is 6h, and combination is paradoxical.

EXAMPLES FOR RATING FOR ITEM 8:
WHAT GETS ME INTO TROUBLE IS—

1. when I procrastinate too long and then end up with mountains of work
2. not being honest
3. my honesty and bluntness
4. when I feel guilty and inadequate
5. when I do something bad
6. drinking too much and neglecting my studies
7. who, me?
8. the police

9. my mood swings
10. I am hypercritical and can be abrasive especially when my aim is at some one who is insincere
11. over commitment
12. things that every teenager does, I just get caught
13. rage & anger
14. that sometimes I don't let people know how I really am feeling
15. always saying what I think—but I don't know if that is "trouble" or just a different life
16. when I don't tell my parents where I am & I abuse their trust
17. trying to be nice to everyone
18. not being sensitive to my wife's or family's needs
19. a large and active mouth with faulty cerebral connections to the restraint centers
20. I try to be funny and I annoy people

Scoring Key for Item 8

1 6d*	6 4g	11 6e	16 6k
2 4c	7 5w	12 3d	17 4l
3 6a	8 2c	13 4i	18 5o
4 7c	9 5k	14 6m	19 7U*
5 2a	10 8b	15 7h*	20 5a

Notes

1. This long response is not more than "procrastination," so not rated up from 6d.
15. Similar to the rejection of stem described in Chapter 2.
19. Joking about one's fault shows acceptance typically at E7.

EXAMPLES FOR RATING FOR ITEM 9:
EDUCATION—

1. is very important if you want to get anywhere in life
2. is good to get
3. is the cornerstone of progress
4. is a must in today's society
5. is one of man's precious heritages
6. is an important aspect of my life although sometimes it is too much to handle
7. is very important but not easy
8. for one's children can be a large expense
9. is essential to everyone, no matter what sex, age, or race
10. is important, but not to all people
11. is very important for a bright future
12. 12 years
13. is a way for self betterment
14. is a lifelong venture
15. is a fascinating experience
16. happens sometimes within institutions, but more frequently without
17. is very essential to me
18. provides tools to live a full life
19. the more you have the better off you are
20. is of significant value beyond the monetary

Scoring Key for Item 9

1 5m	6 6o	11 5b	16 6e
2 3a	7 5i	12 3d	17 4a

3 6j	8 4h	13 6i	18 6k
4 4b	9 4c	14 7h	19 5a
5 6d*	10 6g	15 5d	20 6b

Notes

5. Similar to an example in 6d, "biggest gift given to man."

EXAMPLES FOR RATING FOR ITEM 10:
WHEN PEOPLE ARE HELPLESS—

1. I like to lend a hand
2. I am the first to want to help
3. I feel bad for them
4. it mostly is their own fault
5. they either become depressed or sullen or angry
6. you should help them
7. I am uncomfortable if I can't help
8. they need people to rely on
9. they should be helped to become independent
10. they are unable to do the thing they want
11. they are a real pain in the rear end
12. they have reasons for being that way that go deeper than the surface
13. they should try and pull themselves up
14. I feel very sympathetic
15. I feel sympathetic but rarely lend as much help as I should
16. they rely on friends for guidance
17. one wonders how they became that way
18. I try to be of some assistance
19. they lose hope
20. it is the duty of a progressive social order to lend a helping hand

Scoring Key for Item 10

1 5a	6 4e	11 3U*	16 5l
2 6b*	7 6c	12 7e	17 5e
3 4a	8 5f	13 4g	18 4d
4 6p	9 6k	14 6U	19 5g
5 5h	10 2c*	15 7a	20 7d, 7c

Notes

2. The focus is on one's own response, which is a quick desire to help.
10. Tautological.
11. Hostile tone, characteristic of E3.

EXAMPLES FOR RATING FOR ITEM 11:
WOMEN ARE LUCKY BECAUSE—

1. they can have kids
2. they don't have to deal with the pressures of keeping the "macho" image
3. they don't have it as hard as us men
4. they get nice things
5. they are a necessary part of the world and nature

6. they do not have to chase after boyfriends
7. most of the time they have more time to get their lives in order
8. they get to handle the money
9. it is acceptable for them to have long hair
10. men will do anything for them
11. they get married, and a husband takes care of them sometimes
12. it is acceptable in society for them to be sensitive
13. they are (or rather they *were*), and are now perhaps rejecting this advantage closer to their feelings and biological life
14. they usually don't have to work on cars
15. they have the ability to manipulate men
16. they can see deeper meanings
17. we understand men, but they have trouble understanding us
18. of fate
19. everyone has a little luck
20. we can bring a child into this world

Scoring Key for Item 11

1 4i	6 5d	11 4j	16 6a
2 7b	7 6d	12 6e	17 4b
3 5b	8 3d	13 8b	18 3e
4 2b	9 5m	14 3a*	19 6p
5 7a	10 5g	15 5f	20 5i

Note

14. Cars appear often at E3 (but do not rate on single words).

EXAMPLES FOR RATING FOR ITEM 12:
A GOOD FATHER—

1. is mine
2. is my stepfather, who does his best for me
3. is a good person
4. takes time to be with the kids
5. sticks around & shares the work of raising kids w/ the mother of his children
6. is when he takes care of his child
7. is one who loves, touches, teaches & works on his own issues
8. really figures out his children's needs
9. is a working father
10. can be counted on
11. is a good provider and sensitive to the needs of his family
12. is the loving one, the responsible one
13. is one who treats his children justly and raises them with good values
14. is one who maintains ties with his children even when he is not living with them
15. is someone who cares for you and teaches you about life
16. is a true friend
17. cares for his wife and children
18. should provide his children with conditions for emotional growth, mature self awareness and creative productivity
19. tries to relate to his kids by doing things with him
20. has trust and faith that his children will do what is right

Scoring Key for Item 12

1 4k	6 4c	11 6c	16 4j
2 5c	7 7a	12 5a	17 4i
3 3c	8 5j	13 7d	18 8a
4 5g	9 3f	14 5h	19 6j
5 6h	10 4b	15 6a	20 8b

EXAMPLES FOR RATING FOR ITEM 13:
A GIRL HAS A RIGHT TO—

1. say no when she is in situations that she does not want to be in
2. say what's on her mind
3. protect her body
4. choose her company
5. learn all the same things as a boy
6. the same stuff a man has a right to
7. make her own decisions & live w/ the consequences
8. whatever
9. participate in all sports with boys
10. do anything she wants as long as it doesn't harm anyone (including herself)
11. pursue her talents and interests
12. have an abortion if that is her choice
13. party
14. take on any challenges
15. do a boy's job
16. be a contributing member of the world as is a man in his own way
17. her own body
18. be a full human being
19. be treated equally (as compared to men)
20. drive a truck or be a fashion model

Scoring Key for Item 13

1 6i	6 5d	11 6j	16 8U
2 5g	7 6f	12 5j	17 4g
3 3c	8 5b	13 3b	18 7b
4 5i	9 4l	14 6g	19 6d
5 4m	10 7a	15 4c	20 7d

EXAMPLES FOR RATING FOR ITEM 14:
WHEN THEY TALKED ABOUT SEX, I—

1. set and lissen [sic]
2. pricked up my ears
3. felt uneasy
4. tried to separate truth from fantasy
5. tend to be extremely open
6. sometimes excuse myself from the premisses [sic]
7. quietly & non-judgmentally listen
8. was uncomfortable initially
9. must have been absent
10. go away
11. love it
12. listen and try to help them understand

13. liked to listen to know what others think about it
14. am very interested in how others feel because I don't feel I have the right feeling
15. also got involved
16. smiled inwardly as I thought about my old girlfriend
17. don't like in mixed company
18. normally try to sneak out of the room or act like I don't hear anything
19. analyze what they say
20. get very hot blooded

Scoring Key for Item 14

1 4a	6 4d*	11 3c	16 7k
2 5a	7 7e	12 5e	17 4i
3 5i	8 7b	13 6i	18 6f
4 6k	9 5g	14 8a*	19 6j
5 5k	10 2a	15 5b*	20 3b

Notes

6. Could be 2a.
14. Concern with own feelings and motivations.
15. Or 4b.

EXAMPLES FOR RATING FOR ITEM 15:
A WIFE SHOULD—

1. be supportive and supported, considered equal in decisions
2. be good to her husband
3. carry most of the load of a marriage
4. care for her husband but not be submissive to him
5. hold on to her sense of self while also being a strong partner in a relationship
6. be allowed to have option to work
7. be happy & love being a homemaker
8. clean up the house
9. always be honest, true, and faithful to her husband
10. not pay any attention to people who tell her what she should and should not be
11. have as much patience and kindness as mine
12. take good care of her family first
13. help out as much as the husband
14. be tolerant but firm with her husband and children
15. feel that her role is valued
16. not do all the cooking and cleaning
17. never be lied to by her husband
18. keep the communication channels open within the immediate family
19. be neat, good cook, and appealing
20. give herself what she needs then do what her husband wants

Scoring Key for Item 15

1 7a	6 4l	11 5h	16 3f
2 4i*	7 4m	12 4i	17 5r
3 5c	8 2b	13 5s	18 6f
4 6i	9 4j	14 6b	19 4e
5 8a	10 8b	15 6d	20 7g

Notes

2. Not 2a, which is more vague.

EXAMPLES FOR RATING FOR ITEM 16:
I FEEL SORRY—

1. when I see the homeless people in the city streets
2. that too much affluence has distorted most Americans' goals
3. for myself a lot
4. when I hurt someone
5. when I hurt someone's feelings by not being understanding
6. for self pitying people
7. for people who don't have the wonderful family and friends I have
8. people are such assholes
9. for children whose parents don't care about them
10. that my marriage has ended
11. for people who are not open minded
12. most of the time
13. that I don't have enough time to devote to my family and job
14. for people going thru tough times
15. when people hate others for no good reason
16. for people who can't or won't see the comical side
17. when I see people in pain & hurting
18. for those who don't want to progress
19. for people who don't have confidence in themselves
20. for anyone who has lost hope and enthusiasm for life

Scoring Key for Item 16

1 4b	6 5v	11 6q	16 7b
2 7e	7 6l*	12 4j	17 5d
3 2a	8 3h	13 6e	18 6h
4 5m	9 5b	14 5e	19 6k
5 7a	10 4i*	15 6o	20 8a

Notes

7. Or 5g.
10. Or 5i.

EXAMPLES FOR RATING FOR ITEM 17:
A MAN FEELS GOOD WHEN—

1. he gets home from a hard day's work
2. he does a good job and is recognized for it
3. he does something right
4. he has a good mate
5. he is in bed with a woman
6. he knows he is loved and needed
7. everyone feels good when people support him/her
8. he has a pocket full of money
9. he successfully completes a project on his own
10. he eats
11. he gets along with his wife

12. he's watching football
13. he's secure with his gender role
14. he does something to please him and others
15. he is superior to a woman!
16. he does something he knows is good and right, even if it hurts
17. he is in love
18. he is at peace with his fellow man
19. he's got a woman wrapped around his finger
20. he is a hero in his son's eyes

Scoring Key for Item 17

1 4d	6 6n	11 4g	16 6d
2 6h	7 7e	12 5e	17 4f
3 5g	8 3d	13 6p	18 8a
4 4e	9 6f	14 7d	19 5p
5 2a	10 3a	15 5p	20 5n

EXAMPLES FOR RATING FOR ITEM 18:
RULES ARE—

1. good guides for conduct
2. pick up after yourself
3. to be kept
4. vital for organization
5. do what people tells you
6. rules
7. a pain in the neck
8. made by men, who are fallible, so they should constantly be re-examined
9. to be obeyed—if they are unfair or wrong, they should be corrected—not broken.
10. usually necessary but sometimes irritating
11. necessary but restrictive of freedom
12. necessary, unless too complex, restrictive or ridiculous
13. part of living
14. made to keep people within the boundaries
15. stifling the nation
16. made to be carried out and sometimes broken, it depends on the situation
17. ways for parents to run their child's life
18. for those who make them to break
19. often silly
20. made and we must adjust them sometimes

Scoring Key for Item 18

1 5c	6 2c	11 7c	16 7a
2 2b	7 3b	12 8a	17 5j
3 4a	8 6f*	13 5d	18 6g
4 6a	9 7b	14 4g	19 5j
5 3c	10 6l	15 6i*	20 6g

Notes

8. and 6g*. Rule 3
15. Or 7U, up from 6i, for dealing with "nation" rather than individuals.

EXAMPLES FOR RATING FOR ITEM 19:
CRIME AND DELINQUENCY COULD BE HALTED IF—

1. poverty were eliminated
2. they locked up the criminals for a long time
3. people wouldn't commit the crime
4. more cops were around
5. people understood that crime hurts other people, and if people weren't being hurt themselves
6. many family situations would be improved
7. people would respect one another
8. more people would shoot one another
9. children were taught at an early age what is right
10. people were more caring
11. people followed rules
12. the family took interest in their kids
13. people were better educated from childhood
14. a fortunate mutation made cruelty obsolete
15. there were no rules
16. education & upbringing were improved
17. we rid the earth of humans
18. our well being depended on our contending with natural forces rather than with each other
19. everyone became a Christian
20. they can never be, they can be decreased by speedier and more equal justice; by more uniform punishment

Scoring Key for Item 19

1 5i	6 7a*	11 4m	16 5h
2 2a*	7 6k*	12 5d	17 6a
3 3e	8 3b	13 5h	18 8a
4 3a	9 4f	14 8a	19 5m
5 8c	10 4l	15 4d	20 5a*

Notes

2. "For a long time" might mean longer punishment, which is 4b.
6. Or down to 6U because "improved" is vague.
7. Also like 6o.
20. Rule 3.

EXAMPLES FOR RATING FOR ITEM 20:
MEN ARE LUCKY BECAUSE—

1. they have better pro-league sports
2. they are males
3. some "man", a long time ago, decided men were superior
4. they are granted the respect of individuality more often than are women
5. they have women who love them
6. they can walk away
7. a good man is always desirable
8. don't have to go through the oppression that women have experienced
9. they can pee easily outside
10. they have opportunity to express themselves at work the way that is difficult for women
11. they don't have a menstruation period
12. they do not have to worry about pressures about physical appearance
13. they can walk away from housework

14. they grow up with preference and generally a positive outlook
15. they can play around
16. they are less involved in the basic operation of the home, such as bill paying, shopping, disciplining, and child care
17. women exist
18. they do have more open doors
19. they still have more options for fulfillment in our society
20. when it comes to jobs, they get better ones than women do

Scoring Key for Item 20

1 4p	6 4j	11 4e	16 6d
2 4a	7 5r	12 5g	17 4k
3 6a	8 6c	13 4i	18 5v
4 7d	9 5u	14 7b	19 7f
5 6i	10 7f	15 3c	20 4l

EXAMPLES FOR RATING FOR ITEM 21:
I CAN'T STAND PEOPLE WHO—

1. always try to take advantage and find an angle to everything
2. smoke cigars
3. are loud, rude, and obnoxious
4. are phoney, or very dull, or who aggrandize themselves without justification
5. are picky
6. are stuck up
7. bitch, complain and are selfish
8. can't mind their own business
9. start fights
10. don't leave me alone
11. act superior over everyone else
12. oppose Christ and his church
13. talk about other people
14. pity themselves
15. reject all other ways of thinking and doing besides their own
16. pick their nose
17. talk all the time about themselves
18. talk loud
19. treat others unfairly
20. criticize and condemn

Scoring Key for Item 21

1 6s	6 4f	11 5d	16 3a
2 4e	7 6d*	12 5c	17 4c
3 5j	8 3f	13 4g	18 4a
4 7g	9 2b	14 5g	19 5t
5 4U	10 3c	15 7a	20 5k

Notes

7. A combination of three ideas including one E6 (selfish) is 7g, but the first two words (bitch and complain) here express only one idea.

EXAMPLES FOR RATING FOR ITEM 22:
AT TIMES SHE WORRIED ABOUT—

1. her financial independence
2. being pregnant
3. whether she did the right thing in her life by marry a pastor of the church
4. going to school
5. her weight
6. where I was at night
7. everything under the sun
8. messing up in a game
9. his health
10. looking good
11. if others liked her
12. not having a husband
13. how she could do everything she had to do
14. whether she could get everything finished on time and done well!
15. governmental institutions that clearly did not serve the needs of people.
16. whether his business would be successful
17. the baby's health
18. what people thought
19. making sure we had enough to eat
20. slipping off the edge of the earth

Scoring Key for Item 22

1 6o	6 4d	11 5d	16 5h
2 3b	7 4j	12 5e	17 5k
3 6h	8 4m	13 5g	18 5l
4 4a	9 5b	14 7U*	19 5p
5 4c	10 5c	15 7d*	20 5s

Notes

14. The distinction between the completion and the quality of a job raises the response from 6i to 7U.
15. There is an implicit comparison between reality (institutions) and the ideal (serving the needs).

EXAMPLES FOR RATING FOR ITEM 23:
I AM—

1. comfortable with myself
2. moving up the ladder
3. a sensitive person and a caring person
4. tired of school; I want to graduate and start working
5. a nice guy
6. a self dependent woman
7. happy, healthy and content
8. a truck driver
9. simply a person who wants to know what I'm doing here on Earth
10. just fine
11. a reserved person
12. tired and ready to go to bed
13. a person who feels truly blessed
14. loving and lovable
15. the way I am because of my childhood experiences and my culture

16. anxious
17. attractive
18. feeling better about myself than I ever have but I am still not confident in myself
19. trying to be the best person I could be
20. basically a very happy person

Scoring Key for Item 23

1 4i	6 5h	11 5m	16 3g
2 5c	7 6g	12 4h	17 4a
3 6b	8 4m	13 6f	18 7c*
4 6i	9 7U*	14 6e	19 5f
5 2a	10 2b	15 7f	20 5a

Notes

9. Up from 6m for scope, for putting self in context (Earth)
18. This can be rated 8b for an elaboration on development, but confidence is just a limited aspect of development

EXAMPLES FOR RATING FOR ITEM 24:
A WOMAN FEELS GOOD WHEN—

1. she is liked and accepted for who she is, not as a pretty face or body—but the person inside
2. her husband give her a flower
3. she is treated right
4. she is loved and gives love
5. she does something for her family or friends that helps them
6. she's having sex
7. there is success in her life
8. she is both nourishing and nourished, creatively
9. she gets a good position in something or has accomplished some great thing
10. she's loved and needed and believes that it is real
11. she's appreciated
12. she is looking attractive
13. she is held by someone who loves her
14. she feels beautiful
15. her family are doing fine
16. she is treated as a human being and not like a possession
17. she's with a guy
18. she allows herself to be who she wants to be
19. someone compliments her
20. she can rest

Scoring Key for Item 24

1 6k	6 2a	11 5m	16 7b
2 5q	7 5U*	12 4g	17 3f
3 5a	8 7c	13 5q	18 8a
4 6i	9 6e	14 5b	19 4a
5 5l	10 6j	15 4j	20 2b

Note

7. The broad context of "in her life" raises the rating from 4h.

EXAMPLES FOR RATING FOR ITEM 25:
MY MAIN PROBLEM IS—

1. I'm timid
2. making enough money
3. wasting time
4. my obesity
5. that I fight to much (sic)
6. time management
7. is getting along with hippocritical (sic) people
8. that I am very reserved and find it hard to let people get real close to me
9. that I am a perfectionist and become easily distressed when I don't do my best
10. I am too selfish
11. I judge people too quickly
12. lack of physical enthusiasm in the face of vast mental energy
13. uncertainty as to the meaning of life
14. that I like everything a little, but there is nothing that I can see myself spending my whole life on
15. that I worry over needless things
16. being more aggressive than my mate
17. trying to solve others' problems
18. disliking questionnaires
19. insomnia with resultant tiredness and clouding of mentation
20. suffering when my wife is away too often and I have too few children in the house

Scoring Key for Item 25

1 5j	6 6a	11 6k	16 4e
2 4f	7 5e	12 7c	17 5d
3 6c	8 8a	13 8c	18 3g
4 4m	9 7b	14 6l	19 6U*
5 2a	10 5s	15 5g	20 5i

Note

19. Up from 5p, for expressing both the physiological and the mental aspects.

EXAMPLES FOR RATING FOR ITEM 26:
A HUSBAND HAS A RIGHT TO—

1. faithfulness from his wife
2. go out when he wants to
3. know how I am feeling
4. [erased-sex] work
5. be treated the way he treats his wife
6. be wrong at times
7. be with his male friends sometimes
8. a shared relationship with his wife
9. tell his wife what to do but not get carried away
10. explore and utilize his full potential and be supported and validated in his learnings by his wife
11. do the thing in the house, also
12. whatever he wants but his wife can say no
13. dutch apple pie w/ ice cream
14. neither one has 'rights'
15. think he's the boss But that's only if he's paying the bills
16. want to be treated like a husband

17. be the husband he feels he wants to be
18. be free to spend time with his friends
19. make his wife have sex with her
20. privacy within the partnership

Scoring Key for Item 26

1 7c	6 7g	11 4i*	16 6k*
2 4a*	7 4b	12 6b	17 7h
3 6i*	8 7d	13 5U*	18 6d
4 3f*	9 6f	14 7f	19 2a*
5 8a	10 8b*	15 7U*	20 7d*

Notes

2. This is a little more elaborated than 3a and 3b
3. "I" here is probably the wife. This respondent is female.
4. Should erased words be rated? On the one hand, sentence completions are usual first thoughts, not meditated essays. On the other hand, they are not free association. It is a moot question here. "Sex" is between E2a and E4c, "work" is at E3f.
10. This response might be raised to E9 due to rich a combination. From an E9 TPR.
11. There were about 40 responses in this category, but only 2 from men. This is one of the two.
13. More unique and expressive than the common "dinner" response at 4d, so it can be rated up to E5. From an E5 subject.
15. Do not confuse with 5e. He "thinks he's the boss" but he is not, and his real function is only paying bills. Gentle humor, contrasting harmless self-deception with reality. From a E7 female respondent.
16. Not as clear a role conception as 7h.
19. We do not score the slippage "her," but it shows that this female high school student has a difficulty with role playing.
20. This response is rated high not because of the Western value of privacy but because of the combination with an opposite idea, partnership.

EXAMPLES FOR RATING FOR ITEM 27:
THE WORST THING ABOUT BEING A WOMAN [MAN]—[3]

1. is that sometimes men doubt their abilities
2. to get through pregnancy
3. is having to be divided between being a mother and homemaker and having a career
4. is that you are expected to be soft and innocent and it's sometimes alienating when you choose to act strong and people stand back
5. is you always have to work hard
6. is being oppressed
7. is not knowing whether you are being discriminated against or failing on your own
8. is having to deal with the stereotypes that men are more competent
9. is having to worry about physical appearance—weight. And having period
10. is that they are paid 30% less for jobs than men
11. is putting up with a nagging wife. But you don't have to get married. A wife can be like a parent
12. is you can't spend more time with your kids
13. is being a man
14. you got to pay the bills
15. is that the cultural assumptions about what that means are limiting and for some produce great discomfort
16. is the long day at the office and sometimes not being appreciated for it
17. macho fronts

---

[3]First 10 responses are from females, last 10 from males.

18. is being arrested
19. is people automatically assume your sexist
20. is keeping fit and trim

Scoring Key for Item 27

1 6i	6 5k	11 3c*	16 5w
2 4b	7 7d	12 6k	17 6f*
3 6k	8 6f	13 4g	18 2d
4 8a	9 5d*	14 2b	19 6r
5 4c	10 6h	15 8a	20 5U*

Notes

9. This has elements of both 5d and 4a, so rated at the less frequent category.
11. The second and third clauses do not raise the rating.
17. Not elaborated enough to be 7a.
20. Up from 4a, which is more passive. Somewhat like 5b.

EXAMPLES FOR RATING FOR ITEM 28: A GOOD MOTHER—

1. needs patience
2. is loving and caring, but strict when need be
3. loves all her children just the same
4. takes care of her children
5. love, protect and take care of her family
6. will try to teach her kids to make good decisions on their own
7. is open and honest with her children
8. supports her son
9. is loving, disciplines her children; is active in a ministry, healthy, confident, patient & wise
10. is one who is there for you
11. puts herself last
12. is one who is able to take care of her children & herself & has equal help from her husband
13. gives her family time to be with her
14. tries to understand each child's individual needs
15. is a lucky thing to have
16. has time & patience; she listens, nurtures, & cares
17. is cool
18. gives to her children the skills to be resilient and to take risks.
19. is a good listener
20. loves all the children of the world because she understands what all other mothers go through in the process of life, raising children

Scoring Key for Item 28

1 5b	6 7b	11 5a	16 6h*
2 6j	7 5p	12 7e*	17 2a
3 4c	8 4g*	13 5e	18 8a
4 3b	9 8b	14 6o*	19 5l
5 5g*	10 4e	15 4a	20 7i*

Notes

5. This is not 6h because components are pretty similar.
8. "Supportive" at 5h is more psychological than 4g.

12. First clause stresses competence and independence of mother, about 5U, not 7d. The second clause is 5q. There is no E7 element.

14. Could be raised to 7U, but not to 8a.

16. This has many E5 components, which are different but not strongly contrasting.

20. Broad social perspective raises this to E7, and there is no E8 element.

EXAMPLES FOR RATING FOR ITEM 29:
WHEN I AM WITH A MAN [WOMAN]—

1. I wonder what she really thinks
2. I try & have a good time
3. I feel good inside
4. that I hate, I feel uneasy
5. I will talk to her
6. I like to respect her as a person
7. I feel more content & emotional
8. I sometimes feel safer
9. I fizz just like Robert Preston
10. I wonder if people envy me for being with her
11. I mind my mouth
12. I feel uncomfortable if I don't know him well
13. I feel more at ease
14. I show off a lot
15. I am not always able to say what I would like to say
16. I often feel a lively sexual attraction but I really have no inclination to be philander [sic] or be unfaithful to [name deleted]
17. I conduct myself as a lady
18. a woman is with me
19. I feel physically attracted to him
20. we can talk about sports

Scoring Key for Item 29

1 6m	6 7k	11 4b	16 8c
2 4d*	7 6l	12 6j	17 4a
3 4c	8 5h*	13 7b	18 3f
4 5o	9 6h	14 5a	19 6h
5 2a	10 4h	15 5b	20 4l*

Notes

2. The combination with "try" may raise up to E5. From an E5 TPR.
8. "Safer" shows a comparison, but not the type at 6l.
20. Down from 5c.

EXAMPLES FOR RATING FOR ITEM 30:
SOMETIMES SHE [HE] WISHED THAT—

1. she could die
2. he knew more people with the same interests
3. she never gained weight
4. life could be fair, but knew it wasn't
5. she could have a lot of fancy clothes
6. he was more articulate

7. she really could be anything she wanted to be
8. I had not left home
9. she could escape from the apparently unbearable problems she faced
10. he had less work
11. her life was like Princess Diane
12. there was less pressure
13. time would fly faster
14. she was still going out with him
15. she have more self-esteem
16. women really have equal rights
17. she would respond differently
18. she could let go of things that hurt her and don't benefit her even though she is attached to it
19. her father wood [sic] move away
20. she had worked harder in the past

Scoring Key for Item 30

1 3a	6 6m	11 5m	16 7U*
2 6f	7 6q	12 6s	17 5k
3 4j	8 5j*	13 6i	18 8a
4 8b*	9 7U*	14 4d	19 3e
5 4b	10 5a	15 6m	20 6n

Notes

4. It fits E8b well, though comes from an E6 TPR, so one cannot rely on one response.
8. Between 4j and 6j; the latter has more life-plan sound.
9. Down from 8a.
16. Down from 8c; it just names an issue, not expressing it in a unique E8 manner.

EXAMPLES FOR RATING FOR ITEM 31:
MY FATHER—

1. works hard
2. is my pride and my image
3. is a great father
4. and I have a good relationship
5. is an easy person to deal with
6. is an honorable, decent man
7. is a very gentle and understanding person
8. hasn't seen me in 13 years and doesn't know me
9. is not a real man to me, because he didn't raise his kids even though he could well afford it
10. raised me. He was always working and never talked to me about feelings
11. gives my brother everything he wants
12. is much like myself
13. is a righteous man
14. is one hell of a man for having the strength to keep his family together against the odds
15. is very supportive of his family
16. is handsome
17. is a insulting jerk
18. can be pig-headed and a very bad listener, but more importantly—he is mature enough to retain his child-like qualities & to empathize
19. is terrific. (NOT as a kid but now he is) (When I was a kid he was intimidating)
20. has a special love for me

Scoring Key for Item 31

1 4k	6 6b	11 3b	16 4b
2 6j	7 5u	12 6e	17 2a
3 4a	8 5z	13 5f	18 8a
4 5s	9 6l	14 6h*	19 6r
5 4i	10 7a	15 5q	20 5r

Note

14. Not 8a because there is no conflict or contradiction.

EXAMPLES FOR RATING FOR ITEM 32:
IF I CAN'T GET WHAT I WANT—

1. 1) I try harder, 2) rethink if I really want it, or 3) wait and hope
2. I am depressed for a short time, until I count my blessings
3. I am sad
4. I'm mad
5. I don't get what I want
6. I don't give up until I do finally get it or find/learn something about it that lets me let go of wanting it
7. I feel insecure
8. I find other satisfactions
9. I get someone else to get it for me
10. I get stubborn
11. I keep trying to figure out a way to get it, and change my time-frame
12. I question my desires
13. I am happy
14. I sometimes nag
15. I try some other method of obtaining it \\
16. I usually hold my breath until I turn blue
17. I wait until another day
18. I will often be upset for a while, but then I can change that feeling when I really think about whether I really needed it!
19. I'll be mad inside, but won't let others know
20. I'll try to get what I need

Scoring Key for Item 32

1 8a	6 7f	11 7a	16 3a
2 6c	7 5b	12 7c	17 5g
3 4e	8 6e	13 4m	18 7e
4 2a	9 4h	14 3d	19 6b
5 4o	10 5c	15 5d	20 4j

EXAMPLES FOR RATING FOR ITEM 33:
USUALLY SHE [HE] FELT THAT SEX—

1. with the person she loved was fantastic
2. is immoral
3. was not as important as people said it was
4. is showing caring emotions
5. well, he never talked about it much, but he had a mistress for twenty years. I guess lie felt that sex was a Good Thing
6. a bad thing

7. is a vital part of marriage
8. is needed as much as possible. It enhances the relationship & strengthens the bond
9. was important but not necessary
10. was something to play with
11. was an issue for private rather than public discussion
12. is the man's way of releasing his tension
13. can improve with time
14. was very disgusting and terrible
15. is a natural joining of two lovers
16. was everything
17. was a chore, but not anymore
18. was a wonderful gift from God
19. just another job that a wife has to do
20. was pretty satisfying

Scoring Key for Item 33

1 6e	6 2a	11 6o	16 3b
2 3c	7 5e	12 5k	17 7d
3 5l	8 8b	13 7d	18 5i
4 6b	9 6j	14 4i	19 5o
5 7e	10 3a	15 6c	20 6a

EXAMPLES FOR RATING FOR ITEM 34:
FOR A WOMAN A CAREER IS—

1. exciting
2. an option that she should not feel required to explore
3. the ultimate
4. house wife
5. a plus until she wants children (family)
6. essential for self-identity
7. better than being married
8. a conflict if she is also a mother
9. sometimes very bad
10. more important to their sense of self
11. important if she feels it is necessary, but her family should be her first priority
12. an asset
13. costly
14. whoring
15. limited to what male society allows—e.g. women cannot serve in combat
16. a low on the list of priorities
17. her way out of the home
18. good if this is what she wants in life
19. a struggle, but also a wonderful opportunity for self-expression if needed
20. almost as important as a relationship

Scoring Key for Item 34

1 5e	6 8a	11 6q	16 4a
2 6d	7 4h	12 4f	17 5j
3 4d	8 6o	13 5a	18 6a
4 3g	9 4U	14 2d	19 8b
5 5m	10 6k	15 6t	20 6n

EXAMPLES FOR RATING FOR ITEM 35:
MY CONSCIENCE BOTHERS ME IF—

1. I fudge a bit on the truth
2. I get caught lying
3. I eat too many sweets
4. I am inconsiderate/rude intentionally, especially to friend
5. I let what others say about me influence how I feel about myself
6. I don't balance all debts
7. I treat someone badly
8. I deceive someone into thinking I listened to them
9. I cheat on a test
10. I lose my patience
11. I get confused
12. my empathy is deficient regarding someone
13. I don't follow through w/my promise.
14. I have spoken in anger to one of my kids
15. I compromise my values
16. I cannot respond to the needs, or hurt the feelings, of those who surround me, out of my own self-absorption
17. I do something societably incorrect. But do I listen? I do not
18. I do not stand up for what I believe is right
19. I do something my mom does not like
20. I act bad

Scoring Key for Item 35

1 5a	6 4c	11 5x	16 8c
2 3g	7 5s	12 7c	17 5q*
3 5m	8 6m	13 5t	18 6f
4 6i	9 4a	14 4j	19 5g
5 8d	10 5m	15 6c	20 3a

Note

17. Or 6p.

EXAMPLES FOR RATING FOR ITEM 36:
A WOMAN [MAN] SHOULD ALWAYS—[4]

1. keep smiling
2. stay near her home
3. know what she believes. And then know that if she learns more she can still change
4. be willing to be a full time mother when her children are young
5. wear lipstick
6. do what makes her comfortable
7. look out for herself
8. think her actions thru
9. love herself and be the best she knows and strive to know more
10. try to be herself and not to compete with men and with other women
11. love his wife and kids
12. try his hardest to be a good person
13. pay his bills and guard his good name
14. do his best to think of others and to serve his community

---

[4]First 10 responses are from females, last 10 from males.

15. stick to principles
16. stop and think about what he is doing
17. [S underscored word 'always' in stem]—come now
18. fuck!!!!!
19. be an example for others
20. keep in mind his lease on life is a short term one

Scoring Key for Item 36

1 4e	6 5p	11 4i	16 5a
2 2a	7 3a	12 6c	17 7g
3 8b*	8 5a	13 4f	18 2U*
4 5f	9 7U*	14 7a	19 5h
5 4d	10 8a*	15 6d	20 8U

Notes

3. Or 8c.
9. Combination of 5l, 6c, and 6l; up from 6p.
10. Or 8b.
18. Or higher if understood as a humorous rejection of the stem.

Practice Exercises
for Total Protocol Rating

PROTOCOL A

1. When a child will not join in group activities—he or she has a problem
2. Raising a family—is very hard
3. When I am criticized—I criticize back
4. A man's job—can be easy and hard
5. Being with other people—is good for communication
6. The thing I like about myself is—my attitude
7. My mother and I—get along very well
8. What gets me into trouble is—not obeying my parents
9. Education—is very important to me
10. When people are helpless—I feel bad for them
11. Women are lucky because—they don't have it as hard as us men
12. A good father—is good to his family
13. A girl has the right to—say what is on her mind
14. When they talked about sex, I—listened
15. A wife should—help out as much as the husband
16. I feel sorry—for homeless people
17. A man feels good when—he does something good
18. Rules are—very important
19. Crime and delinquency could be halted if—our cops would do something about it
20. Men are lucky because—they don't have to go through having a baby
21. I just can't stand people who—talk behind other people's back
22. At times he worried about—his education
23. I am—tired
24. A woman feels good when—she is satisfied
25. My main problem is—my study habits
26. A husband has a right to—as much as the wife has
27. The worst thing about being a man—is putting up with women
28. A good mother—feeds her family
29. When I am with a woman—I expect to communicate well
30. Sometimes he wished that—more people liked him
31. My father—is going through some hard times
32. If I can't get what I want—I think about other things

33. Usually he felt that sex—was not the solution
34. For a woman a career is—very worthwhile
35. My conscience bothers me if—I don't know I did something wrong
36. A man should always—stop and think about what he is doing

Scoring Key for Protocol A[1]

1 3a	10 4a	19 4b	28 3b
2 3b	11 5b	20 4e	29 6b
3 3a	12 4i*	21 4g	30 4d
4 5U*	13 5g	22 6b	31 6s
5 5U*	14 4a	23 4h	32 4k
6 5n	15 5s	24 4i	33 5r
7 4g	16 4b	25 5k	34 5e
8 3b	17 5i	26 6e	35 4h
9 5a	18 4c	27 3c	36 5a

Notes

4. This combines 4d and 2a, somewhat like 5c.
5. Down from 6h.
12. Repeat good without adding much.

Ogive Calculation:

E-level	2	3	4	5	6	7	8	9
Frequency		6	14	12	4			
Ogive	0	6	20	32	36	36	36	36

Automatic TPR: E5
Many answers are very commonplace, none very high or very low. Intuitive rating is between E3 and E4, closer to E4. Source, WU student, about 1990.
Final TPR: E4.
The E5 and E6 responses are not strong, and some are popular, while the E3 and E4 responses seem to be more characteristic. In addition, automatic TPR is right at the cut-off point.
Item Sum = 158, E4.

PROTOCOL B

1. When a child will not join in group activities—he's thinking of suicide
2. Raising a family—is very hard
3. When I am criticized—I feel like killing myself
4. A man's job—is valuable to him
5. Being with other people—makes me feel wanted
6. The thing I like about myself is—that I am not a junky
7. My mother and I—get along very well
8. What gets me into trouble is—hanging around trouble makers
9. Education-is important to everyone
10. When people are helpless—I try to help them
11. Women are lucky because—they don't have to work as hard as men
12. A good father—will have a good child
13. A girl has the right to—do what ever they want
14. When they talked about sex, I—listen
15. A wife should—do her duties

---

[1]An asterisk (*) indicates that an explanatory note is appended.

16. I feel sorry—about helpless people
17. A man feels good when—he has done a good job
18. Rules are—strict in some places
19. Crime and delinquency could be halted if—police work hard enough
20. Men are lucky because—they can work hard and make money
21. I just can't stand people who—does bad to other people
22. At times he worried about—his mother taking drugs
23. I am—a good child in school
24. A woman feels good when—she does her work right
25. My main problem is—that sometimes I do bad things
26. A husband has a right to—do anything he wants
27. The worst thing about being a man—is that a man has to go through lots of things
28. A good mother—will have good children
29. When I am with a woman—I feel good
30. Sometimes he wished that—his mother was dead
31. My father—sometimes tells me lies
32. If I can't get what I want—I wait until I can
33. Usually he felt that sex—is not life
34. For a woman a career is—housekeeping
35. My conscience bothers me if—I do something wrong
36. A man should always—be good to a woman

Scoring Key for Protocol B

1 4j*	10 4d	19 4b	28 4h
2 3b	11 3a	20 3d	29 4c
3 2U*	12 4e	21 2c	30 3a
4 4a	13 4a	22 5k	31 5p
5 5k	14 4a	23 4c	32 5g
6 2a	15 4c	24 4h	33 4g
7 4g	16 4e	25 2a	34 3g
8 3g	17 5g	26 3a	35 3a
9 4c	18 6i	27 3e	36 4j

Notes

1. May sound lower than 4j, but still higher than tautological 3f.
3. Global rejection of self: can be raised to 3U because of a little distance in "feel like."

E-level	2	3	4	5	6	7	8	9
Frequency	4	9	17	5	1			
Ogive	4	13	30	35	36	36	36	36

Automatic TPR: E3.
There are several signs of impulsivity; for example, preoccupation with suicide, wishing mother dead, thinking about drugs. Blame is externalized to "trouble-makers."
Intuitive rating: between E2 and E3, probably closer to E3 because many answers are E4. Source, Nashville, inner city youth.
Final TPR: E3.
Item Sum = 134, E3.

PROTOCOL C

1. When a child will not join in group activities—the child does not feel included
2. Raising a family—is a very hard and rewarding experience

3. When I am criticized—I try to listen to what the person(s) is telling me
4. A man's job—is caring for and protecting his family
5. Being with other people—is essential for human growth and development
6. The thing I like about myself is—how much I care for others
7. My mother and I—have an excellent relationship
8. What gets me into trouble is—when I speak before thinking
9. Education—is essential for success
10. When people are helpless—they feel frustrated
11. Women are lucky because—they can control men
12. A good father—spends a good deal of time with his children
13. A girl has the right to—make decisions for herself (boyfriends, sex, etc.)
14. When they talked about sex, I—joined right in
15. A wife should—care for and support her family and husband
16. I feel sorry—when this is not done! [arrow pointing to response above]
17. A man feels good when—he has made others happy
18. Rules are—sometimes needed, but also sometimes a pain in the ass!
19. Crime and delinquency could be halted if—humans understood intentions & motives more clearly
20. Men are lucky because—they don't have the painful job of bearing children
21. I just can't stand people who—are arrogant and put themselves above me
22. At times he worried about—not finding the "right" one
23. I am—caring, affectionate, warm, friendly, and strong-willed
24. A woman feels good when—a man compliments her with flowers
25. My main problem is—my negative attitude toward others
26. A husband has a right to—expect love & support from his wife
27. The worst thing about being a man—the social norms stressing masculinity and downplaying sensitivity
28. A good mother—loves her children
29. When I am with a woman—I try to make her feel as comfortable & cared for as possible
30. Sometimes he wished that—the women he took interest in, took interest in him
31. My father—is a good father
32. If I can't get what I want—I try to analyze why I can't, and a way around it
33. Usually he felt that sex—was just one part of the relationship
34. For a woman a career is—an important vehicle for identity
35. My conscience bothers me if—I hurt someone unintentionally by insulting them or making them feel left out
36. A man should always—treat others with consideration & respect, even if it is not always 2 way—a sign of strong character

Scoring Key for Protocol C

1 5c*	10 6e	19 6g	28 4j
2 6a	11 5f	20 4e	29 6c
34 j	12 5g	21 4f	30 5U*
4 4h	13 5h	22 5e	31 5q
5 6i	14 4b	23 7a	32 7e
6 5a	15 5e*	24 5c	33 6l
7 5h	16 4i	25 6r	34 8a
8 6c	17 5l	26 6a	35 6i
9 5m	18 6l	27 6m	36 6e

Notes

1. lower than examples in 5c. Notice that examples are often more elaborate than category titles.
15. 6c has comparison.
30. Up from 4d for limited mutuality.

E-level	2	3	4	5	6	7	8	9
Frequency			7	13	13	2	1	
Ogive	0	0	7	20	33	35	36	36

Automatic TPR: E6
There is a wide variety of themes, from control (low) to identity (very high), and a predominant concern for relationships. Most of the responses are typical for E6, however, the richness of the protocol and presence of several high level themes, like development, mutuality, and identity, suggests a higher TPR. Source, a Canadian man, probably a graduate student.
Final TPR: E6.
Item Sum = 193, E6.

PROTOCOL D

1. When a child will not join in group activities—he becomes outcast
2. Raising a family—is fun
3. When I am criticized—I draw in
4. A man's job—is never done
5. Being with other people—is one thing I enjoy
6. The thing I like about myself is—my energy level
7. My mother and I—don't really talk to each other
8. What gets me into trouble is—my quick mouth
9. Education—is important
10. When people are helpless—it is sad
11. Women are lucky because—they can stay at home
12. A good father—plays/listens to his children
13. A girl has the right to—say no
14. When they talked about sex, I—listened
15. A wife should—pay attention to her children
16. I feel sorry—for my parents
17. A man feels good when—he achieves something
18. Rules are—to be broken
19. Crime and delinquency could be halted if—punishment was more severe
20. Men are lucky because—they get out of the house
21. I just can't stand people who—lie
22. At times he worried about—his job
23. I am—happy
24. A woman feels good when—given praise
25. My main problem is—communication
26. A husband has a right to—participate in his child's upbringing
27. The worst thing about being a man—is the expectation of funding the family
28. A good mother—plays/talks to her children
29. When I am with a woman—I am more open
30. Sometimes he wished that—he could do it over
31. My father—and I are alike
32. If I can't get what I want—I pout
33. Usually he felt that sex—was good
34. For a woman a career is—secondary
35. My conscience bothers me if—I lie
36. A man should always—do what is right

Scoring Key for Protocol D

1 5v	10 4a	19 4b	28 5e
2 3u	11 4q	20 4j	29 6l
3 6c*	12 5q	21 4i	30 6l
4 5e	13 4e	22 4a	31 4b
5 4a	14 4a	23 4g	32 4b
6 5j	15 4i	24 5m	33 4a

7 6o*	16 3c	25 5f	34 4a
8 4a	17 5c	26 5U*	35 4a
9 4a	18 4i	27 5h	36 5g

Notes

3. Similar to example "I shrink back." Comparison with examples is just as important as checking category headings.
7. "Really" is ambiguous, and may mean nothing more than 3a. However, it is better to assume that people mean what they say.
26. Like 5n.

E-level	2	3	4	5	6	7	8	9
Frequency		2	19	11	4			
Ogive	0	2	21	32	36	36	36	36

Automatic TPR: E4.
There are many popular answers. The sentences are literate, intelligent, and well-constructed, but there are no unusual ideas. Intuitive rating: E5 or E4. Source, a graduate from an Eastern US technological institute.
Final TPR: E4.
Item Sum = 161, E4.

PROTOCOL E

1. When a child will not join in group activities—the child should be steered toward an individual activity at which he/she can become adept
2. Raising a family—is hard these days, many descriptions and changes can work against you
3. When I am criticized—I become stubborn about changing but try to do so eventually
4. A man's job—should be more than just busywork or moneymaking, it should serve to improve his & other's lives
5. Being with other people—I don't know makes me self-conscious and tense
6. The thing I like about myself is—I try to be helpful to others & will be persistent in solving a problem
7. My mother and I—stay in contact through frequent calls and letters
8. What gets me into trouble is—saying something offensive without thinking before-hand of the consequences
9. Education—should provide you with the skills you need to survive and a way to help you get the most out of your life
10. When people are helpless—they should be able to count on someone for support
11. Women are lucky because—they have an easier time making friends with both sexes
12. A good father—should be tough but fair and encourage his kids.
13. A girl has the right to—walk around without being publicly harassed.
14. When they talked about sex, I—listened and made a few remarks but did not talk about my own personal experience
15. A wife should—be responsive to her husband's & child's needs but also take time out for herself
16. I feel sorry—for myself when I think about my lack of success in finding a decent woman or a better job
17. A man feels good when—he gets the admiration of his peers for a job well done
18. Rules are—important as guidelines but should not be taken as absolute
19. Crime and delinquency could be halted if—parents would truly care about their children and give them enough love and attention
20. Men are lucky because—they are more dominant so many goals, wishes, wants, etc. are easier to achieve
21. I just can't stand people who—are overly fashion conscious and act ultra sophisticated
22. At times he worried about—whether he would do anything worthwhile in his life
23. I am—doing fairly well with my life but I have higher aspirations which I have not yet started to strive for
24. A woman feels good when—she's near you
25. My main problem is—inertia, not being able to break free of the status quo to go on to something better

26. A husband has a right to—take time off from being part of a couple all the time
27. The worst thing about being a man—is having to do too many "macho" things to prove yourself to other guys
28. A good mother—should be a good example and care provider to her kids
29. When I am with a woman—that I like, I try to show her my feelings (or interest) subtly
30. Sometimes he wished that—he had a clearer view of his goals
31. My father—is a good parent overall but he is sometimes very irritating in his behavior
32. If I can't get what I want—I get upset for awhile then try to get an acceptable alternative
33. Usually he felt that sex—is a great way for people to enjoy themselves & more productive than watching TV
34. For a woman a career is—a chance to succeed and make the most out of her life
35. My conscience bothers me if—I tell a stupid lie that really wasn't necessary
36. A man should always—try to protect his rights and freedoms

Scoring Key for Protocol E

1 5o	10 5l	19 5d	28 6d
2 7d	11 6j*	20 6a	29 6j
3 6l	12 7a	21 6m	30 6o
4 7g	13 5d	22 7b	31 7b
5 5e	14 7d	23 8b	32 6b
6 6e	15 7c	24 4u	33 5c
7 4a	16 6d	25 8d	34 6e
8 6c	17 6h	26 5j	35 5a
9 6k	18 6c	27 7a*	36 5n*

Notes

11. Not the conventional difference at 5a.
27. Prove yourself to other group.
36. Women's manual.

E-level	2	3	4	5	6	7	8	9
Frequency			2	9	15	8	2	
Ogive	0	0	2	11	26	34	36	36

Automatic TPR: E7.
This man displays a preoccupation with goals and has a long-term view of life, so must be at least E6. Also, he sees things in a larger social context, as in Items 4 and 22, and challenges stereotypical attitudes, as in Items 27 and 21. The ideas are original and complex. Source, graduate of technological institute.
Intuitive rating: E7.
Final TPR: E7.
Item Sum = 215, E7.

PROTOCOL F

1. When a child will not join in group activities—he need to go home
2. Raising a family—is hard to do
3. When I am criticized—I feel sad
4. A man's job—is hard work
5. Being with other people—I feel good inside
6. The thing I like about myself is—being nice to others
7. My mother and I—love one another
8. What gets me into trouble is—talking
9. Education—I feel good about it

10. When people are helpless—I feel sad
11. Women are lucky because—they are women
12. A good father—have good kids
13. A girl has the right to—to have fun
14. When they talked about sex, I—feel good
15. A wife should—take care of her home
16. I feel sorry—when people have no homes
17. A man feels good when—he is [making] money
18. Rules are—[learn] about
19. Crime and delinquency could be halted if—stop that would be good
20. Men are lucky because—they are men
21. I just can't stand people who—talk to much
22. At times he worried about—about a girl
23. I am—happy all the time
24. A woman feels good when—she is having fun
25. My main problem is talking
26. A husband has a right to—to go out
27. The worst thing about being a man—AIDS
28. A good mother—is nice to her home
29. When I am with a woman—I feel good
30. Sometimes he wished that—had money
31. My father—make me sick
32. If I can't get what I want—A car and money
33. Usually he felt that sex—is not good
34. For a woman a career is—is good
35. My conscience bothers me if—I am bad
36. A man should always—be nice

Scoring Key for Protocol F

1 3e	10 4a	19 2b	28 2c
2 3b	11 4a	20 4a	29 4c
3 5e	12 4e	21 3e	30 4b
4 4c	13 4a	22 4f	31 2a
5 4d	14 4b	23 5a	32 3e
6 4e	15 2b	24 3d	33 2a
7 4h	16 4b	25 4a	34 2b
8 3a	17 3d	26 3b	35 2a
9 6o	18 4U	27 5b	36 2b

E-level	2	3	4	5	6	7	8	9
Frequency	8	8	16	3	1			
Ogive	8	16	32	35	36	36	36	36

Automatic TPR: E2.
This is very repetitious, and uses the simplest themes, good, bad, nice, fun, and sad. Many responses repeat or paraphrase the stem, creating a passive impression that results in an intuitive rating of E2, despite the paucity of blatant hostile or crudely impulsive responses. Source, inner-city youth.
Final TPR: E2.
Item Sum = 125, E2.

PROTOCOL G

1. When a child will not join in group activities—find out why
2. Raising a family—is hard work

3. When I am criticized—I hurt
4. A man's job—is his life
5. Being with other people—is fun
6. The thing I like about myself is—I'm friendly
7. My mother and I—were good friends
8. What gets me into trouble is—my mouth
9. Education—is very important to self-esteem
10. When people are helpless—they need others
11. Women are lucky because—we are strong
12. A good father—is understanding
13. A girl has the right to—an education and equality
14. When they talked about sex, I—listened
15. A wife should—be caring
16. I feel sorry—the loners
17. A man feels good when—he's with the guys
18. Rules are—necessary
19. Crime and delinquency could be halted if—I don't know
20. Men are lucky because—they have wives
21. I just can't stand people who—dominate
22. At times she worried about—her power base
23. I am—optimistic
24. A woman feels good when—she is respected
25. My main problem is—I threaten people by being forthright
26. A husband has a right to—be jealous
27. The worst thing about being a woman—is being devalued
28. A good mother—is caring
29. When I am with a man—I am careful
30. Sometimes she wished that—she could start over
31. My father—is dead
32. If I can't get what I want—I get depresed
33. Usually she felt that sex—was closeness
34. For a woman a career is—essential to well being
35. My conscience bothers me if—I am dishonest
36. A woman should always—take pride in herself

Scoring Key for Protocol G

1 5m	10 5f	19 4o	28 4k
2 3b	11 5a	20 4k	29 4g
3 5e	12 5p	21 5l	30 6i
4 4g	13 6k	22 5h	31 4o
5 4a	14 4a	23 5k	32 5a
6 4d	15 4a	24 5o	33 6b
7 5g	16 5f	25 5r	34 4c
8 4a	17 5r	26 5h	35 5a
9 6i	18 4d	27 6i	36 6j

E-level	2	3	4	5	6	7	8	9
Frequency		1	13	16	6			
Ogive	0	1	14	30	36	36	36	36

Automatic TPR: E5.
This woman displays a preoccupation with self-esteem and an obviously related theme, the respect of others. She displays a strong sense of inner life, compatible with the intuitive rating of E5. Source, an older woman returning to graduate school.
Final TPR: E5.
Item Sum = 171, E5.

PROTOCOL H

1. When a child will not join in group activities—they will not want to join because they talks about him or her
2. Raising a family—you can not be real hard on him or her
3. When I am criticized—when you do not like a person and then you curse them
4. A man's job—working with cars
5. Being with other people—like a best friend
6. The thing I like about myself is—I'm cute and friendly
7. My mother and I—we talks about sex sometimes
8. What gets me into trouble is—when they do something real bad
9. Education—being a smarted student
10. When people are helpless—that means they love you and care for you
11. Women are lucky because—they have good men to do for them
12. A good father—good to ther family and haves a job
13. A girl has the right to—have sex sometimes
14. When they talked about sex, I—listen to them so when I grow up I no
15. A wife should—keep the house clean
16. I feel sorry—because some of these people can't help them selfs
17. A man feels good when—sometimes have sex
18. Rules are—good for the schools
19. Crime and delinquency could be halted if—It stop being drugs
20. Men are lucky because—they have good wifes
21. I just can't stand people who—disobey me
22. At times she worried about—sex a lot
23. I am—glad I'm here today
24. A woman feels good when—she get's trow [through] with everything
25. My main problem is—sex
26. A husband has a right to—do what he wants to do
27. The worst thing about being a woman—is she has to have a baby
28. A good mother—is the one who cleans up a lot
29. When I am with a man—I feel comferable [comfortable]
30. Sometimes she wished that—she was lovely
31. My father—is sometimes nice
32. If I can't get what I want—I cry
33. Usually she felt that sex—is fun
34. For a woman a career is—hateful
35. My conscience bothers me if—I do something
36. A woman should always—clean up

Scoring Key for Protocol H

1 5c	10 2b	19 4j	28 3c
2 4U	11 4k	20 4n	29 6f
3 2U*	12 3f	21 3c	30 4j
4 3a	13 3a	22 3c	31 3a
5 4c	14 5o	23 4g	32 4e
6 4d*	15 2b	24 4u	33 4b
7 3a	16 4e	25 3b	34 3b
8 3g	17 2a	26 3a	35 3a
9 2c	18 5a	27 2a	36 3d

Notes

3. Impulsive retaliation and hostility; different from talking about retaliation at 5d.
6. Combination of 3a and 4d, both popular, so rate up.

E-level	2	3	4	5	6	7	8	9
Frequency	6	14	12	3	1			
Ogive	6	20	32	35	36	36	36	36

Automatic TPR: E2

Despite the minimal literacy, enough can be guessed of the meaning of this girl or young woman to rate the protocol very low. Impulsive anger is displayed in Item 3. The source was an inner-city female, and the misspellings and misreadings are typical in that setting. They are not unusual elsewhere also.

Intuitive rating, E2 or E3.

Final TPR: E2.

Item Sum = 123, E2.

PROTOCOL J

1. When a child will not join in group activities—he/she doesn't feel comfortable
2. Raising a family—takes time
3. When I am criticized—my feelings are hurt
4. A man's job—is usually different from a woman's
5. Being with other people—is enjoyable
6. The thing I like about myself is—I am a good person
7. My mother and I—are very close
8. What gets me into trouble is—
9. Education—is important
10. When people are helpless—it is unattractive to me
11. Women are lucky because—they can have children
12. A good father—is mine
13. A girl has the right to—be herself
14. When they talked about sex, I—was uncomfortable
15. A wife should—love her husband
16. I feel sorry—for people who haven't had a strong family
17. A man feels good when—he is successful
18. Rules are—a part of our society
19. Crime and delinquency could be halted if—they hurt others
20. Men are lucky because—they have higher metabolisms than women
21. I just can't stand people who—are selfish
22. At times she worried about—her self image
23. I am—sensitive
24. A woman feels good when—she is liked
25. My main problem is—I'm lonely
26. A husband has a right to—be happy
27. The worst thing about being a woman—is PMS
28. A good mother—is my mother
29. When I am with a man—I am confused
30. Sometimes she wished that—he liked her
31. My father—is a great role model
32. If I can't get what I want—I feel insecure
33. Usually she felt that sex—was pleasurable
34. For a woman a career is—becoming more important
35. My conscience bothers me if—I hurt someone else
36. A woman should always—be honest

Scoring Key for Protocol J

1 5b	10 5c	19 2b	28 4m
2 5l	11 4i	20 4u	29 5m

3 5e	12 4k	21 6d	30 4d
4 5b	13 4i	22 6c	31 6j
5 4a	14 5i	23 6b	32 5b
6 4h	15 4h	24 4l	33 5b
7 4f	16 5g	25 5i	34 5d
8 4u*	17 5f	26 5b	35 5s
9 4a	18 5a	27 6a	36 4h

Notes

    8. Rule 5

E-level	2	3	4	5	6	7	8	9
Frequency	1	0	14	16	5			
Ogive	1	1	15	31	36	36	36	36

Automatic TPR: E5.
This young woman is self-observant and preoccupied with her feelings. Evidently in Item 19 she misread "could" as "should," but overall the literacy is good. The subject is a WU student, tested in the early 1990s.
Intuitive rating: E5.
Final TPR: E5.
Item Sum = 168, E5.

PROTOCOL K

1. When a child will not join in group activities—he/she should not be pressured to do so unless it will be beneficial to him/her
2. Raising a family—should be done in a caring environment
3. When I am criticized—I am hurt, but realize that the criticism could be beneficial
4. A man's job—should not be looked upon as superior to a woman's job
5. Being with other people—makes me happy most of the time, though I also like to be alone
6. The thing I like about myself is—that I work hard to achieve my goals
7. My mother and I—get along very well, and rarely argue
8. What gets me into trouble is—that sometimes I don't let people know how I really am feeling
9. Education—is very important
10. When people are helpless—I try to guide them in ways that will make them able to help themselves
11. Women are lucky because—on the average, we live longer!
12. A good father—is nice, caring, hard-working, and sensitive
13. A girl has the right to—say no, when she's in situations that she does not want to be in
14. When they talked about sex, I—did not get embarrassed
15. A wife should—be faithful to her husband
16. I feel sorry—for people who have not grown up in the comfortable family atmosphere that I have
17. A man feels good when—he accomplishes something that he sets out to do
18. Rules are—to be abided by, so that life is not chaotic
19. Crime and delinquency could be halted if—family lifestyles were better
20. Men are lucky because—they don't have to suffer from pain once a month!
21. I just can't stand people who—get good grades without having to work for them
22. At times she worried about—how others would react to her actions
23. I am—not good at making up sentences
24. A woman feels good when—she is complimented
25. My main problem is—that I get stressed very easily
26. A husband has a right to—lead the household, though the wife must have equal say
27. The worst thing about being a woman—is that they are paid 30% less for jobs then men
28. A good mother—is caring, sensitive, loving, and hard-working
29. When I am with a man—I feel intimidated and sometimes embarrassed about myself

30. Sometimes she wished that—she could be as bright and attractive as her friends were
31. My father—is a wonderful person
32. If I can't get what I want—I work hard until I do
33. Usually she felt that sex—was something that should only be done between two people who love each other
34. For a woman a career is—as important to her as a man's career is important to him
35. My conscience bothers me if—I do something that I know I believe is not right
36. A woman should always—stand up for herself if she is looked down upon by a man

Scoring Key for Protocol K

1 6k	10 6k	19 7a*	28 7b
2 6U*	11 5b	20 4e	29 6U*
3 6l	12 6a	21 3j*	30 5h
4 6e*	13 6i	22 6b	31 4a
5 7a	14 5j	23 5s	32 5c
6 6e	15 4j	24 4a	33 6e
7 4g	16 6b*	25 5g	34 5n
8 6m	17 6f	26 5o	35 6h
9 4a	18 6d*	27 4h	36 5n

Notes

2. up from 5a
4. 5b is too broad.
16. Rule 3. "That I have" is 5a.
18. Or 6a.
19. "Lifestyle" here is a high concept.
21. Or 4i if it means cheating.
29. Between 5m and 7c.

E-level	2	3	4	5	6	7	8	9
Frequency		1	7	9	16	3		
Ogive	0	1	8	17	33	36	36	36

Automatic TPR: E6.

It is unusual for a protocol to display compassion for others as clearly as this woman does in her answers. She has clearly also been touched by feminism. She is aware of her own inner life and also of her relations to others. Her respect for others' autonomy is unusual. The richness and variety of themes here suggest a rating of E7. She is a student at Washington University tested in the early 1990s.

Final TPR: E6.

Item Sum = 193, E6.

PROTOCOL L

1. When a child will not join in group activities—I think they are shy & need encouragement
2. Raising a family—is an admirable & difficult undertaking
3. When I am criticized—I try to stay open minded & learn from the advice
4. A man's job—is no different than a woman's
5. Being with other people—is the best way to spend your time
6. The thing I like about myself is—I'm independent but still need others around me
7. My mother and I—continue to grow closer with the passing of time
8. What gets me into trouble is—stubbornness
9. Education—is essential not only for individuals but for the U.S.
   to remain competitive

10. When people are helpless—I hope that the reason is not that they don't believe they have the ability to try
11. Women are lucky because—today there exists more opportunities to follow their interests in education, sports, jobs, etc.
12. A good father—is a role model for his children to demonstrate patience, love, & open-mindedness
13. A girl has the right to—have any goals, dreams, she wants
14. When they talked about sex, I—listened
15. A wife should—respect & love her husband with an equal's relationship
16. I feel sorry—for children raised in an environment that doesn't foster love or achievement
17. A man feels good when—he's loved & nourished both physically & mentally
18. Rules are—created to keep order
19. Crime and delinquency could be halted if—people were brought up in an environment which fosters self esteem and love
20. Men are lucky because—they don't have to wear pantyhose
21. I just can't stand people who—are close minded
22. At times she worried about—how to keep everything in her life in balance, family, career, etc.
23. I am—always trying to better myself—to be more open minded, patient, and less selfish each year
24. A woman feels good when—she's loved
25. My main problem is—placing goals too high
26. A husband has a right to—love, respect, and an equal partnership in the marriage
27. The worst thing about being a woman—is wearing pantyhose
28. A good mother—is patient & loving and tries to emulate the person she'd like her children to become
29. When I am with a man—I'm usually more at ease since I have more male friends (though my very closest friends are women)
30. Sometimes she wished that—she didn't have to do the adult stuff, paying bills, grocery shopping, & had more play time
31. My father—is not really a part of my life
32. If I can't get what I want—I'll continue to strive for it unless it's clearly an impossibility
33. Usually she felt that sex—was enjoyable
34. For a woman a career is—one choice she can make for her life along with motherhood or both
35. My conscience bothers me if—I judge someone too quickly
36. A woman should always—make her own choices based on her desires not necessarily those of others

Scoring Key for Protocol L

1 5l	10 7a	19 6n*	28 7i
2 6a	11 6i	20 4g	29 6l
3 6k*	12 7a	21 7a	30 6s
4 5b	13 6g	22 7a	31 4h
5 5d*	14 4a	23 7U*	32 7g
6 7j*	15 6e	24 4l	33 5b
7 6k	16 6b	25 6l	34 7e
8 5j	17 7b	26 7d	35 5u
9 6j	18 6a	27 5d	36 6i

Notes

3. "Open-minded" is 6k; "try to learn" is 5a, common and not adding much, so rule 3 suggests staying with 6k.
5. Or 5c.
6. "Need others" as a positive characteristic is a novel idea and a good contrast to independence.
19. 6n is less frequent than 6k.
23. Between 6h and 8b.

E-level	2	3	4	5	6	7	8	9
Frequency			4	7	14	11		
Ogive	0	0	4	11	25	36	36	36

Automatic TPR: E7.
This protocol has most of the major high level themes, with emphasis on open-mindedness. Note also time perspective (item 7), contrast of physical and mental (17), and contrast of independence and connectedness (6), and balance (22). Intuitive E8, or at least E7. Source, woman graduate of technological institute.
Final TPR: E7.
Item Sum = 212, E7.

PROTOCOL M

1. When a child will not join in group activities—he/she may prefer solitary activities; or perhaps is shy and needs encouragement
2. Raising a family—changes your life totally, whereas marriage alone is far less of a change
3. When I am criticized—it hurts; it depends whether it is ME personally or my behavior/ or product I produced—the former is more difficult
4. A man's job—is his identity unless he shares responsibility for other roles, also
5. Being with other people—is energizing, but I often need to be alone to refuel
6. The thing I like about myself is—my advocacy for others. My creativity. My ability to see humor everywhere. My outrageousness
7. My mother and I—didn't get along well; she lived through me, and it made her emotionally ill; it hurt us both
8. What gets me into trouble is—getting angry, and not being aware of these feelings; if I'm aware of the feelings it is much better
9. Education—It's important and does not have to be formal. Some of the finest learning occurs by risking & doing
10. When people are helpless—they hate themselves
11. Women are lucky because—we are closer to our feelings
12. A good father—is a "love"
13. A girl has the right to—protect herself
14. When they talked about sex, I—I paid attention
15. A wife should—avoid shoulds
16. I feel sorry—for people who box themselves in, or who let their life "slip by" without doing something they value
17. A man feels good when—he is adventuresome
18. Rules are—guidelines to be broken if they become barriers
19. Crime and delinquency could be halted if—kids had support and encouragement—even one person who believed in them no matter what
20. Men are lucky because—they are the favored sex in this society
21. I just can't stand people who—are arrogant
22. At times she worried about—others too much to the neglect of her own growth
23. I am—a pretty decent sort
24. A woman feels good when—she is her own person
25. My main problem is—anxiety
26. A husband has a right to—expect fidelity
27. The worst thing about being a woman—the lack of recognition and respect
28. A good mother—is consistent and loves unconditionally; she maintains her separateness from her children, to allow them to breathe and grow
29. When I am with a man—I feel more equal since I've run my own business
30. Sometimes she wished that—there were no time limits
31. My father—is a charming and talented man
32. If I can't get what I want—I look for alternatives
33. Usually she felt that sex—is best with lots of affection and fooling around
34. For a woman a career is—the key to freedom
35. My conscience bothers me if—am too self-centered
36. A woman should always—be able to support herself and children—financially

Scoring Key for Protocol M

1 6U*	10 6h	19 7U*	28 8f
2 7b	11 5a	20 6e	29 7e
3 6U*	12 5e	21 4f	30 6i
4 7U*	13 3c	22 7b	31 5a
5 7a	14 5a	23 4d	32 6e
6 8a	15 6n	24 6a	33 6f
7 8c	16 7b	25 5g	34 5h
8 5k*	17 6U*	26 5f	35 6j
9 8e	18 6c	27 6i	36 5o

Notes

1. Up from 5i; lower than 7d.
3. Up from 5e, like 6b (but not like it enough to put it there).
4. Clear conception of role.
8. A self-aware (E5) response.
17. Like 6p.
19. Up from 6o.

E-level	2	3	4	5	6	7	8	9
Frequency		1	2	9	15	5	4	
Ogive	0	1	3	12	27	32	36	36

Automatic TPR: E7.

There are many unique answers here, and unusual insights. There is a mix of long and short answers, so it is more believable and typical of a truly high protocol than one in which each response is an essay. High themes include valuing aloneness as well as relationships, sex in context of relationships, paradox (22, 9, 18), autonomy (28), and humor (15). Source, woman returning to graduate school to study counseling.

Intuitive rating: E8.

Final TPR: Because there is much richness and diversity with mostly very short responses, this protocol can be argued as E8.

Item Sum = 215, E7.

References

Ansbacher, H. L., & Ansbacher, R. R. (Eds.). (1956). *The individual psychology of Alfred Adler.* New York: Basic Books.

Cohn, L. D. (1991). Sex differences in the course of personality development: A meta-analysis. *Psychological Bulletin, 109,* 252–266.

Erikson, E. H. (1950). *Childhood and society.* New York: Norton.

Fingarette, H. (1963). *The self in transformation.* New York: Basic Books.

Freud, S. (1959). The question of lay analysis. In J. Strachey (Ed. and Trans.), *The standard edition of the complete psychological works of Sigmund Freud* (Vol. 20, pp. 179–258). London: Hogarth Press. (Original work published 1926)

Freud, S. (1961). Civilization and its discontents. In J. Strachey (Ed. and Trans.), *The standard edition of the complete psychological works of Sigmund Freud* (Vol. 21, pp. 59–145). London: Hogarth Press. (Original work published 1930)

Harvey, O. J., Hunt, D. E., & Schroder, H. M. (1960). *Conceptual systems and personality organization.* New York: Wiley.

Holt, R. R. (1980). Loevinger's measure of ego development: Reliability and national norms for male and female short forms. *Journal of Personality and Social Psychology, 39,* 909–920.

Isaacs, K. S. (1956). *Relatability, a proposed construct and an approach to its validation.* Unpublished doctoral dissertation, University of Chicago, Chicago, IL.

Kohlberg, L. (1964). Development of moral character and moral ideology. In M. L. Hoffman & L. W. Hoffman (Eds.), *Review of child development research* (Vol. 1, pp. 383–431). New York: Russell Sage Foundation.

Loevinger, J. (1966). Three principles for a psychoanalytic psychology. *Journal of Abnormal Psychology, 71,* 432–443.

Loevinger, J. (1976). *Ego development: Conceptions and theories.* San Francisco: Jossey-Bass.

Loevinger, J. (1985). Revision of the Sentence Completion Test for ego development. *Journal of Personality and Social Psychology, 48,* 420–427.

Loevinger, J. (1987). *Paradigms of personality.* New York: Freeman.

Loevinger, J., & Wessler, R. (1970). *Measuring ego development: Vol. 1. Construction and use of a sentence completion test.* San Francisco: Jossey-Bass.

Loevinger, J., Wessler, R., & Redmore, C. D. (1970). *Measuring ego development: Vol. 2. Scoring manual for women and girls.* San Francisco: Jossey-Bass.

Maslow, A. H. (1954). *Motivation and personality.* New York: Harper.

Meehl, P. E., & Rosen, A. (1955). Antecedent probability and the efficiency of psychometric signs, patterns, or cutting scores. *Psychological Bulletin, 52,* 194–216.

Peck, R. F., & Havighurst, R. J. (1960). *The psychology of character development.* New York: Wiley.

Perry, W. G., Jr. (1970). *Forms of intellectual and ethical development in the college years.* New York: Holt, Rinehart & Winston.

Piaget, J. (1932). *The moral judgment of the child.* New York: The Free Press.

Selman, R. L. (1980). *The growth of interpersonal understanding.* New York: Academic Press.

Sullivan, C., Grant, M. Q., & Grant, J. D. (1957). The development of interpersonal maturity: Applications to delinquency. *Psychiatry, 20,* 373–385.

Sullivan, H. S. (1953). *The interpersonal theory of psychiatry.* New York: Norton.

PART TWO

ITEM SCORING MANUALS

The scoring manual for each item begins with a *blurb*, that is, a short description of the kinds of responses the item elicits and factors to keep in mind while scoring. The intention is to point out factors that differentiate similar sounding responses that are scored at different ego levels. The user is assumed to be familiar with the concept of ego development (chapter 1) and its manifestations in sentence completions in general (chapter 2).

The blurb concludes with a list of *themes* that run through several levels. People of different ego levels share common concerns. Those concerns are shown in the content of responses at different levels, organized as themes. Within each theme there are sets of similar responses, called *categories*. The list of themes at the end of the blurb is there to help orient the rater, but they need not be recorded in scoring a response. The range of E-levels in which the theme appears is noted; that range tells the levels at which categories belonging to the theme appear. However, examples of the theme will be found in protocols over a wider range, because the responses in a category usually come from more than one ego level.

The categories are groups of responses within themes that are considered equivalent for rating and research purposes. Categories are usually recorded, particularly during training and when checking reliability. However, in rating total protocols, only the ego level of the responses, not the category, is considered. Where two raters agree on ego level but disagree on category, that is considered perfect agreement. Many responses could fit more than one category at a given ego level, so one cannot expect any better agreement.

Category titles are of two kinds: *descriptive* and *exemplar*. Descriptive titles begin with a capital letter and describe the responses that are included. Exemplar titles are *prototypic responses*, often with variant versions indicated; they begin with a dash and a lowercase letter.

In all cases, the examples that follow beneath the titles are taken from actual protocols. There are no hypothetical responses or categories; we did not invent any of the responses (nor, contrary to the assumption of some critics, do we endorse any of the sentiments expressed, even at the highest levels).

The examples are all taken verbatim from real protocols, often with errors of grammar, spelling, and punctuation intact. Most examples are taken from the data gathered with the 1981 form, but some responses in the 1970 manual have been retained even though they have not been repeated in recent samples. (Because many examples in our revised manuals have been supplied by other investigators, and because it was not clear which errors were made by typists and which by the subjects, most errors have been corrected.) Exemplar titles usually, but not always, occur verbatim on one or several protocols; they are mostly correct in spelling, grammar, and punctuation. For every category, answers almost identical to the title or to examples are omitted.

Most category titles are followed by *cross-references* to categories at higher or lower levels (never the same level) that need to be discriminated from the instant category. Those alternative categories should be checked to make sure the closest fit has been found. That is imperative when learning to rate and always helpful.

Certain category titles are preceded by one or two asterisks. The asterisks denote *popular* responses. One asterisk denotes a category that includes at least about 2% of the responses of one large, fairly heterogeneous sample; two asterisks indicate about 5% or more of such a sample.

CHOICE OF EXAMPLES

The purpose of the examples is to indicate both the upper and lower limit of responses that can be scored there. The lower limit may be just one key word out of the title. The upper limit may have an additional phrase or clause added to the title, but one not adding enough complexity to raise the level. Where possible (i.e., everywhere except for the highest ratings), long responses have been omitted. They are almost always unique, so their ratings are not based on solid evidence and do not provide guidance for future raters.

Many examples were omitted in the final editing. Some were too obviously included in the category, and some did not fit logically. Every sample will bring its own unique responses; no usable manual can hope to do more than classify frequent (hence more or less verifiably rated) responses and provide some guidance by means of examples for the other responses.

Although the omissions will trouble some raters, particularly those learning the method, a too extensive manual would be so unwieldy as to invite raters to depend solely on category titles, ignoring the examples altogether, or even to depend on general description of the levels. Our experience is unequivocal that accurate ratings are obtained only by using the manual as presented.

Although we try to give the exact flavor of the response as the subject gave it, that ambition fell before the fact that spelling, punctuation, and grammar are virtually lost arts. Some had to be supplied for intelligibility; moreover, internal evidence showed that some errors had been introduced by careless typing when written protocols were transcribed to computer. Some responses where subjects' errors have been retained are indicated by "[sic]." For the sake of uniformity, responses begin with lowercase letters, and the period at the end of the response is omitted.

THE RATING SCALE

There are eight possible rated *levels* or *stages* (Table 1.1) ranging from E2 (a reminder that this method cannot probe the origins of ego formation) to E9. These new levels replace the old stages, because those stages, called *I-levels*, had become a hodgepodge of stages, transitions, or half stages, and a transitional stage denoted by a different code (Delta) (Table 1.1). To add to the confusion, various users attached ordinal numbers to the scale in a variety of ways and did not always supply a decoding key. Two transitional or half stages, I-2/Delta and I-5/6, were rarely used and are now dropped. One transitional level, Delta/3, was used fairly frequently, but there was never an agreed psychological description nor positive attributes for it, nor was it a statistically reliable rating; it is also dropped. The names of the E-levels are the same as the corresponding I-level stages (Table 1.1). Two levels originally thought of as transitions, I-3/4 and I-4/5, are now full steps, whether called levels or stages. There are no half steps in the new scale. The use of levels and stages as equivalent is a way of evading the philosophical problem of stages, which is beyond the scope of this book.

The E-levels can also be used as a computational code. Confusion should be minimized, provided a new generation

of researchers does not call E2 our first stage. It is the lowest ratable stage, but it is the second stage in our conceptual scheme. The E1 level, like the I-1 stage, designates a period of ego formation not accessible to the SCT method.

SELF-TRAINING IN RATING

Before using the scoring manual in research or clinical application, the rater must master the concept of ego development that is the basis for and the tacit component of the scoring method. To do so, one must complete the training exercises (part I, Appendices A and B) that are designed to substitute for a tutorial workshop. Once the practice exercises are completed, each item should be scored without reference to other items on the protocol before looking at the protocol as a whole. The scoring standards assume that the test has been scored in that way. When handling a number of cases for research or even for clinical purposes, one ordinarily constructs *item response lists*, that is, a list of all the responses to a single item, properly identified. With that list, all responses to a single item are scored for the entire group at once.

Raters can evaluate their own performance in terms of percentage agreement between their ratings and ours for each item. Although the scoring keys give categories as well as levels in order to help the rater follow our reasoning, only E-level is considered in evaluating percent agreement.

PROBLEMS IN RATING

Extreme differences of level are easily discriminated, but adjacent levels are difficult and require reference to the manual even for experienced raters. Faithful checking of cross-references is imperative until the manual is familiar.

Sometimes a topic will occur in categories at one level, skip levels, and then appear again in categories at a higher level. That does not mean the topic will not appear in protocols at intermediate levels. The *skipped levels* are probably an artifact of the limited number of cases in samples used to construct the manual. If one finds a response clearly higher than the low category and lower than the high category, it should be assigned an intermediate rating, even though there are no such categories at the intermediate level. There is no evidence in favor of actual gaps, that is, topics discussed at one level and another higher level but not mentioned in intervening levels.

A frequent problem is what to do with *compound responses*, responses that have two parts, each ratable separately. The temptation is to take the part that corresponds to a clear category, which will often be a cliché or a common expression, and use that rating. In fact, the unusual part of the response, always more difficult to rate, is the more important one. In particular, when popular responses, as denoted by asterisks, occur in a compound response, the populars should usually be disregarded in rating.

As a general rule, two responses differing only by a *negative*—such as a close or not close relationship, or a nice or not nice person—are rated at the same level. In the 1970 manual they were usually included in the same category, but in this edition of the manual they are in separate categories if they represent different themes (such as positive or negative remarks). However, they will rarely be at different ego levels.

So far as possible, the themes are mutually exclusive. However, people (and their products) cannot always be ordered into rows and columns. In a free-response test of this sort, the popular themes may overlap; for example, personal traits and social traits overlap. In such cases, the theme that comes first is chosen for a category that could go either way. Assignment of categories to themes is sometimes arbitrary and ambiguous. The category is the important thing for rating.

Many responses can be included in one of several categories; in most cases, the different categories are at the same E-level. In those cases, either assignment is considered correct when assessing the agreement between two raters. Every response should be read at a *minimal inferential level*, that is, as its writer intended it to be. Where a response fits a category but not the theme under which the category is placed, the category governs.

Themes are not helpful at the highest levels. Almost all responses at the Autonomous and Integrated levels are unique, and most are complex, containing elements scored separately at slightly lower levels. That *complexity* is one of the marks of high ego level. Frequently, the topics either separately or in combination cut across the themes of lower levels. Therefore, themes are omitted at E8 and E9.

Many items include a few *unclassified* responses at some levels, usually E8. Those responses are there for some reason. They do not, of course, include all responses that could not be fit into categories. Either they are the responses that are repeated, even though not often enough to constitute a category, or they are related to the general descriptions of ego levels given in chapters 1 and 2. In most cases, they are high-level responses unique in relation to the particular item but illustrating general characteristics of responses at that level for other items as well.

Many professional colleagues are enthralled with studying the highest possible levels. However, when tests are given to groups of people who have not been trained in SCT scoring or ego development theory, few protocols, even among professionals, are scored at the E8 level and almost none at E9. One can elicit very high responses by special training or special instructions, at least with some groups. However, such experiments change the nature of the test, and the present scoring manual no longer applies. Any claim based on the SCT that a way has been found to "raise ego level" should be viewed with suspicion, particularly if retest instructions are more elaborate than "complete the following sentences."

When a Child Will Not
Join in Group Activities . . .

This stem was chosen to be the first one because it seemed easier to answer than most. It does not make the person answering feel self-conscious, and it is more structured. Content is a better clue to ego level than in many other stems.

At the Impulsive level (E2), the idea of psychological causation is lacking, so the subject looks for a physical or external cause. At the Self-protective level (E3), the child is suspected of bad motives, and force or punishment is often prescribed. The predominant view in the Conformist (E4) to Conscientious (E6) range is that something may be wrong and the child should be helped, not forced. A minority sides with the child's right to be alone. Above the Conscientious level, most subjects recognize several possible reasons, including some healthy ones.

There are three broad topics: why the child acts that way, what to do about it, and the short- or long-term results. Look at those themes as a function of increasing ego level: Causes begin as physical and become more psychological; they begin as confident assertions and become more tentative; they begin as unhealthy and increasingly acknowledge a healthy alternative possibility. Consequences begin as so immediate as to be virtual restatements of the stem and become increasingly long-term projections. Interventions begin almost as commands and increasingly respect the child's autonomy. At the highest levels, answers include so many considerations that themes do not apply.

The responses scored at E9 (Integrated) combine features that would separately be scored E7 and E8, such as three disparate aspects, healthy or not, personal and social considerations.

The stem is the only one for which the wording has changed. It originally read "won't" instead of "will not," but some subjects apparently misread that as "want to."

No special meaning is encoded in the choice of gender for a category title. Many subjects prefer to handle that issue with something like "he/she." To avoid such nonstandard usage, the manual uses either "he" or "she" more or less at random.

Themes:

Causes (E2–E6): they don't like it; there's a problem; she's shy; he lacks self-confidence.
Interventions (E3–E7): make him; persuade her; try to find out why; encourage gently; see what he is interested in.
Consequences (E3–E5): they feel left out; he is unhappy; she is headed for trouble.
Other (E4–E7): I feel sorry; it may or may not be a healthy thing.

ITEM 1: WHEN A CHILD WILL NOT JOIN IN GROUP ACTIVITIES . . .

E2 Impulsive

2-Causes

    a. —they don't like it (4c)
    he or she don't want to play [sic]
    the game is boring

    b. —they are sick (3c, 4e)

E3 Self-Protective

3-Causes

    a. —there is a problem (4b, 5d)

she has a problem
problems

b. Bad motives
it's cause he/she is dumb
he is a loser
he's lazy
he/she is probably spoiled
he is selfish

c. External or physical cause (2b, 4e)
there could be a physical problem

3-Interventions

d. —force him; punish him (4f)
one should make him
he should be yelled

e. Punishments
she would have to leave the room
give him 2 choices, join or sit by himself
don't let him do what he wants—make him sit &
watch the group

3-Consequences

f. Immediate results (4k)
they left out [sic]

E4 Conformist

4-Causes

**a. —he may be shy (5a, 5b)
shy
it demonstrates that he/she is shy

*b. —something is wrong (3a, 5d, 5e)
there may be something wrong
I feel that there is something wrong

c. —he may not want to; she isn't sociable [unelaborated] (2a, 5g, 5h, 5i, 5w)
maybe he/she doesn't want to be bothered
he/she might not be friendly

d. —she is a loner

e. —he may be sick (2b, 3c)
check for possible signs of illness
he might be tired

4-Interventions

f. —coax him; he should be convinced (3d, 5l, 6e)
try and persuade them to join
it is best to try to talk him into joining
I try to convince him/her to join
I prod him to

g. —don't force him; leave him alone [commands] (5p, 5s, 6l)
let him/her be

h. —it's OK (5t)

i. —accept it; let him do what he wants (5t, 5u)
don't get upset

4-Consequences

j. —he is unhappy (5d)
he may be depressed

k. —he is missing fun (3f, 5c)
he loses out

4-Other

l. —I feel sorry for him (7f)
it's frustrating

E5 Self-Aware

5-Causes

*a. —he may be afraid, timid (4a, 6a)
usually they have a problem, maybe they are afraid
they are sometimes depressed or scared
he may be a shy, timid individual
they may have had previous bad experiences

b. —he is embarrassed, self-conscious, uncomfortable (4a, 6a)
he or she does not know the other children well enough to join
he isn't used to dealing w/ children

c. —he feels left out, rejected, unwanted (4k, 6a, 6c)
she may be considered a loser and may not have friends and be excluded from kids her age
it is because the child feels unacceptable in that group
he may not feel able or welcomed

d. —he may have an emotional (psychological) problem (3a, 4b, 4j)
there might be a problem or maybe he/she is just shy
it doesn't necessarily mean he is abnormal
something must be wrong in his development
the child is probably going through an emotionally trying time

e. —something is bothering him (4b)
I will ask him if something is bothering him
this could be the first sign that he is troubled

f. —there may be trouble at home
it shows that he might be neglected at home
he or she might have had some experience at home to promote such behaviors

g. —he is withdrawn (4c)
he is withdrawing from others
may be withdrawn, sign of emotional problem

h. —she may be an introvert (4c)
it may be fearful or reserved

i. —he may prefer to be alone (4c, 6l, 7c)
he may need time for himself
he or she may not feel like it at the time
he is a private person
it may simply mean they are enjoying what they are doing alone

j. —he is not interested; he has other interests
   he will do what he prefers
   he wants to read
k. —she may not understand
   possibly language barrier
   he may not be that level of growth and development
   he (she) lacks some basic understanding

5-Interventions

**l. —he should be encouraged (4f, 6e)
   I encourage him
   try to get the child involved
   one should encourage that person to make an effort to join
   you should encourage them to play with one other child
   I will help him/her get involved

**m. —try to find out why [unelaborated] (6b, 6h, 6k)
   look further for problems
   I ask the child if there is something wrong and can I help him or her
   you should find the reasons why not
   ask why
   his parents or teachers should find out why

n. —I wonder why; I worry about him (6h, 6k)
   I wonder what is wrong
   one should be concern of such behavior [sic]

*o. —try to get him interested (in something else) (7b)
   he should be encouraged to entertain himself
   he should find other interests
   try to make him see the fun involved
   you should find something for him to do

*p. —they should not be forced (4g, 6e)
   that child should not be punished or scolded

q. —someone should talk to him; he should be observed (6i, 6j, 7b)
   I go to talk with him or her and hug him or her
   consult the child and deal with problem
   he should be evaluated

r. —he needs help(6i)

s. —he should be left alone (4g, 6l)
   leave him alone until he comes to you
   I let them do their own thing
   let her alone, perhaps he or she will later

t. —it's his business, his decision (4h, 4i, 6l)
   that is his/her own perogative

u. —he should be accepted; make him feel comfortable (4i)
   he can be made to feel included very easily

5-Consequences

*v. Unfortunate long-term results
   she doesn't learn to work with others
   he will tend to be a "loner" later in life

he is headed for trouble
he/she will not be quick to develop intellectually
he becomes anti-social
he or she will not be a happy person

w. —others may think something is wrong with them (4c)
   he/she is usually considered an outcast
   he will be considered to be a problem child
   he/she is often ostracized
   some of the other children may think that he (she) is weird

E6 Conscientious

6-Causes

*a. —he feels insecure, unsure of himself, inadequate (5a, 5b, 5c)
   he is selfish or insecure
   maybe it is due to lack of self-confidence
   he is probably afraid of rejection
   he is usually shy or uncertain of himself
   he feels inferior
   I wonder if he doesn't feel good about himself

b. —there is, must be a reason (5n)
   there could be several reasons why he doesn't
   there are several things that could be their concern
   there may be an underlying reason

c. —he feels isolated, alienated (5c)
   it is usually because he feels different from the others in the group
   he or she feels detached
   she is either shy or self-conscious and feels better isolated

d. —he is independent (5i, 7c, 8b)
   it is a sign of independence
   I believe in supporting his/her desire to be alone/independent

6-Interventions

*e. —he should be encouraged but not forced; she should be gently encouraged (4f, 5l, 5p)
   I encourage him to join, but then leave him alone
   have the group encourage him with support
   they should be invited gently
   I encourage him to join in, but do not insist

f. —he will join when he is ready, on his own (7a)
   let them be by themselves until they want to join
   one should leave the child alone and hopefully his curiosity will get the best of him and he will join in the activity
   leave him alone. Let him go at his own pace

g. He should be brought in gradually, unobtrusively
   I join the child for awhile, then bring him over to join group

he probably needs time to observe before joining in
*h. —try to find the reason, cause, source (5m, 5n)

I do not pressure him to join, but try to find out why, in a gentle way

he should be talked with to see why he likes to be alone, if he is happy alone

it is advisable to find out what is bothering them so a compromise can be found

one may need to explore the reasons

determine if there is a problem w/ leader

*i. —give him individual attention; he needs guidance (5q, 5r)

he/she may need help in making friends

maybe he/she needs more attention from the group leader (person supervising)

he should be counseled so that it is not a problem in later life

the child may need extra attention (personal) to get him to speak out

he probably needs more encouragement on a one to one basis

he should be urged to participate, otherwise given individual treatment

take her aside and try to engage her in conversation about herself

encouraging them by playing with them and bringing some others to him (her)

find a toy that he may be interested in and play with him until he joins in

j. —he needs understanding (5q)

extra efforts should be made to encourage him and understand his concerns

should be encouraged—understood

k. —find out why and do something to help, work with the child (5m, 5n, 7e)

you should try to find out why, before encouraging them to be involved

it should be determined why & help given where necessary

I try to find out why. Then make a decision from there

l. —respect his wishes (4g, 5s, 5t)

I think his preference should be respected

s/he is best left to do whatever is pleasing to him or her

m. *He needs to learn about the pleasures of group activity*

he probably has not learned to socialize

you should encourage his participation, by explaining the benefits of it

at least let him see what others are doing

E7 Individualistic

7-Interventions

a. —give him time [elaborated] (6f)

maybe he needs encouragement, maybe just time

try to accommodate their interest elsewhere and wait until they are drawn to the group

take some time to understand the child

b. —observe what he is interested in (5o, 5q)

I try to find out why and then work them into an activity at the child's pace

7-Other

c. Individuality as a positive value (5i, 6d, 8b)

he's probably marching to a different drummer

he may prefer to be an "individual"

it just means that child is different in its own way

watch out! He may be the greatest achiever of all

he may enjoy time by himself just appreciating his surroundings and his own mind

d. Three contrasting reasons or ideas

it usually means either of three things; the child is shy or too scared, the child just doesn't like joining in group activities or the child is unable, in some way, to do so

I am concerned of the reason why they won't . . . self-esteem, peer pressures, security, etc.

there might be something troubling him either momentarily or deep down

it may be a problem because extra involvement builds confidence in oneself and introduces people to a better understanding of others

e. Response or value as contingent (6k, 8a)

it may be a healthy or unhealthy sign

it should be checked on to see whether he/she wants to but is too shy (if so, encouraged/helped to join in, if not, left alone)

I would like to talk w/ the child & help him/her do what s/he wants to do to be a happy person

I wonder what's going on w/ him or her and, depending on whose child it is (& other variables), I would invite him or her to participate

f. —I used to be that way (4l)

he may not like the activity or he may not be a social animal—like me

I feel some sympathy because I once was that way

E8 Autonomous

a. It may be a healthy thing or not [elaborated] (7e)

it is "good" or "bad" depending both on the nature of the child and on that of the group

there is a reason. Sometimes observation is the child's style of learning. Other times short- and/or long-term help is desirable to help the child choose active participation

I check to see if she needs anything, how she's feeling AND respond to her need. She may NEED TO BE LEFT ALONE, OR SHE MAY NEED ATTENTION

he may (a) for good reason dislike the group or its activities (b) prefer doing something else (c) be shy & need encouragement

b. Respect for autonomy (implicit recognition of value for group and solo activities) (7c)

it may mean that he has an inner strength and sees a different world

alternate activities allowing and accepting the need for privacy, solitude, or just the child's feeling of separateness (his participation should not be forced) should be scheduled

E9 Integrated

Unclassified

it may be because he feels no identity with the group, is too self-conscious, or has no real interest in the activity

he's probably missing an element in development that would make adult relationships easier—but somebody has to carry the burdens of independent thought & behavior

Raising a Family . . .

This stem was originally the first on the test because it seemed among the most innocuous. A later generation of women, particularly those training to be professionals, seemed to be put off by the question, so it is no longer the lead item. The person may respond in current terms, retrospectively, prospectively, or hypothetically. It draws almost no omissions. Recent subjects write with more candor about the difficulties of raising a family than did those before 1970.

The majority of responses are clichés, but the stem also elicits some touching responses expressive of the highest levels. Contingent and qualified responses, rarely found below the Self-aware level (E5) for other stems, appear at all levels (thus showing that the usual finding is not entirely an artifact of intelligence).

The most common response at the Impulsive level (E2) is hard work, rated E3 because it is also frequent at higher levels. The categories at E2 sound slightly inapropos. Below the Conformist level (E4), most responses are variations on fun and hard work; both responses occur, though rarely alone, even at high levels. Probably both responses imply that the activities of life are divided into those that are fun and those that are hard work.

The hardest and most problematic distinctions are also the most frequent: that is, between "hard" at E3 and "difficult," "job," or "task" at E4. We take the connotations of the word *hard* to be hard work, of *difficult* to be something more like a difficult problem. Similarly, thinking of it as a job or task is seen as less like a wholesale distaste or rejection than simply calling it hard. All those responses are very common and may be given at any level, although they are usually combined with other ideas at high levels. Their frequency and distribution (TPR of persons who give such responses) show they are not diagnostic.

Many responses at the Conformist level (E4), such as "fun" or "difficult," are like responses to other stems at this level. Other categories are stereotyped versions of what are usually Conscientious level (E6) concerns, such as respon-

sibility and contrast of positive and negative aspects. The contrasting elements reveal the conceptual structure of the level: The opposite of fun is hard work rather than problems or sorrow. Father is rarely mentioned.

For the Self-aware (E5) person beginning to turn inward, the opposite of joy may be sorrow or heartache, and the opposite of pleasure may be problem or headache, rather than just hard work. "Fun" is often replaced by "rewarding" or "challenging." Contingencies classed here are fairly concrete: the person, money, help, rather than how one goes about raising a family, as at higher levels. Although the rating does not depend on single words, *experience* is used more often and more meaningfully at E5 than at lower levels; raising a family is an experience to go through rather than just something one does or wants to do.

Conceptual complexity and expression of emotions are distinctive in the responses of subjects at the Conscientious level (E6) and higher. Conceptual complexity can be shown by mentioning at least three distinct traits or attributes in one connection. Another form of complexity is seeing raising children in terms of the relationship between the parents. If cognitively shaded emotions are counted as complex, virtually all high-level responses are complex.

The most discriminating categories at the Conscientious level (E6) are based on new terms, such as privilege, sacrifice, fulfillment, and mutuality. Mutuality is expressed many ways, such as husband and wife sharing an experience or cooperation required. Responses in terms of social class or society are more explicit than at the Self-aware level.

Most of the responses at the Individualistic level (E7) are unique elaborations of themes found at the Conscientious level. Interpreting the stem in terms of watching or experiencing growth and development is exclusively a high-level (above E6) concern, as it is for other stems.

The responsibility accepted as a cliché by Conformists (E4) and weighing heavily on the Conscientious (E6) persons may be partly renounced at the Autonomous level (E8).

One watches, accepts, and learns humility. There is greater tolerance for ambivalence than at lower levels. Feelings are vividly expressed in context of appreciation for complexity.

Examples at the Integrated level (E9) are combinations of elements such as toleration for ambiguity, renunciation of manipulation, time perspective, orientation toward process and development, conceptual complexity, and vivid communication of affect.

Themes:

Favorable (E2–E7): good; easy; responsibility; rewarding; difficult but rewarding; requires commitment.
Difficult (E2–E6): bad; hard work; difficult task; difficult for a single parent; takes both parents.
Other (E2–E7): hostile humor; is what people do; part of life; not as easy as I expected; rewards and drawbacks but fulfilling.

ITEM 2: RAISING A FAMILY . . .

E2 Impulsive

2-Favorable

    a. —is good, OK (4c)
      is very nice

2-Difficult

    b. —is bad, no good
      is a pain
      is a bitch!

2-Other

    c. Redundant or inappropriate associations
      is taking good care of the family
      is like getting pregnant
      have a wife

E3 Self-Protective

3-Favorable

    a. —is easy, not hard

3-Difficult

    **b. —is hard (4f, 4g)
      is a lot of work
      is very hard to do because you don't have a job
      is tiresome
      is rough
    c. —is hard for some people (4f, 4g, 5g, 5h)
      is hard for a teen-age parent
      is hard for a person who don't know how [sic]
      is a hard job without help

3-Other

    d. Hostile humor
      raises your blood pressure
      is like raising herd of cattle
      is easy on ADC
    e. Self-protective attitude
      I want my family to obey me

E4 Conformist

4-Favorable

    **a. —is a responsibility [unelaborated] (6c)
      takes a lot of responsibilities
    b. —is important (5c, 6b)
      is something important to me
    *c. —is wonderful, fun (2a, 5b, 6c)
      will be enjoyable
      is great
    d. —is fun but hard, tiring (5d)
      is a fun job
    e. —is something I look forward to (5f)
      sounds good to me
      is in my future
      is what I plan to do when I am older

4-Difficult

    **f. —is difficult, not easy (3b, 3c, 5i, 5j, 7e)
      is hectic!!
      is stressful
      is difficult and scary
      is a problem
      takes a lot of compromising
    **g. —is a tough job, task (3b, 3c, 5k)
      is a chore
      is a hard task
    h. —takes money (5i, 5l)
      is very expensive and hard to do correctly
      can be costly
    i. —is not for me (5f)
      isn't so important to me

4-Other

    j. —is what people do
      is typical of married people
      is what many couples plan to do after schooling
    k. Concrete reference to own status (6k, 7e)
      It's all right. I'm so used to it now
      will never happen to me
      yes
      no family

E5 Self-Aware

5-Favorable

*a. —takes love, patience (6l)
  with care and patience is important
  work, patient, time, fun
  involves trust, understanding, caring but most of all love
  isn't that hard if you're unselfish and have lots of love to offer
  requires a great deal of patience, I imagine
  takes patience, love and money

*b. —is rewarding (4c, 6a, 6b)
  is a rewarding experience
  should be a very satisfying experience

*c. —is challenging (4b)
  is a hard, challenging job
  is the most challenging job I've ever had

d. —can be a joy and difficult (a pain) (4d)
  has its ups and downs
  can be fun and a mental & physical strain
  has its pluses and minuses
  can be a joy as well as a headache

e. —is an experience (6e)
  can be very interesting
  is a hard and emotionally straining job but everyone should do it
  is an experience I would like to have
  is exciting!
  can be a joyous experience

f. —is one of my goals (4e, 4i, 6j)
  is a long term goal
  is not my goal in life

5-Difficult

*g. Difficult, contingent on person, concrete factors (3c, 6o)
  is tough today
  is very difficult on only one salary
  is difficult without family and friends to help
  can be difficult for a working woman
  is much easier for the husband
  in a city like New York can be hair-raising
  can be a difficult and tedious task in this day and age

h. —difficult for single parent (3c, 6g)
  is not one person's responsibility
  by yourself is a hard job

i. —can be difficult [elaborated] (4f, 4h)
  is very hard financially and emotionally
  can be a major burden on a person
  can be a trying experience
  is difficult work if one is serious about doing it well
  is hard work and lonely

j. —is more difficult than people think (4f)
  is harder than it looks

k. —is the hardest job there is (4g)

is one of the most difficult things in life but it is also fun
isn't one of the easiest jobs in the world

l. —is time-consuming (4h)
  takes a lot of hard work and time
  takes a lot of time and money

5-Other

m. —should be carefully considered
  is difficult, so make sure you're ready before you start
  takes love and planning
  is very simple, just get your priorities straight first
  is a most important decision

n. —is a part of life, love (6b, 7c)
  is not an easy task, but an expected one

E6 Conscientious

6-Favorable

**a. —is difficult but rewarding [one at E5] (5b, 7d)
  is demanding but essential
  is wonderful but sometimes stressful
  is difficult but challenging
  is challenging and rewarding
  seems like a hard and beautiful thing to do
  is both rewarding and painful
  is a rewarding, yet tedious job, according to my father

b. —is the most rewarding, important part of life (4b, 5b, 5n)
  is one of the most significant duties
  is an experience unequalled by any other
  makes life more meaningful

c. —is enjoyable (fun, rewarding) as well as a responsibility (challenge) (4a, 4c)
  is a very demanding but pleasurable experience
  is a big responsibility and filled with satisfaction

d. Enjoyment, outcome contingent on how done
  is not easy, but it can be successful if you take the time and do it right
  is easy, but raising one well takes intelligence and ingenuity
  is fun if you try your best

e. —is a fulfilling experience (5e, 8a)
  can be very exciting and good learning experience
  is difficult, especially today, but very fulfilling
  is a life-enriching experience
  provides one with security and self-worth

f. —is a privilege, blessing, gift
  is not a responsibility but a joy

6-Difficult

*g. —requires both parents, mutual cooperation (5h)
  needs two
  is a wonderful way to share your life and love
  takes the cooperation of all involved
  takes a mother & father together

h. —is demanding; requires devotion, sacrifice (5c, 7a)
   is a hard job, it's very expensive & demanding
   is a responsibility for mature persons
   requires dedication and responsibility
i. —is complex, complicated
   takes more than love
   takes more than time and money
   is something most people know little about, yet continue to do . . .
j. —is not for everybody (5f)
   is not for the weak of heart

6-Other

*k. Personal evaluation, general (4k, 7e)
   the most important responsibility I have
   is not as easy as I thought it would be
   was the greatest accomplishment, so far, for me
   is important to me, but not priority
   is a dream of what I'd like in my future
   takes a lot of work and I appreciate the time and effort my parents put into it
   would be difficult but something I would like to do
*l. Three or more diverse ideas, one at E5 (5a, 7d)
   is a difficult job and takes a lot of concern and love and money
   is a difficult but a rewarding challenge
   is fun, rewarding, frustrating but never dull
   is hard work . . . challenging work . . . pleasurable work
*m. —is a full-time (lifetime) job (7a)
   is a long, probably never-ending process
   is a career
n. —passes too quickly
   is a long process that goes quickly
o. Seen in terms of social class, society (5g)
   today is harder than 25 years ago
   is difficult in an immoral society
   is a rewarding but challenging opportunity in today's society
   is hard, dependent in the cultural background
   used to be expected of one—now is no longer the "automatic" thing to do
p. —(its result) is unpredictable
   is a challenge in which the outcome cannot be predetermined
   I am for raising a family, but they never turn out the way you had hoped

E7 Individualistic

7-Favorable

a. —requires commitment (6h, 6m)
   is a life-long commitment

means having a strong sense of commitment & ability to compromise
   can be done in many different ways, but should involve a commitment of time and love
   is a commitment I'm not quite ready to take on
b. Growth and change (unelaborated) (8a)
   is an ongoing growing experience
c. —is a basic need (5n)
   is a fulfilling and natural thing that should be a loving atmosphere for the whole family

7-Other

d. Three or more diverse ideas, one at E6 (6a, 6l)
   has rewards and drawbacks but can be fulfilling
   is difficult and complex in a society with so many demands, expectations and criticisms
   takes a great deal of responsibility, and self-sacrifices; but the rewards are life-long
   is a source of great pleasure, lasts too short a time, and is unpredictable
e. Personalized description of problem to be coped with (4f, 6k, 8c)
   scares me, since everything will change. It is unfamiliar territory
   is a real joy, especially for me, for I almost gave up hope of having a child
   is one's biggest challenge in life, and one is never really able to evaluate the job he has done
   will be a very challenging experience that I look forward to with excitement & fear
   is an experience that I have not had but an experience that commands my respect

E8 Autonomous

a. Leads parents to grow and change (elaborated) (6e, 7b)
   has been a learning experience, a challenge and my favorite activity in life
   causes me to monitor and sometimes change my values and beliefs and to come out of myself, putting others' comforts ahead of my own
   challenges one to test the theories he has held and to find practical ways to implement his philosophy; therefore it is process in completion of one's development
b. Respect for child's autonomy
   involves a great deal of give and take and understanding of every member's ideals and morals
   means time commitment to the children for talking about problems, but also knowing when a child must act upon his own thoughts and ideas
c. Open acknowledgment of negative affect in positive context (7e)

is a lot of hard work, is filled with worry, is painful but the most rewarding, joyful, fun, loving experience anyone can have

is a full-time job, sometimes frustrating but others so rewarding that the frustrations are forgotten

is burdensome and today seldom rewarding, but I am still glad we had children

E9 Integrated

Unclassified

can break your heart and be wonderful too. One sometimes learns almost too late to accept and love and not try to change

is a fulfillment, including the fascination of seeing new spirits find themselves

When I Am Criticized . . .

Responses to this stem concern what the person does in reaction to the criticism; how he or she feels about the criticism; and evaluation of the criticism, the critic, or the self. The most popular category refers to hurt feelings, and it occurs at every level but is overweighted at E5. Most responses below the Conformist level concern doing and feeling; at high levels, combinations are usual. At the Conscientious level, evaluation is characteristic, and how the person feels about the criticism and what he does about it may be contrasted. The tenuous distinction between active reactions and feelings is blurred, particularly at higher stages, by responses like "I become defensive."

Reactions begin at E2 as simple and concrete. At E3 they are mostly verbal and sound somewhat impulsive, and at E4 they are often passive. Reactions at higher levels tend to include some emotion or some evaluation; at the Self-aware and Conscientious levels, the person, rather than being passive, may use the criticism for self-improvement or stand up to it. Feelings tend to be strongly negative pre-Conformist, muted at the Conformist level, and varied above the Conformist level, tending in the direction of tolerant acceptance of criticism at the highest levels. Simultaneous recognition of positive and negative feelings occurs at the Conscientious level. Insight into negative feelings begins with the Self-aware level but deepens at the Individualistic level and beyond. Most responses at the highest levels express an openness to criticism.

Although there is a general rule against letting single words determine a rating, two categories come close. Sentences that include a clause beginning "even though" are characteristically E7, as for other items. Sentences that state that "I try to curb" some negative reaction are characteristically E6. Variation in wording occurs, as illustrated by the examples given.

Some characteristics not incorporated in category titles may help with rating difficult or ambiguous responses. Answers that tell of sequential reactions—whether doing, feeling, evaluating, or a combination—tend to be higher than those that give a single reaction. Long-term time changes in reaction are rarer and tend to be even higher.

For this item, unlike some others, responses with opposite reasoning can occur in the same category. Some people are more disturbed by unjustified criticism, some by justified criticism (E6e); some people can accept criticism more easily from people they are close to, some from people who do not know them well (E6h).

All the E7 and E8 responses are complex. Particularly at E8, they are more original than the category titles, which must perforce be formulas.

Themes:

Doing (E2–E6): I do what I was told; I criticize back; I ignore it; I try to learn from it; I try not to resent it.

Feelings (E3–E7): I get mad; I don't like it; it hurts my feelings; I take it personally; I am no longer so sensitive.

Thinking, evaluating (E4–E7): I think about it; I analyze myself; I evaluate it.

Combination (E5–E7): it depends; I get mad but appreciate it; I listen, don't like it, and evaluate.

ITEM 3: WHEN I AM CRITICIZED . . .

E2 Impulsive

2-Doing

a. Unquestioning acceptance
I am doing something wrong
I will do what I was told
make you do it right next time
b. —I go in my room (4a)
I like to be alone

E3 Self-Protective

3-Doing

a. —I criticize back (5d)
I mean talk about him
I would call them twofaced
b. —I tell the guy where to go
when you do not like a person and then you curses them
I not play with them

3-Feeling

*c. —I get mad; I become angry (4c, 5e, 5d, 5f, 6e)
I will go crazy
I get mad and hit somebody
I get very angry and upset
it pisses me off
sometimes I get sore
d. —I laugh, feel good (4d, 4e)
I like it
I usually joke about it
I laugh because words are wind
e. —I cry

E4 Conformist

4-Doing

a. —I ignore it; I turn away (2b)
I pay no mind
I don't listen to what they say
I'd rather not hear about it
b. —I keep quiet (5c)
I shut up and take it

4-Feeling

*c. —I don't like it (3c, 5e, 5f, 5h, 6e)
I hate it
I get an attitude
I feel like punching a wall
I do resent it
*d. —it doesn't bother me (3d)
I blow it off
I am not usually upset
I really don't care

I don't get angry
I don't give a damn

4-Thinking, evaluating

*e. —I accept it, try to take it (3d, 5a, 6f, 8a)
I try to find good in it
I take it well because I am used to it
I grin and bear it
I take it in stride
*f. —I listen; I think about it (5j, 6f)
I acknowledge it
it makes me think
I listen, then reflect quite a while
g. —I want to know why (6j)
I try to understand why

E5 Self-Aware

5-Doing

**a. —I try to learn from it, use it constructively, do better (4e, 6f, 6i, 6m)
I try to correct my fault
it teaches me what I am doing wrong, so I can improve
I try to use it for my own advantage
I listen and try to change
I try to accept it in a positive manner
I appreciate it
b. —I stand up for what I believe; I defend myself (6g, 7a)
I usually try to defend myself (unless it was constructive!)
I try to justify myself
I try to prove the person wrong if it is a negative criticism
I fight for my beliefs
c. —I pretend I don't care (4b, 6a)
I keep it hidden, but inside I'm hurt
I can't stand it but try not to let it show
I react inwardly
I appear calm, but am agitated
d. —I retaliate (3a, 3c)
I get mad, then act on it
I become offensive
I usually take control of myself—unless the situation is really out of hand (I would retaliate)

5-Feeling

**e. —it hurts; I feel bad (3c, 4c, 6b)
I feel upset
it bothers me
my feelings are hurt
I get angry or hurt
I believe what they say and cry

I am depressed
I feel deeply hurt and as if the other person doesn't like me

*f. —I don't take it well (3c, 4c, 6b, 6d, 6e)
  I sometimes react poorly
  I am hurt and overreact
  I sulk

g. —I feel embarrassed, self-conscious (6c)
  is hurtful and embarrassing
  I cringe
  I hurt and my face turns red
  I get tense
  I usually get nervous
  I blush

h. —I am offended (4c)
  I feel resentment toward the person who criticized me

i. —I try not to [negative reaction, E3 or E4 type] (6a, 7b)
  I try not to let it bother me
  I try to apply it constructively without getting upset
  I try to change (and not cry)

5-Thinking, evaluating

j. Elaboration of listening (4f)
  I listen and then I say what I think
  I try to listen, but usually feel upset
  I ache first, then I listen
  I just keep quiet, listen attentively, not usually having any say
  I listen and if needed will change
  sometimes I listen, other times I am not interested
  I listen and think about if it is true or false

k. —I analyze myself; it shows my faults (6f, 6i, 6j)
  I try to be self-critical
  I shrug off the criticism if I have personally never felt inadequate in the area of criticism
  I acknowledge my faults
  I reevaluate my actions
  I take a look back at what I did
  I've learned something about me

l. —I deserved it (6j)
  it's usually deserved

5-Combinations

m. —it depends (6m, 6n)
  I react different ways
  it depends on what it is about

E6 Conscientious

6-Doing

a. —I try to curb [negative reaction described] (5c, 5i, 7b)
  sometimes I take it to heart, but I know I shouldn't
  if it is reasonable criticism, I try not to offer excuses

I react in a hostile way, although I try to curb this tendency
I try very hard to accept it at least with outward grace
it's hard for me not to get down on myself
I try not to resent it if I feel the criticism was offered to help me

6-Feeling

*b. —I take it personally; I take it to heart (5e, 5f, 7c)
  I become very sensitive
  I usually take it to heart, but I learn from it
  I learn from the experience, but sometimes I take it personally
  I feel bad when I take it as a personal attack

c. —I feel insecure, rejected (5g)
  I feel attacked
  I feel very insulted and humiliated
  I feel sad and frustrated
  I shrink back
  I tend to withdraw
  I feel guilty

d. —my self-esteem is low (5f, 5g)
  I feel inferior
  I lose my self-confidence
  it is a blow to my ego

e. Reaction related to unconstructive or unjust criticism (3c, 5f)
  for something minor, I become indignant
  I get very mad if they criticize me for the wrong things
  I am offended if it is unjust and not constructive
  it bothers me unless I am pretty sure the criticism is unjustified

6-Thinking, evaluating

**f. —I evaluate the criticism, weigh it carefully (5a, 5k)
  I look to see if it is true
  I try to find out if it's justified
  I determine if it is constructive
  I take it seriously
  I usually think about it to see if it is appropriate
  I try to understand the other person's reasons— again this may be difficult at times

*g. —I get defensive [unelaborated] (5b, 7a)
  my back goes up
  I sometimes act defensive
  I feel defensive
  defenses & explanations come to mind
  I am too quick to justify
  I try to rationalize

*h. —I consider the source (8a)
  it doesn't bother me unless the criticism is from a very good friend
  I try to evaluate the critic and try to improve myself
  I sometimes take it personal depending on who said it

I try to determine if the person is prejudiced or accurate

I analyze the critic's motive

i. Analysis of criticism and response if it is valid (5a, 5k, 7d)

I evaluate the criticism and deny it if I feel inclined or agree with it if it is just

I evaluate it for any real substance, to better myself by

j. —I try to understand where I went wrong (4g, 5k, 5l)

I try to understand why I did what I did

I take a close look at the criticizer, then at myself

I analyze myself to see if I feel the criticism is really justified

k. —I try to be objective, open-minded

I must think it over rationally

I try to objectively decide if the criticism is valid

I become very tense and it is very hard for me to be objective about the criticism

6-Combinations

**1. Negative reaction with acceptance of criticism (7d, 8b)

it hurts at first, but is very positive in the long run

I get angry sometimes but then I realize that they do it to help me

I may reject ideas at 1st but later ponder on it

I am at first angered, then I pay attention

I feel a little shame but I accept it for the better

I get mad but I still appreciate it

I get upset but I try to analyze the situation

I listen, learn & often resent

*m. —I accept it if it is constructive; I try to change if it is valid (4e, 5a, 5e, 5m)

I don't care what other people say unless it is constructive criticism

I don't mind, as long as it's constructive

I can accept it if I know it's based on truth

n. Mutually exclusive either/or reactions (5m, 8c)

I either feel bad about myself or angry at the person who criticized me

I either ignore the criticism or I attempt to correct it

I find it hard to react objectively and not emotionally

I look at it as a way to grow or the person is just jealous

I usually learn from it, but I can also be hurt, depending on how I am criticized

I think about how I can change my patterns (or I get really mad—depends on the person!)

E7 Individualistic

7-Feeling

a. —I am defensive [elaborated] (5b, 6g)

I feel a little bit defensive unless I know the person doing the criticizing quite well

I become angry, afraid, and then try to deny or distort

I try not to feel defensive and see what I can learn

I overreact in standing up for myself but also know that I am oversensitive

I become defensive, then reflective

I often become defensive and struggle against feeling sad

I tend to either become withdrawn & introverted, or defensive

I am defensive and occasionally offensive

b. Response "even though"—(5i, 6a)

my feelings are hurt, even though I know they probably shouldn't be

even though I get angry, I later try to see if the criticism was justified & I can possibly change it

I am annoyed, even when I know it is justified

though I feel bad, it makes me feel that I have an obligation to show I can improve

c. —I am no longer so sensitive (6b)

my initial reaction is to defend my position, but I am getting better at separating my position from my person and therefore at changing my position on occasion

7-Combinations

d. Accept feelings, evaluate, respond [3 elements, one E6) (6i, 6l, 8b)

deep down I'm bothered about it but after quick thought I realize how open-minded I need to be

I try to listen, don't like it sometimes & try to evaluate it fairly

I feel hurt, sulk, think it over; if I feel the criticism is just, I try to change

I usually listen, think about my impressions about the person giving the critique, and decide whether I think this advice is good. I try to listen

it hurts of course—but try to see constructive side. Often seek criticism before go too far out on a limb—especially in business

I ignore it for the moment, but sometimes I think about it later and if I feel it's true, I feel bad

e. Unclassified (3 elements, one E6)

I listen. If the criticism is just I take it to heart, if not I generally let it pass

I usually think for 2 or 3 wks about the validity of what was said, who said it and whether or not I want to modify myself to prevent being criticized again

I evaluate the criticism and make a decision whether I was right or wrong or should make amends

E8 Autonomous

a. —I like to see another's point of view (6h)

I enjoy it. I like to hear what others think of me—good or bad criticism

  *I like because I can learn from others and see in
     myself what the others see in me*
b. —I accept, evaluate, and act accordingly [3 elements,
     2 E6] (7d)
  *I often am initially insulted but then if the criticism
     is valid I am actually grateful because then I can
     change my bad attribute*
  *I try not to show it bothers, then I think about it
     later, first alone, then with someone. (At least I
     try to do that)*
  *I feel at first angry, then insecure and check to see
     what is wrong with what I did (or me)*
  *I can usually take it in good spirit and learn from
     it if it is valid*
c. Alternative E6 responses (6n)

  *I am too inclined to accept it from superiors and
     resent it from equals (or wife)*
  *I bristle. If correct I acknowledge. If not I put on my
     turtle back*
  *I respond openly, either accepting it or defending
     my point*
  *I check to see if it fits—I take what fits & leave what
     doesn't. I try my best to listen to the feelings
     behind the criticism*
d. Unclassified
  *I criticize back (very good at that) then consider the
     criticism when I have time to myself*
  *I know I deserve it, partly deserve it, or don't deserve
     it. The problem is to discover which*

A Man's Job . . .

Some responses take this item to refer to a man's employment; some take it to refer to division of labor in the household; some take it in a more abstract sense, as referring to a man's moral, civic, or religious obligation. Many subjects compare men's jobs with women's jobs or reject the term as obsolete. (Responses referring to women's jobs were not as frequent in earlier, all-male samples; however, times have changed, and these responses come from men as well as women.) There are still very popular categories referring to men's traditional obligation to support their families.

There is a major division between answers in terms of men's jobs as fulfilling responsibilities and in terms of men's jobs as rewarding. Those that cannot be classed as rewards or responsibilities are called *descriptive*. The manual does not distinguish imperative and declarative responses; if they are on the same or closely related topics, they are grouped in the same category. Thus, exhortations may be mixed with descriptions in some categories.

At the pre-Conformist levels, a job tends to be hard work or a way to make money. At the Conformist level, major emphasis is on conventional obligations to family, mostly in material terms as a provider. The Self-aware level continues to emphasize obligation; money may be mentioned, but typically the emphasis is on the less material aspects, such as being a loving father. The extremely frequent categories contradicting the difference between men's and women's jobs are classed here, but examples occur at every E-level. Many responses at the Self-aware level mention the ambiguity of the term. Intangible rewards begin at that level with the idea that the job should be enjoyable. At higher levels, the intangible rewards are further specified: interest, self-esteem, self-expression. At E6, the job may be seen in terms of defining the person, an idea that develops at higher levels to the search for identity.

Themes:

Description (E2–E7): is hard; is taking out the trash; is important; can be done by a woman; is only one part of his life; in a cliché version is to support a family.

Reward (E2–E7): is to make money; is to have fun; is his life; should be something he enjoys; should be interesting; is a means of self-expression.

Responsibility (E4–E7): is to provide for his family; is being a good father; is to provide in more than financial ways; is to work to his potential.

ITEM 4: A MAN'S JOB . . .

E2 Impulsive

2-Description

*a. —is hard (3c, 4c, 5e)
  is to do hard work
  to go and work

2-Reward

b. —is to make money (4b, 4h)
  is to get paid

E3 Self-Protective

3-Description

*a. —is to do outside work, heavy work
  is a trucker
  is cutting the yard
  is to take out the trash
  is lifting heavy objects
b. —is in the house, outside
  is not only outside home but inside as well
  is not at Home

c. —is harder than a woman's job (2a, 4c, 5b)
is hard for a woman to do
is harder

d. Sardonic response
is to act like he knows something
is another man's meat

3-Reward

e. —is to have fun (5g)
is to do what he wants
is chasing girls

E4 Conformist

4-Description

*a. —is important [unelaborated] (5h, 5l)
is very important to him
is a must

b. —is his livelihood, source of income (2b)
is where he makes his money
is his means of subsistence

c. —is difficult, not easy [unelaborated] (2a, 3c, 5e)
is often a hard one
can be tough
is rough

d. —is easy

e. Redundant responses
is a job
is not a woman's

f. Simple personal reference
for me is car mechanics and the stock market
is what I try to do

4-Reward

g. —is his life (5h, 6a)
is part of life
can be his whole life

4-Responsibility

**h. —is to support, provide for, take care of his family
(2b, 5k, 5l, 5m, 6k, 6m, 7d)
is to help feed and clothe his family
is to make a family's living
is to protect his Family
is to be the breadwinner
is to work to pay bills

*i. —is never done (5p)
do not end at 5 pm [sic]

j. —is to help women; treat them right (6m, 6n)
is helping the women take care of their children
is to be a gentleman!
is to make a woman happy

k. —is to head the family
is to raise a family
is to supervise the home

l. —should be done by a man (5q)
is more than a boy can handle
is very tough and a girl should not try it

E5 Self-Aware

5-Description

**a. —can be done by a woman (7b)
IS A PERSON'S JOB [sic]
should be equal to a woman's job
is being replaced by a woman
is better done by a woman
? it's anybody's job

**b. Compared with a woman's (3c, 6e, 7b)
is just as easy as a woman's job
is probably the easier of the two in marriage
is equally important to him as a woman's is to her
is the kind of job women wouldn't be right for (there
aren't many jobs like this though)
complements a woman's and vice versa
should be kept for a man only, and not a woman
who thinks women are better
is usually more profession and hard than a woman's
is just as hard and stressful as a woman's
ends at five
is done when he gets home from work
pays more
should have better pay than his wife's

*c. —varies; is hard to define
can be anything
is not always at work
has no specific definition
may be another man's hobby

*d. —is whatever he chooses, makes of it (6c, 6f)
depends on what he wants to be
is what a man feels is his place to do

*e. Difficulties, specific or qualified (2a, 4c)
is often tiring
can be time consuming
is very demanding
is stressful

f. —should fit his ability (6c, 6f, 7e)
is anything he is capable of doing

5-Reward

*g. —should be something he enjoys (3e, 6f)
ought to be fun
is not always what he wants to do but it should be
is worthwhile, if he is happy
should be enjoyable as well as useful

h. —is important to him [qualified] (4a, 4g, 6b)
is his castle
is usually very important to him
should never be neglected
is the most important part of his life
is often more important than family

i. —is his source of pride (6h)
is important to his ego
always gets to his head
dignifies him

j. —provides security

is necessary in creating a secure home
is his security

5-Responsibility

*k. —is being a good, loving father, husband; keeping family happy (4h, 6l, 6m, 7d)
is to be supportive of his companion
is to help with raising a family
is to love his family
is to be available for his family
is serving God and being a good father
is to provide for his loved ones

*l. —is important for supporting a family (4a, 4h)
is to give his family all necessary support
is bringing money for his family. I'm old fashioned
is important to his family
should pay well enough to raise his family

m. —is to be responsible; is to take care of his responsibilities (4h)
should never get in the way of his responsibility at home
is to be trustworthy
can be quite a responsibility
is to be responsible for himself and his family
should be his main responsibility

n. Virtuous traits (stated simply) (6k)
requires dedication
is to succeed
is to lead
is to care for those who can't
is to love the Lord God with all his heart, soul, and mind
is to be a decent, caring individual

o. —comes next to his family (6a, 6l, 7f)
is secondary to his family life
is to not put his desires before his family's

p. —is to finish it (4i)
is to be completed in the day started, never leave it for the next day
is to do what is expected of him
is never complete at home

q. —is to act like a man (4l)
is to be brave and aggressive
is to be his own man
is to be a leader and motivator

E6 Conscientious

6-Description

a. —is only one part of his life (4g, 5o)
should not be so consuming to become his whole life
takes control of too much of his life
shouldn't be his sole reason for living
does not necessarily reflect on him as a person

b. —is who he is (5h, 7c, 8a)
is to be true to himself
reflects his personality

is very important to his self-concept
defines him
tells lot about him
is his identification

c. —depends on the individual (5d, 5f)
should be chosen carefully to suit the man
is primarily to be a person/to be himself
is to try and be himself and not what his friends want
is only what he makes it by effort, concentration, and true enjoyment
is only as productive as the individual

d. —is an obsolete term (7a)
there is no such thing
is an archaic idea
is no longer a distinct task—the line between male and female roles has blurred
is a phrase I hate

e. —is always considered more important than a woman's (5b)
is higher paying and more influential simply because a man has it
should not pay more than a woman's as long as she is doing the same thing in the same place

6-Reward

*f. —should be interesting, satisfying, rewarding (5d, 5f, 5g)
is sometimes very challenging
should bring satisfaction
is crucial to his well-being
is like a woman's, not necessarily what we want to do. Too often it is the lesser of evils

g. —is a source of self-esteem (5i)
is link to his ego
should fulfill a need to succeed
is that which often provides his sense of worth

h. —should be fulfilling (7c)
is to live his life to its fullest
should be meaningful
should be important to him emotionally
should bring him fulfillment as well as meet financial needs

i. Concern with goals, objectives
should be only a means of allowing him to support his pursuit of his goals
is to pursue his ambitions to the furthest extent (like a woman's)

6-Responsibility

*j. —is to do the best he can (5n, 7e)
is to be the best person he can be
or a woman's job is to be the best he/she can be
is to give his best

*k. —is to provide for his family in more than financial ways (4h, 5k, 7d)
is/should be providing support emotional and financial for his wife

Should only be one form of his support for his family

is to help a mother of his child and stand by both of them when needed

should be not only that of provider but also that of active parent

l. —should not take him away from his family (5o, 7f)

is to make a life for himself & family

must be stimulating and rewarding—yet the family must always come first

m. —is to be a good partner (4h, 4j, 5k, 7d)

is to take care of me emotionally & be my partner

includes helping a woman out with hers

is being responsible for his actions and taking equal responsibility for his children

n. To avoid sexism (4j)

is to treat a woman with the same respect that he is treated

is to know that a man's job can be just as likely a woman's job

is knowing when to let the woman do for herself and when he should open a door for her, or bring her flowers

in 1977 is to make sure both the men & women can do "their thing"

o. Contribution to society

is to hold a responsible job and be involved with community and church

is to support his family and his country

E7 Individualistic

7-Description

a. Culturally (stereotypically) defined (6d, 8b)

can also be done by a woman but society doesn't usually accept this

in a cliché version was and is to support a family

was traditionally the primary financial source for a family

is to be a person primarily and not just a "man"

is not as structured and rigidly defined as it was years ago!

seems a somewhat chauvinistic expression

b. —can be done by a woman [qualified or elaborated] (5a, 5b)

is about to be taken by a smarter woman

is just as hard as a woman's, for there's no difference in jobs

could probably be done better by a woman, since she is less susceptible to do it in a "usual" manner

should be considered no different than a woman's (unless it involves physical labor which requires more strength than a woman has)

can be done by a woman with a few exceptions

should not be any different than a woman's (providing he is capable)

7-Reward

c. A means of self-expression (6b, 6i, 8a)

is a blessing from the Lord but needs to be an extension of a man's gifts and talents

is frequently his identity

must fulfill his desires to accomplish something worthwhile

should be an extension of himself

or woman's job ideally should reflect their personality and be a positive experience

is the most important area of his life, while love for many women is the most important area of their lives

7-Responsibility

d. Securing the emotional welfare of his family (4h, 5k, 6k, 6l, 6m)

is to govern his family and raise it in such a way that every family member's potential is realized

is tough—he must make a living for himself and his family. Offer leadership to the family—and be kind, loving and supportive to the family—[sic]

e. —is to work to his potential (5f, 6k)

ought to enable him to use whatever knowledge is his to possess

is to figure out what he wants from himself & life and try for it

should coincide as closely as possible to his interests and abilities

f. Should be balanced with other areas of life (5o, 6a, 6l)

is one of the three major areas of his life. The other two are his marriage and his health

may be so encompassing that he becomes blind to the other parts of his life which are equally important

g. Complex and contrasting combinations (one E6 element)

is a challenge, a vise of pressure, the source of stability, and too much

to lead with love, compassion and flexibility, along with strength not to be flexible when he's right

is his job: tackle it as a job; don't try to make it your hobby. It's more pleasurable that way

can be anything: dull, interesting, demanding, demeaning, rewarding, stimulating—but hopefully capable of changes if needed

E8 Autonomous

a. Search for identity (6b, 7c)

may be rewarding but cannot provide him with all the opportunities for personal development

is who he is (his ego) unless he has achieved some self-worth beyond that and becomes a person. (I know and admire some.)

is to achieve wholeness, just as a woman's is

is the construction of personally meaningful world

b. Unclassified

a destructive cliché

Being With Other People . . .

This stem has a Conformist pull. Being with others is a Conformist's modus vivendi. For this individual, being with others is fun and makes him or her feel good. That is how one third of the subjects in our samples respond, including people of all ego levels except the highest. Where the response has any other element, it determines the rating.

The main themes for this item are: approval; dislike of being with others, mainly due to discomfort; contingent approval of being with others, including contrast between liking and not liking it at times; and uses of it beyond simple enjoyment or approval.

At lower levels, global approval is likely to be the whole response; at higher levels, more responses express contingent approval or give as a reason some ulterior use of the experience, such as security or learning something. Negative remarks are mainly reports of discomfort in social situations and are mainly at E5 and below.

Contingent approval of being with others occurs at almost all levels; it supersedes blanket approval at higher levels. The terms of the contingency change in accord with level, ranging from being the right people at E4 and below, to appreciation for personal relationships and compatibility at the highest levels.

The most difficult discriminations to make are those involving contingent approval of being with others where it depends on personal qualities of self or others, or mood, or character. It is not so hard to discriminate the level of particular responses as it is to write category titles that capture the basis for the rating. Many examples seem to be almost unique. Thus some latitude for judgment is needed in that group of responses.

Themes:

Approval (E2–E6): is nice; is enjoyable; is needed; is stimulating.

Discomfort (E2–E5): isn't for me; makes me nervous; makes me uncomfortable.

Contingency (E4–E7): is fun if you know them; is sometimes desirable; is great if you're comfortable with them; is fun but being alone is better.

Uses (E4–E7): is a chance to make friends; makes me feel secure; relaxes me; helps me know myself.

ITEM 5: BEING WITH OTHER PEOPLE...

E2 Impulsive

2-Approval

a. —is nice, OK [unelaborated] (4a)
   is fine
   is alright

2-Discomfort

b. —isn't for me (3a, 3b, 5o)
   is not right

2-Other

c. General description of good or bad behavior
   you should not do anything bad
   is good or bad
   is fun when getting trouble

E3 Self-Protective

3-Discomfort

a. —makes me nervous [unqualified] (2b, 5e)
   makes me tense

b. —is hard (2b)
   is hard to get along
   is not easy

E4 Conformist

4-Approval

**a. —is fun, enjoyable (2a, 5a)
   is a nice experience
   is a pleasant way to spend an evening
   is an experience
   is a joy and pleasure
   is good for everyone
**b. —makes me feel good; makes me happy (5d)
   gives me a good feeling
   makes anyone feel good

4-Contingency

c. —is fun if you know them, they are the right people
   (5h)
   makes me happy especially when it's my relatives

4-Uses

d. —makes me feel good about myself (5j)
   can make someone feel better about himself
e. —is a chance to make friends (5k)
   I knows that I have friends [sic]
f. —helps your personality; helps you socially (6i, 7d)
   helps me
g. —makes time pass faster (5d)
   makes the day pass much easier

E5 Self-Aware

5-Approval

*a. —is important, necessary (4a, 6a)
   is something I can't live without
   is something that I could use more of
   mean a lot to me. It is special
   is both fun and necessary
*b. —is interesting, exciting (6a, 6e)
   can be adventurous
   is good if interesting
c. —is healthy, part of life (6b)
   that is life; there are people everywhere
   is good for a person's well being
   is good for both husband and wife
d. —is one of my favorite activities (4b, 4g)
   is what I like the most
   is when I have the best time

5-Discomfort

*e. —makes me feel uncomfortable, a little nervous; can
   be trying (3a)
   sometimes intimidates me
   sometimes makes me nervous
   I tend to be shy at first, but then I'll come around

*is okay, if I know the people. If I don't I feel out of
   place*
makes me shy until I know them
I am always careful what I say or what I do
is not as comforting as being alone
f. —is (can be) boring, tiring
   can be trying at times
   can sometimes be bothersome
   can sometimes be annoying

5-Contingency

**g. —is desirable at times, not at others (6d, 7c)
   sometimes is fun
   *is o.k. for a while but I really prefer spending my
      time with my family*
   can be a pain sometimes
   gets to be a bit much at times
   is usually enjoyable
*h. —is fun if you like them, if they are your friends
   (4c, 6c, 7b)
   makes me feel good (it depends on the people)
   I enjoy good company
   is enjoyable if they are affable
   is great, unless they are boring
   (it all depends on the other people)
i. —has good and bad points (6d)
   can be the best or worst
   has its advantages and disadvantages

5-Uses

*j. —makes me feel comfortable, secure (4d, 6f)
   gives me security
   is comfortable
k. —makes me feel wanted, part of the group (4e, 8a)
   makes me feel important
   makes me feel happy and needed
   gives me a feeling of belonging
   is to share
l. —is a cure for loneliness (7a)
   makes my life less lonely
m. —is better than being alone
   makes me feel better rather than being alone
n. —you learn a lot, new ideas (6a, 6g)
   enlightens me
   helps me expand my vocabulary
   is a good way to learn about them

5-Other

o. —is not important to me (2b)
   is not always necessary to make me happy

E6 Conscientious

6-Approval

**a. —is stimulating, rewarding, educational (5a, 5b, 5n)
   is invigorating to me
   is enriching for me

is essential for keeping my sanity
makes life interesting
makes me happy especially with those different than myself
is important, fun & edifying

b. —is one of life's pleasures (5c)
makes life more enjoyable
is one of the rewards of being human

6-Contingency

c. Enjoyment contingent on (my or their) mood (5h, 7b)
is a great feeling if you feel good
is fun when you want to be
can be great if you're comfortable with them
can be at first difficult if you don't know them or anything about them
can be fun and scary, too, if you're not comfortable with other people

d. Affects me differently at different times (5g, 5i, 7c)
can be fun or uncomfortable depending on the people
can be thrilling or miserable
is fun although energy-draining
is something I sometimes crave and at other times weary of

6-Uses

*e. —relaxes me; brightens the day (5b)
is uplifting
makes me happy to be alive
creates a feeling of unity and friendship

f. —helps me to forget my problems (5j)
lifts my spirits when I am feeling low
relieves anxieties
is pleasant when you need to clear your mind
is good therapy for me
provides me with fun times that ease the pressures of life
is a good release

g. —is a learning experience (5n)
can be enlightening at times
who are intellectually superior to me helps me to learn
teaches me different ideals

h. —helps you learn about other kinds of people, their problems (8a, 8b)
brings different points of view on things
helps to talk things out
helps one to appreciate others
is a good way to observe human behavior
provides you with a better understanding of how people cope with life's events

i. —helps one to a broader view of life, deepens one's personality (4f, 7d)
enriches one's life experience
gives me a feeling of self worth and good feeling
creates a good flow of ideas

enriches each individual's perspectives on life if communication exists
brings new thoughts and ideas, feelings and emotions to life

6-Other

j. Reference to social interaction, socialization
makes me happy. I enjoy talking to new people
is a great opportunity for fellowship

E7 Individualistic

7-Contingency

*a. Contrasted with desire for solitude or privacy; need for both (5l)
can be fun at times but being alone is usually more relaxing
is enjoyable, enlightening, inspiring. I prefer very small groups
is nice but I prefer to react and listen to music
is fun if it is balanced with alone time or time with my wife
in small groups is satisfying; large groups are tedious and boring
was a must for me until recently when I learned to like being by myself sometimes

b. Enjoyment contingent on traits, relation, interaction (5h, 6c, 8a)
is fun when they're "down to earth"
Is enjoyable, especially if you can cause them to be happy or they benefit from it, also if you can
depends on the type of people, mutual interest and my state of mind
can be wonderful if one shares oneself
is comforting when you know and love them well
can be great if you share similar ideals

c. Contrasting reactions (5g, 6d)
can be tiring or very satisfying
can be great or it can be tedious if one hasn't had enough time for themselves
can make you feel warm and loved, but also intruded on
can be stressful for some; for others strengthening
is one of the most fulfilling yet exhausting activities for me

7-Uses

d. —helps me grow emotionally, know myself (4f, 6i)
is rewarding and forces me to grow & change faster
and being myself, as opposed to wife or mother, is enjoyable
allows me to see who I really am
helps me see the way I view myself

E8 Autonomous

a. Opportunity for sharing thoughts, experiences (5k, 6h, 7b)
is sharing yourself and your ideas, and hearing their's

*is a time to give of yourself, meaning sharing your
views and qualities with others*

*makes me feel good because we share ideas, opinions
and experiences*

*must include communication. I love to hear other
people's experience and join in with mine*

*provides feedback as far as ideas & thoughts are
concerned & a feeling of comfort and well-being*

b. Appreciation of other people's worth, one's own
need for relations with others (6h)

*makes me enjoy life more, for there is nothing better
than to see someone else's smile*

*makes me happy because I appreciate their differ-
ences and love to learn from them*

*especially those I care about is one of the things I
treasure most in life*

The Thing I Like
About Myself Is . . .

For some early samples this item was the first on the form, but it proved too threatening for many subjects when confronted with it at the start. It works well in its present position. It evokes a wide range of attributes, with no one predominant, so the item is challenging. Although omission is not frequent, many responses evade or more or less reject the stem; such responses, however, are scorable. The stem has a high pull in the sense that it invites everyone to claim socially approved traits, no matter whether they have those traits in the eyes of others.

A few responses occur verbatim many times: "my personality," "my sense of humor," "my patience," and "everything." The responses "my sense of humor" and "I get along with others," and variants of the latter, occur in indistinguishable form over a wide range. Where afterthoughts or subordinate clauses are added to such popular responses, they govern the rating.

For many subjects below the Conformist level, and for some Conformists, the things they like about themselves are simply given, such as physical features or intelligence. At the Self-aware level and above, responses in terms of passively received gifts are rare. What an individual likes about him or herself is something in which the individual participates actively: interests, efforts, relationships with others, self-reliance. Thus the item illustrates growth in sense of choice and responsibility. The appearance of "my patience" as a category at the E3 level was not anticipated; it probably indicates seeing patience as a virtue more than possessing special patience.

One can see a capsule of moral development in the responses. The idea of morality progresses from not using drugs (E2); to the passive virtue of patience (E3); to being friendly and getting along with others (E4); to more genuinely moral virtues such as honesty, fairness, and sincerity (E5); to following one's own convictions (E6); to being honest with oneself (E7).

The major themes are physical attributes; social traits, explicitly interpersonal; and personal attributes, which may refer to dispositions and traits or to individuality. However, many categories straddle these thematic distinctions. Social traits and personal attributes cover overlapping territory; therefore, we look for explicit interpersonal reference in relation to the social theme.

The hazard of using single words as the basis for rating is illustrated here by the word *open*. To describe oneself as open in some contexts means honest, in others it means outgoing (E5), and in still others it means open-minded or sensitive (E6).

Themes:

Physical (E2–E4): I do not drink; my looks; I'm healthy.
Social (E3–E7): people like me; I get along with others; I like to help others; I am sensitive to others' needs; I try to be nonjudgmental.
Personal (E2–E7): I'm nice; my personality; the way I am; I'm honest; my optimism; I'm honest about my motives.
Evasive (E2–E7): nothing; everything; hard to say; I don't think about myself in such terms.

ITEM 6: THE THING I LIKE ABOUT MYSELF IS . . .

E2 Impulsive

2-Physical

    a. Impulsive or addictive acts
      I do not drink
      that I'm not a junky

2-Personal

    b. —I'm nice, good (4e, 4h)
      cool

2-Evasive

    c. —nothing (5q)
      not much

2-Other

    d. Unclassified
      I am mean

E3 Self-Protective

3-Physical

  *a. —my looks (4a)
      my hair
      my face
      my body
      my smile
      I am cute
      neatness

3-Social

    b. —people like me (4c, 4d)
      that people like about me
      my friends

3-Personal

  *c. —my personality [unelaborated] (4d)
      my good personality
      my hair, eyes and personality
    d. —me; who I am (4j)
      that I'm my own self
      being me
    e. —I'm patient
      when I can be patient

3-Other

    f. Specific actions
      my math grade
      to keep my house clean
      I'll be able to drive soon
      that I actually filled out this survey
    g. —I am lucky

E4 Conformist

4-Physical

    a. —I'm healthy (3a)
      that I am athletic
      my strength
    b. Being a woman, man
      a boy
      being a mother

4-Social

  *c. —I like, get along with others (3b, 5a, 5c, 6b)
      being able to get along with all ages of people
      interest in other people
      that I enjoy meeting people
      I don't hate anyone
  *d. —I am friendly, fun, happy (3b, 3c, 5a, 6i,6j, 7e)
      my social behavior
      I always have fun
      my cheerfulness
    e. —I am kind (2b, 5a, 5b)
      I am generous
      my kindness towards animals
    f. Family background (5d)
      to have a good family, children and even a wife
      I was brought up with better qualities than 90% of
        my class

4-Personal

    g. —my intelligence [unelaborated] (5j)
      my brains
      that I am nice and sometimes smart
    h. —I'm a good person (2b, 5p)
      being able to be polite & decent
      I am a nice person
    i. —I'm responsible (5e, 5i)
      people could depend on me
      being good worker
    j. —the way I am (3d, 5n, 6l)
      the way I dress and operate

4-Evasive

    k. —everything
      that I have a lot of different good aspects
      my whole person
      most things

4-Other

    l. Unclassified
      I'm a type B personality
      myself the majority of the time

E5 Self-Aware

5-Social

**a. —I am caring, loving toward others (4d, 4e, 6a)
I'm not selfish
I am very considerate of others
I care
my warm heart
that I try not to hurt people
my ability to love
I am a very nice, caring person, who is responsible and dependable

*b. —I want (like) to help others (4e)
that I am kind and offer help to anyone that needs it
when I try my best for others
my concern for others
my giving nature
I'm honest, sincere & I like to help poor & sick people
that I love caring for other people

c. —I make friends easily; I like to talk with everyone (4c)
I'm happy, outspoken, outgoing, & a good person to be around
that I am a honest and friendly person
I'm very outgoing & kind to anyone who comes along

d. Relationship with friends or family (unelaborated) (4f)
that I care about my friends & that they are an important part of my life
that I am a very good wife, mother and housekeeper
my feelings toward my son
I am a real friend
that I could get along with my sisters better than most people
I try to be considerate of others in hopes they will return the favor

5-Personal

**e. —I'm hard-working, ambitious (4i, 6e)
perseverance
my devotion to duty
a day's work for a day's pay and when I play it is for enjoyment
I'm not a quitter
I do my best
I'm a go-getter
I am determined to make it for myself and my children

**f. —I'm honest, sincere (6g, 7d)
I can't lie
that I am not a phony
that I'm a straightforward individual
being for real
my openness and frankness

*g. —my sense of humor (6i)
I can be a card
my humorous attitude, quick with a joke

*h. —I am flexible, adaptable, growing [unelaborated] (6d, 7f)
I am very understanding of many situations
that I am open for change depending on my situation
I'm versatile

*i. —my ability to cope with problems (4i, 7f)
my ability to handle responsibility
the ability to make decisions when necessary
making the best of bad situations
my ability to stay calm in time of stress
I always like to have fun, even when I'm down
that I am full of courage
I'm a survivor

*j. Abilities and interests (specified) (4g, 6d, 6o)
my ability to think
my talents & my love of music (singing, dancing, listening to it)
my homemaking skills
my work in the sciences
being able to play the sports I want to well
I am a good wife, mother & professional
1) I'm a good dancer, 2) I'm smart

k. —my self-confidence, self-respect (6k, 6n)
I am not intimidated by anyone
I can count on myself
although people say I can't, I can
I feel my life is back on track and I'm responsible for it
that I feel professionally competent

*l. —I am independent, unique [unelaborated] (6k, 6l, 7g)
I'm original
that no one else is like me
I am an individual
that I feel I can make it on my own
my personality and individuality

m. Efficiency (organizational virtues)
that I have a reasonable amount of knowledge
my organization
my strong will
my intellect & experience
common sense judgment
I am assertive

n. —my attitude, awareness [unelaborated] (4j, 6l)
my personal habits and traits
my basic nature
the way I live my life
my feelings
the way I see the world

o. —I am religious, believe in God
I love G-d
being a Christian

p. My morality (unelaborated) (4h, 6h)
my moral character
my loyalty
I always try to do what's right

5-Evasive

q. —hard to say [unelaborated] (2c, 7h)
   I really don't know
   impossible to explain
   ouch!
   ?
   (I pass)
r. —I don't want to seem conceited
   my charm, wit, genius, beauty . . . (shall I go on?)
   *that I am somewhat smart but not too much to make
      me conceited*

E6 Conscientious

6-Social

**a. —I am understanding, sensitive, a good listener (5a,
      7a)
   my competence, compassion, and ability to love
   my compassion for animals
   my empathy for others
   I am honest and thoughtful of others (altruistic)
   that I am capable, open, and helpful to fellow people
   *that I am a caring person who listens to others even
      though they may be very boring*
*b. —I am tolerant, open-minded (4c, 7c)
   *being able to accept people for what they are, not
      who they are*
   *being able to look at both sides of an argument or
      situation*
   *my ability to relate to people of all different ages,
      races, etc.*
   being able to forgive and maintain caring feeling
   my liberal nature
c. Contribution to society
   my ability to be a good and fair leader
   *I'm generous, and if I can help others to help them-
      selves, it makes me feel good*
   desire to help humanity

6-Personal

*d. —I am always trying to improve, to learn (5h, 5j)
   my ability to change for the better
   *that I am going and try to make an effort to get
      along with everyone [sic]*
   *my ability to overcome my mistakes & grow from
      overcoming them*
   I am finally growing up
*e. —my determination; I usually accomplish what I set
      out to do (5e)
   my ability to get things done and make others feel good
   my strong will and determination
   *the fact that I am not letting a family hold me back
      from obtaining a college degree*
   the fact that I don't settle for mediocrity
   *my ability to solve problems w/ common sense and
      experience*

that I am a doer & not a talker
*I can be depended upon, at least most of the time,
   to honor my commitments*
f. —my ability to set priorities, accomplish goals (7f, 7g)
   I'm proud of my heritage and I have direction
   that I am an intelligent, career-oriented individual
   my constructive abilities
   *my capability to do a good job in anything I under-
      take*
g. —my integrity; I stick to my convictions (5f, 7d)
   my conscientious nature
   my loyalty & set of values I have for myself
   that I will stand up for what I think is right
   *that I have substantially lived up to trust people have
      placed in me*
h. —I am a fair person (5p)
   that I try to be fair and impartial to all people
   my sense of honor and fairness
*i. —my good nature; my optimism (4d, 5g, 7e)
   my general good humor
   my ability to look forward and keep moving
   my equilibrium
   I can laugh at me
   my ability to look for the good in most things
   my positive attitude
   I never give up hope on my dreams becoming reality
j. —I'm easy-going (4d)
   that I can relax more as I grow older
   that I am not hard to please
k. —I am self-sufficient, self-reliant (5k, 5l)
   I can rely on me
   the ability to do it on my own if I have to
   my ability to entertain myself with solitary pursuits
   *that I don't feel so insecure that I would want to be
      someone else*
   my self-determination
   my ability to keep my innermost feelings to myself
l. Self-awareness (elaborated) (4j, 5l, 5n, 7d)
   that I can see my own faults
   my unique perceptions
   *I am beginning to be more realistic as to what and
      who I am*
   I'm learning more about the subject every day
   that I know who I am & what I want out of life
   that I am not afraid of challenges, but am too stubborn
m. —I'm honest with myself [unelaborated] (7d)
   I believe I am honest and sincere with myself
n. —I'm comfortable with myself (5k)
   I like myself
   my self-love
   *that I'm feeling good enough about myself to love
      myself*
o. Thinking rationally (5j, 7g)
   my ability to be rational
   my logical mind
   that I like to think

E7 Individualistic

7-Social

a. Interpersonal ability (elaborate or unique description) (6a)

that I have a feeling of solidarity which makes me want to help others

my empathy, understanding, ability to give

I tend to listen to others' problems and allow them to find a solution

that I feel I could get along with even the most difficult people, because I never put myself first

that I am confident, self-assured, and usually make other people feel comfortable

I am very aware of others and how they relate to me

b. Nonconformity

my ability to be able to try new things and not worry as much as I used to about what people think

(Difficult!) I am not as easily swayed by current trends as many of my peers

I'm a free thinker

I am different, but it doesn't bother me—I don't want to be like everyone else

c. —I try to be nonjudgmental (6b)

that I'm compatible with many types of personalities and am not quick to judge

that I am learning not to impose my views on others

7-Personal

d. —I am honest with myself [elaborated] (5f, 6g, 6l, 6m)

the honesty I have about my feelings

my honesty with myself and my perception of my motives

e. —my zest for living; appreciation of life (4d, 6i)

my joie de vivre

that I know how to enjoy life

my sense of aliveness

my appreciation of nature

I am able to see the world and its experiences in a positive way

that I truly love people and enjoy all interaction, even a good argument

that I have heart. Whatever I do, I tend to give it my all. I also respect other people

that I have an unconquerable will to live

that I can derive pleasure from simple things

f. Adaptability, resiliency (elaborated) (5h, 5i, 6f)

my ability to adapt, stay healthy, both mentally and physically

self-control under stress

that I adapt quite readily to certain somethings that annoy others

"stayed in the game & on the field" and up to now played it with honor

that I remain strong and determined even during difficult times

that so many things have happened to me over my long life that I am seldom surprised or scared about anything

that I have a versatile personality that enables me to mix with a wide variety of people

g. —my creativity, intuition, insight (5l, 6f, 6o)

ability to bore in to the crux; often not appreciated

my independent thinking

the new ideas that I think

7-Evasive

h. —hard to say [elaborated] (5q)

getting harder and harder to find

can't answer—why just one thing

that I do not as a rule feel the need to put this question

Sorry, I don't think about myself in such terms

elusive but is there

7-Other

i. Three contrasting ideas, one at E6 (6o, 8a)

I am concerned about other less fortunate people, serious about school, and concerned about world issues

my acceptance of people for who they are, not for their clothes, looks, or income. Personality & self-worth are important

my consideration for others, my desire to participate, my persistence. (I'm uncomfortable answering this)

my values, personality, ability to get along well w/ others

that I have initiative, stamina and do things well

my good disposition and sense of humor, thanks to my inheritance and good health

j. Unclassified

I have a sense of humor and a sense of the serious

that I consider myself to be both a good mixer and also reasonably self-sufficient

that, even though I am not always great to myself, I always seem to help someone besides me & keep that person w/ a smile

E8 Autonomous

a. At least three contrasting traits, one at E7 or two at E6 (6o, 7i)

I'm open to new experiences and people, slow to judge, intelligent & and am able to overcome difficulties without allowing myself to become negative

my integrity, optimism & patience

my basic outlook on life & the fact that I can take people for who they are. I also like the fact that I can help people w/ most of their problems

that I am becoming less critical and more generous and a bit of a risk taker

my personality, my drive towards mastery, my gifts at growing into my potential

that I seem to have developed some capacity to alter my premises about myself, and thus my behavior, when I get myself in a jam

E9 Integrated

a. Unclassified

that I can let my "child" out; that I don't waste time "judging" the individuals I meet; and that I think independently and creatively

my concern to be honest with myself, a claim that may itself be a delusion

My Mother and I . . .

Almost all subjects interpret this stem as a question about relationships, and the vast majority of subjects express unequivocal, unambivalent positive relationships with mother. Nevertheless, both positive and negative or hostile relationships can be expressed at any level. Ego level puts some limits on relationships, but it is only one factor.

Other aspects of the responses are used as themes: behavior, comparison, distance, and relationship. Comparisons include both comparison of mother with self and comparison of the relationship with mother with other relationships (usually with father). Distance refers primarily to physical distance; psychological distance coincides with relationship. Because positive and negative are not used as themes, most categories will include a negative example along with many positive ones. In a few cases, the negative version is a separate category, as examples show.

The most popular categories—"are close," "get along well" (E4), "are alike," "have a good relationship," and "are friends" (E5)—are not sharply discriminatory. Below E4, the most characteristic responses are behaviors. At E4, the responses are characteristically flat statements, mostly positive toward mother, often clichés. At E5, there is an increase in complexity and away from outright clichés. The complexity is not merely formal; it also refers to the relationship, that is, more responses acknowledge some tensions. At E6, the expression of two sides to the relationship is typical: get

along but disagree, or have changed over time. At E7, the contrasts are sharply drawn and more explicit or more original. Above E6, all responses are unique, so categories are hard to draw. All categories at E7 and E8 refer to relationships, though they may also have other themes represented.

The distinction between behavior in common (E2) and activities done together (E3) is tenuous; the reason for the distinction is that, in theory, the person at the Self-protective level (E3) has a more genuine capacity of interpersonal interaction than the Impulsive level person.

There are very few responses indicating that the person gets along less well with mother recently, so no general statement can be made about what level they should be assigned.

Themes:

Behavior (E2–E6): fight; go shopping; spend time together; talk about my problems; are able to talk openly.
Comparison (E4–E6): look alike; are alike; value the same things.
Distance (E4–E5): are no longer together; never knew each other well.
Relationship (E2–E7): are OK; love each other; are best friends; have accepted each other; don't understand each other but are loving.

ITEM 7: MY MOTHER AND I . . .

E2 Impulsive

2-Behavior

a. Behavior in common (no implication done together)
   (3b, 3c, 4a)
   clean up the house
   have fun
   love to play
b. —fight
   fight sometimes

2-Relationship

c. —are okay
   are alright [sic]

E3 Self-Protective

3-Behavior

a. —talk (4a, 5a)
   talk on the phone
   we talk about sex sometimes
   are like two chatter-boxes
   talk every week
b. —go shopping; went to the store (2a, 4a)
   like to go shopping
c. —do things together (2a, 4a)
   are always together
   had lunch last week
   do the cleaning in my house

E4 Conformist

4-Behavior

a. —spend time, have fun together (2a, 3b, 3c)
   don't spend enough time together
   love to go shopping together
   usually spend hours talking and evenings together

4-Comparison

b. Superficial comparison (5b)
   both don't smoke or drink
   look just the same
   have the same body type (slim build)
   are always late for everything
c. —are like sisters (5b, 5c)
   are like twins

4-Distance

d. —live together; (don't) see each other
   are no longer together
   have not seen her in years
e. —my mother is dead (5d, 5f)
   weren't together for long—she died when I was 11
   have never met

4-Relationship

**f. —are (not) close (5l)
   were never very close
   are bonded together
   have not always been close
**g. —get along well (6e)
   do not argue much
   are on good terms
   try to get along
   are comfortable with each other
   sometimes get along well
*h. —love each other (5m)
   care for each other
   like each other
i. —don't get along [unqualified] (5i, 6j, 6o)
   don't speak to each other
   (step-mother) never get along
   don't communicate much
   don't like each other
j. —are family
   are both blood relatives of my sister

E5 Self-Aware

5-Behavior

a. —talk about my childhood, my problems (3a, 6a)
   like to talk about when I was young

5-Comparison

**b. Global comparison: are alike, not alike (4b, 4c, 6a, 6d)
   have many likenesses
   get along well & we like to talk a lot. We are somewhat alike
   have very little in common
c. Relation with mother compared with other relations (4c)
   are the closest in the family
   were best friends more than mother and daughter before she passed away
   are more alike than my father and I are
   get along much better than my friends & their moms

5-Distance

d. —never knew each other well (4e)
   have never really known each other (she died when I was 5)
   don't know each other very well
e. —are close though separated; miss each other (6m)
   care about each other even though we live far apart
   are close, but talk little w/ each other
f. —I miss her (4e)
   were very close, I miss her very much

were best friends, I wish she could have been around
  for twenty more years

5-Relationship

**g. —are (not) friends (7a)
  are good friends. (She's fun to be with)
  talk like friends
  were never really pals
  were good friends . . . sometimes
**h. —have a good (poor) relationship [unqualified] (6h)
  have a great relationship
  relate well
*i. —don't get along well; often argue (4i, 6j)
  aren't on talking terms right now
  don't always get along
  were not compatible
  had our problems
  don't get along any more
  have been at eternal war
  often provoke each other
*j. —disagree; have differences (6c)
  don't agree on most important issues
  never see eye to eye
k. —(don't) understand each other
  are very close, and have a good understanding
  don't always talk about things that bother us
  usually understand each other
l. —were (not) close at a particular time (4f, 6k)
  were never real close during teen years
  enjoyed my childhood
  were once close friends
  are still very close
m. Mutuality (4h, 6i)
  worry about each other
  need one another, I think
  are very honest to each other

E6 Conscientious

6-Behavior

a. Sharing of ideas, problems (5a, 5b)
  are able to talk very openly
  have difficulty sharing feelings
  often educate each other
b. —work well together
  are very alike, and can't get along well when apart
  are a team

6-Comparison

c. —have different (similar) ideas, values, opinions (5j)
  differ in politics, values, and conviction
  have different ideas but think alike
  are from two different generations
  value many of the same things
  love each other, but have strong individual opinions

d. —are similar (different) in personality, feelings, interests (5b)
  we both share similar traits
  both are worriers
  are like twins, we like the same hobbies and she's
    my role model
e. —get along well although we are different (4g, 7a)
  get along very well and are quite close because we
    are so similar
  have some different views but are still very close
  have a good relationship except she is too old-fash-
    ioned and very critical
f. —are alike yet different (5b)
  are alike in some ways and opposite in others
  have never been close yet we are very much alike
g. —are too much alike, too close (5b)
  clashed because we were so alike
  are so much alike that sometimes I get scared that
    I will grow up to be exactly like her

6-Relationship

*h. —have (don't have) a good, close, open relationship
  [qualified] (5h)
  had a lot of good memorable moments when she was
    alive
  have a close relationship which I value greatly
  have a good relationship based on openness and
    honesty
  have a strong emotional tie
  missed a meaningful relationship
  had a close relationship with many difficulties
  have a turbulent relationship
  were indifferently compatible
i. —respect, appreciate each other (5m)
  support each other
  don't respect each other
  enjoy each other and love each other
  admire each other
j. —argue but get along (4i, 5i)
  friends and bitter enemies
  usually fight but sometimes we have some laughs
  have a love/hate relationship
  sometimes fight but could not live without each other
  cared for one another, yet had our disputes
*k. —are closer now; get along better (5l, 7b, 7d)
  are good friends now; we once hated each other
  have finally become friends
  understand each other more as I grow older
  have accepted each other
  hate each other, though possibly somewhat less now
    that we are grown
  have grown closer over the years
l. —are not as close as I would like
  could improve in how we relate
  can be a lot closer if I just try harder and let her in
  were never very close and I regret that

m. —are closer when we live apart (5e)

get along better now that we don't live together

get along great when I'm at school

n. Contingent relation (7c)

get along when we are honest with our feelings

got along very well until I got married

get along okay but I give in to her manipulations too often

have a pretty good relationship, except when she forgets that I'm an adult

*o. Cannot communicate; lack closeness (4i)

have a friendly, but distant relationship

talk on the surface often

have grown apart in the last several years

did not have a genuine relationship

don't really connect

just kind of miss each other in our communication

p. —can communicate well [elaborated]

can communicate w/ genuine openness

are learning to communicate better with each other

q. Have personality conflicts

are both Capricorns, so there is a power struggle

are still trying to get the other to do it our way

E7 Individualistic

a. Contrast of different aspects of relation (5g, 6e, 8a)

are best friends, but my mom is closed-minded, I finally come to realize

have a special relationship. We don't talk to each other much, but we love each other

agree on most major subjects, but often disagree on little things

contrast in many aspects of personality, but we comfort each other through our understanding

have a very relaxed, good relationship. We accept each other's ideas even though we might disagree

never really understood each other but regardless were very loving

are so much alike in mannerism, but completely different in our points of view

b. Quality of relation or feelings improved over time (elaborated) (6k)

were becoming more tolerant of each other when she died

are getting closer and more compassionate

get along pretty good now that I learned how to deal with her

had problems at first but after I moved out we could not be better—we really understand each other

had very little in common when I was growing up but have a better relationship now

c. —get along better since I had a child (6n)

are not close, but are closer since my daughter was born

have always disagreed until I had my child. Now I seek her advice and help

d. Close relation a result of mutual hardships, problems (6k)

are sharing many of the same emotions since my father & my lover died

e. New realization of relationship or comparison

are probably more alike than I often tend to admit

were so different in our ways. Yet I now realize we were really more alike then I like to admit

f. Unclassified

are growing apart. Her ideas seem antediluvian and do not correspond with my problems or even needs

share a more common psychological ground than my father and I

had a loving relationship. She was a beautiful woman in every sense of the word

E8 Autonomous

a. Role differentiation (7a)

love each other enough to respect each other's private life

now enjoy a relationship that is free of judgment

were never particularly close; friends, but no parental relationship

are reaching the ages that tell me the time is coming for me to become the caregiver and my mother to become the receiver

are not friends like I hoped that we could be as adults. We vacillate between a child/parent/adult relationship rather than maturing together

b. Complex psychological causation; relation or comparison in perspective

are too much alike in our unhealthy mental habits

are close to an extent but I know we are of different generations and I let her believe I conform to her generation

have grown up together and come to terms with our different views in life

c. Complex relation with unique and vivid feelings

get along very well, but I am slightly jealous of her and (I think) vice versa

are so close that my husband gets jealous sometimes of the fun we have together

What Gets Me Into Trouble Is . . .

Content is a better clue to level here than in most items. At low levels, the stem is taken to mean something like "The kind of trouble I get in is . . ." or "I blame my troubles on . . ." At high levels, the meaning becomes more like "My trouble is (I tend to) . . ." At low levels, blame is put on situations or on other people; "trouble" means getting caught. (For a girl, to get caught often means to get pregnant.) At high levels, there is self-criticism. When self-criticism occurs at E4, it often concerns specific actions; at E6, it tends to concern traits or tendencies.

Externalization of blame at low levels may also refer to a situation or physical feature such as body or figure, treated as if it were external to self or as if one were not responsible for its effect. At the Self-aware level, however, the self is acknowledged as responsible. Of course, sex, money, and other characteristic E2 and E3 concerns can be problems for people at any level; when they are mentioned with distancing ("my sexual desires," "depending on the situation"), they are characteristic of high levels.

The most frequently mentioned action is, by far, talking; it is a popular response at E4 and, with appropriate variations, at E5 and E6. At E4 and lower, the most popular version is "my (big) mouth." This could be taken, as "my body" is, to be an externalization of blame, but it seems more appropriate to think of it as an elliptical reference to talking. At E6, the person is not so worried about how much or how loud she is talking, as those at lower levels are, but rather with the appropriateness of what she is saying. There are many traits or traitlike self-descriptions at E6. The most frequently men-

tioned, particularly procrastination and frankness, are listed as categories. A variety of others are grouped together with a few distinctive examples as "Self-criticism: Traits and attributes." A response should be placed in this category only if it does not fit the more explicit categories. Another such category is "Specific interpersonal problems" at E5.

Emotions are not mentioned frequently. Temper occurs at all levels and is classed at E4. Worrying and sensitivity appear at E5, insecurity at E6. Many responses at E5, and especially at E6 and higher, represent thoughtful self-criticisms. However, other responses, sometimes in the same categories, are self-justifying. For example, "frankness" (E6a) includes both saying things I later regret and voicing strong beliefs.

The theme of relationships begins at the lowest level with blaming other people and occurs at the highest level in such terms as expecting too much of other people. We have no distinctive E9 responses.

Themes:

Talking (E3–E6): talking back; my mouth; saying the wrong thing; frankness.
Behavior (E2–E6): fighting; doing wrong; staying out late; laziness; acting before thinking.
Traits (E4–E7): temper; honesty; impulsiveness; being unrealistic.
Relationships (E2–E7): other people; the wrong crowd; pleasing everybody; I'm a slob and my spouse isn't; need for love; insensitive to others' feelings.

ITEM 8: WHAT GETS ME INTO TROUBLE IS . . .

E2 Impulsive

2-Behavior

    a. —being bad (3b, 3d)
      when I act up sometimes
    b. —fighting

2-Relationships

    c. —other people (3g)
      my baby's father
      my sister
      boys

E3 Self-Protective

3-Talking

    a. —talking back; not listening (4a)
      not lissening what I have to do [sic]
      being quick to answer back

3-Behavior

    b. —not doing what I was supposed to (2a, 4e, 6k)
      when I do something that my parents consider wrong
      wrong doing
      doing things that I know are wrong
      running away
    c. —drinking; drugs
    d. Getting caught (2a)
      doing things illegal and my sister telling on me
      being caught while doing bad things
    e. —spending too much money (4f)
      not being able to pay my bills on time
      money
    f. Body leads to sexual trouble (4m, 6s)
      What gets me into trouble is I'm too good-looking
      my need to have more than one boyfriend

3-Relationships

    g. —being with the wrong crowd (2c, 5u)
      when they do something real bad
      being with other people
      hanging around trouble makers

3-Other

    h. —myself
      me
    i. Hostile evasion (5w)

E4 Conformist

4-Talking

    **a. —my (big) mouth (3a, 5a)
      usually my mouth
      my tongue

    b. —talking too much (5a)
      when I talk a lot
    c. —lying (5i)
      when I try to cover up somebody
      dishonesty
      hiding something from others
      lying to people in order to cover my weaknesses
    d. —arguing (6b)

4-Behavior

    e. —staying out late (3b)
      staying out all night without calling home
      coming home later than I am supposed to
    f. Self-indulgence (instances, not as a trait) (3e)
      drinking on St. Patrick's Day
      eating too much ice cream
      temptation
      using my Visa card too often
    g. —not studying; not doing homework (5h)
      school
      not doing my homework because I'm talking on the
        phone
      being late to class
    h. —driving; parking
      traffic ticket

4-Traits

    *i. —my temper (6j, 6l)
      getting angry
      my bad moods
    j. —thinking too much, not enough; my opinions (6u)
      stupidity
      when I don't think
      not knowing
      my head
    k. —my attitude [unelaborated] (6u)
      my relaxed attitude
      my mouth & my attitude

4-Relationships

    *l. —being too nice, too kind (6f)
      I always think of the "other guy" first
      my sympathy!
      that I always try to help everybody
      trying to please too many people
    m. —love (3f, 6s)
      being overly romantic

4-Other

    n. —nothing (5v)

E5 Self-Aware

5-Talking

    a. —saying the wrong thing; speaking at the wrong
      time (4a, 4b, 6c)

that I tend to speak before I listen
telling jokes & telling others of what is going on
my laugh. I am always laughing at the wrong times
I don't know when to shut up
that I open my mouth too soon
speaking up when not asked

b. —saying things I shouldn't; gossiping (6c, 6m)
popping off to others when I feel they have been rude
I often say things which I really don't mean
my say things that I am not sure of [sic]
listening to gossip

c. —being too quiet
I don't speak my mind
not saying everything I think during a fight

5-Behavior

d. —laziness
my laziness & stubbornness

e. The things I do
being wild
something stupid I've done
when I'm bored & have nothing to do. The trouble is then I get mischievish [sic]
when I avoid doing things that must be done
when I follow a group or peer pressure

f. —being aggressive, assertive
being competitive
I am overbearing
my boldness
that I have a tendency to come on too strong

g. —carelessness; not paying attention to detail
my not following directions
careless mistakes

h. —not doing well in school (4g)
failing an exam
the conflict between school and work
my grades or my big mouth
when I get very behind at school
daydreaming during class

5-Traits

*i. —my honesty (4c, 6a)
perhaps being too truthful
being quite open

j. —my stubbornness (6t)
I don't like to back down from an argument
my stubborn persistency (in certain situations)

k. —my emotions; sensitivity [unelaborated] (7e)
sometimes I'm too sensitive & let my feelings get hurt easily
my feelings

l. —worry, anxiety
being too worried about planning for the future all the time

m. —my overconfidence

I believe that I'm right most of the time—even when I'm not!
pride

n. —too little time; hurrying (6d, 6e)
falling behind schedule
when I run ahead of myself

o. —thoughtlessness, insensitivity (7e)
my nonchalant attitude towards grave matters
spending too much time on myself
my decisions based on self-will
selfishness
when I think only of myself

p. Rebelling
doing things I know I shouldn't be doing but do them just to prove people are wrong
going out & not telling my parents where I'm going. But should I?
I speak against traditional rules
my mouth which likes to contradict my parents sometimes just to be the devil's advocate

q. —disobeying God
disobedience to the Word & Spirit of G-d

5-Relationships

*r. Specific interpersonal problems
two bosses on the job
jealousy of my brother
that I'm a slob & my wife isn't
my spending money, too much, claims my husband
yelling at things and people I don't know much about
my husband is a saver and I'm a spender
when I don't tell others where I go or what I do beforehand
not doing things for my fiance

s. —being too trusting; letting others manipulate me
letting women tell me what to do
when my best friend Tracy comes up with a "great idea"
my desire to help people who are sometimes selfish

t. —analyzing others [unelaborated] (8b)
not minding my own business
my being nosey
my criticism
my doubt of others
not accepting every word as being true
my curiosity

u. —being too sociable (3g)
not studying enough because I'm concentrating on personal problems
socializing instead of doing work

5-Other

v. —I don't get into trouble (4n)

w. Evasion (without verbalized hostility) (3i)
circumstantial events
hard to say since it is so rare

E6 Conscientious

6-Talking

**a. —my frankness; I say what's on my mind (5i)
that I am very sincere—I cannot try to say something I do not feel
when I get angry too easily at my friends and say things that I later regret saying
I'm too open & honest—it frightens some people
my temper and bluntness
being too direct in speaking-out
I trust people too much & tell them things I should not
my strong beliefs and my voicing of them
my straight-forwardness
my brashness
telling it like it is
I speak my mind instead of using tact—I sometimes go for SHOCK
  b. —sarcasm (4d)
my smart-aleck mouth
my sharp tongue
my caustic wit

6-Behavior

**c. —speaking (acting) before thinking (5a, 5b, 7e)
my mouth & hyperactivity
when I fail to think before I speak in a tense situation
not thinking before I act (sometimes)
  *d. —procrastination (5n)
deadlines
happily putting things off until the last minute
my waste of time
  *e. —overcommitting myself (5n)
taking on more than I can handle
time—I seem to be late too often and never have time to do the things I need to
trying to do too many things at once
spreading myself thin
not planning my time efficiently
  f. —not being able to say no (4l)
saying yes when I don't have the time
doing things without thinking and doing things because I am afraid to say no

6-Traits

*g. —impulsiveness; snap judgments (7g)
not thinking ahead
not seeing both sides
spending money on impulse
the fact that sometimes I jump to conclusions about people
hasty decisions
  h. —my lack of self-confidence; insecurity
my low self-concept
that I'm hard on myself

when I get swallowed up by self-doubt
I am too critical of myself
  i. —indecision
my lack of will
my vacillating tendencies
my uncertainty at times
I take too long in making quick decisions
obsessing
  j. —lack of self-discipline (4i)
my explosive character
my temper when someone says or does something stupid on purpose
my lack of willpower sometimes
when I fail to discipline my desires
  k. —irresponsibility (3b)
my lack of seriousness
when I am not honest & sincere
usually irresponsibility or an error in judgment
  l. —impatience (4i)
my decreasing lack of patience at home because of college, work [sic]
  m. —I don't express my true feelings (5b)
not able to communicate what my feelings are
that I tend to hide my feelings
  n. —not following my instincts
my habit to not go with what I know, sometimes
ignoring my feelings & intuitions
  o. —taking life too seriously
thinking things through too much, taking everything so seriously
reading too much into a situation or problem
  p. —adventurousness
my restless spirit
my lust for excitement
  q. Self-criticism: traits and attributes
my temper or basic personality
my slow-going nature
compulsive behavior
giving too much & trying too hard
my inflexibility
  r. Backhanded compliments
my willingness to see the good in all men
I am too easygoing
my sense of humor

6-Relationships

  s. —my need for love, attention (3f, 4m)
jealousy and obsession with certain guys
my addiction to people
always wanting a companion
my id
my desire to impress
  t. —wanting things done my way (5j)
imposing my feelings on others
a desire to run things exclusively
my controlling instinct, my opinionatedness

controlling tendencies

6-Other

u. —my point of view (4j, 4k)
my politics
my way of thinking

E7 Individualistic

7-Traits

a. Not coping with reality, with life (general)
trying to be something I'm not
setting unrealistic goals
not always seeing the "gray area" of life
that I can't make up my mind as to what to do with my life/career
wanting what I can't or shouldn't have
taking things for granted, or brushing things aside as unimportant
that sometimes I get too absorbed in something and disregard other things

b. Perfectionism; not living up to expectations (8a, 8b)
taking too long on little projects (perfectionism)
when I try too much to live up to other people's expectations
being too idealistic

c. —guilt feelings (5l, 8a)
worrying and anxiety about the future or past faults
being hard on myself; feeling anxious or guilty

d. —standing up for principles, ideals (8a)
my will for justice, honesty and my curiosity
I have strong personal values, sometimes they may get in the way
standing up for people who usually will not speak up for themselfs [sic]

7-Relationships

e. Consideration of social interactions (5k, 5o, 6c)
that I take all sides in a quarrel because in each side there is some justification
trying to do what I think others want instead of making a decision based on my own priorities

my lack of sensitivity towards other people's feelings and concerns
having difficulty concealing my feelings when I do not like a person or a situation
not thinking before I make decisions that affect other people too
I feel that I've overextended myself to help those who don't seem to appreciate it; but I can't stop helping

f. —isolating myself; trying to be self-sufficient
pretending to not need anyone

7-Other

g. —not thinking of the consequences (6c, 6g)
that I have a habit of wanting to find out things for myself even if it means terrible consequences

h. Unclassified
my priorities. Balancing family, friends, and boyfriend
a low boredom threshold and a cockeyed romantic nature
always trying to meet the need even when it's not in my power to do so

E8 Autonomous

a. Not living up to own ideals (7b, 7c, 7d)
attempting or wanting to control things I can't or shouldn't control
my unwillingness to express my opinion when I feel it will jeopardize my present situation

b. —expecting too much of others; being overly critical (5t, 7b)
my almost constant investigation of my own and others' actions, words, etc.
trusting others to hold up their end of a task. Even though this has caused past problems, I may do it again
I analyze people and life when I ought to live it
on occasion trying to figure out what motivates someone else to do something
my ability to become impatient with myself and others when we don't meet my expectations

Education . . .

There are three major themes in response to this item: education is important or necessary, education has instrumental value, and criticism of education or reservations about its value. The instrumental value is seen exclusively in terms of getting a job at low levels; it is seen in terms of enriching life at higher levels. At the Autonomous level (E8), it may be described as intrinsically valuable. Outright expressions of distaste for education are almost exclusive to the lowest levels; however, criticism of education as an institution occurs at E6 and higher.

This item discriminates relatively well below E4 and above E6. At low levels, education is a *thing* that you *get* in *school*, and then you *have*. At E4, it is described with conventional and uncritical statements of approval, though it may be seen as expensive or difficult, and it is still identified with the classroom. At E6, education is more than book learning, is a means for broadening self or improving society, but also is capable of being improved. Above E6, it is a lifelong process leading to self-fulfillment and new values.

Most subjects say that education is important, and many say no more than that. That response occurs at all levels and is not discriminatory. Many subjects add something favorable or appreciative. A smaller number add something critical. Because the stem is so open, high-level responses show a great variety and are difficult to categorize; hence, judgment must play a large part in their rating. Examples of ambiguous categories are "Personalized commentary" (E6o) and "Unclassified (complex, original, elaborated)" (E8c). A response should be matched against better defined categories before being put in them.

Another difficult set of discriminations concerns categories E5o ("needed for a good life"), E6k ("important for enjoying a full life"), and E7d ("essential for a full life, for enjoyment of life [elaborated]"). At E5, responses speak of the good life without further detail. At E6, the way of expressing the idea is less like a cliché. At E7, the response must be original or elaborated in some way.

When this item appeared near the beginning of a previous version of the test, many people provided the number of years of their schooling. In its present position it elicits few such responses.

Themes:

Approval (E2–E7): fun; good; important today; an important part of life; priceless; a privilege.

Criticism (E2–E7): hard; worthless; hard to get; overemphasized; more than schooling; not what it seems to be.

Uses (E3–E7): good for getting a job; important for a good job; a key to success; important for social goals; essential for a full life.

ITEM 9: EDUCATION . . .

E2 Impulsive

2-Approval

a. —is fun (4f)

2-Criticism

b. —is hard (4g)

is hard work

2-Other

c. Rudimentary definitions (3d, 4j)
I will go to school
when I get my education I go to collage [sic]
is to learn and is to be smart

is I love math
helps in school

E3 Self-Protective

3-Approval

a. —is good
is good to have now days

3-Criticism

b. —is worthless (5h)
is pointless
important but ridiculous
is bullshit

3-Uses

c. —is good for getting a job (4i)
helps you get a job
= Job

3-Other

d. Statement of completed education (2c)
I am in the 10 grade
one semister colledge [sic]

E4 Conformist

4-Approval

**a. —is important (for me) [unelaborated] (5a, 6a)
is a necessity
is the most important thing
*b. —is important in the world today (5a, 5b, 5n)
is needed in any society
is an essential first step
*c. —is important to everyone (5c)
for all
is important for those who want it
is essential for all walks of life
*d. Idealization: is wonderful, great (5d, 6b)
is a dream come true
is fabulous
is beautiful
e. —is one of my goals
is my goal right now
f. —should be fun (2a)
fun as long as you learn with the fun as well

4-Criticism

g. —is hard to get; takes time (2b, 5i)
sometimes seems to take more effort than it's worth
h. —is expensive

4-Uses

*i. —is important to get a good job (3c, 5m, 5n)
is very helpful when you are looking for a job
is the only way to secure a good job

4-Other

j. Formal definitions (2c)
is the systematic training and instruction especially [of] young people
is formalized learning
is an institution

E5 Self-Aware

5-Approval

**a. —is an important part of (my) life (4a, 4b, 6a)
is the first step of life
is a vital part of anyone's life
is a necessity in life
is a valuable part of my life
b. —important for the future (4b, 6a, 6m, 6n)
is the essence of opportunity
is something to help everyone in the long run
is life's basic training that everyone needs
c. —should be available to all (4c)
should be available to everyone because it is a great equalizer
d. —is stimulating, rewarding (4d, 6b)
should be interesting
is challenging
is being valued more highly today, and with good reason
e. —is worthwhile (6b)
is worth the money
is worth all the stress
f. —is never wasted
shouldn't be wasted
g. —you can never get enough of it
is something I'd like more of
should be made mandatory
I want more and am sorry I didn't go to college

5-Criticism

h. —is (important but) overemphasized (3b, 6e, 6f, 6h, 7b, 7h)
is overrated
can help you when you get older, but most of it seems useless
is important to have, but grades are overly emphasized
is full of propaganda
is very important, but isn't everything
has its drawbacks
has been over-used and over-sold
i. Valuable but difficult (4g, 6a)
is important but not exciting or fun
is important but should not get in the way of a person's good times
is difficult to achieve but once you have it you're glad you got it
essential, necessary, hard work

j. —should be taken seriously
   is something I wish I had been more serious about when I had the opportunity of my youth
k. —must be worked for
   is something everyone should strive for
   is only worth what work you put into it
l. —scares me
   is scary when in a classroom setting

5-Uses

**m. —is the key to success (4i)
   is very important if you want to make something out of yourself
   is the way to go up
   is the most enjoyable way to earn "big bucks"
*n. —is a means to an end, a tool (4b, 4i)
   is a very needed tool in today's society
   is a must if you have high goals
   opens doors of opportunity
   is essential for the development of a career
o. —is needed for a good life (6k, 7d)
   is the foundation of a good life
p. —is helpful
   is useful
   can be beneficial

E6 Conscientious

6-Approval

a. —is important [elaborated] (5a, 5b, 5i)
   is so important. High school & college education is the basis for the rest of my life
   is important to a person's well-being and sense of security
   is important in the attainment of my goals
   is important, but should be relevant
   is important to get but too expensive
b. —is priceless, an asset (4d, 5d, 5e, 5m)
   is very important for future goals & achievements
   is a valuable resource
c. —is high on my priority list
   is 3/4 of my life
   is one of the 3 most important things in my life right now
d. —is a gift (7a)
   is one of the biggest gifts given to man

6-Criticism

*e. —is more than just schooling (5h, 7h)
   outside the classroom is as important as inside
   be it formal or informal, is the key to prosperity
   is important but you can also get knowledge from life
f. Should be improved (5h, 7b)
   can be rewarding, when the instructors are interesting

is hard to come by in today's public school system
   in this school system defeats itself. Still, education is essential
   is important for everyone, but standards are falling everywhere
g. —is not for everyone
   is important to me but I don't push it on everyone
   is good for some but not good for others
h. —is not an end in itself; is not enough (5h)
   is not the be-all and end-all of life
   is important, even if it may not appear to be needed directly (e.g. for a job)

6-Uses

*i. —is important in self-development (7f, 8a)
   is vital to a child's development
   is very important if you want to be well-rounded person
   expands your horizons
   is very good to have because it allows you to see things at all perspectives
   is critical for self-esteem
   is necessary to improve an individual's character
*j. Important for social goals (8c)
   is one way to overcome poverty
   is the key to superior cultures
   would eliminate 90% of all criminal activity
   is a crucial dimension to becoming a productive human being
   is still the best hope of the world
   is very important to becoming responsible and compassionate member of society
   is the great equalizer
   for everyone is beneficial for everyone
k. —is important for enjoying a full life (5o, 7d)
   has importance if you want to take your life to the fullest
   is a way of broadening your life
   life's carte blanche
l. —is the best thing we can give our children
   is a child's most important ambition
   The most important goal of any young person
m. —is the best investment (5b)
   or the knowledge gained from my education can never be taken away from me
   is the best investment one can make in oneself or others
n. —is needed for survival (5b)
   should be considered necessary in order for mankind to survive

6-Other

o. Personalized commentary
   makes me feel good
   is important for me to live the kind of life that I want to

*is important but often boring for me . . .
keeps me young*

E7 Individualistic

7-Approval

a. —is a privilege (6d)

*is much needed by everyone. I am very fortunate to
be getting a good education because of the amount
of people who are not*

7-Criticism

b. Not always what it seems to be (5h, 6f)

*does not mean a better life, it just means one more
debt you have to pay off*

doesn't always produce insightful, sensitive people

is what you buy, though learning be what you seek

*can't make people smarter, but only teach them more
information*

c. —should be self-motivated

*is o.k. when you choose it for yourself and are
motivated*

should be self-directed

7-Uses

d. —is essential for a full life, for enjoyment of life
[elaborated] (5o, 6k, 8a, 8b)

*builds one's wealth of knowledge & thus its appli-
cation to life*

*is vital for obtaining the means to enhance one's life
style*

should be a broadening, creative experience

e. —is liberating

is necessary if you wish to live on your own

is the key to more freedom and flexibility

is ultimately the freedom of choice

f. —is the way to achieve your potential (6i, 8a)

opens the doors of human potential

g. —facilitates communication

Is a means of communicating and understanding

should teach how to think and how to communicate

7-Other

*h. —is a process; continues throughout life (5h, 6e)

is extremely useful during one's whole life

*is continuous and I plan never to end my quest for
it, even after schooling*

never ends

*is everywhere. Academic education and its indicators
are being grossly overrated*

E8 Autonomous

a. Leads to self-fulfillment, self-understanding, new
values (6i, 7d, 7f)

*helps a person understand herself and her relation-
ship to the rest of society*

*is so important to become and understand yourself
and those around you. To become a whole human
being*

*along with motivation, are the two most important
elements in the achievement of intellectual goals*

*is the development of the entire man, physical, men-
tal, and spiritual*

b. Education is intrinsically valuable, admirable (7d)

is the search for truth & the quest of life

even at my age is a thoroughly enjoyable adventure

c. Unclassified (complex, original, elaborated)

*is everywhere. Participation isn't. The older I get
the more I learn from sources I formerly over-
looked. I am trying to help my child make this
discovery earlier in life than I did*

*is important to not only absorb material but improve
our place in society and society itself*

*means a lot to me—I'll stagnate if I never do any-
thing creative*

When People
Are Helpless . . .

This stem provides an opportunity for Conformists to give easy, obvious answers and for high-level people to express sensitivity to others' feelings and respect for others' autonomy.

At E2, some responses are just translations of the fact of helplessness, restatements of the stem, or, in some cases, apparently misreadings of the stem as "helpful." At E3, some subjects appear to be guarding themselves against what they perceive as unlimited demands of helpless people. The Conformist lays down rules of conduct, but the Conscientious level person displays sensitivity to feelings (their own and particularly those of helpless people). At high levels, characteristic responses concern preservation of the other person's dignity and independence, an awareness that helping may have its own hazards, as well as complex causes and mixed or contradictory feelings.

At E4, helping is what is or should be done. At E5, feelings are added; one not only helps but likes to. At E6, the person wants to help; such responses are interpreted as signifying that it may not be possible or easy to do so. Obviously, those are tenuous and difficult distinctions, and the discriminatory value of the item lies mainly in other responses.

The theme of "my" feelings also has difficult discriminations. The Self-protective person may express a lack of sympathy; the Conformist typically expresses conventional sympathy. At the Self-aware level, the theme of conventional sympathy is continued, but there are also outright complaints against helpless people. These complaints can be read either as continuing the callousness of some Self-protective persons or as anticipating the introspective self-examination of higher level persons. The data indicate that they are intermediate between those extremes.

This item is unusual in yielding E9 responses: in one case, a subtle paradox; in the other, alternative constructions of the situation with each possibility incorporating high-level themes.

Themes:

My feelings (E3–E7): I laugh; I feel sorry; I get impatient; I want to help them; I feel compassion.

What they are like (E2–E6): they are sick; they want you to do everything; they don't try; they need someone; they feel frustrated.

What should be done (E3–E7): you are supposed to help; I help them; they need encouragement; they should be taught to help themselves; it is our responsibility to help.

Cause or result (E4–E7): they start taking drugs; it is all in their mind; it is their own fault; it is their perception, not reality.

ITEM 10: WHEN PEOPLE ARE HELPLESS . . .

E2 Impulsive

2-What they are like

   a. —they feel bad, sick (5h)
      they are very sick

2-Other

   b. Stem apparently misread as "helpful"
      you should thank them
      they are kind
   c. Redundancies

and do not have anything
they are without help

E3 Self-Protective

3-My feelings

a. —I don't care [Self-defensive responses] (5c)
I laugh
I don't like them
they are boring

3-What they are like

b. —they want you to do everything
they expect everyone to wait on them

3-What should be done

c. —you are supposed to help (4e, 7c)

E4 Conformist

4-My feelings

**a. —I feel sorry, sad (5c, 5j)
it's a shame
it makes me depressed
it is sad

4-What they are like

*b. —they need help (5f)
they need assistance
c. —they are lazy, don't try (6p, 6s)
they give up
they aren't trying hard enough
they might have no motivation

4-What should be done

**d. —I (try to) help them (5a, 5b)
I lend a hand
I would give them anything they may need
**e. —they should be helped (3c, 5f, 5i)
others should reach out [to] them
do your best to help
someone should care
help them!
you should always be willing to lend a helping hand
*f. —they should seek help (5n)
they should consult help
they can get help
they should ask for help
g. —they should try (to help themselves) (6d, 6k)
they could help themselves
they need to push harder

4-Cause or result

h. Simple, specific reasons or consequences (5q)
they start taking drugs
they are not doing the right thing

they are poor
they are at a disadvantage
they are impotent
they are in trouble
they are a hinder to others

E5 Self-Aware

5-My feelings

*a. —I like to help them (4d, 6a, 6b, 6c)
I like to stop in and do what I can
I enjoy assisting them
b. —I try to help them if I can (4d, 6c)
I do my best to try and help
I offer my assistance
I suggest ideas
c. —I feel impatient, angry (3a, 4a, 6n)
it makes me angry because they don't try to change
I don't empathize unless they're children
I don't care, I have my own problems to deal with
it sometimes annoys me
d. —I feel helpless (6c)
I feel like I put myself in their place
I feel uncomfortable
I don't know what to do
e. —I wonder why (6q)

5-What they are like

**f. —they need someone (to help them) (4b, 4e)
they need all the help they can get
they reach out for someone
they usually need a shoulder to lean on
they are more dependent
they need friends or relatives to be there for them
*they need someone who [will] raise the voice for
   them*
*g. —they are afraid, hopeless (6r)
it is a frightening experience
they don't know where to turn
they need a ray of hope
they feel alone
they lack the will to survive
they are often angry
*h. —they are unhappy, depressed; they cry (2a, 6e)
*they become very dependent on others and whine
   and complain all the time*
they often commit suicide
they must feel real low
they tend to feel sorry for themselves
i. —they need to be cared for (4e, 6g)
they need to be taken care of
j. —they are to be pitied (4a)
they are a pitiful sight
I pity them
k. —they may lose control, become irrational
it's scary because they may injure themselves

they tend not to be able to see that the situation can get better
they can be dangerous
they tend to act in extremes

5-What should be done

*l. —they need support, understanding, encouragement (6f, 7d)
they need guidance
I offer encouragement
they should only be helped to an extent
they need a helping hand to get them on their feet

m. —those more fortunate should help (6o, 7c)
the strong should help them
there should always be someone willing to help them

n. —help can be found (4f)
there is often someone to help them
there is help
there's usually something they could do to help themselves

o. —they should remain confident, think positive
they should try their best
they should remain calm & analyze their problems
they should do something about it

5-Cause or result

p. —it is all in their mind (6p, 7e)
they aren't really; people are never helpless
they are not aware of options
it is rare because you can always do something to improve situations

q. Long-term consequences (4h)
it may create lots of problems
they lose out on many things
they cannot grow

5-Other

r. Other people's reactions
most people ignore them
others may consider them lazy or stupid
other people hopefully will come to their aid

E6 Conscientious

6-My feelings

*a. —I want to help them (5a, 7a)
I want to help them but not too directly
I want to come to their rescue
I feel like doing something for them
I feel sorry for them and wish I could help them
I hope that I can help

b. —I feel a need to help (5a, 7a, 7c)
my heart reaches out to them
I feel obligated to help them
I feel the need to talk and spend time to make them less helpless

c. —I want to help but sometimes can't; I feel guilty (5a, 5b, 5d, 7b)
it is hard to know what exactly to do or say
I would like to help them but I am lazy
I feel a mixture of pity and guilt
I feel I should do more to help, but often don't know how
it disturbs me very much, especially if I cannot help them
I feel sad. I wish I could alleviate their pain
I feel I can't truly help them
I would like to help them, but I don't try it

d. —I want to stimulate them to try (4g, 8b)
I don't believe people are helpless; you have to give them the will to fight
I like to try and show them a ray of hope. I try to help

6-What they are like

*e. —they feel frustrated, vulnerable, desperate (5h)
their defenses are down
they feel powerless
they feel like victims
they feel humiliated
they become vindictive and negative
it's demoralizing

f. —their self-esteem is low (5l)
they don't love themself
they don't have self-confidence
when they don't believe in themselves
oftentimes they are insecure and I try to help them as best I can

g. —they need protection; they may be exploited (5i)
they usually became victims
they should not be preyed upon

h. —they feel trapped
they are stuck
when they are caught between a rock and a hard place

i. Concern for their feelings, wishes (7a)
we should try and help them in a way not to offend them
I try to help them in whatever way I can that is most beneficial to the one who needs help
they are sometimes unwilling to accept charity/love
they sometimes fail to seek assistance from others due to their pride
I try to help if they accept it

j. —they should not be pitied
we should never look down on them

6-What should be done

*k. —they should be helped to help themselves (4g, 8b, 8c)
empower them
I try to let them understand what their problems are
they need help that does not keep them helpless

they should ask for or be given help, advice, or encouragement, motivation etc.

I feel they can always do something for themselves to get them out of their rut

they should be taught how to be more self-sufficient

they need to be guided in forming alternatives

I try to think of ways I or they can help them

l. Concern for their dignity, independence

it's good to build their self-esteem

m. —they (should) turn to God, to religion

God is their refuge

n. Help contingent on justified circumstances (5c)

is it because they are victims or because they've not tried to do anything about the situation

I feel sorry for them. I will go out [of] my way to help them, but if they stab me in the back 2 or 3 times, forget it

I get annoyed, unless they are infants or have a similar excuse

like the elderly or sick I feel the need to help them; if they are lazy I feel the need to encourage them

o. —they deserve help (7c)

they deserve to receive help from others such as the government

6-Cause or result

p. —it is their own fault (4c, 5p)

they seem to believe wrong & do all the wrong things

it is often because they choose to be

it is because they do not have the courage to seek help

q. —there is a reason for it (5e, 7e)

it's not always their fault

it is difficult to find a reason

r. —things are hopeless (5g)

they usually can't be helped

they often remain in that condition

there is no point in living

it is not always helpable

s. —they tend to give up (4c)

it's because they have given up

when they give up on themselves

E7 Individualistic

7-My feelings

a. —I feel compassion, empathy [elaborated] (6a, 6b, 6i)

I am sympathetic but unable to devote myself to helping them, the way most women can

I feel sorry for them because they must feel they're powerless to make changes

b. Introspective personal reaction (6c, 8a)

it emphasizes my own helplessness—unless I can help them

I feel sorry for them, try to help them. I hope someone will help me if I'm helpless some day

I would rather do the work for them than wait for them to do it

I also feel as they do—so I try to be strong and give them direction

it scares me & it makes me feel sorry for them. I feel guilty

7-What should be done

c. —it's our responsibility to help them (3c, 5m, 6b, 6o)

it is the strong people's duty to help them

they should be looked after regardless of the reasons for their helplessness

it is my duty as a fellow human to offer my aid

d. —they need social support systems (5l)

society must intervene

other people should be there to help. We are a race, the human race, not just individuals

they become desperate unless society tries to help them

7-Cause or result

e. Complex causation (5p, 6q)

part of it is their perception; the rest is circumstantial

it is usually their perception, not reality . . .

they get frustrated and resist the people who must care for them

it is because they feel discouraged and are not able to see that they have options

f. Helplessness as a social condition

they join the unhappy majority. This global society is rife with helplessness

there's evidence of work still to be done in our world

the gov't will see to it that they so realize, and thusly keep 'em that way

E8 Autonomous

a. Mixed feelings; alternative feelings (7b)

I pity them and admire those who try to change their situation. I have no respect for those who exploit their helplessness

I feel sorry for them, but I also feel helpless because I can't help all the people who are in need of it

they frequently first become depressed and later become angry

they elicit respect when they acknowledge and do what they can, and frustration when they don't

b. They need help toward self-help (elaborated) (6d, 6k)

they should be encouraged but they are the only ones who can do anything about it

others should offer alternatives to gain a sense of
control and direction

it means that they are in need of support regarding
their own self-worth and self-direction

c. —they should make the most of their own resources
(6k)

I try to help them find some inner strength or resources

I want to help in any way I can, especially to let
them see their own resources

they need to see what small steps they can take—no
matter how small

d. Unclassified

they need help. The tricky parts of this equation are
offering appropriate help and accepting it

help usually materializes; it is the faltering and
struggling (but not quite down) who have the
hardest time

E9 Integrated

Unclassified

they particularly need our compassion but may well
find precisely this the greatest burden of their
helplessness

they need others' help to grow and become more
self-sufficient, if there is potential for development. Lacking potential they need protection

Women Are Lucky Because . . .

This stem elicits mostly germane responses, some angry ones, some lighthearted ones, and a few that seem to present a man's rather than a woman's view. (However, "they can make a man happy" was a category in the 1970 manual, based on a female sample.) Those aspects of response have not been shown to be related to E-level; so the rule is to judge the E-level by usual criteria and let humorous, angry, or male-centered responses fall where they may. There are more omissions here than to most items.

Most responses discuss women's privileges or men's requirements and obligations; opportunities are discussed at higher stages. There is another group of responses, harder to characterize, that describe attributes and traits, including being a woman. That theme is referred to as *status*, a term that more clearly applies to Item 20, "Men are lucky because," for which the same themes are used. For both stems, a larger than usual number of subjects comment on the stem rather than complete the sentence. They may deny that women are luckier or criticize the concept of luck.

Categories whose frequency changed markedly from those of the 1970 manual correspond to social trends. "They usually don't have to support a family" used to be a popular category, often expressed in exactly those words. The current sample contained no such answer, and very few that even resemble it. More subjects now mention increased opportunities, par-ticularly with respect to careers. A number of answers do not compare women's advantages with men's, but instead compare women today with women in years past.

That women are allowed to show their feelings (E6) is a frequent response today, echoing the complaint some women make that men cannot or will not talk about their feelings. More subjects now mention that women live longer.

This manual has been loosely coordinated with that for Item 20, "Men are lucky because . . ."

Themes:

Status (E2–E7): they are nice; they are women; they have a nurturing instinct; they are sensitive; they are human.

Exemption (E3–E7): they don't have to work so hard; they don't have to pay for dates; they don't have as many responsibilities; they don't have to prove themselves; they don't have to act "macho."

Privilege (E2–E6): they can have luxuries; they can wear makeup; they can have children; they are pampered; they can talk about their feelings.

Opportunity (E4–E7): they can go out; they have many choices; they have a choice of career or homemaking; they are emerging into a man's world but keeping their own.

ITEM 11: WOMEN ARE LUCKY BECAUSE . . .

E2 Impulsive

2-Status

  a. —they are nice

2-Privileges

  b. Wishes
    sometimes they get everything
    when they found money
    they always go to stores and buy things

E3 Self-Protective

3-Exemption

a. —they don't have to work (as hard as men) (4f)
  they don't have to do physical labor
  they get to stay home
  they don't have to go out to get a job

3-Privilege

*b. Appearance—explicit aspects (5m)
  they have long hair
  they have all these low clothes
  they are pretty
  they get to wear makeup
c. —they can work (outside of home)
  they can get good work
d. —they get the pay check

3-Other

e. —they are lucky
  they are
  of Lady luck

E4 Conformist

4-Status

*a. —they are women; they aren't men
  they were born female
*b. Superiority to men, competitive tone (unelaborated)
  (5a)
  their better [sic]
  they are generally more smarter than most men [sic]
c. —they are, can be feminine
  of their charm and attributes
d. —they are alive (7a)
  they were born
e. —they are the weaker sex
  they are delicate

4-Exemption

f. —they don't have to work unless they want to (3a,
  5e)
  more of them than men don't have to work
g. —they can take it easy (5b)
  they get help if they need it
  they don't have to be jocks
  they don't have to shave every morning
  they don't have to take out the trash
  they can relax
h. —they don't have to pay for dates (5d)
  *they get free dinners and movies (the men always
  pay)*

4-Privilege

**i. —they can have children, babies (5i, 5j)
  they get to give birth

*j. —men take care of them (5g, 6b)
  they usually have a family to depend on
  they have husbands to help them at home
  they can be supported by their husband
k. —they have men; there are men
  they have us males
l. —they can be independent
  today they can make their own decisions
  they can take care of themselves when husband dies
m. —they get, do what they want (5f)
  they can get any man
  we can do anything
n. —children love them (more) (5k)
o. —they have me
  I like them

4-Opportunity

p. —they can go out; they can get married (5d)
  they have men to accompany them
q. Functions in the family—superficial, stereotyped aspects
  they can stay home with the children
  they cook

4-Other

r. —God made them
  they are God's children
s. —I don't know (5r, 6p)
  I'm not sure
  ?
  of what

E5 Self-Aware

5-Status

*a. Conventional emotional differences (nurturing, car-
  ing, strong) (4b, 6a, 6e)
  they are more understanding
  they can be very flexible
  they have feelings & emotions
  they have more love in them than men
  of their level of patience with children
  they are much tougher than men

5-Exemption

b. —they don't have all the responsibilities a man does
  (4g, 6b, 6d)
  too much is expected of males
  they can get by, a man can't
  they don't have to do tough jobs to make a living
  they have less ambitions
  the pressures and demands are less
c. —they don't have to go into the army
  they don't have to fight in a war
d. —men seek them out (4h, 4p)
  men have all the pressure to ask them out

they don't have to worry about finding guys
they don't have to search to get sex
they don't have to propose

e. —they usually don't have to support a family (4f)
they aren't usually considered the breadwinners

5-Privilege

*f. —they can get their own way (4m)
they have power over men (me)
they have learned to play the game
they can make men feel sorry for them
they can use sex to get what they want

*g. —they are pampered, catered to (4j, 6b)
they get so much attention
they are treated gentle
sometimes they could be more respected than men
they get things men can't
fathers always spoil them
most men give them a break instead of treating them equal

h. —they can get away with things (6e)
they can get away with crabbing more
they can get through certain situations in life because of their sex
it's easier for them to be passive if they want

i. —they can give life (4i, 6f, 7d)
they can create miracles: children
God gave them the ability to bear children
they are capable of carrying a life inside of them
they can get pregnant and have the experience to give life to another human

j. —they can be mothers (4i)
God give them the right to be mother
they can fall in love and have children

k. —they can spend more time with their children (4n, 6g, 6o)
they can make raising a family a career

l. —men love, need them
if they're married they have someone that loves them back
men always welcome their company

m. —they have more choice in appearance (3b)
they get the better choice of clothes, guy clothes are nasty
they can make themselves look better
they can wear anything, men's and women's clothing, whereas men must always wear pants

n. —they are allowed to cry (6e)

5-Opportunity

**o. —they have opportunities (now), choices (6h, 6i, 6j)
they can stand up for their rights
they get an education and have a lot going for them
there is a little more progress in the job field
more doors are being open
they can do most anything men do and more

of advantages they have today

*p. —they live longer, are biologically superior
they are healthier

q. —they can make a man happy
they have what men want
they are usually humble and soft-hearted

5-Other

**r. —I don't think they are lucky (4s, 6p)
I can't see why they are lucky
/or are they lucky?
men are lucky
[Women aren't lucky because] nowadays they have to work as hard as a man, to survive

E6 Conscientious

6-Status

*a. Emotional differences: special traits (e.g., intuition, sensitivity) (5a, 8b)
they share a unique quality that men don't, "compassion"
they usually have the ability to understand people's feelings
they are naturally relationship-oriented
they can live in a world of people rather than of objects or machines
they have learned cooperation more than men
they can think and feel some things that men couldn't
we know ourselves better than men (generally) know themselves
they have deeper personalities than men
they have a tendency to have a better insight about life

6-Exemption

b. —less is expected of them; they can be dependent [elaborated] (4j, 5b, 5g)
they are treated differently and more gently than men
they can still hope to be taken care of
not as much is expected, so it's easy to do well
they aren't expected to have a career
in an effort to avoid treating women as inferior, a potential employer might treat them very well

c. —they do not have to compete, be aggressive, take the lead in life (7b)
they do not really have to go out of their way to acquire something, as men do
they can be feminine and vulnerable
they still do not have to take the initiative in personal or sexual relationships
it is more acceptable for them to show weakness than for men
they don't have to prove themselves
it is easier for them to be passive (e. g., when tired, sick, downtrodden)

d. Freedom from responsibilities, pressures (specified) (5b)

there isn't much social stigma to doing/trying anything

they do not have to worry as much about the future as men do

society as a whole puts less pressure on them to succeed financially alone

they can normally escape the pressure of career building

there are less rigid rules for their behavior in traditionally male jobs—less precedent

6-Privilege

**e. —they are allowed to show their feelings (5a, 5h, 5n)

they are generally more in touch with their feelings

they are more open about their emotions

they're not expected to keep up an emotional front

the aren't "supposed to be" hard, uncaring people w/ no real emotions

they are able to speak their minds more freely than men

*f. Childbearing seen as experience, privilege, joy (5i, 7d)

they can feel the movement of a child in their womb

they can experience the joy of giving birth

they are able to know the feeling of having another life inside of them

g. —they can be close to, enjoy their children (5k, 7d)

they have the benefit of being close to their children more than the fathers

they can enjoy raising children

they can offer to their children a very special love

6-Opportunity

*h. —they can fulfill several roles (career and/or family) (5o, 7c)

they can choose whether to liberate or not

they can either raise a family & not work, work, or both

they can have it "all," i.e., career, motherhood, etc.

they became free from their traditional position in society (housewife)

*i. —they have opportunities, freedom equal to men (now); the world has changed (5o, 7c)

these days they can get jobs, etc., that they'd been denied in the past

the affirmative action programs open many opportunities for them at this time

the 20th century has opened a lot more doors for them

society has come to its senses

it's a good time to be female

j. —they have freedom, choices that men do not (5o, 7c)

they can opt to stay in the work force or raise a family easier than men

we can be the stronger or the weaker sex

they are able to make more choices more easily than men

they can be themselves in ways that men are not able to

they have many more life experiences than men

k. —they can lead interesting lives, follow their own interests

they can be who & what they want

times have adjusted better to allow woman to better fulfill their own potential

they are free in choosing their aims in life

l. —they communicate better; they're more open

they tend to be more open-minded

they are able to express themselves

they can talk things through comfortably more easily than men

they can talk to each other in a way that men can't

m. —they can cope better

they cope with pressure better than men

n. —they have grown, gained skills

they are discovering more and more about their self-worth

we have gained skills in working harder (than men) to do better!

we have more of an opportunity to grow in our personal and professional lives

they are becoming more assertive

o. Raising a family in terms of process, outcome (5k)

they are more likely to stay home and watch their kids grow day by day

they are the bearers of the future

they are role models for their families, able to blend in where needed

6-Other

*p. —I don't think either sex is more lucky (4s, 5r)

they are alive—the same as anyone else

there is no such thing as luck, there is time and unforeseen occurrences

they now have more equal opportunities. (Note: neither men or women are in general more lucky than the other)

I don't believe in luck

I don't like this assumption

E7 Individualistic

7-Status

a. —they are human [elaborated] (4d)

they, like anyone else, have the freedom to choose their destiny

they are the other half of a wonderful species

7-Exemption

b. Freedom from male (female) stereotype (6c)

we don't have to deal with acting "macho" or proving ourselves

our culture allows them to be more real

they have made a dent in the social perception of women as intellectually inferior

don't have the ego habits of men

they are freer to establish their own criteria for success than are men

7-Opportunity

c. Can fill several roles, have wider choice of roles (elaborated) (6h, 6i, 6j)

they are emerging into the man's world but keeping some of their own (advantages of both sexes)

they can play both sides of the equality movement

they have more freedom—they can choose to have a career or not, whereas men have less freedom in this area

today they have more career/education opportunities than ever before (but not on par with men)

they seem to have an inner strength that allows them to fulfill many duties like mother, wife, worker, etc.

d. Special relations open to women (5i, 6f, 6g)

there is a special bond between a mother & child that a man will not know

they support one another in ways that men do not support each other

they start from an underdog position and so think more of the have-nots & helpless than men do

7-Other

e. Contrasting E6 ideas (8a)

we can be independent and still be nurtured by men

they often have as many options yet fewer responsibilities than men

they are allowed to be sensitive without criticism while men are expected to be stronger

they have a lot of choices open to them and people don't expect as much from them, so it's easier to be impressive

E8 Autonomous

a. Combination of three contrasting ideas, one at E6 (7e)

they live long lives, are adaptable, intelligent, forgiving, loving, caring, civilized—fair, just—and men love them and they are mothers

we can do, feel and express things more directly. Men have more role constrictions

we can have so many options, emotionally, intellectually, parentally and careerwise

b. Unique or deep emotional experiences (elaborated) (6a)

they are able to feel and understand feelings and needs much deeper than men

women know how to express true feelings to one another without guilt or shame

they are able to have children & in so doing experience something which draws them closer to what "life" is

A Good Father. . .

Responses to Item 12 and Item 28 proved to be more similar than we had anticipated. A few subjects made a point of connecting the responses on the two items; a few more added a parenthetical remark that the answer could also apply to a good mother (or good father, for Item 28). Such responses were likely to be from protocols E6 or higher. Though the exact wording may differ, the following are similarities for Items 12 and 28. Some categories at E3 and E4 refer to taking care of the children; they are very frequent and not discriminating. At E4, the good parent is there when needed. At E5, both parents spend time with their children, take an interest in them, show their love, and listen to them. At E6, responses combine contrasting ideas, particularly love (etc.) and discipline. At E6, good parents love unconditionally, respect their children, "let go," and admit they themselves are not perfect.

At E7 and E8, good parents encourage individuality and autonomy, are nonjudgmental, and transcend traditional gender-role stereotypes. Resisting-stereotypes is rated at E7 for mothers and E8 for fathers; the difference in levels lies in the examples and is hard to translate into category titles. In fact, one category at E6 for Item 12, father treating daughter like son, is a germ of the resisting-stereotypes idea.

A type of response found here and in other items is here called *transcending reluctance*, but it is easier to illustrate than to describe. These responses contain a clause beginning "even though," "even if," or sometimes "even when," when that means "despite." There are not many such responses, but they are reliable indicators of E7 protocols.

Lists of roles and compound answers are more common for these two items than for most others, the many demands on parent (particularly mothers) having become a cliché. Compound answers are rated at the level of the highest element, unless the elements contrast to make a more complex thought, in which case they are rated one step higher.

Categories that are at different levels for mother and father include "fair" (E4 for mothers, E5 for fathers), "loves" (E4 for mothers, E5 for fathers, but frequent at all levels), and "being responsible or dependable" (E6 for mothers, E5 for fathers). Thus, conventional and socially sanctioned role requirements are emphasized at the Conformist and Self-aware levels, whereas characteristics conventionally required from the opposite-gender parent are mentioned most often at the next higher level.

Some responses to Item 12 assume that the question concerns fathers and sons only; presumably, such answers come from men. There are no corresponding answers to Item 28, assuming the question refers to mothers and daughters only.

Because the responses to Items 12 and 28 are so similar, reference to the other manual may help rate difficult responses.

Themes:

Virtues (E2–E7): is good to have; doesn't abandon his child; tries to do the right thing; is dependable; does not dominate; is nonjudgmental.

Help (E2–E7): buys you things; plays ball with his kids; is there when you need him; spends time with his children; provides emotional and financial support; passes on his values by word and actions.

Relationship (E4–E7): cares about his family; loves his family; communicates with his children; loves his wife as well as his children.

Other (E3–E7): minds his own business; is my father; is difficult to define; isn't perfect.

ITEM 12: A GOOD FATHER . . .

E2 Impulsive

2-Virtues

a. —is good to have (3c)
wood be nice for me [sic]
is good for a good daughter
b. Tautology (4a)
is a man

2-Help

c. —buys you things (3e)
I can get all I want
should give his daughter anything she wants

E3 Self-Protective

3-Virtues

a. —doesn't abandon his children (4b, 5a, 5h)
is one that come and see his baby a takes care of
he/she [sic]
is someone who claim their child and take care of
them
never leaves his family
b. —doesn't hit his children
is not a macho jerk
never should spank his kids
doesn't yell at his children
c. —is a good man; is kind (2a, 4a, 5d, 5f)
is great
is wonderful
is nice
d. —should not drink too much
doesn't drink

3-Help

e. —does things with, for his children (2c, 4c)
plays ball with his kids
takes his children camping
f. —has a job, is hard working (4d)
good to their family and has a job [sic]
works

3-Other

g. Unclassified
minds his own business

E4 Conformist

4-Virtues

a. —is what a father should be (2b, 3c)
is a daddy
is the "best father"
knows how to be a father
tries to do the "right thing"

4-Help

**b. —is there when you need him (3a, 5h)
will not let you down
stays around to see his children grow up
is one who helps you in life
is a father who is there
always stands by his children
*c. —helps take care of the children (3e)
takes care of his home
helps the children
plans for his family
d. —provides for, supports the family (3f, 5j, 5p, 6c)
makes a living for the family
is a good provider
e. —raises good children (6g)
is important to having good children
is one who raises his kids right
f. —disciplines his children (6k)
will use correct discipline
scolds his child
g. —is important [unelaborated] (5m)
should be in every family
is the most important thing in a family
h. —teaches his children (5l)

4-Relationship

*i. —cares; cares about his family (5n)
should care about his family, not just his job
j. —is a friend
should be a friend instead of an authority figure
is a male son's good friend
Is not only a provider but a friend

4-Other

*k. —is (like) my father
is what my daughter has
I had one
*l. —is hard to find (6q)
is rare
is conceivable, maybe
m. —is not like mine
is something I know nothing about
n. Unclassified
is not that hard to find
is fun to be with

E5 Self-Aware

5-Virtues

*a. —is responsible; dependable (3a)
never compromises his duties
minds his ship
is a grown-up, not a kid
b. —is fair (6o)

listens to both sides of the argument
loves his wife and children equally
is consistent
c. —does his best, all that he can
   loves his children and tries to teach them as best he can
d. —is a good husband (3c, 7f)
   is the man I want to marry
   respects the mother
e. —is a blessing
   is a gift!
   is an ideal
f. —is a good citizen, good for society (3c)
   is a good Christian parent

5-Help

**g. —spends time with his family [unelaborated] (6j)
   takes care of and spends time with his family
   spends quality time with his family
   spends time, is patient
h. —is there even in hard times (3a, 4b)
   is one who sticks with they family through better or poor [sic]
   keeps in touch with his children even if they are far away
   will stick with their children after a divorce and help them as much as possible
i. —puts his family first
   places his family before his job
   is one who put his child before himself
   will always protect his family at all cost
   is giving to his kids even when he has nothing
j. —is attentive to needs, well-being of family (4d, 6c)
k. —helps his children with their problems
   has to talk with his children and understand their problems
l. —gives advice, guidance [unelaborated] (4h, 6f)
   gives his children guidance through life
   is a wise man over his family
   helps his children make good (wise) decisions
m. —is important [elaborated] (4g)
   played a major role in his children's lives
   is a big step toward a successful life

5-Relationship

**n. —loves his family (4i, 6k, 6l)
   is loving and lovable
o. —shows his love
   is one who is not afraid to show love
   shows that he cares by his actions
   shows affection and sensitivity
*p. —is understanding, supportive (4d, 6c)
   is concerned with his children's feelings
   is one with patience
   is comforting
   is a nurturing father

*q. —listens (talks) to his children (6i)
   is one who takes time to talk with his children
   listens and gives a good hug
*r. —takes an interest in his children; is involved
   takes his family seriously
   is one who pays attention to his children
   wants to take care/play with his children
   is attentive and available
s. —enjoys his children (6r)
   enjoys the time he spends with his children
t. —is respected, loved by his children (6m)
   earns the respect of the children
   is to be admired

5-Other

u. —is what I intend (not) to be
   I'm trying to be
   would be able to show more interest and concern for his children than I do
v. —is difficult to define
   comes in many guises
w. Unclassified
   can handle children without violence
   doesn't always mean good children

E6 Conscientious

6-Virtues

*a. Two diverse qualities (is loving/caring and . . .) (7a)
   is like my Dad. He works hard, is caring, is fun, is really cool. I can't describe it.
   is loyal, loving and there when he is needed
   is loving and sensitive to all's feelings [sic]
   exudes strength and wisdom
   is patient, kind, loving and responsible and understanding
   earns & sees the love of his children—not just their respect
   is loving and caring but fun and consistent
   is compassionate, caring & not afraid of his feelings
b. —is not dominating; is open-minded (7b)
   is to see his children's points of view
   doesn't create expectations for his children
   does not try to live his children's lives
   remembers as well as he can that he was a son not so long ago
   will teach rather than dictate

6-Help

*c. —provides emotional and financial support (4d, 5j, 5p, 7e)
   is a father who is always there spiritually if not financially
   is one who combines provision with constant attention
   is one who provided well for his family both socially and financially

will work and make a living for his family. Spending time trying to teach and play with his children

d. Two contrasting ideas (7a)

has to be understanding, but not too protective

teaches more than preaches

knows when to discipline, when to compliment, and what is right for his daughter/son

will earn his children's respect not demand it

is an understanding person, who listens as well as gives advice

listens to his children before he inflicts an arbitrary ruling

*e. —sets a good example

is a model

is a role for his sons & daughters to emulate

f. Guides [elaborated] (5l)

is patient, kind and always guiding his children in the right path

provides love and guidance to his family

g. Encourages development (4e, 7d)

helps one to become whatever his ability allows

is important for a balanced upbringing

allows his children to develop independence

h. —takes an equal role in childrearing (4d)

takes a major part in raising children

shares responsibilities with a good mother

6-Relationship

*l. —communicates; relates to his family (5q)

is very tuned to his family

is a man who opens up to his children

listens and hears more than words

is honest with his kids

*j. —spends time with his family [elaborated] (5g)

is one who cares for his kids and takes the time to show his love

enjoys being with his children and thinks of himself as part of a team

is at home a lot & is interested in good parenting

spends time knowing this child

spends time with his kids and gives of himself

*k. —is loving but firm (4f, 5n)

is strong and soft @ the same time

shows guidelines to his children while listening to their ideas

is firm but fair

is considerate, yet authoritative

l. —loves you unconditionally (5n)

will always be there when you need him, no matter what you've done

is one that loves his family even when they are not perfect

accepts his kids for what they are

believes in you no matter what

m. —respects his children, their opinions (5t, 8a)

treats his children with love and respect

treats his kids as equals

acknowledges/accepts the feelings of his children

n. —can let go [unelaborated] (8b)

cares—loves—lets go

is one who loves but also can let go when the time is right

o. —treats his daughter like (as well as) his son (5b)

is compassionate to the daughter's needs not just the son's needs

is one who teaches his daughters & sons the same values

places no limitation on daughters because they're women

p. Comparison with a good mother

is as important as a good mother

can double as a good mother

6-Other

q. —isn't perfect (4l, 7c)

is human, not infallible

doesn't come with instructions

isn't something to be achieved easily; takes working at

is mine—faults & all!

r. Unclassified (5s)

loves himself

should be proud of himself

is naturally a good father

can sometimes play and act like a child himself

has a very rewarding job

is a good husband, therefore there is a good family

E7 Individualistic

7-Virtues

*a. Three diverse ideas or qualities (one E6) (6a, 6d)

is caring, nurturing, a good listener and role model

is a person who can admit his mistake, cry and help in child rearing

listens, teaches and allows his children to grow

is one who understands, respects you, & who can talk to & get along w/you

should be knowledgeable, tolerant, flexible, humane

combines love, fairness, and humor; spends time with the family and is an important model

is like my dad—dependable, stable & supportive of the notion that you can do anything

b. —is non-judgmental (6b)

is one who listens without making a judgment

c. —is an unattainable ideal (6q)

finally learns his job when it is too late to use the expertise

never stops learning how to be one

is first a good person. It's difficult to know whether you are one, or have one

7-Help

d. Outcome of child-rearing; values (unique or elaborated) (6g)

tries to pass on his values by word and action
ought to take interest in his kids & encourage them
  to do well, instill self-worth
teaches his children how to be good fathers
should love his kids, and give them a some sense of
  direction—commitment in life

e. Provides for his family's needs (original or elaborated, one E6 idea) (6c)
is supportive when he needs to be, enjoys and loves
  his children when he can, and exhorts them to
  make something of their lives

7-Relationship

f. Shows concern for wife (as well as children) (5d)
makes the mother of his kids feel worthwhile
is sensitive to the competing needs of his wife and
  family
loves his wife first and makes his family top priority

7-Other

g. Transcending reluctance (. . . even though . . .) (6d)
should listen to his children even when they don't
  make any sense
will be there when you need it—better, will be there
  even if you don't need him
is caring and listens to his children even when he
  doesn't want to hear what has to be said

h. Unclassified
is one who loves his child from the heart and teaches
  from the mind
knows the meaning and expression of abiding love
  (so does a good mother)
tries to strike a happy medium between love and
  indulgence

E8 Autonomous

a. —helps his children grow to be individuals (6m)
is a man who lets you grow & lets you make mistakes
encourages his children to become whatever they
  want to become
raises his children for their own sake
loves his children and treats them as full human
  beings

b. —lets go [elaborated] (6n, 7a)
knows the balance between growth, freedom and
  control
accepts responsibility, is conscientious of his role of
  forming his children, and will release his hold on
  his children when needed
plays with his children when they are young and
  pushes them out of the nest as soon as possible

c. Overcomes role stereotypes
allows for deviance (from norms) in relationships
has gone past the role restrictions that modern so-
  ciety imposes on many fathers
is a father who is kind, sensitive, devoid of all male
  "machoisms," and who isn't afraid to show emo-
  tion and say "I love you"
provides a supporting environment for his children
  and acts as a role model for non-stereotypic male
  personality traits

E9 Integrated

Unclassified

accepts the individuality and the limitations of his
  children, recognizes that they too have problems,
  and manages to be sympathetic at a distance

A Girl Has a Right to . . .

The major themes for this item—freedom, equality, choice, and opportunity—are not clearly differentiated. The most similar male item, "A husband has a right to," has some overlapping topics. The theme of freedom covers ground similar to "what he wants"; equality is similar to reciprocity; choice is similar to independence. There is no equivalent in this item to the theme of dominance in Item 26, nor is there a group of responses in Item 26 comparable to those in the theme of opportunity.

Another comparison is with Item 15, "A wife should," ostensibly calling for obligations rather than rights. However, a sizable number of subjects answer Item 15 in terms of rights and choices; there is no corresponding emphasis on obligations for this stem.

Themes:

Freedom (E2–E7): fight; go out; anything she wants; express her feelings; anything that does not infringe on others' rights.

Equality (E4–E7): do men's jobs; everything a boy has; equal opportunity; human rights.

Choice (E2–E7): have a boyfriend; protect herself; say no; her opinion; decide her own lifestyle; overcome stereotyped constraints.

Opportunity (E3–E6): get a job; play football; be happy; develop according to her ability.

ITEM 13: A GIRL HAS A RIGHT TO . . .

E2 Impulsive

2-Freedom

a. —fight (3c)
fight back

2-Choice

b. —get married (5k)
have a boyfriend

2-Other

c. Unclassified
shut the fuck up
play

E3 Self-Protective

3-Freedom

a. —have sex
have sex sometimes
b. —go out; date [unelaborated] (4j)
date as many guys as she likes

3-Choice

c. —protect herself (2a)
speak when she is attacked by someone
scream rape

3-Opportunity

d. —work (4c)
get a job

3-Other

e. Unclassified
go to the store
have friends
sleep late

E4 Conformist

4-Freedom

**a. —do what she wants, likes [unelaborated] (5b, 6a, 7e)
dump a guy when she wants
anything she wants
do whatever she wants (and usually does)
say whatever she wants
do what she wants when she wants
*b. —her privacy
her own private life
have her own room

4-Equality

c. —the same jobs as men (3d, 5d, 6d)
do men's jobs
a job, just like a boy
d. —stand up for her rights
be demanding at times
stand up for her rights just as much as a boy

4-Choice

**e. —say no (to sex) [unelaborated] (6i)
say no to sexual involvement if she wants
make a decision on whether to kiss or not
say no to drugs
say no to a guy
f. —an abortion [unelaborated] (5j, 6h)
g. —her body (6h)
do whatever she pleases with her body
*h. —change her mind (5h)
say no and to change her mind
i. —be herself (5l, 6n, 8b)
be who she is
be myself
j. —go out; date [elaborated] (3b, 5e, 5i)
go out as well as any guy does
date anyone she wants as long as she is over age
date after the age of 14
be with her friends whenever she wants to
spend time on friends and activities other than school work
k. —dress up
look nice
color her hair

4-Opportunity

l. —play in sports; play with cars
play football
compete in sports with boys
play with trucks & cars if she wants to
m. —know (6k)
know the facts of life
ask questions
know what's going on
learn everything a boy does
n. —be loved
love

4-Other

o. Depend on her parents [unelaborated] (6o)
listen to her parents
ask her parents for permission
be supported by her parents
ask her mother's & father's advice
p. Unclassified
go to the girls' bathroom
I don't believe in WL [women's lib?]

E5 Self-Aware

5-Freedom

*a. —express her feelings [unelaborated] (6b)
be angry
cry
express her needs and wants
tell a guy how she feels
b. —(do) anything (4a, 6a)
have freedom
do almost anything
everything
just about anything these days
c. —act like a boy
be like a boy
bare arms (and anything else)
wear pants and be as unladylike as she pleases

5-Equality

*d. —do (have) the same things boys (men) do (4c, 6c, 6d, 7b)
try anything a boy can do
everything a boy has
what a man does
things that are given to boys
e. —ask a guy for a date (4j)

5-Choice

**f. —be anything she wants (to be); choose her own career (6f, 7e)
do whatever she wants in life
be whoever she wants to be
study anything she wants
have a career if she wishes
make her own decisions about any job she wants to have
be what God wants

drive a truck or be a fashion model

**g. —her opinion; speak her mind (6b)
  be heard
  free speech, as does any boy
  voice her opinion

*h. —make her own decisions (4h, 6f)
  choose
  make her own decisions about her school, friends,
    and activities
  to wear what she wants

*i. —choose her own (boy) friends (4j)
  choose whom she dates & marries
  refuse to go out
  love whom she chooses
  do what she wants, including pursue the man I'm
    after
  have a boy as a friend

j. —choose abortion or child (4f, 6h)
  keep her baby or not to keep it
  get an abortion on her own free will
  pregnancy freedom

k. —choose career or motherhood
  become a wife and mother
  get a career before thinking of marriage

l. —be independent; be her own person (4i, 6f, 6n, 8b)
  be as much an individual as males
  live her life as she pleases
  lead her own life
  follow her own ideas and do what she wants

m. —do what she feels is right
  be loyal to herself and her belief
  do what she wants and believe it is right

n. —be a lady, a girl (7c)
  be prissy!
  feel feminine

5-Opportunity

o. —grow up (6m)
p. —happiness
  enjoy her young days
  be a girl and have fun being a kid
  do whatever she wants to do to make herself happy

5-Other

q. Unclassified
  succeed
  be trusted until given reason not to be
  at least one mistake

E6 Conscientious

6-Freedom

a. —do what she wants if it does not hurt anyone, is
  legal (4a, 5b, 7a)
  anything legal

do what she wants as long as it is w/in reason & it
  doesn't hurt anyone including herself
do what she desires w/in bounds of parental agree-
  ment
do what she wants as long as its socially acceptable

b. —express herself [elaborated] (5a, 5g)
  express her feelings, although they may not be ap-
    preciated at times
  express herself more fully than a boy without as
    much chastening
  be expressive yet with a quiet spirit

6-Equality

*c. —the same rights as boys, men (5d, 7b)
  equality
  the same rules as her older brother goes by
  all the privileges given to boys
  nothing more than a guy does
  do everything a boy does. There is no difference

*d. —equal opportunities (4c, 5d)
  the same opportunities as a boy
  compete with a man
  accomplish the same things as a guy
  choose any career, whether male-dominated or not
  strive for any right a man has
  equal access to sports
  equal wages for equal work

e. —be respected; regarded as equal to a man (7c, 8a)
  to be treated with respect, because she is just as
    much a person as any male
  expect as much respect as a man
  have whatever career she wants, and to be respected
  be a contributing member of the world, as is a man
    in his own way
  be a real person in a man's world, to say what she
    really thinks
  be on equal terms with a boy

6-Choice

*f. —choose her own way in life; decide her future (5f,
  5h, 5l, 7d, 7e)
  do anything she wants with her future and her body
  decide about what her life is going to be like
  decide her own lifestyle
  her own ideas about life and how she wants to live
  freedom in every aspect of life

*g. —pursue her dreams, goals
  be ambitious
  life, liberty, and the pursuit of happiness
  pursue her talents and interests
  set her goals high
  expect her goals to be fulfilled
  pursue any aspirations she has for her life

*h. Decide about sexual behavior, her body, abortion
  (4f, 4g, 5j)
  say yes and not get a reputation

be in charge of her activities and her body
have casual sex just the way a boy does
say no to sexual pressure or anything she does not
  believe in
obtain birth control to protect herself
make her own decisions about men and relationships
  i. —say no [qualified] (4e)
say no & not feel guilty
say "no, it's not right for me"
say no to sexual advances without an explanation
say no if she's being pressured about anything
say no and have her no be respected

6-Opportunity

  j. —do what she is capable of (8c)
develop according to her abilities and talents
given a chance to do anything, the right to succeed
  or fail
be anything she wants to be and is willing to work for
  k. —an education (4m)
a quality education
a good education just like boys
  l. —live a fulfilling life [unelaborated] (8b)
a full life
experience life
  m. —mature, develop (5o)
grow and develop at her own pace
become a woman, as a boy to become a man
  n. —be proud of herself (4i, 5l)
love herself & respect herself
feel good about herself, her body, her mind

6-Other

  o. Unclassified
expect loyalty & faithfulness from her family
be honest and sincere in her relationships
do as many assertive things as boys
special privileges, unlike boys

E7 Individualistic

7-Freedom

  a. —anything that does not infringe on rights of others
     (6a)
do anything she wants within reasonable societal
  boundaries, just as a man
do with her life as she wants as long as it does not
  hinder the life of another

7-Equality

  b. Human rights (5d, 6c)
anything that a boy has a right to. (Note: rights
  should not be determined by sex)
a happy life, just as all human beings
be a human being
live in a world w/out war; so does everyone. And
  do what she feels happy [sic]

speak up and share, with pride and respect, in the
  energies that shape our world
go in any direction she wishes in her life. A boy has
  the same right
  c. —be competent but still feminine (5n, 6e)
play boy games as long as she knows she is a girl
  not a boy
and in fact should be tough yet feminine to make it
  in the business world
do anything men can do but still being a feminine
  person in the process

7-Choice

  d. Overcome traditional restraints (specified) (6f, 8b)
do anything "only boys do"
do anything she feels she can do, without society
  restricting her
decide what she wants to do with her life, and not
  let it be settled by tradition
make decisions in life, no matter what country, creed,
  or family pressure is made on her
achieve her goals without stereotypical restraints
change her mind without people saying "typical woman"
  e. Become what she wants (broad view, conceptually
     complex) (4a, 5f, 6f, 8b)
grow at her own pace, physically, sexually, emotion-
  ally, and mentally, but must face consequences of
  her actions
whatever she wants (within certain limits) without
  having to be burdened with the fact that she is a
  girl
excel, strive, be herself, & become a positive thinking
  woman
be the kind of person she wants to be, but to reason
  about about her choices

E8 Autonomous

  a. —be respected as a person [elaborated] (6e)
a good education, to be respected as a person emo-
  tionally, cognitively, and physically
be a person no matter what age, sex, or beliefs she
  has [sic]
  b. Self-fulfillment (uniquely stated) (4i, 5l, 6l, 7d, 7e)
keep her own identity after marriage
equal opportunities to develop all aspects of herself
be herself and become a full human being
be herself whatever that might mean
do anything within the framework of her own indi-
  vidualism
  c. —develop her potentials fully (6j)
develop her potential and enjoy respect of parents,
  peers, society
grow and explore her own development and direction
realize her potential, regardless of the role restric-
  tions society may try to impose
explore her potential

When They Talked
About Sex, I . . .

The manual for this item remains similar to the 1970 version, although the latter was based on responses of girls and women only. In the present sample, virtually no categories, certainly none at all frequent, are given by one gender only.

People can answer in terms of what happens now, what used to happen when they were younger, or what they do as parents or advisors. Sometimes one cannot tell which standpoint they have taken. As an example, "was embarrassed" (E5) is distinguished from "used to be embarrassed" (E7) only by making explicit the time distance.

Responses at both the E2 and E3 levels could be termed impulsive. Possibly, the distinctively E2 categories reflect the fact that many of the protocols at that level come from younger subjects, some of whom may be frightened by the topic or unsure how they are supposed to answer. "Listen" and "join in" are by far the most frequent categories, both classed at E4. All but a few small categories at that level connote actions. At E5, however, internal reactions are the predominant tone, particularly being (or not being) interested or embarrassed. The possibility that one might learn from the conversation is mentioned at E5 but developed more fully at E6. Contingent responses are frequent at E6.

A characteristic high-level response indicates that the person took part in the conversation without revealing anything personal about him or herself. Other high-level responses are conceptually complex.

Probably the hardest distinction to rationalize is that beween "join in" at E4 and "participated" at E5. Whatever its source, it appeared in the 1970 sample as well as the present one. Intuitively, the versions at E5 sound more like active participation, as compared to a somewhat passive tone at E4. Although use of present versus past tense is not a reliable clue in general, it is used to distinguish leaving the room (E2) from left (E4). The latter response is more likely to refer to a past attitude or type of behavior.

Themes:

Participation (E2–E7): leave; ignore them; listened; was interested; offered my opinion; it depends on who they are.

Feelings (E2–E7): get sick; get excited; blushed; was embarrassed; pretended not to hear; used to feel embarrassed.

Information (E5–E7): listened and learned; found they were not informed; thought their attitudes were surprising.

ITEM 14: WHEN THEY TALKED ABOUT SEX, I . . .

E2 Impulsive

2-Participation

a. —walk away; leave the room [present tense] (4d, 5g)
have to move

2-Feelings

b. —get sick; get mad

c. —think it's bad, nasty (3d)

E3 Self-Protective

3-Participation

a. —ignore them (4c)

3-Feelings

b. Direct expression of sexual thoughts or desire

get excited
suggested we have it
get horny
c. —enjoy it, like it (4g, 5j, 6g)
feel good
get happy
had fun
d. —felt ashamed (2c, 4f, 5h)
felt kind of shame
e. —was surprised

E4 Conformist

4-Participation

**a. —listened (5a, 5d)
usually just listen
**b. —joined in; talk with them (5b, 5c)
speak up
talked too
giggle, & chime in
did too
c. —didn't listen (3a)
didn't want to talk about it
was out to lunch
covered my ears
d. —left [past tense] (2a, 5g)
wanted to hide
I left them alone
e. —change the subject

4-Feelings

f. —blushed (3d, 5h, 5i)
listened and turned red
felt I blushed
blushed a bit but listened
g. —laughed (3c, 6g)
usually joke about it
h. —was shy (5h, 5i)
shyed away
i. —don't like it
kind of was scared
j. —thought it natural, normal

E5 Self-Aware

5-Participation

**a. —was interested, listened carefully (4a, 6b)
am all ears
was fascinated
enjoyed listening
*b. —participated (4b)
tried to recall dirty stories
always added my two cents
had lots of questions
contributed to the conversation
c. —listen and join in; listened and participated (4b)

listened and commented if I felt like it
*d. —kept quiet [unelaborated] (4a, 6c)
clammed up
always kept out of their conversation
tend to withdraw
e. —tried to explain; answer their questions (6a, 6j)
usually listen and if necessary give advice
listen, I answer questions if asked
included my knowledge and gather their information
f. —advised against sex before marriage
said that I would wait to get married before I had sex
always applied bible principals [principles]
g. —wasn't there (2a, 4d)
was always sent out of the room
missed it
never was at such a discussion

5-Feelings

*h. —was embarrassed (3d, 4f, 4h, 7c)
feel a little embarrassed to talk about
sometimes get embarrassed
*i. —felt uncomfortable (4f, 4h)
cringed
wonder if I should leave the room
sometimes feel awkward
felt incompetent
felt left out
*j. —was not embarrassed, not uncomfortable (3c, 7e)
was fine
feel at ease
have no problem in joining the discussion
k. —I'm open about sex (7e)
it didn't bother me at all because I'm open about it
l. —was bored; was not interested
'm usually not very interested
m. —remembered
n. Denial
said no
can't relate because it's against my religion
didn't care
we didn't talk about sex

5-Information

*o. —listened and learned (6i)
really listen and try to understand about some things
try to find out things that I don't know
listened & asked questions
p. —already knew about it
listened, but already understood everything
q. —did not understand
think there is something I am missing
didn't know what was going on
don't understand because I don't have any experiences

5-Other

r. —who are 'they'?

E6 Conscientious

6-Participation

*a. —shared, offered my opinion (5e)
  enjoy providing a realistic viewpoint
b. —was interested [elaborated] (5a)
  think its interesting & informative
  was embarrassed, but interested
  become interested because its something I enjoy
  was interested, naturally, but not overwhelmingly so
  am interested. This is life
  was interested in gaining an understanding
  listen with flapping ears and undivided attention
c. —listened quietly; don't say much (5d)
  paid attention without being noticed
  listened but did not offer too many details
  usually listen without becoming involved in the conversation
d. Participation contingent upon how subject is handled (7a)
  join in if they are talking about sex in a manner that is respectable and not obscene
  sometimes don't participate, depending on what frame of mind I'm in
  sometimes listen in or contribute to the conversation if it is worthwhile
  usually listen, and disagree openly if they are biased
  join in any wholesome discussions
e. Listen, enjoy depending on the way it's done (7a)
  enjoyed it if it wasn't just plain filthy
  usually did not like the degrading or crude talk
  usually enjoy it, if it's not perverse
  [S underlined 'talked' in item]—in what way?

6-Feelings

f. Contrast of actions with feelings
  listened shyly through the door
  pretended not to hear
  secretly listened
  was embarrassed but tried not to show it
  asked lots of questions and was sometimes embarrassed
  didn't listen though my interest in sex is keen
g. —was amused; took it lightly (3c, 4g)
  laugh but listen
  I was partly amused and partly embarrassed
  smiled
  interjected with a funny story
  prefer it to be frivolously
  played the game
h. —felt it was personal, private
  got uncomfortable, for that's a personal thing

6-Information

i. —listen for, agreed with their viewpoint (5o, 7f)
  think about what they are saying and look at my view of it
  listened to see if I could relate to their experience
  like to listen and learn people's attitudes about it
  felt eager to hear their views
j. Evaluation of others' information (5e, 7f, 7g)
  found they were not well-informed
  was appalled by their ignorance
  listened to make sure that they were accurate
  was surprised at what some people didn't know
  tried to picture what they were talking about
k. —wondered if it was true (7g)
  wondered if they really did it
  knew they were bragging
  couldn't believe it happened that way!
l. —was curious
  listened with curiosity

E7 Individualistic

7-Participation

a. It depends on who they are (6d, 6e)
  usually give my opinions if I know them well
  blush depending on the company
  was concerned if the audience were mixed

7-Feelings

b. Description of (explicitly) past response
  thought, "How naughty!"
  listened & thought of my own experiences
  giggled at age 12 and was not very interested in their version at [age deleted]
  suppose I joined in
  was really too young to understand and thought it was funny
  was convinced to become a nun
  pricked up my ears, but they almost never did, alas
  used to feel embarrassed
c. Embarrassed (elaborated with E6 idea) (5h)
  felt embarrassed and as if they were thinking of me in particular
  felt embarrassed, for I knew more than they did
  felt a bit embarrassed & inadequate
  was just as interested as anyone, but a little embarrassed
d. Original elaboration of E6 response
  was acutely aware of my naivete
  was confused by the secrecy
  feel lonely and miss that closeness and sharing
  usually get upset if women are put down
  found it fairly amusing, and not terribly provocative
e. —am nonjudgmental, open-minded, objective (5j, 5k)

listened and gave my personal values without judging

assume my role as a physician and become scientific and rather matter-of-factous [sic]

have a tendency to become serious

am opened-minded and also open for advice & guidness [guidance]

7-Information

f. Evaluation of others' attitudes (6i, 6j, 8a)

noted their preoccupation

often wish that they would incorporate some morality before introducing contraception to the young adolescent

was amazed at how little most people know and how many people believe in superstitions & old wives' tales

listened with interest—other people's attitudes on the subject are often surprising

got a sense of how emotionally immature we all are

usually get upset if women are put down

g. Evaluation of others' experience (6j, 6k, 8a)

was amazed at the poverty of their experience

asked myself how come they had so much greater success than I, then realized they were just "talking"

have always said to myself: "talk is cheap"

can most times judge a person's experience by his statements

h. Learn about people's character (8a)

learned something about their attitudes towards humanity

talked about sex and learned more about what kind of person they were

listened carefully, because they said many things that applied to their relationship in general

7-Other

i. Three different ideas, one E6

was amused if it was humorous, bored if it was not, and found it distasteful if in mixed company

frequently thought it was crude, or was bored, but sometimes found it stimulating

am interested provided the discussion is based on knowledge or reveals respect for the complexities of the subject

laughed and listened as any teenager would. I also wondered what it is all about

listened, participated, but divulged no personal information

became more liberal-minded, yet restrict who and when for myself, because I'm worth it

listened attentively, weighed decisions, and projected my feelings

j. Evolution of reaction

got embarrassed. I'm more open now

joined in without any hesitation; I don't feel modest or self-conscious like I did when I first got married

sort of giggled and smiled, but then I started to really think

get really embarrassed; at first I'm squeamish, but I calm down after a while

k. —think of [specific person]

was interested in pleasing my mate

(who's they?) worry for my daughter

E8 Autonomous

a. Concern with reasons, motivations (7f. 7g, 7h)

thought they were being overly outrageous to compensate for what they hadn't done

have a tendency to not believe a great deal of what is said, because men are not always that straitforward on this subject

wondered why: bragging? complaining? trying to impress? lack of self-confidence? attention getting?

listened and wondered why something so natural was such a big source of concern

A Wife Should . . .

The most frequent theme in response to this item is relationship with husband and family, specifically, loving, supporting, and taking care of them. A strong second theme refers to rights and choices, specifically, equality with husband and self-protection. Responses that combine those two themes are characteristic of higher levels.

At the pre-Conformist levels, characteristic responses refer to traditional household duties. A small group of responses express a bitter or hostile view of either women ("not nag") or men ("not be beaten"). These responses are surprising because the stem does not call for such responses, and because the bitter or hostile tone is characteristic of level E3, but these responses may come from any level. E4 is the default rating for such responses, but if any element of the response indicates a higher level, that rating should be given.

The topic of reciprocity is usually found at E6 or E7. Here a category of such responses is rated E7. However, there is also a category at E5; the distinction is that the lower category has a kind of bargaining or quid pro quo implication. Of course in some cases one cannot be sure what the writer intended. These categories are not sharply discriminating; for example, something like "love and be loved" can occur at any level. Although there is no category,

it is reasonable, for example, to rate reciprocity with respect to E5 characteristics as E6.

There are some differences in the answers of men and women and also between the current manual and the 1970 manual. Today there is a greater emphasis on rights and choices of a wife, even among men. Self-esteem was not a noticeable topic in the original manual, as it is now. Even within a category, the answers of men and women may take a different tone. For a woman, being a friend or companion may suggest helpmate; for a man, it may mean a playmate. Where a woman says "be happy," a man may say "be cheerful."

Themes:

Virtues (E2–E6): be good; be understanding; do her best; be a good lover and housekeeper.

Social role (E2–E6): clean the house; work; be a good mother; hold the family together; make her family a priority.

Relation with husband (E3–E7): obey her husband; be faithful; be a helpmate; be an equal partner; support her husband and expect him to reciprocate.

Rights and choices (E3–E7): not have to do all the housework; work if she wants to; be her own person; not be a slave; keep her individuality.

ITEM 15: A WIFE SHOULD . . .

E2 Impulsive

2-Virtues

    a. —be good (4f, 5a)
      be a good lady
      be nice

2-Social role

    b. —keep house; cook, clean (3a)
      take care of the housework
    c. —stay home
      stay home and watch the children
      not be working, they should be a housewife

E3 Self-Protective

3-Social role

a. —know how to cook (2b)
be willing to cook
be a good cook

b. —work (4l, 5d)
have to work too

c. —be a wife (4g)
be a woman to the house
bear children

d. —I don't know because I'm not married
I have no wife

3-Relation with husband

e. —obey (5l)
be obedient

3-Rights and choices

f. —not have to do all the housework (5s, 6i)
be allowed not to cook once in awhile

E4 Conformist

4-Virtues

a. —be understanding (5h)
be caring, loving & understanding

b. —be helpful (5d)
help her husband out if needed

c. —be responsible (5h)
do her duties
not spend all her husband's money

d. —be honest
always be truthful to her husband
be sincere

e. —always be attractive
be lovely

4-Social role

f. —be a good mother, homemaker (2a)
be a good mother & not cause problems for her husband

g. Sardonic responses, tautologies (3c, 6n)
be married
breathe
try to please her husband because if she doesn't he will find someone else to do it

4-Relation with husband

**h. —love her husband, be loving (5i, 6h)

**i. —take care of her husband, family (5h)
care for her husband
always pay close attention to her kids
provide a caring home

**j. —be faithful, loyal (5h)
not play around
not commit adultery

k. —listen to her husband (6f)
listen sometimes

4-Rights and choices

*l. —be able to have a career (3b, 5d)
work if she wants to
be able to work and have a family
be allowed to do it all (work, friends, children, etc.)
have the same employment opportunities as a man

m. —enjoy being one (5w, 6d)
love being a wife
be happy in her marriage

n. —do what she wants (5w)
do as she pleases also

o. —have her own money (5o)
always have a separate savings account

p. Hostile remarks about men, women
castrate her husband if he cheats
be more understanding, less jealous, and most important, less of a nag
love her husband provided he is not an abusive bastard

E5 Self-Aware

5-Virtues

a. —do her best (2a)
try her best at whatever the task
be the best she can be, not more than
be everything she could be and more

b. —be what God wants her to
be a G-dly woman
pray for her family daily

5-Social role

c. —be the backbone of the family
be responsible and love and try to keep her family together
& does play a very important part in the raising of children
be central to family
provide the home's atmosphere

d. —help support the family (3b, 4b, 4l)
help provide for her family and love them dearly

5-Relation with husband

**e. —be supportive
support her husband emotionally & morally
support her husband (not financially)
encourage

*f. —be a friend; companion (7e)
be her husband's best friend
be a helpmate
be a good playmate

g. —be there for her husband
stand by her husband
be there a lot & know when to be elsewhere

h. —be devoted, patient, considerate (4a, 4c, 4i, 4j)
   try to understand her mate
   be devoted to her husband and children first
i. —give, show her love (4h, 6h)
   show her feeling to her family
   always try to demonstrate her love
   tell her husband often that she loves him
j. —please her husband, family (6k)
   make her husband happy
   make home a peaceful place
   compliment her husband
k. —respect her husband
   *respect her husband, not necessarily listen to him
   but respect*
   be proud of husband and children
l. —let her husband be dominant (3e)
   submit herself to her husband
   let her husband feel dominant
   recognize the headship of her husband
   obey her husband to a certain extent
m. Conditional reciprocity (7a)
   be just as faithful and honest as her husband is
   be just as much of a wife as her husband is a husband
   *love her husband and compromise in her marriage
   if her husband is willing to compromise and sacrifice*

5-Rights and choices

*n. —be an equal (6e)
   be her husband's equal
   have equal rights with her husband
*o. —be her own person; be herself [unelaborated] (4o,
   7g, 7h, 7i)
   be true to herself
p. —stand up for herself (7g)
   have rights in the household as well
   be able to take care of herself
   learn how to be more assertive
   be able to voice her opinion
   have the right to say no
   never let her husband abuse her in any way
q. —have time for herself (7g)
   be able to get away once in a while
r. —be loved, respected
   be appreciated
   demand respect from her husband
   always feel loved and safe
   be cherished
s. —share household responsibilities with husband (3f,
   6e, 6i)
   ask her husband for help when needed & get it
   share the housework with her husband
   be there to share but not abused
t. —have a good husband
   feel absolutely comfortable with her mate
   have a husband that she loves

u. —be educated, interesting (6j)
   be well rounded
v. —grow (7h)
   grow as an individual
w. —be happy (4n, 4m, 6l)
   be true, loyal & happy
   always be cheerful
   try to do whatever makes her happy

E6 Conscientious

6-Virtues

a. Idealization of role
   be socially acceptable, beautiful, loving, honest, loyal
   be trusting, honest, loving, understanding, & human
   *be loving, kind, understanding, a good mother &
   homemaker*
b. Sharply contrasted virtues (traits) (7e, 8c)
   *be loving and understanding but should stick to her
   guns!!*
   *be kind, gentle, loving, and strong enough to defend
   her beliefs*
   be loyal, independent, a good mother and supporter
   be a good lover and housekeeper

6-Social role

c. Family as priority (7c)
   *put spouse above all other family and always be
   around for the husband*
   value her husband and kids over career ultimately
   *spend time not only with her children but also her
   husband*
   balance time for house, husband and kids
   give one hundred percent to her husband
d. "Wife" as a role (4m, 8b)
   avoid feeling like a "wife"
   be happy in her family role
   be committed to her role of marriage

6-Relation with husband

*e. —be an equal partner (5n, 5s)
   have an equal voice in financial decisions
   know how to compromise and yet be firm
   participate equally in marriage
   *allow her husband to help with household chores
   even if she doesn't like the way he performs them*
   encourage a relationship to be a partnership
   be a complete marriage partner in all ways
f. —communicate with husband (4k, 7a)
   talk freely with her husband and should listen
   encourage her husband to be open, honest
   *always communicate her feelings to family members
   as calmly and clearly as possible*
   be honest in her relationship
   *be truthful to her husband & listen to what he has
   to say*
g. —consider husband's needs (7d)

understand a man's needs
allow her husband to enjoy his free time
understand and forgive trivial faults

h. —be loving [elaborated, with E5 idea] (4h, 5i)
love her husband but not mother him
love her husband and child and make time for them
be loving, caring, and interesting to the husband
build up her husband w/ adoration and praise

6-Rights and choices

*i. —not be a servant (slave) to husband, family; not obey (3f, 5s)
love and honor, but not necessarily obey, their husband
not be a maid in her own home
love her husband, but don't become a slave for him
be supportive without being submissive
never stand for any abuse, whether physical, mental, or financial

*j. —pursue her own interests (5u, 7h)
have other interests besides her husband and family
have a life of her own
do what she needs to feel fulfilled
do more than being a housewife

k. —please her husband, but also please herself (5j, 7c)
be considerate of her husband but never be taken for granted
be able to make herself comfortable while making her husband & kids comfortable too
be supportive, but also have a say-so as to what goes on in the family
not only take care of her family, but enjoy her life as well
make her husband happy in any way possible as long as it's not damaging to her

l. —feel good about herself; maintain her self-esteem (5w)
not feel like she can do it all, or worry about it either
love herself
always do what she needs to do to maintain her self-respect

m. —know what she's getting into
make sure her husband knows what she wants before marrying him
know her husband's views on abortions/career/ childraising etc. well in advance (and vice versa)

n. Rejection of stem (4g)
not let anyone "should" on her
never say should—
is another phrase that immediately gets me ready to argue

E7 Individualistic

7-Relation with husband

a. Reciprocity with husband (5m, 6f)

communicate her needs to her husband and learn to understand her husband's needs
participate with her husband to the degree possible in his activities—and vice versa
complement the husband, in a mutually co-dependent way
give 100% to her husband, as he to her
respect and support her husband, fully expecting him to reciprocate
be everything a husband should be. No less. No more
try to meet halfway emotionally—and so indeed should a husband

b. —work to improve the marriage
work at this to beat the odds—50% divorce rate
keep the passion in a relationship
make an effort to keep the marriage healthy

c. —balance interests of self, husband, children (6c, 6k)
find the right balance between her desires & those of her husband
cherish her children while still keeping her husband as the number one person in her life
love herself, her husband and children and find time for all
be a good mother, an understanding wife and her own person
respect herself, her husband, & her children

d. —be sensitive to her husband's emotional needs (6g)
try and understand her husband's feelings
be in tune to her husband's feelings & thoughts— communicate with him
know the needs of her husband on a physical & emotional level
be considerate of her husband's ego
take an active [part] in her husband's development
help her husband be sensitive to his children

e. —be (your) best friend and lover (5f, 6b, 8c)
be married to a husband who is as much a friend as a lover
respond to her husband on all planes—intellectual, spiritual and physical

f. Maintain relationship despite obstacles
support her husband (not materially) at all times— even when she doesn't agree with him
stand by her husband, even though he is sometimes wrong; there are limits, of course, but he feels more of a need to be in charge

7-Rights and choices

g. Put herself first, then her family (5o, 5p, 5q)
fulfill her own self and thereby be a better wife
think about her own needs more than her husband's
be a woman true to herself first
first of all be a person

h. —keep her individuality [elaborated] (5o, 5v, 6j, 8b)
be an individual also

be loving, loyal, but should always have a mind of her own

[be] caring to her husband but also should not be a complacent stereotypical wife

be aware of herself and her needs in order not to be drowned in daily tasks

i. —maintain her independence within the marriage (5o, 8a)

balance her independent life with her family life

be her own person, also stand by her husband as much as possible for encouragement

be sure not to constantly subjugate her needs to those of her husband

lead a rewarding life, both in the outside world and at home

be a loving & independent partner

E8 Autonomous

a. —maintain her own identity (7i)

be kind, loving, and giving & understanding to the husband without losing her sense of self

maintain her sense of self—occupy self & get involved with other things (besides husband and children)

support her husband emotionally because he needs it, but she should not relinquish her own goal

be prepared to struggle to continue to evolve in her own right and be prepared to support her husband in his attempt to do the same

b. Define her own role (6d, 7h)

be fulfilled with her life, doing whatever is required to achieve that fulfillment

not try to be all things to all people (I could wish but I cannot prescribe)

try to develop herself as a person and not be "only" what is expected of her

c. Original responses, contrasting several facets (one at E6) (6b, 7e)

be faithful, loyal, herself—independent, fun, wise, tolerant, caring, adaptable—and sexual

feel free to be a woman as well as to enjoy life and her job

listen to her husband's problems and dreams and strive to combine hers with his

be her husband's best friend, team-member and encourager; but she should also be fully her own person

I Feel Sorry . . .

This stem was included on the presumption that responses beginning with *for* would express pity for others and be characteristic of Conformist and lower ego levels; responses expressing guilt or regret for mistakes would begin with *about*, *because*, or *when*, and occur particularly at the Conscientious level; and responses concerned with social issues would begin with *that* or *about* and occur at high levels. The progression from pity to guilt to social issues is not altogether wrong, though it is only probabilistic, but the connection between word choice and the thought expressed is not true. Most responses at all levels begin with *for*, though some thoughts might more logically be expressed in another way. For example, "I feel sorry—for people that stare at the handicapped" would make more sense if rephrased "that people stare at the handicapped." There are many such responses, and they are scored in terms of what the writer is assumed to have meant.

Responses in terms of concrete situations or events are typical of E2 and E3. Undiluted self-pity is one characteristic of E2 level. Most responses at E2 name another person, but that occurs so frequently at slightly higher levels that it is classed E3.

The typical Conformist response is mention of a general group of unfortunates, such as people who are sick, poor, homeless, or helpless. Similar categories are mentioned at E5, but at E5 other responses relate to inner feelings. At E6 and higher, one typically feels sorry for those who for some reason are mistreated or are suffering unfairly.

Responses at E5 differ from those at E4 by less self-pity and more self-criticism. However, contrary to expectation, feeling sorry for bad deeds may occur at any level. At E3, the bad deeds are either concrete (like having sex) or vague (like doing wrong). The most frequent expressions of guilty feelings include the cliché about hurting someone's feelings, a category that is not very discriminating and is scored E5. By E6 and higher, the sense of responsibility is clearer and expressed in less clichélike terms. At E7, many responses refer to causes and consequences of behavior and to regret over own past mistakes. Responses concerning characterologic limitations are typical of the highest levels.

Responses concerning character traits, typically rated E6, are so varied that it is hard to write category titles that will be both sufficiently inclusive and correctly interpreted. In rating, use specific categories for responses that can fit them, and judge other characterologic weaknesses last. Some simple answers of that type would best be classed at E5 rather than E6. We have not found an unambiguous rule to substitute for judgment and general knowledge of the levels when rating unusual answers.

There are no new themes at the highest levels, but there are elaborations of themes found at E5 and E6. Concern for social issues is a theme beginning at E5 and running with increased frequency through E8. It is not designated one of the predominant themes because most of the responses can also be classed under other themes.

Homeless people, now the prototypic poor folks to feel sorry for, partially replace racial minorities, especially what used to be called Negroes. A new subtheme that occurs at more than one level concerns special sympathy for women and women's problems; that is true of men as well as of women subjects. No similar responses express special sympathy for men.

There are more categories for this item than for most others. In a few instances first-person responses, like "when I'm lonely," are listed in categories under the others theme, because there were not enough cases to constitute a category under the myself theme, and the response seemed clearly similar to others in the category.

Themes:

For myself (E2–E6): for myself; I don't make more money; for myself at times; for myself too much.

For others (E2–E6): for no one; for my sister; for poor people; for people less fortunate than me; for the underdog.

About my inadequacies (E3–E7): when I do something wrong; when I hurt someone's feelings; that I didn't stay in college; when I have been insensitive to those I love.

About others' inadequacies (E3–E7): for losers; for snobs; for people who don't try; for people with low self-esteem; for people who are limited.

Other (E3–E7): for you going through these tests; my mother died; for the world; for great cultures long gone.

ITEM 16: I FEEL SORRY . . .

E2 Impulsive

2-For myself

a. —for myself (4a, 6a)
   when I am sad
   about myself

2-For others

b. —for no one

E3 Self-Protective

3-For myself

a. —when things don't go my way
   if I am being disappointed
   for myself when I fail a test
b. Because I don't have (certain things)
   I don't make more money

3-For others

c. For specific people (4f, 4i)
   for my sister
   for Rosie
   for my parents
d. —for (some) people
   for people sometime
e. Personal pronouns
   for her

3-About my inadequacies

f. —when I do something wrong [unelaborated] (5m, 5n)
   when I make a mistake
g. —about things I did
   that I had sex
   that I got pregnant at such an early age
   for all the bad things I have done

3-About others' inadequacies

h. For specific groups (hostile or belittling tone) (4f, 4h)

the nerds of this world
for losers
for fat people
for stupid people

i. —for people who get in trouble
   when people do wrong things

3-Other

j. Hostility toward test or testers (5aa)
   for the person that has to correct this interview
   for the sucker who is going to try to make any sense of this

E4 Conformist

4-For myself

a. —for myself sometimes (2a, 6a)
   for myself when something goes wrong

4-For others

**b. —for the homeless
   for people who don't have a place to live or any food to eat
   for people or animals who are homeless
   for the derelicts & children who live in the streets
**c. —for poor, underprivileged people (5a, 6b)
   for people who are sick or poor
   for starving people in India
*d. —for the sick, handicapped (5d, 5k, 5l)
   about my cousin, who is paralyzed
   for the mentally ill
   for people who are deaf
*e. —for helpless people, people who can't help themselves (5b, 5q)
   for people who completely rely on others
   for people that can't make it on their own
f. For specific groups of unfortunate people [demographic or physical variables] (3h, 5k, 5l)
   for criminals
   for single people

for Vietnam veterans
for people who don't live in the United States
for people who want to work but can't find a job
for all the aborted babies

g. —for animals
when the dog got hurt
for the birds & fish in Alaska (oil spill)

4-About others' inadequacies

h. —for snobbish people (3h, 5w)
for people who are conceited
for people who never listens [sic]

4-Other

*i. Specific family situations (3c, 5i, 7d)
my mother died
for people who don't get along with their parents
for couples who can't have children
for young girls who get pregnant
for single parents
when I think about my marriage

j. Frequency
sometimes
for a lot of things
never

E5 Self-Aware

5-For others

*a. —for those less fortunate (than me) (4c)
for people who have less than me
for people who didn't have the same advantages I've had

*b. —for neglected children, children from broken homes (4e)
for all deprived children
for unloved children
for children that are at the mercy of whoever will take care of them

*c. —for victims of abuse (6c)
for abused people or animals
for battered spouses

*d. —for people who are hurt, unhappy, suffering (4d)
for all the unfortunate people in this world (which is a lot)
for everything that suffers
for those in despair
people in pain

e. —for people with problems, troubles (6b)
for my friend who is having a difficult pregnancy
for people who are under a lot of stress
for people born with odds against them
when people are in poor circumstances

f. —for people who are lonely, alone (6l)
when I'm lonely

g. —for people who are not loved, have no one [unelaborated] (6l)

for anyone who does not have family
that some people are not loved
for people without close friends
for girls who don't have dates

h. —for people who lose loved ones
for families of missing children
for people who have lost friends

i. —for people who have bad marriages (4i, 7d)
about my divorce
for couples who have broken up
that my friend is having marital problems

j. —for old people
for old people because they are going to die soon
for the elderly
for senior citizens who are always alone

k. —for dying people (4d)
for terminally ill people
when someone dies even if I don't know them
for those who have no chance to live

l. —for people with AIDS (4d)
for innocent people who are affected by Aids

5-About my inadequacies

**m. —when I have hurt someone, been unfair (3f, 6f, 6g)
for the little retarded kid I used to chase and knock down
when I hurt someone intentionally
when I unintentionally hurt someone's feeling
when I insult somebody in fun and they take me seriously

n. —when I have done something wrong [elaborated] (3f)
when I do wrong to myself or someone else
when I know I've done something wrong and didn't mean it
for the mistakes I had done in the past
when I displease God
if I intentionally do wrong

o. —when I cannot help someone
when I can't help a friend
because I cannot provide my children with their material needs
when there is a bad situation I can do nothing about

p. —when I don't do my best
when I know I could do better and don't
that I got a bad grade on my history exam that I studied so hard for

5-About others' inadequacies

*q. —for those who don't help themselves [sense of choice implied] (4e)
for those who can't ask for help
for those who feel helpless
for people who say they can't
for people who don't try things

r. —for people who can't adjust to (cope with) life (6j)
for people having difficulty getting along with others
for people that are misfits
for people who give up on life
for people who live under fear

s. —for people who can't change, grow (6h)
for those who do not believe in personal growth
for people whose defenses keep them from growing

t. —for people who use drugs
for those who live in the world of drugs
drunk drivers and their victims

u. —for those who are ignorant (6r)
for ignorant people who think they know it all

v. —for people who feel sorry for themselves (6k)

w. —for selfish people (4h, 6o)
for people who have no capacity to give

x. —for people without faith (6v)
for those who do not know God
for the unsaved
for people lost in a world of sin

5-Other

y. —about the state of the world (6p, 7e)
for innocent persons caught up in this evil world
for the world
for our destructive society
about the complexity of this modern world

z. —when bad things happen [unelaborated] (7f)
when I read or hear any sad story about a tragedy
for good people in bad situations

aa. Value of test questioned (3j)
that I came to [school] today, and have to take this test instead of learning something

E6 Conscientious

6-For myself

a. —for myself too much (2a, 4a)
for myself—yuk!
for myself too often
for myself when I'm tired

6-For others

*b. Lack of opportunities; controlled by circumstances (4c, 5e)
for the homeless who can't help being homeless
for the people in the Holocaust because I had to read a book about it
for fat children, because it is usually not their fault
for people who feel trapped and helpless
for people who have no chance at an education
for those people who want children but can't

*c. —for the mistreated, the underdog (5c)
for people that stare at the handicapped
for the downtrodden masses

for those unfairly denied the necessities of life, or justice
when I see someone being taken advantage of
for innocent people who are hurt
for the people who have to put up with the people who mock others
for children that are at the mercy of problem adults

6-About my inadequacies

d. For lost opportunities (7a)
for a lot of things that I have & have not done
that I didn't stay in college fifteen years ago
that I did not study harder in [school]
much of my life was spent in a vacuum
when potential—in any domain—is unrealized

e. —that I don't have enough time
that I have limited time, resources and energy
when I should of done something, but procrastinated

f. —when I get angry, am cross with my family (5m)
when I lose my temper with my child
after saying something mean, in anger

g. —when I have let someone down, disappointed someone (5m)
letting down my mother

6-About others' inadequacies

h. —for people who have no goals, no direction (5s, 8a)
when people don't take their lives seriously
for people who sit back and let life pass them by
for those of us that do not have the motivations to try and improve our lot in NYC
for those that think that life has no meaning
for those who let life slip away by default

i. Failure to achieve goals, ideals
for those who don't know how easy it is to succeed
for people when they feel they have no future
for people who are underachievers

j. —for people who do not enjoy life [in general terms] (5r, 8a)
for those who are oblivious to the simple wonders of life
for people who do not live fully
for people who seem to enjoy being miserable
for chronic complainers, they miss out on life

k. —for those with low self-esteem (5v)
for people who can't accept themselves for who they are
for people who don't have a good sense of self
for people who are insecure
for people who don't see how beautiful they are

l. —for people who have not known love, have no one [elaborated] (5g)
for people who cannot fall in love
for those people who do not have someone to share their lives

m. —for people who can't express their feelings (7b)
   for those who can't feel sympathy, compassion, love, kindness, & empathy
   for people who run from their feelings
   for those who can never express themselves freely

n. Contrast of physical and mental
   the children who were abused by their parents, physical & mental. They have no say about it
   for people who are physically and/or mentally disabled

o. Unkindness, hate, lack of trust between people (5w)
   for bigots
   for people who walk in total darkness full of hurts, hate and know no peace
   those who discriminate against others
   when I hear or witness brutality
   that people aren't more unselfish

p. —about injustice, oppression (5y)
   when the innocent victims of war-torn nations have nowhere to go
   (I feel sad) for all those who are unjustly persecuted
   when an individual doesn't get something that he really deserves
   that the world is often unfair, violent, etc.
   for people who take advantage of others through the positions they are in
   for those women who are forced into prostitution by some low-life bully who should be thrown to the lions

q. —for narrow-minded people (7b)
   for people who are strongly opinionated
   that people in general are so close-minded and prejudiced

r. —for uneducated people (5u)
   for people who don't take education seriously
   for people who don't know the meaning of education

s. —for people who allow themselves to be dominated
   for people who don't have the guts to be individuals
   people who do not think for themselves
   for women who live thru men

t. —for those unable to be honest with themselves
   for people who are phony, who don't know themselves, and try to please everyone all the time
   for people who have to lie in order to feel good about themselves

u. Characterological weaknesses
   for people who are interested in money—more than excitement
   for people that have no will power
   for people who can't be alone
   for people who are afraid to grow up
   for the person who is constantly teasing others in order to build himself up
   for people who cannot laugh at themselves
   for people who cannot admit their mistakes or say "I'm sorry"

v. —for those who do not have a personal relation with God (5x)
   when people bluntly reject Jesus
   for people who have shut themselves off from God's love

E7 Individualistic

7-About my inadequacies

a. Personal shortcomings, elaborated (6d)
   that I didn't learn to appreciate my parents before I did
   for myself when I can't stand up for what I believe in all the time
   when I have contributed to someone's pain by being insensitive
   when I've hurt someone or deceived myself
   that I am just now learning to have self-respect for myself
   that I waited so long to formulate goals for myself
   that I have not set myself free to enjoy my life as much as possible and do all that I would like to
   that I don't always make the most of opportunities to help people

7-About others' inadequacies

b. —for people who limit themselves (6m, 6o, 6q)
   for all of us when we don't just "go for it"
   for those who do not question & explore!
   for tight-minded, very conservative people because they shut themselves out of so many of life's pleasures and good people
   for people that go against their own feelings and principles in order to please the society
   for people who are limited in thinking, i.e. right, wrong, good, bad

c. Difficulties with relationships, communication (5r)
   lack of communication destroys a relationship
   for people who don't believe they can have a close relationship
   for men & women. Relationships are tough

7-Other

d. Family situations, elaborated (4i, 5i)
   for people who are not happy with themselves or their family
   for my father at times, because he still seems insecure after all this time
   for women who are trapped in a marriage because of their insecurities
   for my parents who work so hard for the children and never have a vacation

e. Social issues, elaborated (5y)
   for great cultures long gone
   when I see the pain some women go through in their personal lives

for those people who are on drugs, because they hurt themselves as well as their loved ones

that the people of the earth are not working together or respectful of differences

that we have destroyed our world in the way we have

f. —that bad things happen [unique, elaborated] (5z)

for others and for myself when something negative happens that is undeserved

when something unexpectedly debilitating or tragic happens

g. Unclassified

& repent after an offense

only for the innocents and rarely for man

is a statement I hate

for people that have been victims, no, not sorry, but I know how it feels

but never guilty

for myself, but I try not to show it or let it influence my actions

E8 Autonomous

a. Loss of purpose, values, or zest for life (6h, 6j)

for those who are walking and living but are really dead in hope, dreams, etc

when I haven't had the good sense of enjoying the day, weather notwithstanding

b. Lack of objectivity or perspective

for people who can't see reality

for the person that is blinded by hate or ignorance

c. Coping with inner conflict or contradiction

for the disadvantaged and particularly the negro [sic] to the point that I am outraged and intolerant of prejudiced people

that my anxieties often make me so difficult to live with

that people have to experience pain in order to grow

for those who are unable or unwilling to accept change and/or permanence

d. Search for identity

for anyone who has been beaten out of his/her own identity

who lose their potential for life through a frantic search to find themselves

for today's women, who have to find roles for themselves that have never existed in history and may be roads to unhappiness

A Man Feels Good When . . .

In this manual, almost no categories are specific to just one gender. Themes are the same for this item as for Item 24, "A woman feels good when . . ." but not all categories are the same. The predominant theme for this stem is accomplishments and achievements. In order to differentiate ego levels, one must note slight variations in this theme, from vague accomplishments, to doing something well, to doing something worthwhile or difficult.

Direct references to sexual gratification can occur on protocols of any ego level, more than for other items; such a response, even though classed at the Impulsive level, should not be considered pathognomonic. Many responses also relate to being loved or in love. Combinations of those themes do not occur at the lowest levels; mentioning sex in relation to love or in combination with remarks about achievements occurs in responses higher than E4.

Personal appearance, which is mentioned at all levels for women, is not mentioned for men. Being complimented is also more prominent for women than for men.

Themes:

Gratification (E2–E7): he has sex; he's got a few beers in him; he wins something; he is doing what he wants to do; he follows his conscience; he expresses himself in some way.

Accomplishments (E3–E6): he gets a job; he accomplishes something; he succeeds; he accomplishes something worthwhile.

Relationships (E3–E7): he is with a woman; he is with a woman he loves; he makes a woman happy; he knows he's loved by the person he loves; his accomplishments help his family.

Identity (E6–E7): he feels like a man; he can stop being macho and just be himself.

ITEM 17: A MAN FEELS GOOD WHEN . . .

E2 Impulsive

2-Gratification

*a. Direct reference to sexual gratification (3a)
  after sex
  he has an orgasm
  he gets laid
 b. —he feels good (3c, 4a)
  he doesn't feel bad

E3 Self-Protective

3-Gratification

 a. Reference to sensual gratification (2a)
  he's got a few beers in him
  he gets his back rubbed
  he's just out of the shower
  he has a full stomach
 b. —he has what he wants (5c)

he is taken care of
he is treated good
c. —he is happy (2b, 5b)
he has fun

3-Accomplishments

*d. —he has money, gets paid (5h)
he can make money
his boss gives him a raise
e. —he is working
he gets a job (any kind)

3-Relationships

f. —he is with a woman [no implication of continuing relation] (4e, 4f)
he has more than one woman
they are with a lady [sic]

3-Other

g. Evasion (6q)
he has finished his survey
I don't know, I'm not a man

E4 Conformist

4-Gratification

a. —he is well, healthy (2b, 5j)
he wakes up without a hangover
b. —he wins something (5f)
his sport team wins
he has won a game of racquetball

4-Accomplishments

*c. —he accomplishes something [unelaborated] (5f, 5g, 6f, 6g)
he shows what he has accomplished
he can accomplish what he wants
d. —his work is finished (5e, 5f, 6f)
his day at work is ended
he completes a task

4-Relationships

*e. —he has a family; has a good woman [continuing relation implied] (3f, 5k)
you tell them they are going to be a father
he gets married
he sees his first child
he knows there is someone waiting for him at home
he has a good relationship
*f. —he is in love; he is with a woman he loves (3f, 5k)
he finally meets the woman of his dreams
he is with someone he cares about
g. —his family is happy [unelaborated] (5l, 5q)
he has a happy home life

his family is happy and healthy

E5 Self-Aware

5-Gratification

a. —things are going right; everything is going his way
life is good to him
b. —he is content, satisfied (3c, 6c)
he owns his own house and lives comfortably with his family
c. —he is doing what he wants to do (3b, 6e)
he is doing what makes him happy
d. —he has no worries, no problems
he is not in trouble
he is not threatened
e. —he relaxes, watches sports (4d)
he sings
he hits a golf ball

5-Accomplishments

*f. —he is successful (4b, 4c, 6f)
he has been promoted
he proves himself
he excels
he has successfully completed a task
he does something a woman cannot do
his career advances
*g. —he has done something well (4c, 6g)
he is at his best
he knows what he's doing
does a good job, goes out, their team wins
*h. —he is a good provider (3d)
he makes a good living for his family
he "puts the meat on the table"
he can take care of his home
i. —he does the right thing (6d, 6i)
he practices what is good & right
he knows he made the right decision
j. —he is taking good (physical) care of himself (4a, 7b)
exercises and looks good for it
he works out in the gym
he can be strong
he feels strong

5-Relationships

**k. —he is loved; he knows he is loved (4e, 4f, 6l)
his woman cares
he finds the woman who will share his life with him
he is loved at home and happy at work
he has love and money
*l. —he has helped someone, made someone happy (4g, 7d)
he has done a good deed
he treats his wife nice

he is able to help others as well as himself
he comes through when needed
he makes a woman happy

*m. —he is complimented, praised (6h, 6m)
    he gets 'strokes'
    a woman builds him up
    he is recognized for his goodness

n. —he is appreciated, admired (6h, 6m)
    he is understood
    he is recognized
    he's seen as important
    his wife is proud of him
    a woman treats him as if he were the most important
       person in the world

o. —women cater to him, pay attention to him
    his wife meets his needs
    women are crazy about him
    he is pampered by a woman

*p. —he is in control, in charge
    he thinks he is a leader
    he can take advantage of a woman
    don't ask! He feels he has power
    when he has his family in subjection & job security
    he thinks he knows everything or has everything
    he dominates women
    he is in charge of his life & destiny
    he feels empowered

q. —his children succeed; his family is happy [elaborated] (4g)
    he sees his children following after the better things
       in life
    he first hears the word "daddy" from his child
    he takes pride in himself and his family

r. —he is with friends
    he's around people and things he enjoys
    he has people he cares for

s. —he is hugged; he hugs someone

t. —he makes a woman feel good
    he's satisfied a woman sexually

E6 Conscientious

6-Gratification

a. —he feels good about himself (7c)
    he has self-esteem
    he loves himself
    he is proud of himself

b. —his ego is given a boost
    his ego has been satisfied

c. —he feels secure (5b)
    he is self-confident
    he feels competent

d. —he follows his conscience (5i, 7f)
    he does what is correct, and does not just conform
    he does the right thing, regardless of what other
       people thought of him or his actions

he helps a person, or stands up for what he believes
in

e. —he enjoys his job (5c)
    his work absorbs him

6-Accomplishments

**f. Sense of accomplishment for having fulfilled goals
    (4c, 4d, 5f)
    he has a sense of accomplishment as a human being
    he fulfills his duty
    all of his goals are met
    he accomplishes something that he has wanted for
       a long time
    he can conquer and move on to a new challenge
    other people respect him and he meets his expecta-
       tions
    after fulfilling his responsibilities

**g. —he accomplishes something worthwhile, difficult
    (4c, 5g, 7a)
    he is productive
    he makes a good business deal
    he has solved a difficult problem
    he accomplishes something w/ his own two hands
    he has faced his most fearsome challenge!
    he's done something constructive
    he has done something he can be proud of
    he is doing something significant and important by
       his own standards
    he has worked hard for something and succeeded
       where he wasn't expected to

*h. —he is praised (appreciated) for a job well done
    (5m, 5n)
    his family tells him they are proud of him
    he is recognized for doing good work
    he is given encouragement and positive criticism
    his contributions are appreciated

i. —he has done his best (5i)
    he has completed a task to the best of his ability
    he's done what he thought was best

j. —he has a good job and a good family (7g)
    he enjoys his work and has a good family life
    he is doing something he loves and is in love with
       someone
    he has job security, then usually his home life will
       be happy
    everything goes well at the office and he has made
       love w/ his wife

k. —he is independent
    he doesn't have to depend on other people financially
    he knows he's his own man

6-Relationships

*l. Reciprocity in love (5k)
    he knows his wife is his partner and not his obstacle
    he shares loving times with his family
    his mate shows her appreciation and affection

the people he cares about feel good at the same time
    he feels good

m. —he is respected (5m, 5n)
    people around him are proud of him
    he receives respect for his integrity

n. —he feels needed
    he is wanted and is somebody
    he feels he's the backbone in a relationship
    he is relied upon
    he is useful

o. Trust
    he knows that he can always trust somebody
    he knows who his friends are & has good friends
    a woman trusts him and believes that he has more than sex on his mind

6-Identity

p. —he feels like a man (7e)
    he does something that is considered masculine or "macho"
    he thinks he's being manly!
    a woman accepts his ideas; his male vanity's appeased

q. —men differ (3g)
    men are different, therefore they feel good at different times

E7 Individualistic

7-Gratification

a. Self-fulfillment, self-expression; creativity (6g, 8a)
    he is productive, secure, and free to make choices, and to provide a good living for those he's responsible for
    he lives up to capabilities and goals he has
    he can relax at night knowing he is where he wants to be in his life at that time
    he can express his feelings and he knows his identity
    he has created something from his own head and hands
    he has expressed himself in any way
    he has successfully completed an undertaking of his own initiative
    he has an opportunity to demonstrate his competency
    he is appreciated for being himself

b. Combined mental and bodily satisfaction (5j)
    he's physically fit and mentally stretched
    he is in good health, productive, content
    his body feels good and when he is satisfied with his accomplishments
    he's raised a good family, accomplished his goals, made love to a woman, had a good day skiing, sailing, etc.

c. —he is at peace with himself (5b, 6a, 8a)
    he feels complete
    he is in control of his life

his life is in balance
he can live comfortably within himself

7-Relationships

d. Mutuality of interests of self and others (5l)
    can accomplish what he wanted and can give to others
    his needs—emotionally & physically—are met with a mutual effort
    his work world and leisure world (family & friends) support each other
    he has a good life with a wonderful [woman?] whom he can understand & enjoy
    his accomplishments also improve his family's lot
    he has accomplished something for his office, his family, his future
    he is able to demonstrate his competence to people he cares for
    he finds true companionship

7-Identity

e. Implied criticism of male stereotype (6p)
    he does something that pleases him—just as a woman would
    he can stop being macho and just be himself
    Same problem with this question as in #14. Sounds like a commercial for an aftershave—sorry, you won't get a macho answer out of me
    he is able to feel like a man, whatever that means
    If this is intended to say something about men that is not true about women, I don't feel qualified to answer
    he acts like a person, and not the usual ego-inflated male superior image
    —you ask as though I can speak for men
    he begins to learn to break out of the stereotypes society presents to men—

f. —he is true to himself (6d)
    he is being true to his nature, honest with himself—as do women
    he knows he is accepted as he is, by a woman
    he's allowed to be himself
    he is himself rather than living according to others'/society's expectations

7-Other

g. Conceptual complexity (6j)
    he has been strong and gentle at the same time
    he is relaxed and aroused at once
    a woman likes to be with him but does not cling
    he puts a lot of effort into a new activity (mental, physical, professional, or whatever), and achieves some sort of breakthrough
    he can provide for the well being of his family (psychologically as well as economic)

E8 Autonomous

a. —he finds inner peace, fulfillment [elaborated] (7a, 7c)

his heart is light & his conscience is clear

he uses his talents and skills constructively, avoids excesses and constantly increases his understanding of life

he feels whole, the same way a woman feels good when she is whole

b. Unclassified

he has achieved a goal, but most achievers are never content with what they have done and constantly seek greater heights with corresponding recognition

he can "let his kid out," and just horse around without exposure to ridicule or criticism

Rules Are . . .

Responses to this stem can be classed as favorable to rules, critical of them, or ambiguous with respect to favorableness. The ambiguous ones are here divided into those that are neutral with respect to the value of rules, giving descriptions or definitions, and those that are mixed, giving positive and negative aspects. They are not necessarily ambiguous in meaning. Many responses, however, are hard to classify in these terms. Is saying rules are guidelines (or flexible) favorable, critical, or neutral? Some subjects go on to elaborate, but when they do not, the answer depends on the connotations one reads into the response.

Whether the person has a predominantly favorable or predominantly critical attitude to rules is not a reliable clue to ego level. Mixed responses predominate at higher levels. Flat-out rejection of rules is too rare to generalize about. Examples are given at E3 and E5, but the examples at E5 actually come from higher level protocols. Such responses should be judged by other criteria.

Characteristic E2 responses show a failure to generalize about rules. Neutral responses at E2 and E3 are not ambivalent but are concrete examples, like "to do as your told by a cop," or descriptions, like "regulations."

The predominant theme at the Conformist level is a bland acceptance of the rules: important, necessary, made to be followed. However, the cliché "made to be broken" is surprisingly frequent. Although favorable responses are in toto more frequent than critical ones, "made to be broken" is more frequent than "made to be followed." Together the categories for those two clichés account for about one fifth

of the responses in a large, diverse sample. When they occur in combination with other responses, only the other one is scored. They are not diagnostic, occurring at least from E3 to E7.

At E5, rules are often evaluated somewhat critically or are put in a wider social perspective. At E6 and higher, there are more ambivalent messages. Many subjects find a way to state advantages and disadvantages of rules, or they give reasons for their response. Thus, conceptual complexity becomes an important aspect of the response.

All responses classed above E6 are qualified in some way; they cannot easily be classed as favorable or critical, hence themes are not used. For example, at E7 some subjects confront the conflict between the needs of the individual and those of society. Several high-level responses, grouped in other categories, share expressions of concern that other people not be hurt or oppressed by a rule or by a rule change. To say that rules restrict freedom is typically an E6 idea; to perceive that rules make freedom possible is typically an E8 idea.

Themes:

Favorable (E3–E6): good for people; made to be followed; guidelines; necessary to maintain order.
Critical (E2–E6): always broken; stupid; made to be broken; often not right; not set in stone.
Neutral (E2–E5): to help clean up; regulations; flexible.
Mixed (E5–E6): both good and bad; a necessary evil.

ITEM 18: RULES ARE...

E2 Impulsive

2-Critical

  a. —always broken (4i, 5n)
    never follow

2-Neutral

  b. Concrete examples or admonitions (5i)
    to help clean up the house
    not to sex that much or do drugs
  c. Repetition of stem (3c)
    rules

E3 Self-Protective

3-Favorable

  a. —good, OK (4e, 5p)
    very good for people
    good for the schools

3-Critical

  b. Deprecatory comments (5j)
    stupid at times
    bad in most cases
    senseless

3-Neutral

  c. Definitions (2c)
    what you can and can't do
    regulations
    whatever is put down

E4 Conformist

4-Favorable

**a. —made to be followed; to be obeyed (5o)
    nice when people follow them
    to be followed with no 'ifs' & 'and' about it
    regulations we must abide to
  b. —not to be broken (5o)
*c. —important [unelaborated] (5a)
    important in everything you do
*d. —necessary; needed (6l)
    essential
  e. —usually good; sometimes necessary (3a, 5p)
    good to an extent
    for following at certain times
  f. —for protection [unelaborated] (6d)
    for your safety
    made to insure safety and should be followed
  g. —made to keep people in line (5a, 6a, 6b)
    great for the bad
    important so that people won't "get away with murder"
    designed to discipline people
    things made up to control people

  h. —for everyone (5b)
    everywhere

4-Critical

**i. —made to be broken (2a, 5o)
    easy to break
    rules and must be broken
    not always made to be obeyed
    to be gotten around

E5 Self-Aware

5-Favorable

*a. —important in any society, in our civilization (4g, 6a, 7c)
    a necessary part of life and a society
    to keep us civilized
    necessary in groups of people
*b. —made for the general good (4h)
    made for good & practical people
    meant to protect the majority
    made for your own good
    made to give everyone a fair chance
*c. —guidelines [unelaborated] (6c)
    helpful in setting limits
    sometimes broken but help guide us
    norms
  d. —part of life (6e)
    important in life
    necessary in all games, including life
    made to be lived by !!!
  e. —made for a reason
  f. —useful
    here to help us
  g. Acceptable if sensible, reasonable
    good when in moderation
    acceptable when commonly agreed upon
    necessary but must be fair to everyone
  h. —to be respected
  i. Altruistic and prudential rules (2b)
    to be loving, caring & helpful to anyone
    not to give in when you set a rule for a child
    very important, therefore you should read them very carefully

5-Critical

  j. —sometimes ridiculous, wrong (3b, 6j, 6n)
    often pointless
    often not right
  k. Self-conscious or reasoned rebellion
    for someone else, not for me
    red flags to me, made to be broken, points of rebellion

a totally false and inadequate basis or method for directing human behavior

l. —unnecessary
getting out of hand

5-Neutral

m. —flexible, changeable [unqualified, unelaborated] (6c, 6g, 6i)
made to be revised
sometimes flexible

n. —not always followed (2a, 6h)
important, but I don't always follow them
good but cannot always be followed
made, but who really follows them
seldom followed, often broken

5-Mixed

*o. —made to be followed, as well as broken (4a, 4b, 4i)
good some of the times, but were made to be broken
made so it can protect people; made to be broken
except in certain situations, not made to be broken
important but at times should be disregarded
meant to be kept but are often broken
necessary, but breakable

p. —sometimes good and sometimes bad (3a, 4e)
sometimes necessary, sometimes not
both good & bad

q. Value relative to situation (7a)
good if fairly administered
made to be broken in certain special circumstances
needed in some settings but not all

E6 Conscientious

6-Favorable

**a. —necessary to maintain order, organization (4g, 5a, 7c)
needed and keep New York in order
made to govern behavior in some way
necessary to avoid chaos. However, I do not always follow them
a way of ordering one's life, necessary in a society for structuring and guidelines
made to control any kind of bureaucracy
structural guidance

b. Necessary because of human fallibility (4g)
made in place of morals for the weak
needed for children
needed when people don't exercise self-discipline or good judgment
useful to simplify interactions w/ others
for those who don't understand right and wrong, those who mess-up the smooth moving system

c. Guidelines (elaborated) (5c, 5m)
often not as rigid as they may first appear
guides, but not set in granite

guidelines for behavior, which may be outdated or counterproductive
important to establish boundaries
often quite stupid, but we need them (some of them) as guidelines
there to be flexible and be guides, not barriers
a guide to live by, not an end in themselves

d. For protection (elaborated) (4f)
made for the safety of yourself as well as the safety of others
necessary to allow equality when interacting
necessary to keep people from infringing on other people's rights
made to protect and be fair to everyone
Laws are made to protect the innocent, but more often help the guilty get away with more

e. —a basis for life (5d)
am important part of life—but not of ultimate importance
very necessary for existence

f. —made by people
man-made power symbols
made by men and therefore need to be looked at carefully
directly affected by the public's support of them

6-Critical

*g. Subject to change (5m)
not set in stone, except the Ten Commandments, and even these are questioned
required but should be frequently re-evaluated
to be questioned
subject to interpretation
constantly in need of revision
important but should be flexible
always evolving

h. —to be bent (5n, 7a)
made to be broken or at least stretched!!
sometimes broken, often bent

i. —confining; restrictive (5m, 7c)
inhibiting, sometimes
at times too rigid—they need to be flexible
inflexible

j. —not always fair, just (5j)
created to make people more "equal" than they really are
not all "golden"
vital but must be just
only good if they are fair to all

k. Biased; for the rulers, the powerful
meant to keep certain groups oppressed
in a school, a way for the faculty to look powerful
imposed by the people who have political power
enforced for some and ignored or changed for others
a must in this biased world
made by the rich to be broken by the rich

6-Mixed

*l. Necessary, qualified by negative statement (4d, 7c)

a necessary evil

necessary in many areas, a necessary evil in other areas, and evil in still others

sometimes ridiculous, but necessary

important, practical, & silly all at the same time

sometimes necessary but can be broken

necessary but not necessarily right

important, but seldom followed

m. —to be followed if just; to be broken if unjust (7b)

there for guidance, but can be broken if it is unjust, such as Jim Crow

valid only when they are just

n. Broken or observed according to one's own values (5j)

should be disobeyed if against personal morals

only applicable if they make sense to the person following them

to be followed within the bounds of a person's own good judgment

o. Unclassified

more valuable than I used to think they were

sometimes important for non-apparent reasons

good in principle, often bad in practice

a vexation at best, and not very important

far less necessary than is usually supposed

made to be broken, except don't kill, steal, cheat (and other basics)

E7 Individualistic

a. Situations justify exceptions (5q, 6h)

necessary, but so are exceptions

made to be broken in extenuating circumstances

too general and should be specified for the individual

for providing structure, but should be flexible to the needs of people

b. —to be followed, evaluated, and changed (6m, 8a)

made to be evaluated, and if they are not for the good of all, changed

made to be followed and changed if they prove to be inadequate

to be followed most of the time and to be broken when an exception warrants it

c. Necessary for order but may be too restrictive (6a, 6i, 6l, 8a)

essential in an organized society, but sometimes too restrictive

sometimes made to be broken if the action does not harm anyone else

necessary for order but they should not be used to oppress or hurt

often overly picky and not flexible enough, but necessary to provide order

d. Comment on stem

made to be broken. (This may be a cliché, but it's true)

made to be broken. (I don't really believe this—too good to pass up)

meant to be broken. (Sorry, but I really mean it!)

e. Unclassified

important in helping me not get bogged down in petty decisions

E8 Autonomous

a. Three or more ideas, one at E6 (7b, 7c)

laws made by people to make society a more organized place (to limit conflict)

rules and I dislike them but usually try to maintain them and am always making new ones to live by

there to guide and direct but not to suppress &/ or oppress people

within reason a good structure—if you know how to use them

most effective when the governed people have collectively made them up

not cast in concrete but guidelines to be changed when they are no longer realistic

fences which make games possible and keep people from each others' throats

helpful if conscientiously drawn. They guide those who need them and are useful reference points for those who need them less

b. Protection for freedom

to provide structure within which freedom abides

excellent guides to help civilized people live in freedom

Crime and Delinquency Could Be Halted if . . .

This stem, originally used for males only, has the merit that it does not make people self-conscious, as some more personal items do. Presumably, everyone recognizes the impossibility, but some interesting and revealing responses are given.

The predominant tone of the categories at the Impulsive and Self-protective levels is punitive. Particularly at the Self-Protective level, some responses are so vindictive and merciless that one wonders whether they are meant as sardonic. In any case, they would still be scored E3.

Typical of the Conformist level are responses implying that crime and delinquency stem from inadequate influence of traditional institutions: family, church, and school. The two most popular categories at this level continue the punitive theme of lower levels, but the tone is law and order rather than vigilante. However, these answers are not discriminating with respect to ego level.

The major emphasis at the Self-aware level is understanding, caring about, and helping people in general and delinquents in particular. The remnant of the punitive theme is a call for parental strictness. Interest in causes of delinquency begins at this level. A popular but nondiscriminating category at this level states that they cannot be halted.

At the Conscientious level, the tone of the responses changes away from punishment or retaliation: Reasons should be understood; parents and teachers need to be better educated, and social institutions need to be altered to prevent crime. Rehabilitation and counseling supplant punishment. A category stating that the world or people must come to an end first is popular and nondiscriminating; it is scored E6.

Above the Conscientious level, the complexity of the issues is recognized and dealt with in various ways. Social issues—such as prejudice, poverty, and discrimination—are addressed more directly than at lower levels.

There are many compound answers at all but the lowest levels, that is, answers with two or more scorable parts. The higher clause should then determine the rating, particularly if it is unusual. Many answers, for example, combine a call for stronger punishment or restoration of the death penalty with some higher level response. Where the two clauses form a clear contrast, such as stricter laws and increased privileges for poor youths (carrot and stick) answers, the score is one step higher than that of the higher of the elements.

Responses calling for alleviation of poverty occur at all levels, sometimes in quite similar terms. To the extent that this concern relates to ego level, there is a continual series, making the discrimination of level difficult. Generally, the answers at higher levels are a little more sympathetic and original; not all shades of meaning can be captured in category titles, however, so the rater must extrapolate.

Some people misread the stem as "should be halted if . . ."; such responses should be rated on ego level only. The rater's task is to discern what the respondent means, if at all possible.

Themes:

Punishment (E2–E4): more jails were built; there were more policemen; laws were strictly enforced.

Impossible (E3–E7): there was nothing to steal; all men were saints; they can't; there were no people.

Child rearing (E4–E7): people brought up their children right; parents cared; parents were better educated; the family unit was stronger.

Social conditions (E4–E7): children had other outlets; everyone was educated; the system was changed; everybody was on the same economic level.

Individual responsibility (E3–E7): people would stop it; people cared; there were strong moral values in the home; there was more love; the criminal has to want to stop behaving that way.

Other (E2–E5): you do something bad; I don't know; there is no answer.

ITEM 19: CRIME AND DELINQUENCY COULD BE HALTED IF . . .

E2 Impulsive

2-Punishment

a. —they locked them all up; more jails were built (3a, 4b)
you will go to jail

2-Other

b. Illogical response (except "should" responses) (5q)
you do something bad
I am doing wrong
it happen to me
you do it

E3 Self-Protective

3-Punishment

a. —there were more policemen (2a, 4b)
b. —criminals and delinquents were killed (4a)
you killed all the bastards who do it
they are got rid by the authority
a hangman's rope was used again
c. Primitive and indiscriminate reaction
everyone in the world were given a lobotomy
people who commit crimes have that same crime committed to them
everyone was killed

3-Impossible

d. —there was nothing to steal

3-Individual responsibility

e. —there were no criminals; people would stop it (4m)
no one commited crimes
everybody join in and try to stop it
people quit doing those types of things

E4 Conformist

4-Punishment

**a. —the death penalty was reinstated (3b)
they brought back capital punishment
**b. —laws were more strongly enforced; punishments were stricter (2a, 3a, 5b)
punishment was quick and sure
police work hard enough
(halted?) more punitive steps were taken
laws were different, and more strict
punishment fit the crime
people/children are punished right away in their youth

4-Impossible

c. —everyone was perfect (5c, 6b, 8a)

man was not sinful
all men were saints
d. —some rules weren't made; there weren't any laws
everything were legal

4-Child rearing

*e. —people brought up their children right (5e)
parents taught their kids what to do and not to do
we had better parents around today
*f. —children were trained, taught right from wrong (5l)
they were taught better
g. —parents were strict; there was more discipline
parents would control their children
parents are stern with their children from day #1
we set limits at an early age

4-Social conditions

h. —youths had other things to do than hanging in the streets (5j)
we had more facilities (YMCAs etc.) to keep youth off the street
children had other outlets
more people had something to occupy their time
i. —more jobs were available (5i, 5k)
j. —the drug problem could be solved (5k)
drugs & alcohol were unavailable
drugs and drug users were eliminated from the earth
drugs were legalized
k. —something was done about it
we work to solve the immediate problem
someone really get down to their business

4-Individual responsibility

*l. —people cared (5d)
people didn't hate each other
people cared for the delinquents in the first place
m. —people would obey the laws (3e)
every child would mine [mind]
people obeyed rules
n. —people thought before they did things
you would stop to think of the consequences of crimes

4-Other

o. —I don't know
(I cannot solve this problem)
I don't understand
????
p. —it could; possible

E5 Self-Aware

5-Impossible

a. —they can't
I feel that they could never be completely eliminated

you could have a snowball fight in hell

b. —we lived in a police state (4b)

more communism was enforced

the laws were stricter like they are in Saudi Arabia

c. —people changed (4c, 6b, 6k, 8a)

man's personality changed to a more caring one

human beings were different than we are

5-Child rearing

**d. —parents cared; parents were more interested in their children (4l, 7a)

parents were more loving—less abusive

parents took more time to listen to their child's needs

*e. Parents or community were more responsible, concerned (4e, 6l, 8b)

we worked harder together as a community

parents were more conscientious in raising and educating their children

society would be more interested in youth

the parents take responsibility in raising their children

more dedicated staff existed

f. —parents could be helped to straighten out their lives

people understood their own selves

there are not so many broken homes

parents had been loved

g. Help given in early childhood (4g)

we reach people soon enough

there was less child abuse in this country

5-Social conditions

*h. —people were better educated (6c)

I don't think they could ever be stopped, but education would help them

all were educated

schools were better

education were stressed more

i. —poverty was abolished (4i)

everything was free

there was no deprivation

the cost of living weren't so high

j. —the right programs were in effect; enough help were available (4h, 6f)

more programs for young children were available

the prison rehabilitation system was more effective

we meet the needs of youth

we spent more time working with and educating the poor

there were more places for people to turn to

criminals & delinqents got help

k. —we eliminate the causes (4i, 4j, 6g, 7c)

we focused on problems—jobs, poverty—rather than symptoms—drugs, etc.

we considered all the factors

5-Individual responsibility

*l. Morals and values (4f)

there were strong moral values in the home, school & workplace

morals and rules were taught to the criminals before they became thieves

parents spent more time with their children & instilled more values in them

everyone had the same set of morals

*m. —people believed in God

if we start teaching children about God and his love

people would study and apply Bible principles

people became more involved spiritually

God was the head of every home

man turned from self to God

n. —there was more understanding, communication

people listen

everyone tried to help & understand each other

o. —everyone was satisfied with what they had (6i)

people felt their needs were met

p. —people were willing to report crime

every one would stop being afraid of taking a stand

5-Other

q. —it hurts other people [read as "should" instead of "could"] (2b)

it goes beyond the limitations

our children are to have a better future

r. —there is no answer

? if I had the answer I would change the world!

E6 Conscientious

6-Impossible

*a. —there were no people; the world came to an end

Jesus returned and ruled with an iron rod

a nuclear bomb annihilated civilized man

we were all robots

*b. —this were Utopia (4c, 5c, 8a)

we lived in a fictional world

this were a perfect world

we could start civilization all over again and create a utopian society

6-Child rearing

c. Parents and teachers were better educated (5h)

parent education began at children's birth

everyone in this country were educated to be better parents

6-Social conditions

*d. —the system changed

punishments fit the crime & unjust laws were changed

the educational system would be better

our economic society was restructured

we restricted personal income limits

we lived in small, homogenous societies

our judicial system worked

*every facet of American society was reviewed, re-
thought & redone*

e. —everyone had equal opportunities (7b, 7d)
   the world wasn't prejudiced
   inequalities in society were reduced
   *people took more interest in children & if laws were
   enforced on an equal basis*
   equality of education were truly pursued

f. Rehabilitation and counseling were emphasized more
   (5j)
   *the people who do it learn that it will not get them
   further in life*
   *there were more programs to rehabilitate these peo-
   ple who commit these crimes*
   *there were more strict sentences and more effective
   rehabilitation*
   *the criminal's life style is analyzed, helped and cor-
   rected*

g. —we knew what caused them; more were known
   about it (5k, 7c)
   we understood them
   *there was more understanding of the needs for these
   actions*
   *more research was done to find out the reasons
   behind this and hopefully it can be controlled as
   a result of the research*

h. Government did (not) do something (specified)
   the authority really wants to
   the government didn't condone
   corruption would decrease

i. —there was less greed; we were not so materialistic
   (5o)
   greed and hate did not exist
   society was fairer, less materially minded

j. —guns were outlawed

6-Individual responsibility

*k. —there was more love; people would help each other
   (5c, 7e)
   *people had more understanding and caring for each
   other*
   people were more compassionate
   people could live in harmony and inner peace
   men respected each other
   *our society stopped punishing and judging and
   started helping and caring more*
   brotherhood and altruism were a part of all mankind

l. —family and community worked together [unelabo-
   rated] (5e, 8b)
   families & schools worked together
   *police & parents could work together and listen to
   their children's cries for help*

m. Contrasting elements, one E5 (8c)
   *parents were more concerned and there were no
   street drugs*
   *families gave enough love and discipline, punishment
   was sure and swift, and drug abuse was halted*

*there were stricter laws regulating drugs and if wel-
fare was fixed up*
*there was capital punishment and schools where
students can take up a trade*
*parents strived towards setting good examples, car-
ing enough to discipline*
people were not poor and also if they followed laws
*the world were just and people were genetically
equal (That's too big a question)*

n. —people had more self-esteem
   *people would grow up and take responsibility for
   themselves*
   people respected their own worth and that of others

o. Adults respected, trusted young people

E7 Individualistic

7-Child rearing

*a. —the family structure was stronger (5d)
   *if the family unit was a place for encouragement,
   support, & love*
   more emphasis was put on family life
   families lived and worked as a loving unit

7-Social conditions

b. Socio-economic conditions improved, were equal-
   ized (6e)
   *there were alternatives for poverty stricken teenag-
   ers*
   *if everybody on earth could be on the same socio-
   economic level*
   people had a better life to look forward to
   *there was a greater distribution of wealth and edu-
   cation, housing, employment for the world's poor*

c. —the reasons for it were dealt with; social and en-
   vironmental changes were made (5k, 6g)
   *society as a whole were less apathetic, and respond
   only when something happened to them*
   we could find their roots & cure the causes
   *lived in a society where there was no motivation for
   crime and delinquency*
   *society tried to solve the basic problems that led
   people into crime*

d. Reference to equal opportunity or to prejudice
   (elaborated) (6e)
   *resources were distributed more equally and family
   life was healthier for most people*
   *everyone had sufficient opportunity for growth and
   development*
   *people (adults) were more understanding of teenag-
   ers and didn't stereotype them*

7-Individual responsibility

e. Solution has to come from within the delinquent (6k)
   *the criminal/delinquent wanted to stop behaving in
   such a way*

compassion, love & joy were more abundant in the hearts of the criminals & delinquents

E8 Autonomous

a. Essential nature of humans or society could be changed (4c, 5c, 6b)

the criminal intent was taken out of all minds, which is unrealistic

people could have a new heart (spiritually) and then would control themselves

the very nature of man, which is to choose his own way rather than God's, could be reversed

we still lived in bands/tribes in the forest sharing a subsistence level of economy with no private property or trade with other groups of people

b. Family and community worked together [elaborated] (5e, 6l)

the family unit, school, and society as a whole addressed their need upon each other

the planet were more healed; and people were ready to work together to solve problems

your children are consistently dealt with, encouraged to be self-sufficient, loved, respected, taught to love themselves and given self-worth

c. Recognition of complexity of the problem, direct or indirect (6m)

we knew the magic formula for each child to raise them without injuring them. Also if poverty could also be eliminated

all people's psychological, social and economic needs were met

. . . I can't finish this statement. Humanity is too variable and complex to think this generality could be true

there was a healing of the broken family & justice in inner cities and in the third world

we attended to the needs (educational, emotional, physical, etc.) of the individual

Men Are Lucky Because . . .

Categories in the 1970 manual for this item implying that women cannot participate in common male activities (such as some sports) are now rare or absent, reflecting the fact that women can do many things that were once almost exclusively male prerogatives. Whereas the idea that men are not as apt to be discriminated against did not occur in the 1970 manual, it is now a popular category. It occurs from E3 to E7 and so does not indicate ego level. Presumably, it reflects increased awareness rather than increased discrimination. That men dominate, control, or rule the family is a less common response than it used to be.

Most subjects take the stem to ask in what ways men are luckier than women, but a few interpret it to mean luckier than animals, or than boys, or than men in times past. Some subjects make a point of connecting answers to Item 20 with that to Item 11; for example, they may criticize the idea of luck or criticize the stem. We have not included such answers in both manuals; so some guidance may be found in the Item 11 manual.

Criticism of the stem occurs at E6 for both items, but stating that men are not lucky, or not luckier than women, occurs at E6, whereas the statement that women are not lucky occurs at E5. The difference is plausible, for it is a popular truism that men are luckier. To state that women are luckier, or as lucky as men, presumably requires some independence of thought, which is more characteristic of E6 than E5.

Common themes are used for Items 11 and 20; however, the category referring to superficial appearances occurs under privileges at E3 in Item 11, under exemptions at E4 in Item 20. Subjects say that women are lucky because they can adorn themselves, men because they do not have to. Greater emphasis on status differences in Item 20 than in Item 11 mirrors the real-world status superiority of men.

Themes:

Status (E2–E6): they are smart; they are men; they are head of the house; they are considered superior.

Exemption (E3–E7): they don't have to claim a child; they can't get pregnant; they don't have the responsibility for kids; they've never had to fight for equal treatment; they don't have the conflict of raising kids with their work.

Privilege (E2–E7): they can beat on women; they control women; they have women; they are freer than women; we live in a male-dominated society; they are given expectations to achieve, so more encouragement.

Opportunity (E4–E7): they have more sports activities; they have more career choices; they have the best of both worlds, career and family; they have opportunity to express themselves at work; the world provides them greater opportunities for self-realization.

ITEM 20: MEN ARE LUCKY BECAUSE . . .

E2 Impulsive

2-Status

a. —they are good to look at (4g)
b. —they are smart (4c)

c. —they work, have jobs (4l)
   they do not have to go to school

2-Privilege

d. —they can beat on women

e. Blatant sexuality
   they can screw girls

E3 Self-Protective

3-Exemption

a. —they can't have an unwanted pregnancy (4e, 4f, 5h)
   they don't have to claim a child
   they can have sex without getting pregnant
b. —they can get out of trouble easier than women (4h)
   they are aloud to act however they want and dont get in trouble for it [sic]

3-Privilege

c. —they control women, get what they want (5a, 5b)
   they get to be on top
   they can go out and find girls very easy
   they can tell their wives what to do
d. —they make money (4l)
   they have ladies and money
   of their money

3-Other

e. —they are lucky (5t)
   we just are
   women are unlucky
   they aren't unlucky

E4 Conformist

4-Status

*a. —they are men, not women
   they're men, but big deal
   they are men and were born that way
*b. —they are strong, physically stronger (than women) (6b)
   they have upper body strength
c. —they can do more things (2b, 5o)
   they have talent
   they are a natural with handling cars, appliances
d. —they are alive (5c)
   they exist

4-Exemption

**e. —they don't have to go through periods, childbirth (3a)
   they don't have to suffer through menopause
   they don't get cramps
   they don't have PMS
**f. —they don't get pregnant, have babies (3a, 5h)
   they women's have to have the babys not them [sic]
*g. Appearance, clothes (2a, 5e, 5g)
   they have less fat cells
   they don't have to shave their legs
   they don't have to look good all the time

they don't have to buy makeup
they do not have to wear panty hose
it doesn't take them long to get dressed
h. —they have an easy life; fewer troubles, worries, responsibilities [unspecified] (3b, 5f, 5g, 5q)
   they have fun
   they have all the breaks
i. —they don't have to do the housework
   they do not have to clean up
j. —they don't have to stay home; they can get away from children (5f)
   they can pick up and leave when they get sick of the family life
   we can put a baseball cap on & walk out of the house
   they aren't cooped up at home all day

4-Privilege

**k. —they have women; there are women (5m)
   they have us (women)
   these more women out there [sic]
*l. —they get better, higher paying jobs (2c, 3d, 5k, 5v)
   job promotion
m. —they can choose dates (etc.); don't have to wait to be asked(6m)
   They get to ask the girls out
   they can always choose the woman they want
   they propose marriage
n. —they can get married (6i)
   they have good wifes [sic]
o. —they can do what they want [unelaborated] (5o)
   they can do most any thing
   they can come and go as they please

4-Opportunity

p. Participation in specific masculine activities
   they can fly jet fighters
   they can be priest
   they have more sports activities

4-Other

q. —of a lot of things
   they can obtain certain things
   they have almost everything in their favor
r. Biblical reason
   they were the first ones created
s. Evasion of stem (6n, 6o)
   I'm not a man
   ?
   don't know what this means
   I don't know

E5 Self-Aware

5-Status

a. —they are the head of the house (3c, 6f)

they should be in control
they are providers
they are the bread winner of the family
b. —they are the dominant sex (3c, 6f, 6g)
c. —they are part of the human race (4d)
   he is made different from any other animal
   they are human beings
   they live in a wonderful world
d. —they are brave, take chances
e. —they age gracefully (4g)
   they age better than women
   they still make the rules & they are considered attractive as they age

5-Exemption

f. —they can avoid responsibility, blame [elaborated] (4h, 4j, 6d, 7a)
   they can get away with irresponsibility and live with themselves
   they usually aren't bothered with the kids
   they usually don't have to justify their actions to their family
   they are not responsible for "life and death" matters
g. —they don't have to worry about their appearance (4g, 4h)
   we are not judged by our looks as much
   they don't have to worry about becoming pregnant & losing their shape
h. —they don't have to worry about pregnancy (3a, 4f)
   they don't have to worry about having children and worrying about menstruation
i. —they can get away with bad behavior (3b)
   they can take charge & do things w/o being talked about [that] if a woman does she is talked about as being bad
   they are not accountable for "sins"
   we can act up and not be put down
j. —they can protect themselves
   they can walk at night alone
   they can walk down the street without being hassled
k. —they work only eight hours (4l)
   their job is not a 24 hour a day job
   they work & bring home the $ & nothing else

5-Privilege

*l. —they are freer, more independent than women (6h)
   they are self-reliant
   they have more freedom within their family: example, stay out late
   they can isolate themselves easier than women can
   they have the room and freedom to roam
*m. —they have women to take care of them, help them (4k)
   they are pampered
   women often cater to their needs
   they have good women behind them

they have people that care about them
n. —they have more rights, choices
   they are treated better
o. —they can do what they want, go where they please [elaborated] (4c, 4o)
   they can go places whenever they want and not act too fearful
p. —they can be aggressive, demanding, assertive
   they have power
   they seem to have more energy
   they go out and make things happen
q. —they are carefree (4h)
   they seem to have more fun
   they can be playboys
   they know how to enjoy life
   they are able to be silly, self-absorbed and selfish
r. —girls want them
   women can't live without them
s. Male cameradie (8a)
   they have each other
   they generally don't have to deal with female politics
t. —of fate (3e)
   luck was in the stars for them
u. —they can pee standing up
   they can stand up in gas station restrooms
   they don't have to wait to go to the bathroom

5-Opportunity

**v. —they have more (career) opportunities, advantages (4l, 6k, 6l)
   the working world expects them to be there
   they generally earn more than women for the same job
   they usually have more time to study
   it is easier for them to get a job & be promoted
   they do not have as many obstacles
   his needs have always been accepted 1st
   every day is another opportunity
w. —they can be fathers
   their biological clock has no time limit
   they help bring life to being

E6 Conscientious

6-Status

*a. —they are considered superior; they get respect
   they often command more respect, get paid more, & are picked for important jobs
   they are automatically taken more seriously, in every aspect
   they are perceived as more powerful
   'stereotypically' they don't get bullied around
   they do not have to prove themselves, as women do
   they have social status
   no one questions their right to be
*b. —they are more stable, stronger emotionally (4b)

they don't seem to have as much guilt as women
they are not as sensitive as women
most of them do not believe in emotional ties
they can control their emotions—they don't cry in public
they seem not to base their decisions on emotions, more so on reality
people do not expect them to feel a lot
they don't have as many mood swings
they are a very strong group

6-Exemption

*c. —they are not as apt to be discriminated against, judged by others (7e)
there is less prejudice against them in the work force, and they can go to the bathroom standing up
they are more free to do what they want to without having a name put to them like women do
they are seen as just people without their sexuality being a factor
they've never had to fight for equal treatment
they're not downgraded about women they see like women are
they are not as apt to be sexually harassed

d. —they are free of household, child responsibilities, worries (5f)
they do not feel the responsibilities of family life (household, nurse maid etc.) as a female does
they can too easily remove themselves from a difficult situation, as opposed to working things out (i.e., families & marriages)

6-Privilege

*e. Advantages given men by society (7b)
society's rules are not as strict for them
not as much is expected of them
cultural mores offer them more options in life
this society enables them to fulfill their dreams
they don't have all the stereotypes & images to uphold about the way they act and look
they have history & momentum on their side
they can take more initiative in our society
society sees them as better suited for most "status" jobs

*f. —they make decisions, make the rules (5a, 5b)
they still control many resources/much power, although that's changing, as it should
they've always had the opportunity to be in control
they are generally the most powerful due to the "good ole boy" network
they are expected to be leaders
they are in the driver's seat

*g. —it's a man's world (5b)
our culture favors men
we live in a male dominated society

we have the advantage of living in a patriarchal society

h. —society allows, encourages their freedom (5l)
their parents let them be more independent than daughters
they are encouraged to be independent & not to let failure stop them
they are free to do many things that women would feel uncomfortable doing, e. g., going out alone
the assumption is they can & will be self-sufficient

i. —they have women to love, share with; they are loved by women (4n)
of their capacity to love and think
we have the privilege of loving & caring for a wife
they have women for companions
they get to enjoy women!

j. —their roles are clearly defined
society feels they should have certain jobs

6-Opportunity

k. —they are better able to get ahead, achieve more, shape their own lives (5v)
they can be driven internally to achieve a goal
they climb more easily up the corporate ladder
they have an opportunity to become part of the system
they control their own destiny
it's sometimes easier to choose a career and not be pressured

l. —they can pursue a larger variety, more interesting careers; they can have career and family life (5v, 7a)
they have the best of both worlds, career and family life
they have so many diverse opportunities to make a living
they have a satisfying family and professional life

m. —they have the initiative, the advantage in dating [elaborated] (4m)
they are in control over the progression of their relationships with women
it is easier to find the "right" person than it is for women to find the right man
they are allowed more freedom in relationships
they don't seem to have to worry about their relationships as much as women

6-Other

*n. —they are not luckier than women (4s)
for what reason?
they can wear pants when it's cold. I've always thought women were luckier
are we really?
—I don't feel lucky

o. —question not answerable (4s)

*(I think the lucky questions are not really answer-
able. No one sex is luckier than the other)*
—*(meaningless for me)*
—*can't complete—I don't believe that men as a
group are luckier than any other group (women,
children, dogs)*
p. —they think they are
they have a supremicists view of themselves

E7 Individualistic

7-Exemption

a. Freedom from career-family conflicts (5f, 6l)
*they don't have the conflict of raising kids with their
work*
*they don't have to think if they want a career or a
family, they almost automatically get the career
and the family is optional*
*they have the luxury to detach from domestic life
completely when work occupies their minds*

7-Privilege

*b. —society teaches, expects them to achieve; social
structure favors them [elaborated] (6e)
*they don't have to cope with the passive expectations
of femininity*
*society's expectations of them as to child-rearing,
relationships, and everything except work and
sports, is so low that they easily meet those expectations*
*they are respected for their accomplishments more
readily than women are*
*they are given expectations to achieve so are often
given more encouragement*
*they do not have to struggle for the "right" to blaze
new territories*
*they were raised from little on that career and edu-
cation was important*
*others assume that they "can do" in times of physical
and intellectual stress*
c. —they can be themselves, grow, give to others (8b)
they are more free than women to be themselves
*of their chance to live and grow and have relation-
ships*
they have the ability to give to people
*(of women—joking) they can live their lives to the
fullest if they choose*
*being born a human is a unique opportunity for
growth*
their roles allow them to be themselves
*they are afforded so many chances for growth and
development*
*They can protect, care for, and provide for their
families*
d. Recognition of individuality

they are able to maintain their individuality
*they have been encouraged to be individuals but
usually they fail to do so*
e. —they have an unfair advantage (6c)
*society allows them more individual freedom than
women. This should be changing, but I think it is
true today*
*unfair though it may be, the system is stacked in
their favor*
*they enjoy the top places in our society (even though
they might not deserve them)*
*their wants and desires are more readily accepted
into society*

7-Opportunity

f. —they can use their knowledge, express their talents
*their bodies are made such that they can use them
to do a great many things in the physical world*
*they have opportunities to develop their potentials,
albeit not always adequate or successful*

7-Other

g. Contradictions and paradoxes
*they have so much freedom in planning their lives—
woman's lib notwithstanding*
*they are placed in the dominating position, even
though they are usually morally weaker*
*women still let them believe they are the stronger
sex*

E8 Autonomous

a. Less subject to trivial problems and worries (5s)
*they can do what they want more; women seem so
trapped into dull & petty roles*
*they don't have to deal with gossip or social pres-
sures or problems of friends quite to the extent
that women do*
*they don't have to worry about makeup and dress
style, otherwise men and women are equally lucky,
assuming fate is to be considered a valid concept*
*they have fewer negative feelings than women (such
as fear and envy)*
b. Self-realization, self-development (7c)
*the world did & still does provide greater opportu-
nities for self-realization*
c. Complex, original elaboration of E6 ideas
*they are usually socialized to go after the things they
want, to use anger without as much guilt*
*in our society, career goals and sex roles are not
that far apart*
*we can generally get away from the tedium & the
racket by going to work, and feel good about our
value*

I Just Can't Stand People Who . . .

Probably many people have thought of this very question, because there are many brief answers, even as high as E6. The themes chosen form a gradient: from annoying personal habits; to trivial faults, socially but not really morally reprehensible; to traits that are debatable though usually pejorative; to what are generally agreed to be moral defects. (Unfortunately, thematic decisions in this case put the manual-makers into an uncomfortably judgmental position.)

Annoying behaviors are prominent from E2 through the Conformist levels (E4 and E5); however, not everyone will agree that some of the behaviors, such as being a politician or sending out questionnaires, are reprehensible or annoying. Peccadillos are prominent at E3 through E5. Traits are important at E4 and all higher levels. In some cases, these could be rephrased without much change of meaning to be favorable traits: "aggressive" could become "assertive," "criticize" could become "uses critical intelligence," "won't stand up for their beliefs" could become "agreeableness," and so on. The predominant interest in moral defects at level E6 fits well with its designation as the Conscientious stage. Some of the objected-to traits at that stage also have moral overtones. The moralistic tone is less prominent at the highest stages.

The two most popular topics are some versions of conceit and looking down on others, peaking at E5, and insincerity, peaking at E6. The former goes from "are snobbish" (E4f), to "think they are better than others" (E5d), to "care only about status" (E6f), to "are intolerant" (E7f). The latter goes from "talk behind your back" (E4g), to "are two-faced" (E5s), to "are hypocrites" (E6m). Particularly in the latter case, the progress from behavioral description to characterological description is evident.

Many responses include lying or cheating along with some other thought; in such cases the other part should govern the rating.

Themes:

Annoying behaviors (E2–E5): make me mad; pick their nose; show off; are boring.

Peccadillos (E3–E6): talk too much; boast; put others down; pontificate.

Traits (E2–E7): fight; are stupid; are conceited; are bossy; are selfish; are narrow-minded.

Moral defects (E2–E7): are mean; steal; are unfair; are insincere; are bigoted.

ITEM 21: I JUST CAN'T STAND PEOPLE WHO . . .

E2 Impulsive

2-Annoying behaviors

    a. —make me mad (3c)
      I hate

2-Traits

    b. —fight
      fight, cuss and use bad words

2-Moral defects

    c. —are mean, nasty (5v, 6n)
      laugh at me and people
      does bad to other people [sic]

E3 Self-Protective

3-Annoying behaviors

    a. Annoying appearance or personal habits (4e)

chew with their mouth open
pop their gum
whistle loudly
piss all over the toilet
stare
b. Smell
   are dirty and not clean
c. —give me a hard time (2a)
   call me names
   tell on me
   disobey me
   get on my nerves
d. —send me questionnaires
   bug you to death to finish their damn survey
   make up questionaires

3-Peccadillos

*e. —talk too much (4a, 5a, 5h)
   are blabber-mouths in class
   talk too much & start trouble
f. —are nosy
   mind my business
g. —are lazy (5n)
h. —nag

3-Traits

i. —are stupid (5r)
   are crazy
   act silly
   ask the same dumb questions day after day

3-Other

j. Unclassified
   are really smart
   babble—are dweebs, dipsticks (that constitutes the
      majority of people in world)

E4 Conformist

4-Annoying behaviors

a. —are loud (3e)
   lack certain manners or talk loud on streets
   have big mouths
b. —show off

4-Peccadillos

*c. —brag; boast (5d, 6b)
   praise themselves
   brag when they have nothing to brag about
*d. —think they know it all (5i)
   think they no so much & don't no anything at all
      [sic]
e. —smoke; drink too much (3a)
   drink and drive
   drink alcohol
   take drugs

4-Traits

*f. —are conceited, arrogant, snobbish (5j)
   are cliquey
   put on airs
   snub me
*g. —gossip; talk behind your back (5s, 6m)
   talk about people and they are no better than them
h. —can't stand people (6u)
   seem to reject me
   can't stand me

4-Moral defects

**i. —lie; steal (6l)
   aren't honest
   tell tales
   cheat and lie

E5 Self-Aware

5-Annoying behaviors

a. —are boring (3e)
   are dull & pompous
b. —are politicians
   run this country
   are liberals
   are agitators
   are "rednecks"
c. Are against (for) religion
   have no regard for God
   make a "show" of their religion

5-Peccadillos

*d. —think they are better than others, than they really
      are (4c, 6b)
   have big egos of themselves
   think they are so great and no one else matters
   aggrandize themselves
   are smug
*e. —belittle others (6n)
   patronize others
   are insulting
   cut down other people
   treat me like a child
   look down at military personnel
   make fun of others and treat them as inferiors
   talk about me as though I'm not even there
*f. —complain; whine (6c, 6h)
   are eternally pessimistic
   always gripes [sic]
   lament over nothing
g. —feel sorry for themselves
   are hypochondriacs
   feel completely victimized
   are full with self-pity and excuses
h. —talk and say nothing (3e, 6a)
   ask tons of questions just to talk

just talk w/o thinking first
tell the same stories over & over
talk too much and do too little

i. —won't listen; don't come to the point (4d, 6e, 7a)
interrupt me while I'm talking
ask for advice and don't follow the advice
are not good listeners or self-centered in conversations
interrupt without knowing what the conversation is about
ramble when they speak

j. —are obnoxious, overbearing (4f)
are vulgar
are ostentatious
are crude & pushy
butt into a conversation
come on strong—are so positive

5-Traits

*k. —always criticize
berate others
are always finding fault with others
preach
are cynical and sarcastic

l. —are aggressive, bossy (6i, 8a)
want to impose their rules
are intimidating

m. —judge others [unelaborated] (7b)
judge too much

*n. —refuse to try (3g, 6j, 7e)
have no initiative
think that they know everything and cannot learn anything new
repeat the same mistakes over and over
have no goals
give pat answers without really looking at the questions
don't care
won't help themselves
refuse to think

o. —won't stand up for themselves, their beliefs (6s)
don't speak their mind
follow blindly
let other people run their lives

p. —have no confidence (6j)
think they are inferior to me
have no self-esteem

q. —have no sense of humor
can't take jokes, who are mean
never do anything wild & crazy once in awhile
never laugh

r. —are ignorant (3i)
are incompetent

5-Moral defects

s. —are two-faced (4g, 6m)

say one thing and do another

t. —are unfair (6r, 7b)
unfairly criticize other people
are unjust and violent

u. —don't care about the world's problems, people in need (6d)
don't help others and are greedy
do not fight for human rights
complain about things and don't try to change them

v. —hurt others [unelaborated] (2c, 6n)
neglect their children
are unkind

5-Other

w. Unclassified
accuse me of something I haven't done
fight for a wrong reason
won't look me in the eye
think their children are angels
have no social skills

E6 Conscientious

6-Peccadillos

a. —talk about things they don't know about (5h)
speak authoritatively from ignorance
tell me "my reality"
pontificate
posture

b. —brag about their achievements (4c, 5d)
always seem to have to outdo everyone at someone else's expense
have to let you know they are very important in their business or profession

c. Complain without a good reason (5f)
complain about money when they have more than is necessary
always says they fail a test and then gets 90 [sic]
complain about everything, nothing that you do pleases them

6-Traits

*d. —are selfish, self-centered (5u, 7a, 7d)
are wrapped up in themselves
are on ego trips
don't think about others
are egocentric
say "I" a lot
have no respect for anyone but themselves
are self-absorbed

e. —are self-righteous, always right (5i, 7a)
are opinionated
are always blaming others
are wrong and they won't admit it

f. —care only about status, material things
drop names

brag about material possessions
care only about clothes and becoming friends w/
popular people only
spend their whole lives worried about keeping up w/
the "Jones"
are totally materialistic
are pretentious

g. —are shallow, impulsive, emotional
stay mad
see everything as clear-cut black and white
don't think before they do something
say the wrong thing at the wrong time
have no discretion

h. Negative view or approach to life (5f)
talk too much (especially about others or negative
things)
always talk behind other people's backs and never
have anything positive to say
are negative & complain
who are angry at the world in general

i. —are manipulative [unelaborated] (5l, 8a)
obviously conniving

j. —can't make decisions (5n, 5p)
are indecisive or self-deprecating

k. —are unrealistic
spout weird fanatic theories about UFO's killing
JFK, whales who telepathically control the eco-
logical net of the Earth, etc.
constantly play mind games and basically live in a
total fantasy world
refuse to acknowledge reality

l. —are not honest with themselves (4i)
deceive themselves and others

6-Moral defects

**m. —are hypocrites, phony; try to be something they're
not (4g, 5s)
are not sincere
lie & pretend to not understand something when they
do
act fake
change the way they are to fit in with a new group
are flashy and artificial
pose

*n. —are cruel; purposely hurt others (2c, 5e, 5v)
mistreat others
abuse children or sexually abuse anyone
carelessly hurt their friends
don't care about animals

*o. —are irresponsible, unreliable, untrustworthy
break promises
think they can say and do whatever they like
welsh on commitments
never get their assignments completed
don't carry their weight
inconsistent and incompetent

p. —are prejudiced (7f)
discriminate based on race or creed
are biased
are racist
won't accept people for what they are
have personal hatred against other people
label others
are chauvinists

q. —are inconsiderate (7c)
are rude to waitress
are discourteous
carry one-way conversations and have no respect
for what you have to say

*r. —take advantage of others; have no regard for oth-
ers' rights (5t)
try to get over by stepping on others
lie & use people
try to get other people to do their work for them
don't respect privacy

s. —are opportunists (5o)
kiss ass
are maliciously sly
try to sneak 12 items into the 11 items or less line
lie to achieve

6-Other

t. Three contrasting elements, one E5 (7g)
jump to conclusions without listening to the situation,
who are conservative
are noisy, vulgar and put other people down

u. Rejection of stem (4h)
(nobody really)
(there are some people I can't stand a bit, but not
many that I can't stand 100%)
say they just can't stand a certain type of person
There are people I can't stand, but I am not sure
that I can categorize them into groups

v. Unclassified
do things well that I do poorly
litter and destroy public property

E7 Individualistic

7-Traits

*a. See things only from their own viewpoint; are
closed-minded (5i, 6d, 6e)
are arbitrary & inflexible
are hypocrites, narrow-minded and cruel
are narrow-minded & rigid
refuse to even hear ideas, thoughts, beliefs, etc.
self-righteously refuse to consider other positions

b. —are judgmental; judge people unfairly (5m, 5t)
pass judgment on others before they get to know them
have excessively rigid principles
view justice as an absolute
judge others harshly

c. —are insensitive to other people's feelings (6q)

don't care about how their actions affect other people

refuse to acknowledge my feelings

cannot greet you with a friendly smile and chat pleasantly for a moment, showing some interest in you

d. —are self-centered [elaborated] (6d)

"know everything" while avoiding knowledge of things unpleasant

put others down as a result of their own insecurities

are totally concerned with "finding who they are" and "being myself"

are mistrusting, self-centered and always negative

e. —don't make an effort to solve their problems (5n)

give up on trying to make things happen (home, work, life in general)

are static and are resistant to change

constantly sit and complain and whine and don't do anything to try to help themselves

won't make any effort to adapt

due to no mental illness can't make a decent effort to make something of themselves

assume they know before making an effort to understand

sit back and react to life

allow their talents and abilities to evaporate by laziness and apathy

7-Moral defects

f. —are intolerant, bigoted (6p)

make fun of others because of a difference in looks or ability to do something or personality

7-Other

g. Three contrasting elements, one E6 (6t)

have terrible body odors, harm others, and don't try to help themselves

are selfish, phoney and long winded

smokes a lot, lies constantly, puts on a fake plastic front to hide whoever she really is [sic]

are completely self-centered, sanctimonious, and lie

h. Unclassified

destructively rebel instead of constructively not conforming

E8 Autonomous

a. —are manipulative [elaborated] (5l, 6i)

manipulate, who do "holy" things for ulterior motives

are manipulative, etc. In general, those who do not have good intentions

insist on trying to change me without my consent

exercise power over others by manipulating them

b. Unclassified

are shiftless, lazy, & dependent, & have no respect for themselves & therefore can't respect others

lack compassion, humility, and general caring for others; though its their "behavior" I can't stand, not them

don't want to grow, mature, and expand their personality

are not in intellectual and/or emotional control of themselves

adopt a do-gooder pose out of a feeling of guilt or who blame every sin on society or parents

with total conscious awareness can cause another being pain, sadness and/or death without conscience

At Times She (He) Worried About . . .

Many female subjects take the stem to refer either to self or mother, and mother is often said to be worried about the subject; in either case, this is a self-centered response. Male subjects less often construe the person as father. (However, in an earlier form of the test, this item came after one directly referring to father, and in that case it was often taken to refer to father.) Because the stem pulls for self-centered responses, those that might a priori seem to indicate low ego level are not pathognomonic. Many of the responses classed at low levels may reflect adolescent concerns as much as low ego level, because, on average, adolescents have lower ego level than older people. There are many omissions and evasive responses ("everything," "nothing") to this stem, classed E4.

People of all ego levels worry about self, other people, and "things." What distinguishes the levels are some distance from problems of the moment, discriminating important from unimportant worries, time perspective, and distinguishing one's own view from someone else's. Concern for social and world problems is found at E5 and higher.

One characteristic low-level concern is sex. In girls and women, it is usually in terms of getting pregnant or dates and marriage. Similar concerns at higher levels usually are couched in terms of relationships, at least among women.

At E4, worries tend to be about concrete things: appearance, particularly weight; grades; health; and money. The most frequent category of response just mentions a specific family member. At E5, worries often have a more interpersonal reference, but appearance is still a major concern. Frequent concern over the future shows growing time perspective. Many subjects refer explicitly to trivial or unnecessary worries, in effect, criticizing themselves for worrying.

At E6, worries are conceived as problems, decisions, or choices, rather than just concrete things. Living up to standards is implied in many responses at this level. At E8, there may be concern for abstract and intangible aspects of experience, such as zest for life, or meeting people's expectations.

Among the categories that do not discriminate well are those referring to money, to immediate concerns, and to the future. "What people thought" (E5) discriminates surprisingly well from "what people thought about her (him)" (E6), although of course not perfectly. Themes are less helpful for this stem than category titles, because it is difficult to tell whether some responses refer to the subject or to someone else, and many categories contain answers appropriate to other themes.

Themes:

Self (E3–E7): me; her grades; her future; what people thought of her; what he was doing with his life.
People (E3–E6): boys; her children; what people thought; her home situation.
Things (E2–E6): it; money; unimportant things; financial problems.
Other (E4–E7): nothing; dying; nuclear war.

ITEM 22: AT TIMES SHE (HE) WORRIED ABOUT . . .

E2 Impulsive

2-Things

   a. —it; things (4j, 4k)

E3 Self-Protective

3-Self

   *a. —me (4b)

b. —getting pregnant
her period
not seeing her period

c. —sex [unelaborated] (5j)
aids
me going out and having sex with anybody
sex and drinking

3-People

d. —girls; boys (4g)

E4 Conformist

4-Self

*a. —grades; schoolwork; job [unelaborated] (6b)
me in math
school
how she was doing in class
her term papers

b. —himself; herself (3a)
herself more than others

c. Appearance (concrete references) (5c)
being short
his weight problem
her face
her hair
her figure

d. —my safety; my late hours (6m)
when her children was coming home [sic]
my whereabouts
me going places by myself

e. —bad breath; perspiration

4-People

**f. —his family (6k)
me and sister
my son and daughter
his family back home
her children
his future girl (wife)
where were her children

g. —other people (3d)
his girlfriend
friends

h. —her husband going out on her
where is her husband

4-Things

**i. —money (5p, 6o)
bills
where her next dollar was coming from

*j. —everything (2a)
anything
many things

k. —little things (2a, 5o)
little problems
the smallest things in the world

4-Other

*l. —nothing
nothing under the sun

m. Immediate concerns
drugs
being cut from the football team
what to make for dinner
drinking
smoke!
his fuel supply

n. Evasion
(She who?)
don't understand
?
—(stupid question)

E5 Self-Aware

5-Self

**a. —the future; life [unelaborated] (6a)
getting old
the future too often
growing up

*b. —health
my welfare
my cold
getting ill

*c. —her appearance; her looks (4c)
what she looked like while out on dates
the clothes he wore
being unattractive

d. —being liked; getting along with people (6d, 6l)
being disliked
whether or not people would come through for her

e. —getting dates; getting married (6l)
whether he was going to call
whether her relationship will last
finding the right husband
whether she would marry him
why no girl liked him

f. —doing, saying the right thing (6h)
how I'm doing
going wrong
what she might have said wrong
how to say something

g. —getting things done (6i)
*whether or not she could do everything she wanted
  to do*
all the things she was trying to handle

h. —being successful; making it in the world (6j)
becoming a failure
*whether her smarter friends would get Cum Laude
  and she wouldn't*
accomplishments

i. —my behavior
how to behave
myself when I make mistakes

getting in trouble but sometimes the fun was worth it
j. —her sexuality [standards or control implied] (3c)
having an abortion
her virginity
me and my boyfriend getting "too serious"
having sex without birth control

5-People

k. —others' health, welfare
his patients
his addiction
my family's well being
her friends drinking & driving
l. —what others thought, said (6c)
what her parents would think
who was talking about her
m. —his children's future (6a)
her children making it in this world
her children when she was gone
n. —everyone else
everyone but me

5-Things

*o. —unimportant, silly things (4k, 8d)
needless concerns
irrelevant things
things that she does not have to
p. —feeding the family (4i, 6o)
where the next meal was coming from
how she was going to get some money to feed her family
being evicted, not having food on the table

5-Other

q. —death; dying [unelaborated] (6n)
if she would live or die
r. —the world (6r)
the future of the world
the planet
everyone in the world
s. Quips
being so ravenous she would eat the refrigerator
not worrying enough
the weather
the beings from outer space who were constantly landing in his backyard
t. —balancing priorities
balancing all her responsibilities
balancing the different aspects of his life
u. —her sins
life's evil forces

E6 Conscientious

6-Self

*a. —the future [elaborated but passive tone] (5a, 5m, 7b)

love, drugs, sickness, dying and what's ahead for her
growing old alone
the future and what it held for her
what the next day would bring
what would happen when he got older
*b. —his career; finishing school; getting a job (4a)
if she would make it in her career
passing her exams
his grades and the college process
not doing well in school
losing his job
*c. —what people thought of him, her (5l, 7d)
how others treated her or looked at her
being a failure in other's eyes
the impact of his statements
other people's opinion too much
d. —being accepted (5d)
whether she "fit in" or not
being left alone without anyone to help her get along rough times
whether her friends would reject her
e. Personality traits or inner states
my stability
feeling embarrassed
his sincerity
f. —his identity [unelaborated] (7b, 7e)
being a full person
his masculinity
being herself
g. —being a good parent (7a, 8b)
how good a mother she would be
if she was doing the right thing raising her children
h. —making the right decision (5f, 7c)
whether boarding school was the right decision
doing the moral thing
the decisions he had made in his past being right or wrong
her choices
i. —doing a good job, his best (5g, 7a, 8b)
if her performance was not as good as it could be
living up to her ideal of what she should be
if I were doing the best I could
whether or not his work was acceptable or not [sic]
being able to handle all of her various "roles"
his effectiveness as a person
j. —reaching goals (5h, 7a, 7b, 7e, 8b, 8c)
having the opportunity to pursue his goals
whether she was making the most she could out of life
inadequacy; whether I can really achieve a certain goal

6-People

*k. —family problems (4f)
how she should have handled that problem with her children

having a handicapped child
how I would grow up
how his children would be as adults
her home situation
*l. —her relationships (5d, 5e)
if I truly loved her
pleasing his parents
the friends she had chosen
whether or not people really liked her
conflicts between his colleagues on the job
m. —safety [elaborated] (4d)
her kids growing up and being safe
n. Death of family members or friends (5q)
having to face an unexpected death
losing some of the people she loved

6-Things

*o. —financial problems (4i, 5p)
who is "she"? I worry about financing my children's
educations
finances
making a living
making ends meet
his retirement security
p. Time limitations
meeting deadlines
having enough time to do everything
why time went by so fast
where her quiet time would fit in
q. —things that were out of his control
things that might never happen, and that was very
foolish
things she could do nothing about
just anything she could because it was such a habit

6-Other

r. —social problems; nuclear war (5r, 8e)
the violence in this country
inflation
what kind of world this will be with pollution, nuclear
war, etc.
children that are hurting
the future of society and, indeed, of civilization
s. Disclosure
what his mother would think if she knew what he
did
someone finding out

E7 Individualistic

7-Self

a. Feelings of responsibility (elaborated) (6g, 6i, 6j, 8b)
how to be a mother, wife, & professional all at once
her ability to endure in the face of crisis
what to do next instead of what he had done

everything, the house, work, her child, and then she
decided things will happen and go with the flow
whether she had enough emotional goods to go
around
the future, her mortality, would she accomplish her
goals
spending enough energy on her family
b. Existential concerns (6a, 6f, 6j)
the future and what it will mean
no life of her own and lost opportunities
what he was doing w/ his life
the whole reason for being
his own worth

7-Other

c. Then versus now (6h)
the things in life he had done wrong and how to
correct them
her future & whether past decisions affected her still
appearances but now she's worried about life &
death
d. Implied or explicit comparison of two points of view
(6c)
things, even though she believed "worry" was un-
productive
not being able to make it, but who cares, there's
always something else
what others think, but I told her not to
[what] others would think of him; then he took a
look at the others
all the problems in the world, so he wouldn't have
to look at his own
what others thought of her. This made her try to be
someone she wasn't
my mental health because I liked being alone
pleasing others without consideration to how it was
affecting his life
how she is treated, but she doesn't know how to treat
others
e. Unclassified (6f, 6j)
her identity and her goals
how I internalized people's feelings and actions

E8 Autonomous

a. Enjoyment of life; loss of zest for life
the future so much she forgot to enjoy the present
losing her dreams and ideals and falling prey to
daily "ruts" and monotony
b. —whether she could meet the standards expected of
her (6g, 6j)
living up to the image of her older brothers and
sisters
her personal failings as judged by the standards of
her main associates
his own lack of capacity to handle the job he has
attained

c. —realizing his, her full potential (6j)
the possible decline of his creative powers
her life's destination
utilizing the full potential that lay within her power
d. Little things rather than big ones (5o)
the most nonsensical things, which occupied so much of her time that she neglected what was truly important

little things that seemed momentous because they seemed so close to her
e. Combination of broad social and personal concerns (6r)
money, health, the state of the world, and whether her son needed new shoes right now
a war which destroyed the world before she fulfilled her dreams

I Am . . .

Most responses to this stem can be classed as referring to one's circumstances, traits, feeling states, or identity. All of these terms are used here broadly, not in any restricted or technical sense. Feelings include physical states as well as emotions, particularly at E4 and lower.

The largest single category describes circumstances in matter-of-fact terms, the kind of demographic information that can be recorded on a checklist. Responses in this category, scored E4, account for a large proportion of cases below E4 and rarely occur above E6.

Other kinds of responses that occur frequently are variations on "lucky," "happy," or "me," such as "who I am" or "what I am." Because such phrases are nondiscriminating, if there is another element to the response, it should govern the scoring. Surprisingly, "lucky" by itself tends to occur most often at E6, contrary to assertions in the 1970 manual. (Our data do not permit us to decide whether the difference is in the times or in the manual-making process.)

Most of the respondents sound cheerful and self-approving. Only at E3 are there many responses of negative hedonic tone, though differentiated self-criticisms are frequent at the highest levels. At E4 and lower, many responses refer to feelings of the moment; at higher levels, most people refer to longer term characteristics. Thus "happy" is rated E4, and "a happy person" is rated E5.

The interest in differentiated character traits and differentiated emotions that flowers at the Self-aware level is illustrated by the large number of categories at that level. Where a response fits a category with specific content, it should be so rated. For the many unique responses, there are categories that refer to trait descriptions in general, according to number of different ideas, and so on. Most of

the illustrative examples cited occurred more than once; others sound like what people often say about themselves and others.

Although the source and gender of the respondents was concealed during manual making, most categories have responses from both men and women and from different subsamples. However, preoccupation with "contrasting roles" (E5) is exclusively a female (in fact, a mother's) preoccupation; and students in a religious college are over-represented among those who answer that they are servants or children of God.

Although this item is not the most sensitive indicator of ego level, it has been retained because it is similar to some other approaches to the self. Emphasis on self-esteem in much of the psychology of self is at variance with what this item reveals, namely, that shallow self-approval and self-rejection characterize the pre-Conformist levels, whereas complex self-appraisals characterize the post-Conformist levels, often nonevaluative or including both positive and negative features.

Themes:

Traits (E2–E7): nice; a good person; too fat; a happy person; sensitive; emotionally independent.
Feelings (E2–E7): fine; tired of this test; happy; glad to be alive; thankful; too impulsive and self-conscious.
Circumstances (E3–E6): a man; going to graduate; too busy.
Identity (E4–E7): myself; a child of God; unsure what I am going to do with my life.

ITEM 23: I AM . . .

E2 Impulsive

2-Traits

a. —nice (3a, 5b)
a nice person

2-Feelings

b. —fine, o.k. (4g)
feel good today

E3 Self-Protective

3-Traits

*a. —a good person (2a, 4d, 5b)
cool

b. —boy crazy (4k)
a sex crazed maniac and part-time worker at a clothing store

c. —crazy; stupid

d. —lovable, lovely (4b, 5o)
a lovely person

3-Feelings

e. —tired of these questions (4h. 5s, 6i, 6l)
wondering why I am doing this

f. Self-rejection (4a, 6d, 7b)
always mean
a selfish person
very ugly

g. —worried, depressed [diffuse] (4l)
a worried mom
very uptight right now

3-Circumstances

h. —careful whom I talk to
very careful with whom I play with [sic]

E4 Conformist

4-Traits

*a. Appearance (3f)
too short
overweight
beautiful

b. —friendly; easy to get along with (3d, 5b, 5j)
a warm person
laid back
very outgoing person
polite

c. —smart; not smart (5d)
bright
an intelligent Black woman
sensible

d. —honest, dependable (3a, 5e)
trustworthy

a good & decent person
a responsible man

e. —strong; assertive (5c, 5g, 5h)
always certain of what I want
powerful

f. —average, normal (5bb)
a well-adjusted person

4-Feelings

**g. —happy [immediate feelings] (2b, 5a, 5n, 6f, 6g, 7c)
a mother and I'm happy

*h. —tired [unelaborated] (3e, 6i)
bored with daily routines
sick of nursing school
sleepy

i. —feeling good about myself (5a, 5g, 5n, 7c)
happy with who I am

j. —hungry (5z)

k. —in need of a partner (3b, 5t)
happy that I have a boyfriend, [name]
always sad because I don't have a steady boyfriend
alone

l. —worried [specified] (3g)
not worried about sex
worried about getting an incurable disease

4-Circumstances

**m. Demographics: name, age, sex, occupation, marital status . . .
in the tweltfh grade
not a teenager
a Capricorn
Jamaican
healthy
5 ft 2", of average intelligence, married, and have two children
pregnant

n. Role or function in family (5x, 5y)
a good mother
a single parent

4-Identity

**o. —me [unelaborated] (6n)
what I am
myself

p. —somebody special
wonderful
a magnificent person
somebody

q. —. [Period]

E5 Self-Aware

5-Traits

*a. —a happy person (4g, 4i, 6f, 6g, 7c)

in a good mood most of the time
happy with my life, right now
happier each year
*b. —caring, kind, understanding (2a, 3a, 4b, 6b)
  a good friend
  a loving, warm person
  a samaritan
  a soft touch to charities
  a person who feels a concern about everyone
*c. —hard working, ambitious (4e, 6m, 6j)
  struggling so hard to get everything in life to take
    care of me and my child
  a determined person
  going to be somebody important
  a competitor
  not quitting anything
  a person with many goals and a person set on achiev-
    ing those goals
d. Abilities; achievements (4c)
  honoured to be on varsity lacrosse as a sophomore
  #2 in my class
  getting better at my job
  very cheerful, fun to be around, can do anything that
    I want to if I put my mind to it
  talented
  a woman who is just as capable as any man
e. —serious; sincere (4d)
  real
  too serious sometimes
f. —trying to do my best (6h)
  striving to be the best I can
  trying
  trying to do what is right
  a person who tries to be fair to everyone
g. —in control; self-confident (4e, 4i, 7d)
  my own boss
  a calm person
  my own person
  everything I want to be and more
  in charge of my life
h. —able to take care of myself; independent (4e, 7d)
  bound to succeed
  able to deal with my problems
  a survivor!
  happy, healthy and self-empowering daily
i. —shy; an introvert (6d)
  timid
  extremely unassuming
j. —funny (4b)
  a fun person
k. —an optimist
  optimistic towards the future
l. —lazy
m. Character trait (single idea) (6b, 6d, 6e, 6p)
  a positive person
  a modern person
  very open-minded about most things

a good listener
a private person
a leader
a very cautious person
very spontaneous
compulsive
a very flexible person
organized

5-Feelings

n. —glad to be alive (4g, 4i, 6f, 6g)
  glad to be alive & whole considering my life expe-
    riences
  glad to be a woman
  thankful for life
  a femme soul—I love it
  young and full of life
o. —in love (3d)
p. Feelings about school (graduation, vacation)
  glad the semester is almost over
  very nervous whenever I have to take a test
  anxious to graduate
  happy here at [school]
  looking forward to our vacation next week
q. —proud
  proud to be in school even at age 34
  proud of my family
  proud of being a Puerto Rican woman
r. —unsure, insecure [unelaborated]
  confused
  going through a really rough time
  unsettled
  very self-conscious sometimes
s. —at a loss to answer these questions (3e, 6l)
  trying to think of answers, I can't
  taking a heavy-duty psychological test presently
t. —lonely (4k)
  lonely but content
  a person who feels lonely easily
u. —hard on myself (6d, 7b)
  too negative about myself
  upset with myself
v. Thoughts, feelings about the future (vague, general)
  scared of the future of my children
  afraid of getting older
  a girl who has many dreams
  very excited about my future

5-Circumstances

w. Reference to future status
  going to graduate at the end of this year. (I hope)
  ready to make it as a successful recording artist
  going to be an accountant
  trying hard to graduate and get a good job
x. —looking forward to marriage, family (4n)
  getting married May 27, 1989

very happily married, and anxious to start a family
y. —lucky to have my family (friends) (4n, 6f, 7e)
   happy to have people who love and care for me
   very happy in my marriage
z. Immediate actions (4j)
   here
   filling out this form right now
   alive
   drinking tea

5-Identity

*aa. —a child (servant) of God
   one of Jehovah's witnesses
   a Christian
   a child of G-d, a mother, a wife, a daughter
   truly happy God found me in time!
bb. —a human being (4f)
   a whole person
   therefore should be respected
   as much a person as anyone else
   just a normal human being
cc. Contrasting roles
   a mother, a student, a friend, and a confidant
   a woman, mother, wife, nurse & student & teacher,
     therefore I'm tired

E6 Conscientious

6-Traits

a. Interests
   a person who loves nature to the fullest
   interested in people
   an avid reader
b. —sensitive (5b, 5m)
   over-sensitive
   very emotional when it comes to others
   a sincere, sensitive, affectionate person
c. Contradictory attributes (7a, 8a)
   eager to be friendly but shy with new friends
   *a caring person who likes to help people out and I
     also can be a person who can be sneaky and
     spiteful*
   an easy going, stubborn, opinionated, caring person
   *observant, frank, sincere, & hot tempered and stub-
     born*
   productive, but feeling burnt out
   *as good as I try to be but can be as bad as I want
     to be*
   intelligent but insecure
   usually optimistic but realistic
d. Differentiated character trait (often somewhat self-
   critical) (3f, 5i, 5m, 5u, 7a, 7b)
   usually honest with myself
   overly conscientious
   a procrastinator
   too much of an introvert at times

very honest and open—sometimes to a fault
somewhat of an iconoclast
still basically shy and reserved, a private person
*e. Character traits (two different ideas, one E5) (5m,
   7a)
   somewhat law abiding, good natured person
   shy, impulsive, & determined to become a nurse
   considerate, generous, honest, and intelligent
   a very loving, outspoken person
   a person with dignity & a strong value system
   I am insecure, flirty, fairly pretty, not very outgoing

6-Feelings

*f. —lucky, thankful (4g, 5a, 5n, 5y, 7c, 7e)
   a blessed man
   so grateful
   fortunate
*g. —content, satisfied (4g, 5a, 5n)
   doing pretty well at this point in my life
   usually content with the way I am
   clean & serene
   at peace
   *the only person I know who doesn't need "every-
     thing"*
*h. —trying to change (5f, 7f, 8b)
   learning more about myself
   growing—I hope
   a young woman learning & experiencing life
   trying to put my life back together
   trying to be a better Christian and a better person
   changing rapidly
i. —tired [elaborated] (3e, 4h)
   under a lot of stress currently
   tired of nurturing my husband so much
   tired of working so hard
   drained most of the time & a bit unhappy

6-Circumstances

j. —busy (5c)
   a very busy person who is frequently lonely
   too busy
   swamped with homework
k. Benign humor
   the all-being master of time, space and dimension
   demonically possessed by Richard Nixon
   therefore I think?
   the great I am
   and you are too
l. Speculation about the test (3e, 5s)
   wondering about this study
   interested in what this test is about

6-Identity

*m. —concerned with my direction in life (5c, 8b)
   deciding who I am

a good old country boy trying to make something out of myself

a person who enjoys life and knows what my goals are

determined to get my doctorate

very unsure about what I am going to do w/ my life

searching for new things to try

finally setting my life in order as of from today

*n. —me [elaborated] (4o)

an original

myself, not my mother, father, brother, cousin, or friend, just ME!

unique

me, take me as I am

who I am. And that's great!

basically the same person I always have been

myself and try to be no other

o. Social consciousness

a philanthropist

upset with the structure of false democracy

a guy who likes to see good things being done

an idealist

a young Latino with a conscious understanding of the disadvantaged positions of all third world people

I am a liberal person who hates war, prejudice and people who are afraid to be what they are

p. —complex [unelaborated] (5m)

dynamic

q. Body and soul

at best a man with a self, and at worst making above minimum wage

a human being with supernatural soul & free will

E7 Individualistic

7-Traits

a. Character traits (three diverse ideas, one E6) (6c, 6d, 6e, 8a)

[age], happy w/ my life, strong willed, soft hearted, and an only child

a very conscientious and considerate liberal person

honest, trustworthy & most always very happy with who I am & what I stand for

beginning to become happy, joyous & free, and very grateful for this

an intelligent, sensitive person trying to keep from becoming stagnant

7-Feelings

b. Self-accepted self-criticism (3f, 5u, 6d)

too impulsive and self-conscious

always spread too thin and always unable to find time to adequately complete one task

a perfectionist & cannot stand when things are not carried out the way they should be

what I am: a good enough person but don't try me too hard

almost invariably apprehensive of intellectual inferiority

occasionally aloof because I'm actually not sure what to do

c. —happier (about myself) than I used to be (4i, 4g, 5a, 6f)

more content with myself than when I was younger

d. —self-sufficient [elaborated]; emotionally independent (5g, 5h)

happy that money has never influenced my life to make me disregard important things

self-motivated and self-relying

emotionally independent and physically dependent

e. Gratification in interpersonal relations (5y, 6f)

grateful for health, supportive family & opportunities for growth

a whole person because I love people (family) and they love me!

happiest when I know I can trust people

7-Other

f. Psychological causation; growth (6h, 8b)

a combination of past experiences & everything around me

a positive, growth-oriented person

E8 Autonomous

a. Inner conflict (6c, 7a)

getting more stable with age, with less conflicting thoughts and emotions

confident in the way I look, but scared to death of everything else

a child inside a man's body

alternately self-confident and uncertain about myself and sometimes amazed at the swings those perceptions and feelings take

excited about the future and apprehensive about the future

an interesting person, full of paradoxes

b. —developing [elaborated] (6h, 6m, 7f)

on my way up the ladder of self-fulfillment

a woman who came late accepting herself as a woman

proud that by trial and error, I am continuing to learn about and experience the beauty of life on earth

a very organized person now, even though I was very messy as a child

a devoted person on the path to reaching my real potential

A Woman Feels Good When . . .

At low ego levels feeling good often means an immediate bodily sensation; at higher levels it tends to refer to a frame of mind and a longer term. In general, the higher the level, the more interpersonal the emphasis.

Major themes are gratification of sensual or other wishes; accomplishments, beginning with looking good and proceeding to work and achievements; relationships; being loved and needed; and identity.

Direct reference to sexual gratification is more likely at the lowest and highest levels than at intermediate ones. This creates a difficult problem, because most confusions or misreadings involve only small differences in rating, whereas in this case the difference may be between E2 and E6. Crude remarks are usually at low levels; sexuality often is expressed in terms of a relationship at high levels.

Categories referring to being complimented and looking nice account for a major proportion of responses at E4. The category "she is loved" occurs at all levels, is not differentiating, and is classed E4 as a compromise. Variations on those E4 categories are the most frequent responses at E5. Task completed at E4 becomes accomplishment at E5. At E6, accomplishment is the most usual response, always elaborated in some way, usually with reference to goals or duties.

At E7, categories referring to individuality, roles, mutuality, and communication of feelings are similar to those of other items. Many responses integrate or contrast feeling good about personal appearance with an entirely different thought. Thus, concern for appearance is not replaced but supplemented by other concerns for women at high levels. At E8, all responses are original and most are conceptually complex. Individuality and identity may be clearly expressed.

There were many more responses in the 1970 manual to the effect that women feel good when they make a man happy, despite the fact that it was based entirely on women; the present manual also includes men. A few such responses are retained here.

Themes:

Gratification (E2–E6): she has sex; she gets new clothes; she is complimented; her needs are met; she feels good about herself.

Accomplishments (E3–E7): her work is done; she looks attractive; she accomplishes something; she creates something original; she is seen for her ability, not her sex.

Relationships (E3–E7): a guy takes her out; she is loved; she is appreciated; she is in love with a man who loves her; she is accepted as a person.

Identity (E5–E7): she knows what she wants; she has reached her potential; she is true to her self.

ITEM 24: A WOMAN FEELS GOOD WHEN . . .

E2 Impulsive

2-Gratification

a. —she has sex [unelaborated] (6c)
   being kissed on her neck

she gets screwed
b. Resting; eating (3e, 5h)
   she gets a nap
   she gets enough to eat
c. —she feels good (3d)

E3 Self-Protective

3-Gratification

*a. —she is given something she likes (5a)
she is going shopping
she has a rich husband
she gets new clothes
you give her diamonds

b. —she gets what she wants (4c, 4d, 5g, 5u)
she gets everything
she gets to go
she buys something she likes

c. —she's through her period
there off there period [they're off their period]
at the beginning of the month

d. —she is happy (2c)
she is having fun

3-Accomplishments

e. —she has her work done (2b, 5h)
she gets home from work
the housework is done

3-Relationships

f. —she is with a man [no implication of continuing relation] (4n, 5s)
she meets someone special
a guy takes her out
she finds herself a nice looking man

g. —she has a man (4n)
she has a boyfriend
she is married

E4 Conformist

4-Gratification

*a. —she is complimented, praised (5c, 5m, 5p, 6f)
a man gives her a compliment
she is whistled at

b. —she feels secure [unelaborated] (6a, 6d)
she's accepted
she has financial security

c. —everything goes her way (3b, 5f)
she gets her way

d. —she has money (3b)
she gets the alimony check
she has money and has good looks

e. —she is healthy
she is physically fit
she exercises

f. —she has had a bath
she takes long bath

4-Accomplishments

*g. Concern with appearance of self or house (5b, 5c)
she looks good

she loses weight
she gets dressed up

*h. —she is successful; she has done a good job (5j, 6e)
she does her work right
she makes it to the top
she puts on a great party

i. Meeting vague standards (unelaborated) (6e)
she does what is right
she pleases her husband
she's satisfied
she is proven worthy
she is useful

j. —everything is going well at home (5d)
she can take care of her family
all's well with her dear ones

k. —she wins (5k)
she defeats a man
she is in control

4-Relationships

**l. —she is loved (5n, 5q, 6i, 6j, 6k)
she is cared for
a man cares about her
she is loved, truly loved
her children love her

*m. —she is in love (5q, 6i)
she loves

n. —she has a good man [continuing relation implied] (3f, 3g, 5s)
she is in a good relationship
she has a good caring mate
she can find a husband who doesn't cheat on her & just be satisfied for her only
her man is faithful

o. —she has had a baby; she is pregnant
she gives birth
she becomes: mother
she successfully breast feeds
she holds her child

E5 Self-Aware

5-Gratification

a. —she is treated well (3a, 6l, 6m)
her needs are met
she is pampered
she receives comfort

b. —she knows she looks good (4g)
she fits into everything she tries on
she looks, feels and smells good

c. —she is complimented about her looks (4a, 4g)
she is told she looks nice

d. —her family is happy (4j)
when she knows her children are happy, healthy
her husband loves her and her kids are happy

e. Accomplishments or development of her children
when her children accomplish something good in life
she has raised her children well

f. —things are going right (4c)
there are no problems to worry about
life is good to her
nothing goes wrong
one day goes perfect!

g. —she is able to do what she wants (3b, 6b)
she's doing what makes her happy
she does what makes her feel good

h. —she can relax [elaborated] (2b, 3e)
she has had some sleep after a long and stressful day
she can be herself & have time to herself

i. —her life is in balance (6g)
she balances everything
there is harmony in her life

5-Accomplishments

*j. —she has accomplished something (4h, 6e)
she's done something she's proud of
her hard work is reflected in her surroundings
she finishes something she started
the day has been fruitful
she does creative things—cooking—cleaning—furniture arranging

k. —she is better than, as good as a man (4k)
she surpasses the egotistical man who is chauvinistic
she has accomplished the same thing as a man
she is respected in a 'man's world'

5-Relationships

*l. —she has helped someone
she has done something good for others
she does for her family
she makes a man she loves happy
she comes through when needed
she shares of herself
she comforts an injured child
she can spend quality time with her child

*m. —she is appreciated, admired; men pay attention to her (4a, 6f)
she's noticed
her family tells her they are proud of her
she is praised as a good mother
she receives a well deserved compliment
her husband appreciates & helps her
people listen to her

*n. —she knows she is loved (4l)
she knows she is cared about
her husband treats her like a newlywed bride after 7 years
she feels loved

o. —she is respected, treated like a lady (6j, 7b)
she is treated as one

she's given attention and respect
she is told she looks pretty and is smart

p. —someone she loves compliments her (4a, 6f)
her husband tells her she looks nice every now and then
she is praised by her loved ones

q. —she is hugged, romanced (4l)
she is caressed by a gorgeous man
she is dancing with someone fun and good looking
men pour on the chivalry
she is loved and touched

r. —she is needed, wanted
she feels needed and appreciated

s. —she is with the man she loves (3f, 4n)
she's found someone she likes

t. —she is with friends, family
she has a family
her family is coming home
she is in a good company

5-Identity

u. —she knows what she wants (3b)
all she has hoped for comes true
she sets a goal in her life that she wants

E6 Conscientious

6-Gratification

*a. —she feels good about herself; she likes herself (4b, 7d)
she has self-respect and high self-esteem
she likes being who she is

b. —she is able to be selfish (5g)
she treats herself to something

c. —she has just made love, had orgasm [elaborated] (2a)
she has just made love with a man she loves
a man brings her to a level of sexual and emotional satisfaction
she's reached a goal, is praised, and when she's having sex with the man she loves

d. —she feels secure [elaborated] (4b)
she can have a feeling of security and freedom to do as she chooses
she has security and comfort
she's got a sense of security & love

6-Accomplishments

**e. Sense of accomplishment for having fulfilled goals, duties (4h, 4i, 5j)
she gets what she wants and hasn't hurt anyone in the process
she has done what she thinks is right
she is allowed to achieve her goals
she meets a challenge
she creates something original

she's accomplished something noble, and when she looks good!

she has accomplished something that is important to HER

she has done something a woman usually doesn't accomplish

she does what she set out to do

she can accomplish more than what she expected

she's able to provide a sense of kindness, warmth to others

she completes a goal, achieves, has fun, enjoys company

she knows she has done her best

f. —she is complimented for something she has done (4a, 5m, 5p)

her husband notices the work she does

she is appreciated for an achievement

she is recognized for her abilities

g. Combination of career and family (5i, 7a, 7e)

accomplishes her professional & personal goals

she accomplishes her career goals as well as establishes a family

h. —she is independent

she can manage on her own efforts

she is self-reliant

she can be happy with or without a man

6-Relationships

*i. Reciprocity in love (4l, 4m)

she is in love with a man that equally loves her

she has happy, loving relationships with people

the bond between her and her husband is strong

she is nurturing and nurtured

loved honestly and allowed to love in return openly

she has a long, honest and open relationship with a man

j. —she is loved and appreciated (4l, 5o)

she is loved and respected by friends and family

k. —she is loved for herself (4l, 7b)

she knows she's loved for who she is and not for what she's done

she is loved for herself and not for what she can give

l. —she is supported, understood (5a)

she is loved and supported

she gets the moral support she needs

she's found a man who understands her

someone is there to support and encourage her

m. —she is treated equally (5a, 7e)

she finds a man who will treat her equally

she is treated justly

6-Identity

n. —she knows who she is [unelaborated] (7d, 7f, 8a)

she is affirmed for who she is

o. —she has reached her full potential (8a)

she is able to fulfill her potential

she is able to demonstrate her competencies

p. —women are individuals, different

not having a man presume what makes her feel good

women are individuals that feel good at different times

E7 Individualistic

7-Accomplishments

a. Contrasting aspects, one at E6 (6g)

she is cared for, has people who she cares for and feels fulfilled in what she's doing

her womanhood is respected and she is supported and accepted as an equal

she accomplishes her goals & dreams and is loved and loves back

she loves others and respects herself

she is physically & mentally healthy

she is seen for her ability, not her sex

she is complimented about her looks, intelligence & cooking

she knows she is being feminine and intelligent at the same time

she knows she is loved and has the opportunity to grow

a) she gets a raise, b) drives a great car, and c) has fantastic sex

she feels loved, is assured about who she is and what she does

7-Relationships

*b. —she is treated (loved, accepted) as a person (5o, 6k)

she is taken as an individual and not type cast

she's noticed for her achievements and loved for being 'herself'

she's loved for who she is

men treat her with respect, respect for her mind and opinions

she's treated as a human being and not an object

she is accepted for what and who she is

a man cares about her feelings and likes her for herself, not just for sex

people see her as a person

c. Mutuality of interests of self and others

her talents for achieving as well as nurturing are appreciated and valued

a man is sensitive and supportive

she leads a life that is useful to herself and others

she has accomplished something meaningful to her and she probably feels even better if it means something to others also

7-Identity

d. —she is true to herself (6a, 6n)

she is free to be herself

she's doing what's right for her

she is doing something significant and important by her own standards

e. Role conception (6g, 6m)

she is able to do everything which is expected of the ideal woman (maintain a full-time career, be a perfect mother, housekeeper and wife)

a man doesn't treat her as a toy but as an intelligent person but protects her and cherishes her at the same time

she's not just a mother & a wife but something that is important to her as an individual in the outside world

you treat her as an equal and not 'as a woman'

f. —she knows who she is [elaborated] (6n, 8a)

she knows who she is and what she wants

she is healthy and has a good sense of self and knows what she wants and how to get it

she knows who she is and where she's going

E8 Autonomous

a. Achievement of individuality (6o, 6n, 7f)

has a stable sense of her self

she knows who she is and lives her life to the fullest today

she is aware that she is also an individual

she can be a full person, doing and being what she wants

she appreciates her uniqueness, accepts the totality of her experiences, (past and present, good & not so good) as positive lessons and lives in life

b. Unclassified

her sex life goes well, and when in all respects she and her husband are "sympatico"

she has everything she has dreamed of and is still able to find time to sleep

My Main Problem Is . . .

Responses to this stem can be classed broadly as behaviors, relationships, obligations (particularly in relation to school and family), feelings and thoughts, and self. Themes are less useful to raters than those of other stems, because many responses at all levels can be construed as related to more than one theme. For women, this is particularly true of relationships to men.

Relationships are important at all levels; behaviors are important from the beginning through the Conscientious level. Obligations are particularly prominent at the Conformist level. Feelings, including thoughts, are prominent at the Self-aware and Conscientious levels.

Self themes are more prominent at higher levels than at lower ones, not because people at high levels are more self-centered, but rather because they are more self-critical and have more distance from self. Thus, above E6, the need for achievement may itself be criticized, at least implicitly. However, all the E7 categories are tinged with some sense of striving, which is not true of the E8 categories. Themes are not used for E7 and E8 categories.

Some of the categories at E5, such as "Interpersonal concerns" and "Specific situations," cover quite diverse ground, as illustrated by the examples. Some examples represent responses that were repeated almost verbatim several times.

Contrast of the unclassified response at E8 with the similar category at E7 illustrates the difference in levels: At E7, the person understands his or her problems as a result of poor parenting, whereas at E8 the person no longer wants to use that as an excuse.

Themes:

Behavior (E2–E6): fighting; my mouth; being on time; talking without thinking; procrastinating.
Relationships (E3–E6): boys; getting along; solving other's problems; good family relationships.
Obligations (E3–E4): getting a job; getting good grades.
Feelings (E4–E6): my temper; I worry too much; no self-confidence.
Self (E4–E6): my weight; myself; my tendency to withdraw.

ITEM 25: MY MAIN PROBLEM IS . . .

E2 Impulsive

2-Behavior

   a. —fighting; misbehaving (4j)
     that sometimes I do bad things
     back talking

E3 Self-Protective

3-Behavior

   a. —my mouth (4a, 5a, 6f)

     my big mouth
   b. —sex (5o)
     sex because aids
     I am a nymphomaniac

3-Relationships

  *c. —other people (4d, 6g)
     my step-mother
     my friends
   d. —(not) having a boyfriend, girlfriend (4e)
     been [being?] with the man I'm with

e. —men; women
  too many girls like me
  I treat men too good & tend to get walked on
  boys

3-Obligations

f. —getting a job (4f)
  a good job
  that I'm out of work

3-Other

g. Hostility, sarcasm directed toward test (4n, 6t)
  this
  finishing trite sentences
  there are too many answers to each of these questions

E4 Conformist

4-Behavior

a. —talking (too much, too fast, etc.) (3a, 5a, 6f)
  overtalking myself
b. —getting up; being on time (6a)
  not be able to do things in time
  waking up in the morning
c. —smoking; drinking

4-Relationships

d. —getting along with people (3c, 6g)
  to get along with my father and mother
  relating to people
e. Concrete problems related to dating, marriage (3d, 5o, 5w)
  that my boyfriend loves to drink and I don't
  that I'm a slob and my wife is neat
  trying to find the right guy

4-Obligations

**f. —money; financial problems (3f)
  bills
  a lack of financial stability at this time
  the rent
**g. —school; finishing school; studying (5k)
  English classes
  test taking
  doing math
  my grades
  that I don't apply myself more with my studies
  finishing papers
  getting into the nursing program
h. —doing chores (6c)
  cleaning up
  I don't like to cook
  having to work
i. —raising a family (6g, 6i)

trying to raise my child without his father being around
j. —being good; doing the right thing (2a)
  when I make mistakes
  obedience

4-Feelings

*k. —temper; impatience [no implication of control] (6d)
  I am always mad
  I have little patience
l. Wish for freedom
  not having the kind of freedom I want

4-Self

*m. —my weight; appearance (5p)
  eating
  overcoming my weight problem

4-Other

n. —nothing; don't have any (3g, 6t)
  dont no [sic]

E5 Self-Aware

5-Behavior

a. —speaking without thinking (3a, 4a, 6f)
  I have a big mouth, I can be too insulting sometimes
  talking when I don't know what I'm saying
  my inability to keep a secret
b. —expressing myself (my feelings) adequately (6h)
  sometimes not saying what I think
  not expressing my true feelings
  talking in groups
  sometimes I hold back what I have to say, even if it will benefit me

5-Relationships

*c. Interpersonal concerns (unelaborated) (6r, 6w, 6x, 8a)
  I worry too much about what others think
  I need to be needed
  I don't care enough
  accepting criticism
  worrying what people have to say
  I do not alow [sic] to everybody to tell me what to do
  acting haughty or smartassed in social situations
d. —involvement in other people's problems
  I let everyone dump their problems on me
  I try to help everybody
  trying to please people
  stop caring too much about other people and think about myself
e. —dealing with other people's faults
  too many people are greedy

about male chauvinists
tolerating people who don't accept me
that I cannot cope with people who are phonies
enough people don't care for the soul salvation
f. —communicating [unelaborated] (6h)
getting a point across to other people

5-Feelings

*g. —I worry about everything; nervousness
I worry too much about things I can't change
letting little problems that don't mean nothing bother me [sic]
I fret too much
I worry too much and plan too far ahead
stress
anxiety
I feel tense when I think of everything I have to do
so many phobias
security
fear of what tomorrow will be like
I fear being wrong
h. —life; my future (6l)
my career
I am not sure of my future
i. —being moody, depressed, lonely
having no one to rely on
emotional
j. —I'm too shy, self-conscious (6e, 6j, 6w, 8a)
I am not personable enough
I am very shy and don't make friends easy
k. —concentration; confusion (4g, 6b)
I daydream a great deal
study habits (or lack thereof)
l. —trusting people too much
I am very trusting
m. —love
I'm in love & she isn't
falling in love, or thinking I am
that I miss my father a lot
n. —boredom; routine
being stuck in a dead end job
that I am 15 pds overweight, bored w/life, sick of school and tired
o. —fear of pregnancy; inability to become pregnant (3b, 4e)
my biological clock is ticking
p. —my health (4m)
getting old
my headache
the fear that I am having about sexual diseases
poor eyesight
my cholesterol
q. —lack of energy
my slowness
my inactivity
that I'm exhausted all the time

5-Self

*r. Backhanded compliment (7b)
I am too popular
caring too much for people
I'm too friendly and end up being hurt
I am too nice for my own good
I work too hard
s. —myself; my attitude (6k, 6x, 8d)
my pride
I tend to be put myself first [sic]
I am immature
not always having things my way
t. —people don't understand, appreciate me
people don't recognize my talents & good qualities at school
that people don't care too much for me because they think I am some strange person
I give the impression of cunning ruthlessness
u. —poor coping skills (6o, 7d)
I want things to go smoothly
I cannot solve my many problems
v. —letting go (6q)
letting go and having fun

5-Other

w. Specific situations (4e)
trying to remember where I put things
not be able to go to church more often
getting prepared before the children awake
working late nights
I take too much medication
I have no college education & can't get one at this time
being away from Steve to complete my education
I speed too much and get caught
watching too much T. V.

E6 Conscientious

6-Behavior

**a. —lack of time [unelaborated] (4b, 7a)
scheduling my time
trying to be superwoman
taking on too many projects
saying no to time demands of others
overcommitment
too little time; too many course requirements
*b. —procrastination; indecision; disorganization (5k)
having too many choices and not being able to choose
that I mull things over & over
I am not centered
indecisiveness (I think)
I see both sides of the issues
inconsistency

that I don't always follow the advice I seek until too late

c. —laziness; lack of self-discipline (4h)
I like to be laid back
self-control. I spend too much money
I don't give it all I got
that I am too impulsive and controlling
controlling my need for sweets

d. —temper; patience [emphasis on control] (4k)
trying to be considerate & patient enough with people
my bad temper, I think about things after I have done them
I get mad when people don't think before they act or speak

e. —not being assertive enough; being too aggressive (5j)
I don't always take charge when it is needed
that I am shy and I don't speak out for what I want
I'm too easygoing

f. —lack of tact; being outspoken (4a, 5a)
my arrogance
I sometimes say things which is the true but hurtful to others [sic]
I'm acrimonious with my sarcasim [sic]

6-Relationships

g. —having good family relationships (3c, 4d, 4i)
dealing with my parents
talking too much and not being consistent with my son

h. —communicating [elaborated] (5b, 5f)
trying to stay on the same wave length as my husband and have good & open communications
not being able to truly express myself in a relationship

6-Obligations

i. Concern with responsibility, outcome of child rearing (4i)
at the moment, is raising my oldest daughter's self-esteem

6-Feelings

**j. —lack of confidence, assurance; feeling insecure, inferior (5j, 6j, 8a, 8d)
self-esteem
self-doubt
a negative self-image
I am pessimistic about my own capabilities and abilities
my inability to accept praise
remembering I am competent

k. —expecting too much of myself, others (5s, 7b, 8d)
being too hard on myself
trying to fit people into a particular mold

accepting the fact that not everyone is good
accepting myself for who I am
that I tend to over-criticize people

l. —choosing goals, priorities, career (5h)
I don't know what I want to be
deciding what to devote my life to
"staying," believing I really can accomplish my goal

m. Concern with achievement, knowledge
not keeping up the standards of my family and myself
that I am pessimistic about my personal accomplishments
trying too hard to succeed

n. —lack of motivation, ambition
I try too hard to get along, without exploring outside possibilities
motivating myself when I feel like relaxing

o. —facing, coping with problems (5u, 7d)
my tendency to binge when hurt or pressured
fear & not trusting the universe
that I never face a problem head on
to cope with difficulties of the world

p. Conflicting needs, desires (8b)
being pressured between family & work
being able to separate my deep closeness for my children long enough to complete my studies undisturbed

q. —taking things too seriously (5v)
being over-sensitive
I can't take things 'too' seriously

r. —understanding, knowing myself, others (5c, 8a)
sorting out my emotions
not understanding why she doesn't love me
understanding other people's prejudices

s. —I am too stubborn, compulsive
I am very stubborn and don't give in even when I know I'm wrong
that I am too bull-headed, too determined

t. —figuring out my main problem (3g, 4n)
right now is that I can't define it
that I have so many
I didn't know I had one. I do have lots of little ones, though

u. —the way I think [unelaborated] (7c)
I analyze a lot

v. —this materialistic world
living in a dog-eat-dog society like New York City
this corrupt world we live in

6-Self

w. —my tendency to withdraw (5c, 5j, 8a)
I can't get close to people
my quiet nature—I am not as open as I would like to be
avoiding involvement

x. —self-centeredness (5c, 5s, 8a)
selfishness

lack of real morals
my lack of empathy
that I sometimes avoid people whom I have judged to be uninteresting

E7 Individualistic

7-Obligations

a. Lack of time (elaborated) (6a)
I need a hundred years to accomplish all that I want to
I want everything I accomplish today to have been accomplished yesterday
getting everything done for school & work & "being there" for my family too
stress due to pushing myself too hard at work

7-Feelings

b. —perfectionism (5r, 6k)
over-conscientiousness
am a work-aholic
I get too intense about my goals
that there are at least a dozen things I'd like to excel in

c. —thinking too much [elaborated]; thinking instead of doing (6u)
that I tend to criticize my own thoughts too much
an old anxiety-provoking thinking habit
directing more energy from a mental place into physical reality—action and risk
that I think about too many things too much, too deeply, & all at the same time!

d. Lack of realism, realistic coping (5u, 6o)
I still think of myself as 15
worrying about 'tomorrow,' instead of living life one day at a time
not being truthful with myself & others

that I talk too much; I go into too many little details that are unnecessary & unwanted

7-Other

e. Result of poor parenting (8e)
emotional immaturity due to growing up in a dysfunctional family
I received some poor parenting in my youth and I often doubt or don't realize my potentials

E8 Autonomous

a. —problems developing intimate relations (5c, 5j, 6j, 6r, 6w, 6x)
that I am not as sensitive to how my wife perceives my actions as how I ought to be
not being empathetic to others' problems
I'm afraid to get close enough to let someone hurt me

b. Contradictions and paradoxes (6p)
that I make important things trivial and trivial things too important—problem w/perspectives
a combination of feeling inadequate with arrogance

c. Meaning of life
being stuck in the mud of my existence
that I do not know the reason for my existence

d. Identity, self-worth (5s, 6j, 6k)
my lack of confidence in what I can accomplish. I depend on my looks for everything
I have had to learn self-worth even though I don't always have a man around. (Mother was of the old school.)
identifying w/ the failures of my parents, accepting my family, especially my mother, as well as what I have in common with her

e. Unclassified (7e)
not letting bitterness, or blame of others for my neuroses, hinder my success

A Husband Has a Right to . . .

Although this item was originally used for men only, it is now used for both men and women. Many responses are the same for men and women, but others are given chiefly by one gender or the other. Many seemingly illogical responses, given chiefly by women, give husbands' obligations rather than rights, as if the stem read "A husband should by right—" or "It is right for a husband to—." Such responses should be judged according to ego level, not according to their logical fit to the stem.

Attitudes toward traditional gender roles affect responses to this stem along with ego development. There is a correlation between them, but not a perfect one. Generational differences are among the confounding factors. The theme of dominance has categories up through E5, reciprocity at E5 and higher.

Responses scored at the lowest levels represent traditional machismo values; those at the highest levels represent the values of mutuality and communion. At the intermediate stages there are intermediate attitudes, but also some expressions of extreme egalitarian or macho attitudes. In the latter case, placement is accounted for by other elements of the response, chiefly conceptual complexity.

There is constant temptation to rate higher those whose attitudes are like one's own, which results in errors. The rater must be open to the possibility of macho or egalitarian responses at any level, although empirically the greatest overlap is at E5 and E6. At E5 and higher, responses reflecting conventional masculine role usually have a less peremptory tone than similar responses at lower levels.

Other topics where one may be tempted to let personal opinions influence the rating are those of infidelity, divorce, and sexuality in general. By themselves, they afford no reliable information about ego level, though the manner of expressing such attitudes can be a valid indicator. For example, references to sex at E2 imply a purely physical relation, whereas more conventional expressions of sexual wishes, whether or not monogamous, are rated E4. References to sex at higher levels are usually put in the context of a loving relationship.

The stem invites from men claims to self-indulgence, sexual and otherwise, as well as claims concerning the structuring of relationships within the family. Self-indulgence ranges from "do what he wants," a popular but nonetheless discriminating category at E3, to claims to individuality and humanity at E7 or higher. References to specific, concrete prerogatives occur over a wide range and are classed E4 as compromise.

Despite the impersonal wording of the stem, many women respond as if we asked about their relationship to their own husbands. More people decline to complete this stem than most. Some formulate their objections explicitly (typically rated E7). Others express their objection to it in other ways, including irony: A man responded, "be sacrificed to family"; a woman responded, "clean, cook, and wash. HA, HA!" and another, "protest his wife's bad cooking. Hey let him cook himself." Such responses occur in protocols rated E5 to E7, and should usually be rated E6.

Themes:

What he wants (E2–E6): drink and smoke; a night out; make love to his wife; relax; love and respect.
Dominate (E3–E5): give orders; rule the family; make decisions.
Independence (E2–E7): talk; leave; cook; privacy; pursue his own interests.
Reciprocity (E5–E7): equality; same as a wife; expect fidelity.
Be human (E4–E7): be kind; be himself; an equal voice in raising children; be a person.

ITEM 26: A HUSBAND HAS A RIGHT TO . . .

E2 Impulsive

2-What he wants

a. Sexual rights (blatantly expressed) (4c)
   screw around
b. Impulsive acts (4d)
   drink and smoke
   fight

2-Independence

c. —talk (5h)
   speak

2-Other

d. Tautological responses
   do what a husband has a right to do
   have a wife
   be a husband

E3 Self-Protective

3-What he wants

*a. —do what he wants [unelaborated] (4a)
   leave his house when he wants
   do whatever
   go wherever he wants
b. —a night out (4b, 5j)
   go out somewhere when he wants to
   go out
c. —a little fun (5b)

3-Dominate

d. —tell his family what to do (4g, 4h)
   say over his wife
   cut up his wife's credit cards
e. —yell at his wife; beat his wife, kids (5m, 5q)
   scold his wife

3-Independence

f. —work (4f)
   work all night
   work for a living
   go to work
g. —leave his wife
   walk out on a marriage if he's not happy
   get a divorce

E4 Conformist

4-What he wants

*a. —do what he wants [simple, concrete qualification] (3a, 6b)
   do whatever he wants to on his day off from work
   play golf and go fishing
   watch any t.v. show he wants to at night

*b. —go out with the boys (3b, 5j, 6d)
   come home late
   spend some nights out with his friends
c. —make love to his wife (2a, 5a)
   his wife
   make love to his wife whenever he wants to
   monogamous sex
   ask for sex
   say no to making love
   have headaches too
d. —eat, sleep (2b)
   sleep late some weekends
   go to sleep when he wants
   demand meals
   a good dinner after a hard day's work

4-Dominate

*e. —take care of his family
   provide things for his wife and children
   protect his family
f. —support the family (3f)
   receive support from his wife financially
   be the bread winner
   budget the bills as much as the wife
*g. —be head of household; lead, direct his family (3d, 5e, 5g)
   be the man of the house
   manage his household
   take charge
   wear the pants
   be the boss
h. —say no; make rules (3d, 5e, 5g)
   make demands
   have the last word

4-Independence

*i. —cook, clean (5d)
   help the wife out a little, it's not a crime
   do the dishes
   cook and clean if that's what he wants
   stay at home if he so desires
   take out the garbage

4-Be human

j. —be good to his wife; a good wife
   be kind
   gives his wife a surprise

4-Other

k. —I don't know (7f)
   Im not no husband [sic]
   (I don't have a husband)
   ?
l. —nothing (7f)
   nothing, we are separated

E5 Self-Aware

5-What he wants

   a. —love his wife (4c, 6a)
     love and care for his family
     do nothing but love his wife
     love his children
   b. —be happy (3c)
     keep his wife happy
     do what's best for him, and to happiness
   c. —relax; rest
     be tired
   d. —stay home and raise the kids or go to work (4i)

5-Dominate

 *e. —make decisions [unelaborated] (3d, 4g, 4h, 6g)
     make his own decisions
     make decisions for the family
 *f. —know what his wife is doing (6i)
     know everything that goes on in the family
     question his wife
     know if his wife is cheating
     know where his wife has been & how much money
      she spent
   g. —discipline his children; control his family (4g, 4h)
     rule his household with love
     control his household and make rules if he abides
      about it too
     ask his wife not to have a job

5-Independence

**h. —his own opinions; express his feelings [unelaborated] (2c, 6c, 6h)
     his own opinions and choices
     talk, as long as I can talk too
     share his feelings with others
     cry
     assert himself
     be heard
     speak his mind
     say what he wants, I don't always have to listen
 *i. —privacy; have time to himself
     a room of his own
     be able to have some space
     say "Look, I want to be alone tonight"
   j. —go out alone; do things by himself (3b, 4b, 6d)
     leave home for a while to regain his cool
     go on vacation alone
     some time away from his wife
   k. —freedom; be his own person (6c, 7a, 7g)
     let his wife have her freedom
     certain freedoms from his wife
     exist
   l. —do what he thinks is right, best

5-Reciprocity

   m. —discuss with his wife; argue with, criticize his wife (3e, 6h)
     tell his wife what her wrong doings are
     question his wife about attitude
     praise his wife
     talk to his wife but not beat her
   n. —be with his family; enjoy his wife, children
     hang out with his wife instead of the fellows
   o. —equality; be an equal partner (6e, 7d)
     do all the chores that his wife does
     equal participation in the family organization
     expect family cooperation
     share all the responsibilities along with his wife
     be treated fairly

5-Be human

 *p. —be himself (6c, 7g)
     be true to himself
     be himself first & foremost
   q. —complain; be in a bad mood (3e)
     get mad and have a bad day
   r. —a peaceful, orderly home
     expect help in maintaining a good home
     take pride in his home

E6 Conscientious

6-What he wants

 *a. —expect love; be loved (5a)
     a warm and loving relationship
     love and respect from his wife
     expect truth and love
     expect love if he gives love
   b. Qualified "do what he wants" with an awareness of rights and feelings of others (4a)
     anything he wishes as long as they are within the rules of behavior of men
     do basically what he wants to as long as it doesn't hurt his wife or others
     do whatever he feels, in agreement with his wife

6-Independence

   c. —have a mind of his own (5h, 5k, 5p)
     have his own thoughts and feelings apart from his wife's
     be sensitive as well as machismo
   d. —have his own friends (4b, 5j)
     have friends both male and female

6-Reciprocity

**e. —the same as a wife; no more than a wife (5o)
     do anything his wife can do and vice versa
     expect from his wife what he gives to her
     nothing more than equal participation in a marriage
     receive back what he puts into a marriage

do nothing unless it is agreed by both—the wife and himself

*f. —request, expect certain [conventional] things of his wife (8b)
ask his wife to help with the housework
ask for what he needs
ask his wife to bear children
expect his wife to be responsible
expect me to tell him where I'm at in case he needs me
expect support from his wife

g. —share in decision-making; make the final decision on important matters (5e)
make a final decision after talking enough w/ his family
consult his decisions with his wife

h. —express his opinion [elaborated] (5h)
express his most personal feelings to his wife
express his opinion, not demand
speak his mind if he listens to both sides
his beliefs even if it contradicts with mine

i. —know what his wife feels, thinks (5f)
understand and listen to his wife's point of view
know his wife's goals or ambition

6-Be human

**j. —be as close to his children as his wife is
see his kids after divorce
help decide whether he wants a large family or a small family
an equal voice in raising children
fight for custody of the children if the mother is unfit

*k. —respect his wife, be respected
expect to be respected by his wife
respect and love
be treated well, if he respects his wife
be respected as an individual
respect his wife

l. —be honest; expect honesty from his wife (7c)
demand honesty from his wife
be honest
monogamy
expect love, honesty & attention from his wife
honest communication

E7 Individualistic

7-Independence

a. —pursue his own interests; retain his individuality (5k)
have freedom as an individual
have outside interest·, such as hunting
be an independent person but not live two separate lives
define his own idea of success and reach for it
express his individuality within the relationship
privacy within the partnership

b. —grow
his own spiritual, physical, & societal growth
explore and grow and take risks

7-Reciprocity

*c. —expect loyalty, fidelity (6l, 8b)
expect a loyal, faithful, caring wife
love his wife without feeling the necessity to ward off other men

d. Partnership (elaborated) (5o)
be part of a team w/ his wife—the team must be greater than the individual
tell his wife about his feelings, problems, dreams
the same rights he and his wife have agreed to live by
be consulted by his wife on matters affecting their partnership

e. Reciprocal communication with family members
openly clarify the feelings of himself & his wife about all things

f. Rejection of 'rights' as presented in stem (4l)
nothing, necessarily; a relationship should be determined by two people
be a person. Nobody is guaranteed any rights in a relationship

7-Be human

g. —be a person; be human; make mistakes (5k, 5p)
whatever a person has a right to
be a person just like a wife has a right to
have faults
have his needs as a human met

h. Elementary role conception
create his own role as husband
expect a larger role than just providing for others
choose what will work the best for him because we all have that right

i. Reservations about rights over wife
order around his offspring, not his wife
whatever he wants but his wife can say no
sexual gratification (within reason) in marriage
take charge of the house, but not his wife
expect things from his wife but also understand why things aren't always right

E8 Autonomous

a. —expect mutuality in marriage
demand the kind of respect he gives to his wife
develop his part of a relationship
serve his wife self sacrificingly, and desire the same from his wife

b. —ask for, expect emotional support from his wife (6f, 7c)
expect his wife to be willing to listen and understand
the support (physical, emotional, spiritual) of his wife
expect commitment in the form of support from the wife

The Worst Thing About Being
a Woman (Man) . . .

For this item, more than any other, the men's and women's versions elicit different trains of thought. It was impossible to consider all responses together without regard to gender. The same themes are used for the male and female forms, but most of the categories are different. However, the two manuals are aligned so that similar categories are given the same letter.

Some popular categories in one gender are rare in the other: Women mention being considered inferior or being discriminated against very frequently, whereas men do so extremely rarely. For some topics, such as various versions of too much responsibility, the corresponding categories are the same or similar; both genders feel unfairly burdened. For other topics, corresponding categories carry complementary meanings, such as needing to be the aggressor versus playing the passive or dependent role.

In some cases, what sound like similar categories actually carry complementary meanings. Beginning at E5, both genders object to the imposition of gender stereotypes. In men, that is chiefly an objection to having to live up to the image; in women, it is an objection to being expected to live down to the image (granted that the opposite meaning or an ambiguous one can be found in some cases of each gender). Proportionately more men than women object to the stereotype; the proportion increases with ego level for both; and the greater proportion of males holds for every ego level. The different ways of objecting to gender stereotypes do reveal differences in ego level; category titles capture those differences fairly well for women, less so for men.

A few categories mean the same thing for both men and women but are placed at different levels. Saying there is nothing wrong with being a man peaks among Conformist men, whereas saying there is nothing wrong with being a woman peaks among Self-aware women. That accords with the general, thus conformist, belief that men have it easier than women.

Some changes in emphasis are understandable in terms of changing times. More women complain of their multiple obligations than earlier; fewer complain of being tied down at home. Fewer men complain of the draft than in 1969. Men used to complain occasionally about being dominated by women; now they are more likely to complain about "women's lib" (perhaps with the same meaning).

Some changes are hard to explain. Although menstruation was a frequent response in the 1970 manual, it did not reach 10% of that sample. Today, the number of women who give menstruation as a response is more than 20%. The difference possibly reflects changes in what women are willing to talk about. Men now frequently complain about not being allowed to show emotions or weaknesses, which was rarer in the earlier sample.

Some categories can be assigned to either of two levels, but for the sake of simplicity are assigned only to one. For women, sexual exploitation and worrying about pregnancy (E5a) could have been E6, being discriminated against (E5k) is about as frequent (relatively) at E4, being considered or feeling inferior (E5j) could have been E6, being what's expected of you (E5l) could have been E6, and emotional vulnerability (E6m) could have been E5. In those cases, a particular response may have an element that would justify assigning to the alternate level.

Women's Themes:

Physical aspects (E2–E6): you can get pregnant; the curse; being weaker; you have to look good all the time.
Responsibility (E2–E6): staying home; too much work; you are responsible for almost everything; the drudgery of housework.

Social roles (E3–E7): putting up with men; not making as much money; discrimination; overcoming social stereotypes; juggling career and family.

Human aspects (E2–E7): bad behavior; troubles; being emotional; you can't do things men do; emotional vulnerability; not being recognized as a person.

Evasion (E3–E7): don't know; nothing; I love it.

Men's Themes:

Physical aspects (E4–E6): shaving; you die younger; being a slave to sex.

Responsibility (E2–E6): paying bills; you have to work; being depended on; providing for a family; being tied down to a job.

Social roles (E3–E7): putting up with women; being what's expected of you; pressure to succeed; stereotyped roles are hard to play.

Human aspects (E2–E7): getting drunk; hardships; you get the blame; you are expected to be strong; you are not supposed to show emotion; being stereotyped as a man, not a person.

Evasion (E3–E7): don't know; nothing; unimportant; question has no meaning; I like it.

ITEM 27: THE WORST THING ABOUT BEING A WOMAN ...

E2 Impulsive

2-Physical aspects

a. —is that you can get pregnant (4b, 5a)
is she has to have a baby
is that she be's the one to get pregnant

2-Responsibilities

c. —always staying home (4d)
staying home with the children
is you can't go know where [sic]

2-Human aspects

d. Bad behavior (5p)
is drinking

E3 Self-Protective

3-Social roles

c. —putting up with men; being bossed around (4i, 5u)
is men
is we have to take lots of stuff
you are put upon
d. —is trying to find a man (5y)

3-Human aspects

e. —is hardships, troubles [unspecified]
that we go through too many problems

3-Evasion

g. —I don't know (5z, 7h)
is I have no idea
h. —answering these questions

E4 Conformist

4-Physical aspects

**a. —is menstruation [unelaborated] (6a)
going through menopause
is cramps

female problems
is being cranky once a month
is having the "monthly friend"
*b. —is childbirth, labor (2a)
is childbearing pains (I suppose)
is the uncomfortable 9 months of carrying a baby, that is, being pregnant
is having children

4-Responsibilities

*c. —is too much work, responsibility [unspecified] (5h, 6d)
work work work
is full of burdens
is being depended on from many people
is that her work is never done
is she has to do it all
d. —is being tied down (2c, 6g, 6h)
not being able to be totally free
e. —is the housework (6e)
is having to cook and clean house and all the others that follow
f. —raising the children [unelaborated] (5h)

4-Social roles

g. —is not being a man (5t)
being 2nd to men
is not being one of the guys
is being a woman
h. —not making enough money (5k)
is the job market
unequal wages
we get underpaid as compared to men
i. —is being taken advantage of (3c, 5a, 5f, 5u)
is that a woman always loses
men take advantage of their feelings

4-Human aspects

j. —is worrying, being emotional (5y, 6m)

of the nerves
is that she crys for everything [sic]

E5 Self-Aware

5-Physical aspects

*a. Sexual exploitation; worrying about pregnancy (2a, 4i)
  taking garbage talk from men
  being responsible for the birth control method
  is that many times they are looked upon as sexual objects
  is getting pregnant when it is not wanted
  is dealing with the sexual double standard
  is that many times in order to get ahead men will proposition you

*b. —being physically weaker; physical problems
  is breast cancer
  can't compete physically with men as well as another man
  is her biological time clock
  is being fragile
  is that we are considered weak

*d. —is staying attractive (6b)
  wearing hair rollers to bed
  is having to wear pantyhose
  is the importance of appearance
  is we get fat easier

e. —is growing old
  is losing beauty
  sometimes wishing you were young again

f. —being raped
  being afraid of rape

g. —is your hormones
  is having active hormones that work against her

5-Responsibilities

h. —is responsibility for home and children (4c, 4f, 6d)
  is having to be responsible for almost everything
  is that you are expected to do all the work in the house
  is bearing a child and all that goes with it

5-Social roles

**j. —being considered inferior; feeling inferior to men (6i)
  is not always getting respect
  is being always put down for being a woman
  is she has 2 jobs & is not treated with equal respect as a man is
  is the social status that we were given many years ago
  is to continually prove that we are worthy

**k. —is discrimination; not having equal rights (4h, 6h)
  she has to fight subservience
  prejudices against her

having so many men in higher positions
is the inequality between the sexes
is that I am sometimes a second-class citizen

*l. —is being what's expected of you (6f)
  is the number of things she is required to do well
  is the fact that everyone expects you to wait on them
  is that you must handle a lot of pressure from men
  is she is expected to marry
  is that men expect too much of you
  is that we have to be so careful about our reputation & relationships

m. —is being criticized, misjudged
  is having to always prove yourself
  is she's the blame usually

n. —is competition with other women
  is having to deal with women they feel that have to compete sexually with you [sic]

o. —is male chauvinism; sexism
  is having to deal with male egos
  the chauvinistic macho men
  most men look upon women as objects—it's what society conditions them to believe

p. Stereotypical faults of women (2d)
  is we gossip
  talking too much

r. —is being dependent; waiting to be picked (6j)
  is feeling helpless
  is having to be afraid to ask a guy out

t. —is having to act like one (4g)
  is always trying to be feminine
  is if you don't like being a woman

5-Human aspects

u. Being misused or mistreated (3c, 4i)
  they are treated as slaves
  is having someone always trying to run your life
  is a man abusing you physically

v. —it's a man's world; you can't do things men do
  is trying to compete in a man's world
  is that I couldn't play little league
  is having to be cautious about where you go alone

x. —is not to be able to have children; is losing a child (6m, 7d)
  to give up a chance to raise their children

w. —is being taken for granted
  is when your husband feels housework is not working
  is the low prestige and nonexistent pay of being a housewife/mother

y. —loneliness (3d, 4j, 6m)
  is being a lonely wife
  is being alone

5-Evasion

*z. —is nothing (3g, 7h)
  is that I cannot see anything bad about being a woman who said being a woman was bad at all?

E6 Conscientious

6-Physical aspects

*a. —menstruation [elaborated] (4a)

is PMS

is going through menopause, menstruation, and pregnancy

is the menstrual cycle, and the mood swings and pain that accompany it

getting monthly periods, twice a year would do nicely

b. —is that you have to look good all the time (5d)

is having to wear miserable shoes and uncomfortabe clothes when dressed for work

is the pressure to look like a "10," which is ridiculous

is being judged for your looks

6-Responsibilities

*d. Burden of responsibilities (specified) (4c, 5h)

is having to work, take care of her children & husband, & do housework

always having to be blamed for things at home

is the social & economic pressures of raising a family

having to feel like you can do it all and being pushed to do so

is we have a lot more responsibility when we are single & raising kids

is the inequity of task responsibility

is being the default parent

e. —is the routine, drudgery of housekeeping (4e)

6-Social roles

*f. —being judged by, overcoming stereotypes [general] (5l, 8a)

is the stereotype that she should be a homemaker

is people placing you in a category before they know you

the roles you are expected to accept

is the old "sex role" that goes along with it

have to prove yourself a lot and many times expected to give way to men

is trying to fit an image that men want

*g. —is that society puts limitations on her (4d, 7a)

is that society feels that she should be the one to stay home & look after the kids

is that rules and other things in society are more easier to follow for men

is our society, parents, etc., socializing us to be a certain way

is that there are many social stigmas attached to the way a woman must behave

is that others give limitations. I don't feel any

is being stifled by the system because you're a woman

is that her role is affected by culture very much

is not being able to do a lot of things that society says is unacceptable behavior

*h. Limitations in opportunities, jobs, careers (4d, 7a)

is not being offered jobs because you are a woman and not a man

is that it is a man's world and we won't get the opportunities that men get

is being paid for the same job as a man but getting less

*i. —men don't take you seriously; they assume you aren't competent (5j)

is not being viewed as being knowledgeable or self-sufficient

is being trivialized

is dealing with men who think women are inferior

is having to prove we are capable of using our brains for more than shopping

j. —is playing the passive role (5r)

not being allowed to be in control

is the subordination

k. Role conflict (unelaborated) (7a, 8a, 8b)

the many "hats" you must wear

is being torn in several different directions at the same time

is having to choose between career & family

is having so many conflicting needs

6-Human aspects

m. —is emotional vulnerability (4j, 5x, 5y, 7d)

is having your heart broken by insensitive males

getting so much hurt by love, we take it hard

is becoming overly absorbed in emotions

is we care too much

is your heart sometimes rules

n. —not understanding men (7b)

I don't know, if I were a man half of my life I would have a comparison

is not being able to see how the "other half" lives

is not knowing if a man is sincere

E7 Individualistic

7-Social roles

a. Restriction or confusion in woman's role (6g, 6h, 6k)

is having to juggle career & family & wanting to do each one well

is that the world expects you to act like a 'girl' instead of an equal even as an adult

is that society prevents her from achieving her full potential

is the role strain & conflict in being mother/lover/employee

is that when you have children, a career is no longer that important *is learning to stay on the cutting edge of what society will accept*

is living in a society that devalues women

b. Men's misunderstanding of women (6n)

is that some men are barbaric in their beliefs about woman's role in society

is having to deal with social problems which no male can understand

is having to endure really stupid insecure men

7-Human aspects

c. Being recognized as a person

is that many people distinguish you as a woman versus a person (e.g., in a career, for your intelligence, etc.)

d. Personal tragedies and emotional problems (uniquely expressed) (5x, 6m)

is having the ability to be a mother taken from her

is being vulnerable to sexual assault and making the decision to keep the unborn child

is being left alone with all the roles of mother, widow, adult daughters

is breaking-up of a relationship and starting all over again

f. Contrasting aspects (8b, 8c)

menstruating—lower wages—social stigma —(MOM) having to cater to men—do "lady-like" things

is she is mostly responsible for the physical and emotional well being of her children

is that men can take advantage of women, sexually & intellectually

7-Evasion

h. —I love it; I like being a woman (3g, 5z)

is nothing, it's great being a woman

escapes me—I wouldn't want to be a man

E8 Autonomous

a. Criticism of socially imposed stereotypes (explicitly stated) (6f, 6k)

is being classified as nothing more than an object to reproduce and act like a servant

is that some people still stereotype you as weak, innocent, etc., and don't believe you can really do a good job

is our legacy of the traditional female sex role where we were taught to be dependent & accommodating, & arriving at adulthood where the opposite is expected

is being weak, vulnerable, trapped, trying to counteract stereotype

aside from physical discomfort of menstruation/ menopause is that often the assumption is she "can't do"

b. Inner conflict (6k, 7f)

is balancing vanity and meaningful work

is the limitations she voluntary places on herself

c. Embracing paradox (7f)

is the awesome responsibility of children. (It is also the best)

is like the worst thing about being a man—you're not perfect

ITEM 27: THE WORST THING ABOUT BEING A MAN . . .

E2 Impulsive

2-Responsibility

b. —paying bills, taxes (5s)

income tax

2-Human aspects

d. Bad behavior (5o)

is liking to smoke

getting drunk

getting shot

abandons his family

E3 Self-Protective

3-Responsibility

**a. —is having to (go to) work (4c, 4d)

they have to work harder

is having to make a living

is finding a job

b. —having to support a family [unelaborated] (5h)

3-Social roles

c. —putting up with women; being bossed around (5p, 5q)

is all nagging and complaining he has to hear

is being bugged by women

d. —is trying to find a girl (4l)

is that girls can say no so easily

3-Human aspects

e. —is hardships, troubles [unspecified]

is the harsh penalties

is that a man always has to do things

f. —is living

is have to live in this rotten world

is living in the city

3-Evasion

g. —I don't know (4m, 5z, 6s)

?
h. —filling out these forms
having to complete sentences like this

E4 Conformist

4-Physical aspects

*a. —shaving; physical appearance
is baldness
is a developing beer belly
is having to wear a necktie

4-Responsibilities

**c. —is (too much) responsibility [unspecified] (3a, 5h)
is that all the responsibilities are on you
being depended on
you be the one to take care of things
is the responsibility to work after high school
d. —he has to work all his life (3a)
is that you have to work so long before you retire
e. Specific chores
is having to commute to work
is you have to fix all the cars
is having to take out the garbage

4-Social roles

g. —Is (not) being one (5t)
shouldn't bother a man who's really a man

4-Human aspects

k. —you get the blame (6l)
is you can't cry your way out of trouble
l. —is finding the right woman (3d)
finding a decent woman
that we can pregnant the wrong woman [sic]

4-Evasion

**m. —is nothing (3g, 5z, 7h)
has not come to my attention

E5 Self-Aware

5-Physical aspects

b. Physical limitations, illnesses
is blood pressure problems
is the threat of impotency
is the constant fight against physical decay
c. —you die younger; life is too short (6p)
is the lower life expectancy
e. —is growing old [unelaborated] (7e)
f. Genital pain
getting kicked in the nuts
is jock rot

5-Responsibilities

**h. —is responsibility of providing for, raising a family (3b, 4c, 6d)
is trying to take care of everything, family, car, and house
is that he is responsible for being the breadwinner
is that one day I'll have to support a family
i. —being drafted; war
is worrying about getting drafted
is like when the war broke out, men can be recruited

5-Social roles

j. —being considered inferior; feeling inferior
is when you are not respected by others
**l. —is being what's expected of you; pressure (6f, 6h)
is social pressure
being expected to be Super Person
is being expected to treat women differently
is that often times your potential is thought to be more than actual
is that much more is expected from you than from women
m. —is being criticized, misjudged
is always being thought of as the heavy
is the people are always evaluating you
is being misunderstood
n. —is competition (6g)
is wondering if you can make it in this world
the struggle to make a living
is the pressure to compete
o. Men's faults (2d, 6q, 6r)
is false pride
is being too aggressive
is his greed
that he makes mistakes
p. —women's faults (3c)
is being distracted by women
is cold women
is that many women expect you to treat them like gods
q. —is women's lib (3c)
is affirmative action for women
is getting called chauvinistic because of Women's Lib
s. —paying for dates, alimony (2b)
is having to pay alimony if divorced
it's expensive to date
t. —not being a woman (4g, 6n)
you can never experience childbirth!

5-Human aspects

v. —being expected to be strong (6f, 6m)
is expecting to be strong all the time
u. —having a bad experience with a woman
is being rejected by a woman

when his heart is broken
is to have a divorce

w. —is being taken for granted
   is you work all the time and hardly get credit for it

5-Evasion

z. —is unimportant (3g, 4m, 7h)
   is not very bad
   varies

E6 Conscientious

6-Physical aspects

c. —is sex drive
   (in a way) is having a desire for sex at certain times
   when a wife has little or no desire
   is you're always on the chase even if you don't really
   care
   being a slave to animal desires
   his weakness for women

6-Responsibilities

*d. Burden of responsibilities (specified) (4c, 5h)
   is sometimes you feel the whole burden of just about
   anything is left up to you
   is that you are expected to know everything about
   running a house
   is the physical and mental stress, which exceeds that
   of a woman, at least in our society
   is responsibility for all who do not carry theirs
   is the uncertainty of providing security for the family
   are the pressures brought about by unemployment
   is having to make all the decisions in a relationship

e. —being trapped, tied down in a job
   is the pressure of career success, negating the option
   to really do what he wants
   is getting trapped in an unrewarding and going
   nowhere career or occupation
   one can get tied down eight to five
   is his perpetual commitment to his profession
   is that at the present time a man is pressured into
   occupations for monetary reasons

6-Social roles

**f. —living up to the stereotype, mold, image [unelabo-
   rated] (5l, 5v, 7a, 8a)
   is that in order to be "a man" one must be big and
   strong and ugly
   is the stupid stereotyping conducted by some women
   is his society-based sex role
   is the masculinity myth you must uphold
   is cultural expectations of a man's role in the family
   is being expected to act in the typical macho, stupid
   way that most men do
   is the pressure of maintaining a strong virile image

**g. —the pressure to succeed, prove himself (5n)
   is knowing you must succeed with no help from other
   sources
   is the constant leadership expectation that is de-
   manded
   is that society says you have to be a success or you're
   no good
   are the pressures caused by living in a man's world
   is failing to reach his goals
   is the expectations of our culture

h. —pressures of society [elaborated] (5l)
   is having to associate with all the jocks and studs
   is the way the world sometimes changes his goal
   is having to worry about conformity
   is the expectations heaped upon his shoulders by
   society
   many people think you enjoy sports

*j. —having to take the initiative
   is it's hard to find women who take you out
   is the responsibility of being the "aggressor" of the
   two sexes
   is the pressures of "playing" a dominant role
   is having to ask for dates
   is wanting, sometimes, to have the attractions of a
   woman

k. —not enough time with your family
   is not being able to see children actually grow up
   the pressure that can be applied at work to take time
   away from the family

l. —is discrimination; not having equal rights (4k)
   is not being able to sweet talk another man (police)
   out of a problem
   is that women have an unfair advantage in gaining
   custody of children

6-Human aspects

*m. —you are not supposed to show emotion, have weak-
   ness (5v, 7a, 7c)
   is that you can't express sensitivity
   he is not allowed to cry
   is trying to hide his vulnerability
   is being taught not to show feelings
   is not always being respected for being sensitive

n. —not understanding women (5t)
   is not knowing what it's like to be a woman
   is not be able to know what a women is thinking & why
   is not knowing what women today want

o. —growing up [elaborated]
   slowness of maturing and the characteristic short-
   sightedness and quick temper
   is forgetting how to be a boy
   is growing up too late

p. —not enough time to accomplish things (5c)
   is that there never seems to be enough time to do
   all the things you want

concern about future
of 55 is the sense of how much remains to be crammed into one's life
is that our society demands too much of his time, talent & treasures!

q. Self-criticism (general) (5o, 7c, 7g)
  is not having his priorities in order
  is probably my concept of being a man
  is knowing that you will make mistakes
  is that not all his thoughts or actions are positive

r. Male chauvinism; negative male stereotypes (5o, 7b)
  is being over-sexed and being too dominating toward women
  is that all the girls think you're a bucket of lust
  is that it is assumed you are cold—uncaring, sexist, macho—
  is living down the indignations [indignities] that other men have done
  is being stereotyped as chauvinistic

6-Evasion

s. —question has no meaning (for me) (3g)
  is another false statement, since I see no "worse thing about being a man"
  ? What's so bad about being a man—or a woman
  is the attitude that one sex is better than the other

E7 Individualistic

7-Social roles

a. Living up to stereotypes, elaborated; multiple role demands (6f, 6m, 8a, 8b)
  is that one HAS to be "masculine" in order to live comfortably among men
  is that he represents power & strength and therefore many demands are placed on him
  is being stereotyped as a breadwinner, decision maker, leader, dominant, etc.
  that the stereotyped roles are often hard to play
  is the socialization that we have to be cool & are not to be expressive or tender
  is the stereotypic macho-stoic expectations
  is trying to be beyond the popular opinions of manhood

b. Guilt over male advantages (6r, 8a)
  is to live in a society that frowns on the abilities of women
  is having to deal with other men that think men are a superior gender
  not letting women know you prefer to be one
  is the idea that females are taught to feel they can and must alway be dependent on you
  is being justifiably envied by those who are not

7-Human aspects

c. Being a person, maintaining individuality; human frailties (6m, 6q)
  is that complete individuality is impossible—goes for a woman too
  is being stereotyped as a man & not just be a person
  is having to often times be put into "male role expectations" when you just want to be yourself
  is constantly being on call whether the problem is congenial or not
  is that men have to make many decisions for which they are not equipped

e. —growing older [elaborated] (5e)
  is that it becomes harder to compete as one grows older
  is not growing spiritually & emotionally
  is the need to maintain his self-esteem at any age

g. Sense of perspective (time perspective or priorities) (6q)
  is being responsible for things that often seem petty
  is sometimes living up to your pride, you have to know when to swallow a little
  is that we are reared to be too competitive
  so I thought as a child, was that he might have to go off to war and get killed

7-Evasion

h. —I like being a man (4m, 5z)
  There is no worst thing—it's great

E8 Autonomous

a. Criticism of socially imposed stereotypes (explicitly stated) (6f, 7a, 7b)
  is the phase, which some outgrow, of needing to measure up to the social concept of manhood
  is having to be tough, and then because you are tough, you are told you have sexual hang-ups
  is not being able to [be] openly emotional without being termed gay (although, as far as I'm concerned, nothing wrong with being gay)
  the virtually mandatory requirement that one be assertive to gain respect when with a group of people
  is that society expects so many physical things out of a man and brands him a weakling if he can't do them
  are the artificial standards of success imposed by society
  is the rigid, tight-lipped role one is forced into, in our society
  is that the cultural assumptions about what that means are limiting &, for some, produce great discomfort

b. Inner conflict (7a)

*is admitting past mistakes, and realizing exactly who
and what you are*

*are the burdens of "self-guilt" that can develop when
he fails in things that social norms expect of him*

*is that you can easily come to expect too much of
yourself and others*

c. Embracing paradox

is often the best thing about being a man, women!

*at that point is the same thing as our major oppor-
tunity—that we need a new way of understanding*

is no worse than the best thing

d. Unclassified

*is lack of real gut communication between each
other, as it appears women have*

A Good Mother . . .

This stem draws many high-level responses, but it also has popular categories that are nondiscriminating: for example, loves her children, takes care of her children, listens to her children. This was the longest item in the 1970 manual, perhaps because it allows for a wide variety of responses.

One problem in rating is that some common responses are ambiguous in import. Does the answer "cares for her children" mean that she loves her children or that she takes care of them? Further, does the respondent identify self with the parent or the child? If such information were available, it might affect the scoring, but one must go with what is written, not read more into it.

At the Conformist level, the characteristic responses are broad, conventional compliments and clichés. Interest in the development of the child and in the long-term future outcome of childrearing appear at E6. Separation, individuality, and independence are mentioned in increasingly clear ways at higher levels. The need to strike a balance between mother's needs and the needs of her children is mentioned at E7 and E8.

Criticisms of mothers, statements about what a good mother should not do or be, refer mostly to peccadillos and are less common and less condemnatory than the hostile statements about fathers for Item 12. There is no category for Item 28 corresponding to the E5 category for Item 12 stating that a good father is loved or respected by his children, presumably because that is taken for granted.

Although the numbers are small, there seems to be a difference between "A good mother—is a good wife" at E3, and "A good father—is a good husband," which is rated E5 but could have been called E4. At E5, both mother and father are described as putting family first, but the category is more frequent for mother and explicitly includes unselfishness. At E7, a good mother is described as considering herself too. The corresponding category at E7 for good father has him recognizing his wife's rights. There is no category for a good father recognizing his own rights, no doubt because that is taken for granted. Although these observations refer to a relatively small number of cases, they echo the traditional role of wife.

Themes:

Virtues (E2–E7): is good; is a good wife; does what is right; is self-sacrificing; does her best; is not carried away by stereotypes of being a mother.

Help (E2–E7): lets her child have what he wants; takes care of her children; is there when needed; devotes time to her children; is a good example; teaches independence.

Relationship (E4–E7): loves her children; listens to her children; is aware of her children's needs; considers her own needs too.

Other (E3–E7): is my mother; can fill many roles; is not necessarily a super-mom; grows with her family.

ITEM 28: A GOOD MOTHER . . .

E2 Impulsive

2-Virtues

   a. —is good, nice, sweet (3a, 4a)

is always good

2-Help

   b. —lets her children do (have) what they want

gave a child what he or she wants

E3 Self-Protective

3-Virtues

a. —is a good wife (2a, 4a)

3-Help

*b. —takes care of, looks after her children (4d, 4j, 4k, 5a)
always looks out for her family
feed their family
c. —takes care of the house (4d)
is the one who cleans up a lot

E4 Conformist

4-Virtues

a. —is wonderful, an asset, good to have (2a, 3a, 5d)
is the best thing that can happen to a child
b. —does what is good, right, proper (5c)
rears her children in the way he/she should go
trains her children well
c. —is fair, impartial; loves all her family equally
treats all children equally
d. —stays home; is always there (3b, 3c)
is one who stays home and takes care of her kids
should not work, and stay home with her family

4-Help

*e. —is there when needed (5e)
stands by her family
is always there to lean on
is one who understands and helps her children out
f. —helps, guides, teaches children; teaches right from wrong (6e, 6g)
is one who teaches their children how they behave
teaches her children about good and bad
g. —provides for, supports her family (5f)
h. —provides a good, happy home (5j)
helps provide a good environment at home
will have good children
would love her kids and keep them happy
i. —is important, necessary

4-Relationship

**j. —loves, understands her children (3b, 5m, 6k)
loves
takes care of and loves her children
is an understanding person
*k. —cares about, worries about her children (3b)
l. —is (also) a friend (5s)
is a loving one & a friend

4-Other

*m. —is (like) my mother; is me

is the kind of mom I want
n. —is hard to find (6q)
is a rare breed

E5 Self-Aware

5-Virtues

*a. —is unselfish, self-sacrificing; puts her family first (3b)
provides for her children before herself
acts selflessly
b. —is, should be patient, thoughtful, considerate (6b)
is kind, gentle & loving
is caring, open, patient, and understands
c. —does what's best; wants the best for her children (4b, 6a, 6i)
tries to meet the needs of her family
d. —is a blessing, a treasure, a precious possession (4a, 6a)
is a virtuous woman
is a gift!
an ideal

5-Help

**e. —devotes time to her family (4e)
loves her children and does special things for them
plays with her children
is a mother who spends quality time with her children
is available when a child wants to talk to her
f. —is supportive; supports emotionally (4g)
is always there and always supportive
g. —protects her children
watches out for her children
h. —does not restrict her children (6c, 6f, 7g, 8a)
listens, gives good hugs, and never asks too many questions
teaches her children the right way and lets them make their own
doesn't make her children feel guilty
i. —doesn't spoil her children; is strict (6j, 8b)
disciplines her children
sometimes says NO
will punish when necessary
j. Outcome of child-rearing: healthy, happy, well-behaved (4h, 6e)
is important to a happy childhood & adulthood
is usually reflected in her child
helps her child to become a good adult
k. Religious; encourages religion in child
will train her children in accordance with the Bible
loves her family and God

5-Relationship

**l. —listens to her children; is attentive; is one you can confide in (6i)
is loving, caring, and willing to listen to problems

is one you can talk to and trust
listens
*m. —shows her love (4j)
surrounds her child with love
praises and hugs
*n. —nurtures her children
is nurturing and protective for children
o. —is interested, concerned, devoted to her family (6i)
cherishes her children
knows what is going on in her kid's life
involves herself with her family
p. —is open with her children (6p)
q. —shares responsibility with father
is equal in a relationship and has help raising kids
should take an equal share in raising her children
has to communicate well with her husband
r. Does not have certain specific flaws (implied criticism)
loves and keeps her temper
should be open to her children. And not be such a worry wart
is to learn to keep her mouth shut—sometimes
doesn't complain
doesn't always resort to physical punishment as a means of disciplining children
doesn't run her children's lives

5-Other

s. —can fill other roles (4l)
is one that is loving, understanding, nurse, teaches, best friend, father, caring, etc.
can also be a career woman
is the same as a good father
does not have to be a housewife
t. Source
is self-made
is naturally a good mother; parents are either naturally good parents or not
u. —is happy; enjoys her life (6r)
is satisfied with her role
is one who has children and really wants them
v. —is hard to define; is many things
who knows
comes in many different packages
w. —is my goal, what I hope to be

E6 Conscientious

6-Virtues

a. —does her best, all that she can (4b, 5c)
cares for her children & gives the best she can offer
is also as good a woman as she can be
is a mother who gives 100% to her kids
b. —is, should be consistent, dependable, responsible (5b)

is loving, consistent and gives her time and attention to her children
loves, cares for, and takes on a great responsibility in raising her children
c. —is, should be tolerant, accepting, broadminded (5h, 7a)
loves her children always and accepts them for what they are
is one who isn't bias [sic]
is someone who is easy to talk to and willing to listen to you without always giving advice or criticism
is flexible

6-Help

d. —is a good example, role model
does not ask for what she can't model
e. —teaches her children values (4f, 5j)
passes her values on to her children by her words and actions
f. —encourages development of her children (5h, 7b)
will allow her children freedom within limits to develop
means her children have a good start for the future
g. —offers guidance [elaborated] (4f, 5h)
is loving, nurturing, and offers guidance
is always there to offer advice
h. Contrasting aspects, one E5 (7c, 7h, 8c)
cares for her children—emotionally and physically
stimulates her children intellectually, teaches them good manners, and gives them plenty of love and support
nurtures her children and only asks that they be the best they can be
loves her children, protects them, & teaches them morals
should be caring and understanding and not be afraid to disagree with her children and be ready to apologize when she's wrong

6-Relationship

*i. —is aware of her children's needs, problems, feelings (5l, 5o)
is in tune with her children
is sensitive to her children's needs
empathizes with her children
is open-minded, and remembers how she felt when she was young, and changes with the times
j. —uses both love (understanding, patience) and discipline (5i, 8b)
loves and cares for her children without spoiling them
must balance firmness and understanding
should be patient & kind but be consistent in disciplining
k. —loves her children unconditionally (4j)
never stops loving and helping their family

believes in you no matter what
is understanding and will stick by you wrong or right
never gives up on her children
loves you even when you've done wrong

l. —provides love [original, elaborated] (8b)
loves & cherishes her children's love
plants seeds of love in her children
provides love & unity for a family

m. —respects her children; gives them the feeling of love, security, being wanted
is the one that can give love, support, and respect to her children
cares about her children, respects their feeling
makes her children feel proud of themselves
encourages self-esteem in her children

n. —knows when to let go; allows children to grow up (7f, 8a)
is one who puts her kids first, and gives them opportunities to grow
can let go
gives her children distance
is one who lets her child grow—emotionally as well as developmentally

o. —sees each child as an individual (7f)
helps her children to be loving of whoever they may be no matter how different they are
is a mother who loves a child for who and what they are

p. —communicates with her children (5p)
has a friendly open relationship with her children
tries to develop a good relationship with her children

6-Other

q. Difficulties and imperfections of motherhood (4n, 8d)
should be able to apologize when she is wrong to her children
is not necessarily a super-mom
is hard to find—just like good fathers—we all fall short

r. —is relaxed, self-confident (5u, 7a, 8d)
makes judgments without worrying what others will think
takes initiative and makes decisions that stick

E7 Individualistic

7-Virtues

a. Resists stereotypes (6c, 6r)
should teach her son how to make cookies & play baseball (both with her daughter)
is compassionate and does not get carried away by the stereotypes of her being a mother

7-Help

b. —teaches independence, self-sufficiency (6f, 8a)

is one who gives her children enough room to make their own decisions
gives her children both freedom and support
values a child as an independent person
same as for a good father (should teach how to be self-sufficient and allow their children to be themselves)
supports & loves her kids while letting them own their own responsibilities

c. Several aspects, two E6 (6h, 8c)
can understand her husband's, son's, or daughter's problems, even though they themselves may not realize them, and solve them
nurtures her family & understands their needs & is in agreement with the father
helps to give her children love, discipline, understanding and some form of religion to help them in the growing up process
is a great listener who tries not to be judgmental but lovingly sensitive

7-Relationship

d. —considers herself also
looks out for herself first so she can care for the others who need her
takes time for herself

e. —balances her needs and her family's, children's
tries to meet her children's needs, yet is mindful of her own, also
has a balanced personal & family life

f. Separation as a developmental phase (6n, 6o, 8a)
can separate from her children & let them lead their lives
sees her children as individuals separate from herself
loves and "lets go" without losing the relationship
cares, nurtures, teaches, and releases her children

g. —loves but does not overprotect (5h, 8a)
is nurturing but not overly stifling
is warm without smothering her children
loves her children but leaves them alone to fly

7-Other

h. Contrasting aspects, with gentle humor (6b, 8c)
realizes that the job of raising children is goal-oriented & time-limited and retirement benefits are great
corrects, loves, nurtures, teaches, understands, resents, and grows from the experience
is a bandage on a hurt knee, a cool hand on a feverish forehead, a concerned conversation when there is anger, a soft lap and a hug when there is fear

i. Unclassified
is loving, patient, & non-judgmental
is a good listener even when no one is talking

is a good listener, and someone who grows with her family

E8 Autonomous

a. Encourages individuality, autonomy (7b, 7f)

allows her children to develop according to their own potential

gives to her children the skills to be resilient and to take risks

gives her children healthy messages, permission to be themselves, and lots & lots of unconditional LOVE

lets go, loves without demanding conformity to her own ideals and standards—and helps to guide if possible

b. Both love and discipline (original, elaborated) (6j, 6l)

is one who treats her child as a small adult; who can love, teach, encourage, respect, allow space, consistently discipline, and give a child a sense of self-worth

c. Several aspects, including respect for child's unique identity (6h, 7c)

is kind, consistent, tender, sensitive, and always aware a child is master of its own soul

appreciates her children as individuals, allows their explorations in life with supportive boundaries, and enjoys the experiences they share together

d. Accepts her limitations (6q, 6r)

is a goal that's very difficult to reach—I don't think that a really good mother would ever feel she was a good mother

is not always perfect and it is better if she does not pretend to be

When I Am With a Man (Woman) . . .

Although for most items the rating is the same whether the subject is a man or a woman, that is not always true for this stem. In a few cases, the rating for a man's answer differs from that for the corresponding woman's answer: To feel like a man is E4, whereas to feel like a woman is E5. Most categories, however, include answers from both men and women, as indicated in titles and examples. In many cases, it is clear whether the answer is given by a man or a woman. Sometimes the use of the active or passive voice varies with whether the respondent is a man or women; if not, the rating is the same.

Answers varied so widely that themes are hard to draw and are not mutually exclusive. We began by differentiating actions from feelings. People have feelings about actions, and many responses express both. In addition to positive and negative feelings, many responses express the contingency on which the feelings or actions depend. Many categories, particularly at higher levels, refer to thoughts more than to feelings; they have been classed as introspections.

Although feelings may be expressed at any level, in general, lowest levels describe actions; at the next higher levels, they describe corresponding feelings. At still higher levels, similar feelings are expressed as contingent on the person, the situation, or the relationship. At the lowest levels, answers refer primarily to actions and feelings of the moment; going up the scale, an increasing proportion of the responses refer to aspects of the situation or people that extend beyond the date or the occasion, such as enduring traits or attachments, comparison with other occasions, standards of conduct, or shared interests.

Below E4 being "with" implies primarily a sexual relation, and at E4 and higher it implies primarily a social one. At the highest levels, sexual, social, and professional relations may be contrasted. Expressions of reciprocity occur at higher levels.

Themes:

Actions (E2–E6): I talk; I make out; I'm a gentleman; I'm a different person; I talk more openly.
Positive feelings (E3–E7): I go wild; I feel happy; I feel secure; I enjoy his company; I feel more comfortable.
Negative feelings (E2–E7): I'm scared; I get nervous; I keep my guard up; I sometimes feel self-conscious; I am nervous but feel good.
Contingencies (E5–E7): I feel good if he loves me; that I love, I can be myself; I no longer feel ill at ease.
Introspections (E4–E7): I am myself; I like attention; my feelings don't change; I respect her as a person.
Evasions (E2–E4): I am never with a man; it's none of your business; she is my wife.

ITEM 29: WHEN I AM WITH A MAN (WOMAN) . . .

E2 Impulsive

2-Actions

a. —I talk [unelaborated] (5c, 6b)
   we talk
b. Crude sexual reference (3a, 3c)

I like to fuck the shit out of her
I get hot

2-Negative feelings

c. —I feel bad, sick, afraid
   sometime I be scared

I feel funny
I want to run away
I don't fill write [feel right]

  d. Crude hostility (3e)
I am mad
he's an ass
I want to shoot him

2-Evasion

  e. —I am never with a man (woman)
  f. —I do nothing (6a)
we don't do nothing [sic]
no big deal

E3 Self-Protective

3-Actions

  a. —I kiss, neck, make out with him (her) (2b, 5e)
I feel like kissing
I love to talk be around him and kiss I love to cook
for he [sic]
  b. —I (don't) act nice, right, like I should (4b)

3-Positive feelings

  c. Sexual pleasure (impulsive tone) (2b)
I want his bod!
I want sex and love
wow!
I go wild

3-Negative feelings

  *d. —I am nervous, shy [unelaborated] (5n, 6k)
I humble myself
I feel nerves [sic]
  e. —I get bored, angry (2d)
I don't trust many only want one thing [sic]
he better not hit me

3-Evasion

  f. Evasive, sarcastic responses
I am with a woman
I don't know about that
I am not with a man
I usually breathe
it's none of your business

E4 Conformist

4-Actions

  a. Conventional sex-role manners (6r)
I like to be treated like a lady
I try to be a gentleman
I treat her like a woman
I let him open doors
I like him to suggest where to go
  b. —I am on my best behavior (3b, 5f)

I like to look nice
I am polied [polite]
I watch my language
I try to be courteous and kind

4-Positive feelings

  **c. —I feel happy, good (5g)
I feel great
it's ok
I feel very good about myself
  d. —I have fun, a good time (5d, 6h)
I like to have fun
  e. —I love him (her); I feel loved (5j)
I feel like the whole world just revolves around us
I like to hear love songs
I like to [be] close and intimate
  f. —I feel like a man (5l)
she makes me feel like a man

4-Negative feelings

  g. —I am careful, on guard (5b)
I don't want my wife to find out!
I watch every move he makes
I am very careful what I say and do
I lie a little
I am more discreet
I always say "Cool it!"
  h. Concern with what others think
people stare at me
I get a guilty conscience of what my mother would
think if she saw me now
I think everyone will say oh look at them two [sic]

4-Introspections

  i. —I want to be respected; I respect her [unelaborated]
     (7k)
I respect everyone
I try to show respect
  j. —I am myself [unelaborated] (7h)
I try and be myself

4-Evasion

  k. —I am with (think of) my wife (husband)
it means I'm at home!
I am usually with my husband
she is my wife
  l. Specific situation or actions
I have to walk faster
normally we go to the movies or we go to eat

E5 Self-Aware

5-Actions

  a. —I act different (6l, 6n)
I'm a totally different person
I act like a little girl

I find myself not acting like me
I tend to perform better

b. —I don't know what to say, do; I talk less, too much (4g)
I am sometimes at a loss for words
I clam up
I don't get much chance to talk

c. —I like to talk, to share (2a, 6b)
I want to be really heard
we share joys and pains
I try to keep a good conversation going

d. —I laugh (4d)
I laugh too much
I laugh more than when I'm alone

e. —I flirt (3a)
I feel flirtatious

f. —I want (try) to be pleasant, charming, interesting (4b, 6m)
I try to make sure that we both have a good time
I like to talk about things other than child rearing

5-Positive feelings

*g. —I enjoy myself [unelaborated] (4c, 6g)
I like to enjoy my time with him
I love it

*h. —I feel safe, secure
I feel protected
I feel sheltered

i. —I am confident
I feel I can handle it
I feel successful

j. —I feel cared for (4e)
it's important to know he cares
I feel needed
I want to be cared for
I feel I have something to care for

k. —I feel special, excited (6h)
I feel proud to have him
I feel there is nothing or no one can hurt me anymore
I feel marvelous
sparks fly

l. —I feel feminine, like a woman (4f)
I feel good and attractive
I am conscious of being a woman!

5-Negative feelings

*m. —I feel uncomfortable, self-conscious (7c)
I sometimes feel awkward
I am confused
I feel inferior
I sometimes feel that I am not attractive or smart
I sometimes feel intimidated

n. —I feel nervous sometimes, somewhat (3d, 6k)
I tend to be a bit shy
I feel kind of scared

on a date, I become much more shy

5-Contingencies

**o. —it depends on the man (woman); I'm happy if I like him (her) (6j, 7f)
I feel good if he is totally mine
who loves me, I feel great
varies with the woman
if she is someone I am close to, is enjoyable
I may or may not find her interesting

5-Introspections

p. —I want, give attention (6c)
I do not always give her enough attention
I only think of him

q. —I like to be pampered
I treat her like a queen
I enjoy being treated like a woman
I like to be complimented

r. Sincerity as issue
I try to be very honest about my feelings
I sometimes feel good, and sometimes feel he is being dishonest with me

E6 Conscientious

6-Actions

a. —I act the same (2f)
(boy) I try to act myself and talk to him
I am little different from when I am with a man
I act normally
(boy) I try to act normally, but sometimes I don't
I don't think I treat them differently from a woman
I speak as freely as if I were with a woman

b. —I can talk more openly, easily (5c)
we converse freely
I tend to communicate easier than with a man

c. —I try to make her (him) feel comfortable, important (5p)
I like to make her laugh
I like to make her feel good about herself
I feel good making him feel good
he's the only one I see & I make him feel special
I try to cater to her needs, and show respect

d. —I listen
I like to listen & then give my views
I let him do most of the talking

e. —I like to compete, to control
I feel overshadowed
at times it's a battle of wills
I like to watch their expressions & challenge their ideas
I am challenged
I enjoy playing mind games

6-Positive feelings

**f. —I feel relaxed, comfortable (7b)

I don't feel uncomfortable
I want us both to be comfortable
I am comfortable and at ease, and if he's good looking then I may end up "with" the man
I feel comfortable because most women are very sensitive & affectionate
I feel comfortable & I don't let my emotions control how I act

*g. —I enjoy her (his) company, conversation (5g, 7a, 7f, 8b)

or a woman from a foreign country, I like to ask a lot of questions
I want good conversation
I feel companionship
we talk, share thoughts, and get along fine
I like to know that we could be good friends
it's just like any other human, therefore I enjoy their company (most of the time)
I stare at her eyes and enjoy the moment
I am in good company

h. —I feel alive, complete, stimulated (4d, 5k, 8b)

I perk up
I melt
I usually feel sexual energy between us
the whole world seems just a little brighter
I am happy, fulfilled
that I love, I feel whole
time is forgotten

i. —I like to get to know, learn from him (her) (7a)

I like to know about their interests
I look for her point of view on a wide variety of subjects

6-Contingencies

*j. —it depends on the woman (man) [elaborated] (5o, 7f)

I usually am self-conscience [sic] about how I look unless I know him well
that I love, I can be myself around him
I feel scared, if it is the first time
who is warm, loving, and tender, I feel likewise
whom I love, I don't hide the feeling if it's mutual or not
I like it when she is appropriately affectionate
if it is not my husband, it's the same as being with a woman
I feel good about myself, if he's a good person
who is boring, I'd rather be home
I feel good if we are compatible
I enjoy her if there is not great "date" pressure
I may feel awkward or at ease, depending upon who it is and my relationship with her
who loves me, I feel feminine

k. —other than my husband (wife), I'm nervous (5n)

I am rarely at ease, unless he's my husband
I feel uncomfortable unless I am related to them

6-Introspections

*l. Compared with feelings while with same sex (5a, 7b)

my feelings don't change
I feel more mature
I note attraction to opposite sex
I am friendly as I am when I'm with a girl
it is usually no different than being with a woman
there is always an underlying sexual tone that is not present when I am with a man
I am generally more open & honest with my feelings
I'm always more self-conscious than with women

*m. —I wonder what he (she) thinks (of me) (5f)

I wonder if he is telling me the truth
I study him very well
I wonder if he sees me as I am or if he is dreaming
I wonder how she feels about me
I am always trying to impress her with my attractiveness

n. —I am aware of the differences (5a)

I am aware of his maleness
I am sometimes aware of our sexuality
I am aware of being a woman
I am conscious of her sex but not ill at ease
I often wonder what it is to be a woman

o. —I think of sex (7l)

I want to do the nicest thing known
I like to have a good time, not have him want to make love
it does not necessarily mean it's for sex
I want to talk first, drink and have sex
I am sexually aroused! Just kidding
I feel no sexual pressure
I don't like to talk only about sex

p. —I feel we are equals

I expected to be treated as an equal
a peer, she's treated equally
I try to view them as an equal

q. —I compare her (him) with my model (wife, husband)

I find myself hoping to find a good husband and a good father for my children. Someday I hope I will
I wonder if he is able to pay the mortgage

r. —I am reserved, old-fashioned (4a)

I get on the reserve side, a little afraid at times too
I am aware of proper etiquette
I try to keep a gentle, quiet spirit & be discreet & pure
I want her to lead the way
I tend to act like a Victorian gentleman

E7 Individualistic

7-Positive feelings

a. —I like to know his (her) feelings, beliefs, values (6i)
   I try to see his real personality hidden under the surface
   I search for his qualities as a human being
   I try to probe her values about life
b. —I feel more comfortable (6f, 6l)
   I usually find close relating easier than with men
   I more easily allow myself to be nurtured
   I enjoy being playful

7-Negative feelings

c. Feelings of discomfort (elaborated) (5m)
   I feel a little shy at first, but then confident (especially if he is an older man)
   sometimes I feel awkward because of the gender difference especially at work
   I am a little nervous and tense, I don't want to make a bad impression
   I tend to either 'clam-up' or put on an act, never act myself
   I am often ill-at-ease until we can find a subject of mutual interest to talk about
   I feel trapped more than I need to
d. Conflicting feelings
   I don't allow myself to act on any feelings except for my wife
   I feel a closeness and yet strangeness because of his differences, but I like that
   I am nervous, but feel good
   there can be at times this feeling of both excitement, anticipation, and dread
   I often hold back my emotions and the thought of sex becomes important

7-Contingencies

e. Change over time
   I now try to develop an entire relationship, not one just based on sex
   who is a relative stranger I feel as shy as in dancing school in my youth
   now I feel just fine. It was not always so
   I am usually more 'at home,' more comfortable (not as true now as formerly)
f. Enjoyment contingent on person being interesting, intelligent (5o, 6g, 6j, 8b)
   that I like and admire and can talk to easily, I enjoy myself
   I am usually aware of his sense of humor first and his intellect second
   I enjoy her company if attractive and intelligent
g. Subject's reaction contingent on feelings of others

mold my conversation and habits to the mood of the individual
I like to feel that he is just as glad to be with me
I am ever conscious of how my overly jealous husband views it

7-Introspections

h. —I remain myself [elaborated] (4j)
   each can be his/her own being
   I am myself and let her know it
   I work on just being a person with another person, but. . . .
   I want to feel I can be myself, not what he wants me to be
i. Contrasting ideas, one E6 [minimally elaborated] (8c)
   I like to feel competent and feminine
   I try to treat her as an equal, yet show her courtesies like opening the door
   I want him to be open, outgoing, courteous, and respectful
   I feel that I should be receptive to her feelings and thoughts
j. Appreciation of the other
   I wonder if he can handle me (who I really am)
   I want her to feel that she is being admired for whatever admirable qualities she has
   I want to make him feel desirable
   I don't think I can generalize about this—everyone is different
k. Treat the other as a person (4i)
   I want to be respected as a person
   I treat him as an individual
   I hope that she feels I regard her as a human being
   I want to talk with her and rather know her more mentally rather than physically
l. Sexual fantasies (6o)
   I can't help but picture her nude
   I wonder what kind of lover he is

E8 Autonomous

a. Interaction, reciprocity (beyond enjoyment of date)
   at first I'm nervous—then I get to know his personality and if I can reach him—I usually make a friend
   I enjoy interacting with her, giving and receiving attention
b. Original expression of enjoyment (6g, 6h, 7f)
   who loves me, my whole heart and soul feel involved—there's no such feeling like it
   that's a charming and beautiful woman, I find it a life-enhancing experience
c. Contrasting elaborated ideas (7i)
   I enjoy her company incrementally with the combination of her good looks, intelligence, creativity and sexiness

*I will frequently have some kind of sexual fantasy
tho I have no interest in a 'real-life' affair*
*I find myself concentrating on not letting my stereotypes
get in the way of communication between us*

d. Role differentiation: business vs social, sexual vs.
personal relation, etc.

*if I know him I feel comfortable. If I don't, uneasy
(depending on whether the situation is personal
or social)*
*friend I can talk about anything, wheras it's been so
long since I've had a lover I'm apprehensive about
what it might be like*

Sometimes She (He) Wished That . . .

The fact that the stem for men differs by one word (*he*) from that for women (*she*) does not create a problem here; most categories have responses from both sexes. Most responses of girls and women begin with "she," of boys and men with "he." That, plus the content of responses, suggests that they usually express their own wishes. When the response begins with "I," the "she" of the stem may mean mother; thus, it gives the mother's (supposed) wish for her. However, change to first person may also be just semantic slippage. But a subject may be thinking of anyone.

Finding themes for this stem was particularly difficult. Because there are such ambiguities in responses, themes also are ambiguous. Arbitrarily, responses are classed in four themes. Hostile and destructive wishes occur mostly at low E-level. Moderate wishes for changes in situation are expressed throughout the range, beginning with having more things. Fanciful wishes for escape or transformation are prominent beginning at E4. Altruistic wishes are rare and occur mainly at high levels.

The distinction between change in one's situation and escape is clear at the extremes: wanting to be rich versus wanting to fly. Many other responses are unclear, however. Wish for escape or transformation usually refers to self, but change in situation or things can be either self or other. Desire to change the past falls under escape transformation. Wishes with present and future reference are usually classed as situational.

Some people, like the fisherman's wife in the fairy tale, waste their wish on hostile or self-destructive thoughts. These thoughts are most frequent at E2 and E3 and rare at E6 and higher. In principle, a depressed person at any level might give them, but in our experience they are also signs of low level. Some hostile remarks directed at the test or the testers are difficult to distinguish from more humorous barbs that are classed as evasions or jokes at higher levels.

At E5, altruistic wishes appear, though rarely, and, again, ambiguously. The wish that people would be kinder may be altruistic or merely self-centered. At E6, subjects often want to escape the burden of responsibility and express that wish in fanciful terms. At E8, inner conflict is shown by retracting or renouncing a wish as soon as it is expressed; just saying it is impossible occurs at lower levels.

The topic of marriage is less frequent than one might expect. A small number of males and females wish they were married. The boys and men were younger, of lower social class, and of lower E-level than the women, but numbers were too small to draw conclusions. The rating of E4 is a compromise.

By contrast, the wish to be single or never to have married came from women (mostly) and men in several samples and at several levels. The wish to have a boyfriend (for girls) or a lover also came from males and females in many samples; it is nondiscriminating because it came from all levels.

Another difficult discrimination involves the responses that wish for changes in traits, mostly rated E5 or E6. Generally, the rating should be guided by where the traits are normally rated in other items. At E5, many of the traits are action tendencies; at E6, the traits often have more abstract and inward reference.

Themes:

Hostile, destructive (E3–E4): she was dead; she hadn't had a child; I was not around.

Situations, things (E3–E7): she could have her own way; he didn't have to work; life was easier; he had more time; she could do more interesting things.

Escape, transformation (E3–E7): I'll be happy; she was someone else; her problems would disappear; he could start over; life was simpler.

Altruistic (E5–E7): the world was at peace; people were kinder; people were less prejudiced.

ITEM 30: SOMETIMES SHE (HE) WISHED THAT . . .

E2 Impulsive

a. Unclassified
he will never say have sex with him
I wouldn't do the things I do

E3 Self-Protective

3-Hostile, destructive

*a. —she was dead (4a)
I would disappear
she was never born
I was dead, things get so bad
he could jump off the building

b. —she didn't have a child (5l)
I would have gotten on birth control pills
he did not have kids

c. Hostile responses or wishes (4q, 6v)
stupid question
he never partook in longitudal studies of personalities [sic]

3-Situations, things

d. —she could have her own way (5g)
everything goes her way
I could get whatever I want
she could have everything
his wishes would come true

e. —he would leave (4o, 5e)
he would go away and never come back

f. —they would stay
I stay with her
he hadn't left
he would stay all night

3-Escape, transformation

g. —I'll be happy

E4 Conformist

4-Hostile, destructive

a. —I was not around (3a)
I would move out of the house

4-Situations, things

**b. —she was rich [unelaborated] (6b, 6c)
his lottery #'s would come in
she would some day marry a millionaire

*c. —she didn't have to work; he had finished school (6e)
he had quit the job
she didn't have to go to school
I didn't have to work so much
he had already graduated from law school
her dissertation was finished!

d. —she had a boy friend
he had more girlfriends
she was loved
she has that impossible man
he would call
she would meet a nice guy
he could have a lover

e. —she was married
he was grone and married [sic]
got married sooner
she finished school, & was finally married
she had remarried after her husband's death

f. —people would help her (6u)
she could be taken care of
someone else would do the dishes
I would help her more
she gave me more attention
he received more credit

g. —she could go home (5e)
she could be at home
I would come home

h. Parental admonitions
his grades were better
I would clean my room
I wouldn't stay out so late
I wouldn't talk back

i. —she was working

4-Escape, transformation

*j. —she was prettier; he was taller
she was slim
she could dress better
she had different hair
he could eat a lot and not get fat

*k. —she was older, younger (6t)
she was grown
she could be little again

*l. —she were someone else (5m)
she was in my shoes
I would be like her

m. —she was a boy, man
he is a lady
I was a boy

n. Health
she could walk again
she were healthy

o. —she could be alone (3e, 5e)
I would leave her alone
everyone would go away
they would leave him alone
he would just go away and leave her alone

p. —she was not married (5l)
he was single
I was not married

she never married my Dad

4-Other

q. Evasion (3c, 6v)
who is he?
?
don't understand
I don't know
this questionaire hadn't arrived
this test wasn't so long

E5 Self-Aware

5-Situations, things

**a. —life was easier; things were different
I would have a better life
life could have been different
everything was straightforward
b. —she could sleep late, relax
he could go fishing more often
c. —her family life was different
my brother & I would get along
her husband could control his temper
family was closer
he had a more normal upbringing
d. —she had children
she had a baby sister

5-Escape, transformation

*e. —she were someplace else; she could run away (3e, 4g, 4o, 6d)
she could get her own apartment
I could move and get away
he was living in Hawaii!!
f. —her problems would disappear (6s)
there would be no problems in the world
she was never born because of all the problems she's had
he could chuck it all
he had no worries
g. —everything was perfect, possible (3d)
he could fix the unfixable
he could change the world
it could last forever
she could have it all, love, money, and happiness
he could always feel as happy as he sometimes feels
h. —she was smarter, different (7a)
I would change
he had talents in more areas
i. —he was a better person [vague] (6n)
he could do better
she could be a better person than she was
j. —she hadn't said (done) that (6j)
she hadn't made that mistake
he'd done the right thing
k. Traits: action tendencies (6m)

I would stop being so impulsive
I talked more
she was stronger/hard
she wasn't so shy
I was not lazy
she had more energy
she was more outgoing
he could have been more assertive
l. —she had waited to marry, to have a child (3b, 4p)
she had lived by herself before she married
he waited to get married
she had pursued a career before a family
m. Desire for fame or glamour (4l)
she would be President some day!
he was secretary of state
he was Rasputin

5-Altruism

*n. Altruistic wishes (6u, 8c)
she could do more to help people who are hungry
the world was a better place
there was more understanding in the world
more people would be happy with life
she could do more for her family
guilt didn't exist
everyone loves God

E6 Conscientious

6-Situations, things

*a. —she had more time
there was more leisure time and less work
she had more time to herself
he had more time to spend with his family
b. —he was more successful (4b)
she had done more
he had more time to accomplish his goals
c. —she could afford more things (4b)
he had enough money to take care of his entire family
he had new tools to work with
d. —she could travel, take a vacation (5e)
she could take a trip by herself
she could take a few days off to be by herself and think
e. —she had finished school and had a job (4c)
f. Wish for better relationships
she had the opportunity to be very close to someone
her family had been warmer
certain people would write her more frequently
she could see her old friends again
g. —he could be himself [unelaborated] (7c)
people would just look at him for what he is, not how much he has
he could please himself
h. Reason for wanting things different
he could afford to be in politics

she were as free as a college girl
she was never a woman because of all the problems we have

6-Escape, transformation

*i. Time was different
   time would slow down
   the children would stay young
   things would progress faster
   he had enough time to devote 100 percent of his energies to each project
   he could live forever
   there was more time to each day

*j. —she had done some things differently [vague, unspecified] (5j, 7f)
   she had made more careful decisions in her life
   she could change the past
   he had taken a different road in life

*k. Dissatisfaction with education or career (7b)
   she would have gone to college
   she had pursued another career
   her job was more challenging
   she'd gone back to school & not gotten married & NOT had kids (SOMETIMES)
   he had educated himself for a profession
   Sometimes I wished that I was back in college
   he had gone into business

l. —she could start over [unelaborated] (7f)
   he could do things all over again
   she could begin her life over & not make the same mistakes
   she could undo some of the things she did
   she could disappear, or start over again
   her life has started out differently

**m. Wish for more (less) of specified traits: inner states (5k)
   I were not so serious
   he was more sensitive
   she could gain some self-respect
   she could be all that God intended
   she wasn't so self-conscious
   I'd not been such a tom-boy or so independent
   I was not prone to emotional expression
   she didn't worry as much as she did
   he was more stable in life
   he was more patient
   he were straight
   he was not so darned straight
   I was more conforming
   I was a little moderate with my restrictions
   she'd be more disciplined
   she was very simple

n. —she was a better person [specified] (5i)
   I was the perfect daughter
   she knew how to meet people a little better
   he was a better father

o. Wish to be more independent, mature, self-motivated
   she was no longer a child but a woman and on her own

p. —he knew more; she could see into the future (7a)
   he understood everything there was to understand
   he had a firmer grasp on world affairs
   she knew the outcome
   he had all the right answers to his children's questions

q. Fairy tale fantasy
   she had magical powers
   she married the Prince & lived happily ever after
   he were invisible
   it was all a bad dream
   she could take a week's vacation from the world

r. —she could fly
   she were free to fly

s. —he did not have so much responsibility (5f)
   she wasn't under pressure so much
   he hadn't undertaken the book
   he could get out from underneath the mountain of undone things

t. —he had lived in another era (4k)
   he had lived in the 19th century
   she lived somewhere else, in another time

6-Altruism

u. —people were kinder, more considerate (4f, 5n, 8c)
   people would show more respect for each other
   he would be more nurturing
   there were no prejudice
   the world was more forgiving
   there was more love in the world

6-Other

v. Humor (mocking the question) (3c, 4q)
   she would not belch with her mouth full
   he could fuck everyone he was attracted to
   he had any three wishes he wanted
   he had some idea what this will prove to anyone
   grandmothers ruled the world

E7 Individualistic

7-Situations, things

a. —others understood her; she understood others (5h, 6p)
   people would not hound her about her temper
   I would conform more to her way of thinking
   we would understand her viewpoint more

b. —she could do more interesting things (6k)
   he'd be free of daily routines
   he didn't have to spend so much time on detail

c. —she could be herself [elaborated] (6g, 8a, 8b)
   people would expect less of her, and just let her be herself

he could throw off all the "masculine covers" and just be himself

people accepted her for who she was. She wanted a chance to prove herself

7-Escape, transformation

d. —life was simpler
  life wasn't so challenging
  life would not be so frustrating
  life were not so complicated
  it would all be less confusing
e. View of life as a whole
  her life was more spontaneous
  she could change her entire lifestyle
  he had chosen a life of craftsmanship, art, or other form of manual expression
f. —she could change the past; she could start over [elaborated] (6j, 6l)
  she'd married a prince, instead of a frog
  he could recover his youthful self-confidence
  she had taken more risks
  he could have loved a bit more and worried a bit less
  she could start all over again and try harder and live slower
  she had chosen another, more traditional avenue
  she had taken life (e.g., education, relationships) more seriously
  he had learned how to live sooner
  he had had a childhood, and that he had learned to play

E8 Autonomous

a. Coping with inner conflict (7c)
  he could be a tree & free himself from all his mental turmoil
  he was less ambitious, that he had a greater talent for contentment
  he'd (I'd) had earlier/better knowledge of how a male parent and husband really best functions
  she could stop worrying for just a little while and just have some hedonistic pleasure
  she was smarter or else too stupid to know the difference
  she did not see life at a depth she does because it would mean less responsibility
b. Renunciation or retraction of wish (7c)
  all problems would go away, even if this was unrealistic
  he could relive his life; other times he was glad that he could not
  he were young again, but he knew that was a dumb kind of wish
  she had things she would not be happy with if she had them
  I would be just like my sisters; now she's glad I'm not
c. Social problems, abstract (5n, 6u)
  there were not so many tight, closed-in minds in the world
  people were less prejudiced & that she had greater faith in God
d. Unclassified
  she could do a better job making every second in life count

My Father . . .

Most subjects respond to this stem by saying something nice about father. Smaller numbers mention something unfavorable about him, give a concrete or neutral fact, or say something about their own relationship to father. At high levels, they tend to combine those facets. Usually, the rating does not depend on whether the subject does or does not love, or praises or criticizes father.

We use the themes *characteristics*, *relationships*, and *activities*, and include both favorable and unfavorable remarks in the same category to a greater extent than with other stems. Where possible, descriptive categories have been unpacked to be a series of exemplar categories; alternatively, they are richly illustrated with examples. Within an E-level, the exemplar categories are given first, followed by a descriptive one to cover possibilities for which there are not enough replications.

At the Impulsive level, characteristic responses are either unqualified rejection of a bad father or tautologies. It is somewhat surprising that unmodulated rejection or criticism of father occasionally appears even on high-level protocols. Describing father as a nice man is a popular response, but is not very discriminating; it is rated Self-Protective (E3) because it is relatively more frequent among pre-Conformists.

Banal idealization of father is very popular at the Conformist level, along with neutral and simple remarks about the relationship with father. To see father as having good and bad moods or being nice at some times and not at others may seem to be a recognition of complexity, but it may be a failure to recognize complexity by asserting that he is a good and bad guy alternately.

Beginning at the Conscientious level, there are many responses combining favorable and unfavorable characteristics, typically connected with the word *but* or some equivalent expression. The terms of the contrast become increasingly complex at higher levels, enhancing the impression of father as a real, three-dimensional individual.

Conception of fatherhood as a role is foreshadowed by simply saying he was a good or inadequate father (E5). At E6, he is declared to be a good example, or, in the argot of the day, a role model. Only at the Individualistic level do the responses seem to be based on a real conception of fatherhood as a role. Some responses at the Autonomous level convey a sense of a long-term life plan. Others encompass elements of inner conflict or complexity.

Some high-level responses have a tragic tone or are very moving. One high-level theme echoes the complaints of many women about their marriages: that men cannot express or deal with emotions. However, in the current samples, this complaint also comes from sons.

Although our sample was not suitable to make precise comparisons of answers of men and women, some trends were striking. There are no exclusively male or female topics. There is a trend for more women to give unreserved praise of father, for more men to give matter-of-fact descriptions. More women give answers indicating lack of contact with father; it has been suggested elsewhere that fathers after divorce are more likely to stay in touch with sons than with daughters.

Themes are omitted at E7 and E8, as many responses cut across themes. At E6, the category "Appreciation, admiration, respect" says something about the subject's relationship to father, but most of the responses give father's characteristics. The examples serve as a guide.

One category is retained from the 1970 manual even though there are no examples exactly like it in current samples: "is the head of the family, the man of the house" (E4).

Themes:

Characteristics (E2–E6): is a pain; is a nice man; is strong; is a caring person; is strict but fair.
Relationships (E3–E6): is good to me; and I don't get along; loves me; is a role model for me.
Activities (E4–E5): is a good provider; loves to fish.
Other (E2–E6): is my father; I don't have one; died when I was young; had a hard life.

ITEM 31: MY FATHER . . .

E2 Impulsive

2-Characteristics

*a. —is mean, bad [unqualified rejection] (4e, 5n)
  stinks
  is crazy
  is a pain in the ass

2-Other

b. —is my father

E3 Self-Protective

3-Characteristics

**a. —is a nice (good) man (4a)
  is nice

3-Relationships

b. —is good (nice) to me; gives me what I want (5a)

E4 Conformist

4-Characteristics

**a. Simple idealization (3a, 5a, 5b)
  is a good person
  is a wonderful dad
  was a beautiful person
  is a great man
  is terrific
  is a gentleman
b. Appearance; physical comparisons (5d, 6e)
  is getting old
  and I look just alike
  wears glasses
  was a strong man
c. —is okay
  is cool
  is alright
d. —is an alcoholic
e. —has a temper; has good and bad moods (2a, 5j)
  is a grouch
  can be alright, but sometimes when he yells he really
    scares me

4-Relationships

f. —and I are (not) close; (don't) get along well
  [unelaborated] (5r, 5s, 7a)
  doesn't care for me
  and I was close when I was small [sic]
g. —is strict, not strict (5w)
  is really hard on us
  was a strict and good man
  is a disciplinarian

*h. Lack of contact (5aa, 5cc)
  is often gone
  is not in my life
  lives far away
  will not talk to me
  left at age 2
  is divorced from my mother
i. —is easy-going; is easy to get along with (5h)
j. —is the head of the family, the man of the house

4-Activities

*k. —is a hard worker, good provider (5m)
  worked hard all his life
l. Occupations (5h)
  is a good mechanic
  was a working man
  was a CPA
  is retired
m. Specific activities
  does all the house chores
  likes to BBQ on weekends
  has remarried
n. Shared activities
  is my sports buddy
  and I like to do things together

4-Other

*o. —is dead (5dd)
p. —I don't have one; I don't remember (5z, 5cc)
q. —is sick (7e)
  is very sick right now (physically)
  is blind
  is chronically mentally ill

E5 Self-Aware

5-Characteristics

**a. —is a caring (generous, kind) man (3b, 4a, 6b, 6c)
  is a decent person
  is giving
  has been very gracious and helpful
  is a gentle person
  is a great guy, always helping others, ex: Little
    League
*b. —is the most wonderful man in the world; is the
  best person (4a, 6i)
  was my first love
  is # 1
  is the best dad in the world. He is loving and un-
    derstanding
  is my favorite male figure
  was a saint
  is the greatest!

c. —is intelligent, capable (6h, 8b)
was really creative
is the sharpest man I know
is a kind man, very intelligent too
is not as smart as he used to be
was a genius & a GOOD man

d. —has a strong, interesting personality (4b)
has a terrific personality
was an interesting man
is a very strong, strict person

e. —is quiet (7a)
doesn't talk much
was quiet and hard-working

f. —is religious, righteous (6b)
is a loving & Godly man
was gentle, kind, and a lover of God

g. —is funny, has a sense of humor
has a great sense of humor and at times he's my buddy instead

h. Positive or neutral aspects of personality or lifestyle (unelaborated) (4i, 4l)
is a very professional person
is very business oriented
is a very peaceful type of person
is a responsible man
is a perfectionist

i. —is complex [unelaborated] (6a)
is strange
is a very puzzling man
is unpredictable

j. —worries; is lonely, unhappy (4e)
is hurting inside
was a confused man
is a very insecure person

k. —is old-fashioned, narrow-minded (6a)
is very close minded
was too set in his ways

l. —is stubborn
is strict and stubborn
is a very negative person

m. —is a workaholic (4k)
is a driven man who should take more time to relax
is motivated by his work

n. —is selfish, stingy (2a)
is very selfish and self-centered man
was a horrible, stingy person

o. —is immature, irresponsible
can be a foolish man
lacks discipline
has never "grown up"
is a man, but not a responsible or caring one

p. Simple negative characteristics and traits (2a, 4i, 6o)
was & is a difficult person
was very cold and cruel

gets uptight a lot and begins handing out ridiculous punishments
is a meek man
is too critical and moody
is very wrapped up in himself
is the hardest person to get along with
is about, and still as cynical as ever

5-Relationships

*q. Evaluation of father as parent (elementary role conception) (6j, 6m, 7d)
takes care of me
spent time with me
is not a father to me
is a very family-oriented man
should have spent more time with his wife & kids
could have been a better one
never took me to a movie or the circus
tries HARD to be a good father and grandfather
doesn't know how to play with children quietly
is very protective

*r. —loves me; I love him (4f, 6m)
is a very affectionate man
doesn't love me. Never loved me
& my mother love me very much
was a nice man and we loved each other

s. —and I have a close relationship; are best friends (4f, 6m)
and I don't get along the way that I would like to
is also my friend

t. —enjoys, loves, is close to his family (6d, 6m)
was a man who cared about his family
is not close to our family

u. —is an understanding man; understands me (6e, 6p)
listens
was a good man, very understanding & funny

v. —is important to me (6k)
is a very important figure in my life
is a very special person to me
is one man I will always remember

w. —is an autocratic (aggressive) person (4g)
is bossy
happens to be a strong-willed man
tries to act like he knows everything and whatever he says is right

x. —mistreated my mother; is dominated by my mother (6n)
did not help my mother the way he should have
takes a lot of grief from my mother

y. —doesn't communicate (7a)
is not feeling enough
never shows he cares
and I don't communicate very well

z. —is a stranger; I don't know him (4p)
and I do not have any association at all
did not exist until age 15

is dead and I never knew him
never knew me
aa. —is missed (4h)

5-Activities

bb. —is busy, active; enjoys activities
loves Maine
still remembers how to have fun
likes drinking and politics
is happy today
loves to fish
cc. —was hardly ever at home (4h, 4p, 6l)
gives good hugs but is away [a] lot
spends a lot of time out of the house not with his family
led his own life
was rarely home and not nice when he was

5-Other

*dd. —died [mentions when] (4o)
passed away one year ago

E6 Conscientious

6-Characteristics

*a. Complex personality (opposed, disparate traits, "but") (5i, 5k, 7b, 8a)
is a good father, but wasn't always a good husband
could have been much better were it not for his alcohol
was devoted to his family, yet authoratative [authoritarian?]
is a respectable, admirable but stubborn man
is great but hard for me to talk to
is a very loving man but irresponsible
is talented & difficult & 75 yrs old
is a strict but loving person
was wonderful but undemonstrative
is a serious intellectual & yet humorous as well
is smart but isn't sure what he wants to do with his life
was very warm & loving, but too much of a martyr
is strict but fair, and I love him
is distant but generous and caring
was a good man but passive
was the boss in our family but not a tyrant
was a wonderful man but he believed that a woman's place was in the home
b. Devoted, dedicated, sincere (5a, 5f)
had totally gray hair when he was 21 and is dedicated to his profession
was an idealist
was a very trustworthy and honest man
was the best person I ever knew. He never pretended to be anyone other than himself
says what he thinks and I love him for it

c. —is a sensitive person (5a)
is quiet & sensitive
d. —enjoys life; cannot enjoy life (5j, 5t)
is a very angry and confused man
tried to be a person who was happy go lucky
e. —is (not) like me, we have a lot (little) in common (4b, 5u)
although being too conservative, still thinks alike like me
's life has been a complete opposite of mine
f. Too virtuous
is too much of a perfectionist
was too quiet. I never knew what he was thinking
is a kind, loving, caring man, but sometimes allows others to take advantage of his goodness
was generous to a fault
g. —can't cope; isn't realistic (7c)
lives in a fantasy world
fails to see the causes of his unhappiness
just cannot handle life well
h. Appreciation, admiration, respect (elaborated) (5c)
is a wonderful person who is very individualistic
is creative, energetic, & easy to be around
was a pretty modern man for his time
is a renaissance man
is a gentle man & very talented musician
is not someone I really love; he's a man that I respect
is a man I have no respect and compassion for at all
works hard for his family and has a good set of values
continues to achieve new heights
is a wise, good-hearted, and kind man
through discipline has bettered his life & ours
is intelligent, hardworking, and in love with his family; to me that is a great man

6-Relationships

i. —is a wonderful man, and I love him (5b)
is the sweetest, nicest, caring man I love
is a beautiful soul, I love him
j. —is a role model (5q, 7d)
is an inspiration to me
is a hard worker and a good example
was a good guideline for me to follow
k. —had a great influence on me, taught me a lot (5v)
contributed much to my self-esteem
helps me through my problems and is with me at my triumphs
helped to build my independence
l. My feelings toward father despite separation (5cc)
I wish I knew him
I don't remember him too well. I loved him—but he could have been a much better man
left my family when I was young and I can never forgive him for that

died at such a young age and I miss him and his sense of humor

m. Father's feelings, attitudes toward me (5q, 5r, 5s, 5t, 7a)

I love him very much. He did all he could for me when he was alive

supports me in my ambitions

patronizes me

was disappointed that I didn't want to be an engineer (like he is)

is very busy, but loves us tremendously

thought I could do anything I put my mind to

is proud of me

n. Father's relations to others (5x)

tries to relate to other people, but often finds it difficult

can't help his actions, but I know he loves my mother

is a good person towards almost all people

was difficult to relate to

has always played by the rules and now may be getting screwed over

o. —can be difficult, has shortcomings, but I love him (5p)

is sometimes very stubborn or unpredictable, but most of the time I love him deeply

p. —and I don't understand each other, have differences of opinion (5u)

and I get along well even if we don't see eye-to-eye

is someone who I can't relate to

/ I have purposefully lost touch with each other

q. —won't let me grow up; treats me like an adult

was over-protective

r. Father (or my relation with father) as changing over time

has mellowed w/ age

has learned to let me make my own decisions and I have become closer

has changed a lot after he became a X'n [Christian]

is struggling to change

was dictatorial and often unfair but our relationship has changed to more mutual respect

6-Other

s. —had a hard life

is a good person that has had to overcome many obstacles in his life

E7 Individualistic

a. —does not express feelings; is hard to get close to (4f, 5e, 5s, 5y, 6m)

is out of touch with his and other's feelings

loves me, but has a hard time showing it

is a good man but not as close to me as I'd like

is someone I will never really get to know

is uncomfortable talking about personal things

b. Complex quality of interpersonal relations (F's or mine) (6a, 8a)

is a kind, sweet man who unfortunately didn't talk to us

tried to give me more than I knew enough to take

is too wrapped up in his job to understand me

could be more sensitive and adaptable to change

was a loving, caring, religious, ethical disciplinarian

is very strict but gets along with my mother who is open minded

was dictatorial and often unfair but our relationship has changed to one of more mutual respect

might/could probably share in more of life's joys if he came out of his shell

often goes along with my mother's ideas. When he stands up for himself we get along better!

is too busy being a "good guy" to be involved with me

doesn't understand me, but cares for me very much. He just doesn't give me space

c. Cannot deal with emotional needs (6g)

is very unaware of his, or others', emotional needs

was not there for me emotionally, most of the time

was more supportive intellectually than emotionally

is learning that he has physical limits but no emotional ones

d. Role conception (5q, 6j)

is perfect for the job (of being a father)

is a father only biologically

was not the role model he should have been to me when I was a child

figure, in the absence of a real one, was my grandfather

is alive but his role as a father is deceased

e. —is a source of concern to me (4q)

is dying a very slow death; it is painful for both of us

E8 Autonomous

a. Composite responses, with E6 elements, some conflict or contradiction (6a, 7b, 7c)

is a very conservative man, who loves us but didn't grow with us

is the hero I've always admired but sadly realized his human inadequacies

did the best he could with what he had, and his lack of emotions affected my upbringing

is a good man who strove for ideals and accepted his setbacks

is a man of great intellect but who is quite terrified of his own fears and vulnerabilities

b. Love of learning

is unending in his search for knowledge and his efforts to help others

was a man who had a great belief in education, although he himself only went to sixth grade

If I Can't Get What I Want . . .

This stem presents a childish thought in childish words. How does one handle the frustration of a wish? It draws low-level better than high-level responses. The response may be in terms of emotions, behaviors, or thoughts. Cutting across those general themes, apart from expressions of anger, the response may express acceptance, perseverance in seeking the desired thing, substitution of something else, or reasoning one's way out of the situation. At low levels, acceptance, perseverance, and purely emotional reactions are frequent; at high levels, substitution and reasoning predominate. All those themes, both high and low, are found at E5 and E6.

Below E5 many subjects seem to interpret the stem as "If my parents won't give me what I want . . ." Going up the scale, an increasing proportion of the subjects take the topic as an abstract situation, part of the human condition, rather than a reference to intrafamily conflict. A few subjects seem to misread the stem, omitting the negative; those responses are from many levels and are rated according to content without reference to the misreading.

At the E2 level, there is no program for dealing with ungratified wishes. The person rebels, denies, or gets mad. At E3, frustration is still hard to take, so one gets angry or gets the wish one way or another. The predominant type of response at E4 is passive acceptance, but there are also many perseverance responses. Simple expression of moderate dysphoric feelings is classed E5 but is nondiscriminating. At E6, there is a thoughtful working over of the situation, consideration of alternatives or reasons, contrasting of emotional reactions, or acceptance of what one has. Conceptual complexity rather than new themes characterizes the highest levels.

At E6 and higher, a compound response with two contrasting ideas is usually rated one step higher than the higher idea alone (according to rule 2 in chapter 4). There are a number of such responses at E5, E6, and higher, but most did not incorporate enough similarities to frame distinctive categories; hence judgment must be used.

Themes:

Emotional Response (E2–E6): I get mad; I cry; I pout; I am disappointed; I feel frustrated.

Behavioral Response (E2–E7): I rebel; I keep begging; I try harder; I try another way; I accept the situation only after I have tried again; I work on other angles.

Cognitive Response (E2–E7): I don't want anything; I forget it; I do without; I accept the fact; I reconcile myself to what I have.

Other (E3–E7): I would get a car; I usually do; it depends; I make the impossible possible.

ITEM 32: IF I CAN'T GET WHAT I WANT . . .

E2 Impulsive

2-Emotional Response

    a. —I get mad (4a)
       I feel bad

    I'm pissed off

2-Behavioral Response

    b. —I rebel, run away
       I just walked out
       get bad

2-Cognitive Response

   c. —I don't want anything; I won't get anything (4o)
     I would not want anything else
     I don't want it

E3 Self-Protective

3-Emotional Response

   a. —I'll throw a tantrum, have a fit
     I throw myself down & pound my head on the floor
     I yell
     I will throw stuff
   b. —I cry

3-Behavioral Response

   c. —I get it one way or another (4g, 4n, 5d, 5e, 7a)
     I start to cry, then I get what I want
     I bribe the person
     I will go thru the extreme so that I do
   d. —I keep begging for it (4h)
     I bother them until I get it
     I beg & crying works with my father

3-Other

   e. Simple wishes: Stem misread as "If I can get what
     I want" (4m, 6l)
     I would have a job and my own apartment
     I would get a Porche
   f. —nobody can
     I make sure nobody else can
     you can't

E4 Conformist

4-Emotional Response

  *a. —I get upset, angry (2a, 5a, 6a)
     I sometimes get upset
  *b. —I pout, sulk
     I always feel sorry about myself
     I look sad and pout
     I just give the silent treatment
  *c. —I don't worry about it; it doesn't bother me (5l)
     I say ok
     I don't get upset
     I don't throw a tantrum
   d. —it bothers me; I worry
     it disturbs me
   e. Simple dysphoric feelings
     I feel sad
     I feel awful

4-Behavioral Response

  **f. —I try harder (5c, 5f)
     then I try again
   g. —I take it; I fight for it (3c)
     I do it myself
     I steal it

   h. —I'll ask my father, someone else (3d)
     I'll charm him for it
     I ask my boyfriend or some other boys
   i. —I pray for it (5m)
     I usually ask God for it

4-Cognitive Response

  *j. —I get what I need; I don't need it (5j)
     I settle for what I need
   k. —I forget it (5h, 5l, 6g)
     I think about other things
   l. —I give up (5h, 5l)
     I let go
   m. —I'd be happy [Stem misread?] (3e, 6l)
     I'd be the happiest girl in town

4-Other

   n. —I usually do (3c)
     I can usually find a way to get it
   o. —I just don't get it (2c, 5h)
     when I want it, I just don't get it
   p. Unclassified
     I would want a wonderful husband, children, a home
     and to be through w/ school

E5 Self-Aware

5-Emotional Response

  *a. —I am disappointed, depressed [distance from
     dysphoric feelings] (4a, 6a, 6b, 6c)
     I fight for it, then I get disappointed
     I just get really upset and try to console myself
     I usually kick & scream (I am just kidding). I get
      upset
     sometimes I want to cry
   b. Feelings with interpersonal reference (6b)
     I feel hurt
     I dislike the person who prohibited my getting
     I take it out on someone else
     I feel rejected

5-Behavioral Response

  **c. —I keep trying (until I do) (4f)
     I persist until I get it
     I get determined to get it
     I work to eventually try to get it
     I won't give up
  **d. —I try another way (3c, 7a)
     I work around it
     I find other alternatives
     I'll figure something else out
     work harder another way to get what I want
   e. —I find a way (3c)
     there has to be a way to get it
  *f. —I work for it (4f)
     I save and buy

I work harder for it to happen
I try to get it on my own
*g. —I wait until I can (6d)
I wait
I do without it until I can get it
I ask at a later date
right away, I don't mind waiting

5-Cognitive Response

*h. —I do without (4k, 4l, 4o, 6g, 7d)
life moves on
I make do
I just go on my way
I go without it until I can
*i. —I accept it (the situation) [unelaborated] (4k, 6g)
I adjust
I resign myself to it
then I just have to live with it
j. —I settle for what I can get (6e, 7d)
I'll take what I can get
I'll get what I can
k. —I compromise
I may make concessions
I compromise, for the time being
l. —that's that (4c, 4k, 4l)
oh well
too bad
then that's the breaks. Maybe I'll get it later
that's life
m. —it is for the best, God's will (4i)
so what? Life isn't fair always, and only spoiled people get what they want all the time
God has a better idea
I thank God for what I have
n. —I try to find out why
I wonder what I've done wrong
There is a reason for it

E6 Conscientious

6-Emotional Response

*a. —I feel frustrated (5a)
I get frustrated, and then try to get it again
b. —I feel resentful, impatient [distance or control implied] (5a, 5b)
I get furious on the inside but pretend I don't care
I become very upset but I try not to act like a spoiled brat
I primarily complain but realize my selfishness later
I sometimes act immaturely
I feel dissatisfied with my life
c. —I am unhappy but soon get over it (5a)
I pout for a little while, then go back to normal
naturally I am disappointed but I compromise
I often get depressed for several days before getting over it and trying again

it takes a while to let go of it
I tend to get upset initally, but I accept it in the end
d. —I am patient (5g)
I'll be patient until I do get it
I just wait patiently until I can get it or I just forget about it
I wait until something better comes along
now, I get it eventually

6-Behavioral Response

**e. —I'll try for something else (5j)
I get the next best thing
then I go to "Plan B"
I find a substitute
then I try another thing important
f. —I accept it only after I have tried again (5d, 7a)
I try again, then adjust
I accept it, after debate, & go on

6-Cognitive Response

g. —I accept it (the situation) [elaborated] (5i, 7d)
I try to be philosophical
I'll eventually get over it
I try to make the best of it
I very rarely complain
I don't let it make my life miserable
h. —I appreciate (am satisfied with) what I have, can get [unelaborated] (5i, 7d)
I have to reconcile myself to what I have
I use what I have
I have to make the best of what I can get
I thank the Lord up above for what I do have
i. —I rationalize, convince myself I don't want it (7d)
I try to talk myself out of it
I decide it wasn't worth it
I settle too easily for second-best
I sometimes deny that I want it
I usually feel pretty badly, then rationalize it away
j. —I change what I want (7c)
I try to want what I can get
I ask God to change my desires
I alter my expectations

6-Other

k. —it depends on what it is
I get upset or depressed depending on what it is
I try to explain why that is important to me
I do without and try later if it is still worth pursuing
I'll decide how important it is and whether or not to work hard toward it
I will keep trying for it if it is important to me, or give it up if not
it depends
depending on what it is, I may be unhappy or I may not care
l. Unclassified (Stem misread?) (3e, 4m)

I would want the capability to be more tolerant
I would have the perfect man that could understand
*   me, & relate to my feelings, & have a good career*
*   to take care of me*
I would wish for good health, peace, money

E7 Individualistic

7-Behavioral Response

   a. Different approaches to the same goal (original or elaborated) (3c, 5d, 6f)
then I try to subterfuge my way into it
I spend time trying to think of creative ways I can
I wait patiently and work on other avenues or "angles"
right now, I can wait till I do get it by working for it
I try the back-door approach
   b. —I sometimes manipulate people (4h)

7-Cognitive Response

   c. —I rethink my goals [elaborated] (6j)
I readjust my priorities
I alter my needs and goals
I would like to think I could accommodate to reachable goals
I think about ways I can get it, or decide if it's worth wanting
   d. —I try to be content with, accept what I have, can get [elaborated] (5i, 5j, 6g, 6h)
I try to be flexible & understand why not
I accept it and try to figure out if it was the best thing that could of happened
I stew a bit, but then become resigned to it
I accept the fact and look for something else
   e. Evaluation of situation and self (8a)
I try [to] analyze why I didn't get what I want and if my expectations were unreasonable
I examine how important my "want" was & is
it takes me a while to re-evaluate my priorities

7-Other

   f. Contrasting reactions (one E6) (8a)
I get annoyed or sometimes I resign myself, depends on the situation

I wait, try harder, or sometimes decide that I can do without it or that it just isn't for me
then I haven't tried hard enough or I want something beyond my reach
I settle for waiting or I accept the fact that I won't receive whatever it is
I am usually disappointed, but then I don't care after a while
I get frustrated, then philosophical
I'll do without it or I'll change my methods so as to get it later if I can't get it now
I generally blow it off although I feel frustrated for a brief period
I just wait until I do, & if I really can't, then I forget about it
   g. Combination responses with unique elements (8a)
I make impossibles possible
I go on living because it won't change my life
it's never very traumatic—I'm pretty flexible
I work harder to get it. I like to challenge myself
I tend to pout and withdraw; but I'm trying to be more flexible & trust God's plan
I try to accept it and then renegotiate later
I have other fish to fry and put on the fire
I don't let it become an obsession with me and continue with life
I just try for something else, I have to have a sign to be more aggressive
right away, I wait patiently. If there [is a] problem I try for something else just as good or valuable

E8 Autonomous

   a. Evaluation of the situation: 3 elements and 2 E6 ideas (7e, 7f, 7g)
I try to reason whether I needed it or was entitled to it. If I am entitled to it, I feel as though I am boiling—& feel choked
I let it go unless it is very important and impinges on my moral values or my children
I wait, reevaluate the need, reassess the approach to make it possible, if necessary
I re-examine my desire for it, my need for it, and the methods I used to achieve it
I adjust to this without much difficulty and often with some relief—as long as I am sure

Usually She (He) Felt That Sex . . .

This stem elicits both positive and negative remarks about sex at every level; so, by itself, favorableness is not a clue to ego level. However, there are few negative responses from subjects above E6. By far the largest number of responses from both genders express unconditional approval of or enjoyment of sex. Unfavorable views of sex come mainly, but not exclusively, from females.

Age is also a factor, as young subjects may express childhood prohibitions. Disapproval and prohibitions account for many of the responses below E4. However, responses indicating sexual inexperience are not rated lower; thus, "is going to be beautiful" is rated the same as "is beautiful" (E5). A few high-level responses are given even by young or inexperienced subjects.

Although there are many ways of expressing approval of sex at E4 and E5, they are not sharply differentiating with respect to ego level. At E4, the remarks are quite bland; on average, more enthusiasm is expressed at E5. Beginning at E5 and increasingly so at E6, contingent attitudes are expressed, that is, there are "right" partners and appropriate times and places. At E6, emphasis shifts to appropriate feelings, particularly love, of course.

Many people have a feeling of privacy about sex. Some say so, but probably some of the bland expressions of approval are ways of avoiding self-revealing statements. Categories that do not fit the four main themes are grouped as "Other." Most of them have an impersonal tone. This is one of the few items for which there are clear E9 responses, uniting personal and impersonal ideas in a complex way.

Most categories include responses from both sexes, but many, perhaps most, are predominantly given by one or the other.

Themes:

Favorable (E3–E7): a game; is good; important part of marriage; expression of love; brings a couple closer.
Unfavorable (E2–E6): was bad; boring; overrated; exploitive.
Contingent (E3–E7): for married people; OK with the right person; for lovers; once a pain but now enjoyable.
Private (E2–E6): is his own business; shouldn't be discussed; was a private matter.
Other (E4–E7): is routine; should be taken seriously; something I would learn about later; something others enjoyed more than she.

ITEM 33: USUALLY SHE (HE) FELT THAT SEX . . .

E2 Impulsive

2-Unfavorable

a. —was bad (3c, 3d, 4i)
is not good
was a no-no

2-Private

b. —is her own business (5t, 6o)

E3 Self-Protective

3-Favorable

a. —was a game (4b)
was a play
b. —is all there is (5c)
was the only thing in life

3-Unfavorable

c. —was wrong, a sin (2a)

was a crime
d. —was nasty, not nice (2a, 4i)
was violent
was very disgusting and terrible

3-Contingent

*e. —is for married people (5q, 6n)
is for older people
is wrong when a minor

E4 Conformist

4-Favorable

**a. —is good (5a)
was a good thing
was nice
*b. —was fun (3a, 5b)
sounded like fun
was a lark
*c. —is important, necessary (5e, 6c)
is important & fun
was the most important
d. —is normal, natural, healthy (5f, 6c)
is a wholesome act
e. —is OK
f. —was good for [something]
is good for the body
was good for a person
was necessary socially

4-Unfavorable

*g. —is unnecessary, unimportant (6j)
is not all in life
*h. —is boring
is pointless
is not worth it
is tiring
is monotonous
i. —is dirty (2a, 3d, 5t)
was dirty to talk about
repulsive
is disgusting
j. —is uncomfortable, painful
felt bad
was harmful
k. —was not what she wanted (5l)
was forbidden for her
was something she'd never try
was not for him

4-Other

l. —is routine, common
was taken for granted
was a normal everyday occurrence
m. Evasion
I don't know

—who is he?
?

E5 Self-Aware

5-Favorable

**a. —was great, wonderful (4a)
can be wonderful
was interesting
was magnificent!
**b. —was enjoyable, pleasant (4b)
is a positive experience
*c. —was special, the greatest (3b)
was his favorite pastime
was everything in the world
was the best part of living
was fantastic
was the only fun way to exercise
was the greatest leisure activity
d. —is exciting, stimulating (6a)
was passionate
was thrilling
e. —was an important, necessary part of marriage, a relationship (4c, 6h)
was part of married life
was the most important thing in a woman-man relationship
was the completion of a relationship
f. —was (an important) part of life (unqualified) (4d, 6c)
is something one can't do without
was a very important thing in her life
is part of everyone's life
g. —was part of being a woman, a man
is important in being a man
h. —was an act of love (6b)
was love
meant love
i. —was a gift
was part of God's design
was fantastic and the best gift of life
j. —was (is going to be) beautiful (6h)
was a beautiful experience
k. —is relaxing, a release (6a)
relieved her tensions
made her an easier person to be around
was an outlet
was a means of "cooling off" only

5-Unfavorable

*l. —was overrated; was unappealing (4k)
wasn't that good
was not what it was cracked up to be
wasn't satisfying
was disappointing in practice

*was played up out of proportion to its fundamental
    role*
ok, I really don't enjoy it
was adequate, but not spectacular

m. —was overemphasized, overpublicized
    could be overdone
    was his only preoccupation
    was being exploited too much in American society

n. —was one-sided (6d)
    was the only thing on her boyfriend's mind
    was only enjoyed by the man
    was to satisfy himself only

o. —was an obligation, a chore
    was her duty
    was a burden because she is so tired all the time

p. —is, could be a problem
    would ruin their relationship
    was still dangerous
    interfered w/ her friendships with guys

5-Contingent

*q. —is OK, good, with the right person, circumstances
    (3e, 6e, 6i, 6n)
    would be great with her boyfriend
    was unnecessary when it was not desired
    *okay as long as she felt it was the right time and
        she wanted to do it*
    is right in the context of marriage
    wasn't right until you did it with the right man
    had its place
    was fun in moderation

r. —was not enough
    something she wanted more of
    was over too quick
    was a good thing but it wasn't enough

s. —could wait
    was good but to wait till your older

5-Private

*t. —was not to be discussed (2b, 4i, 6o)
    was taboo
    hard to talk about to children
    *wasn't something you would talk about with your
        parents*
    was a topic he'd rather not discuss
    was best kept in the bedroom

u. —was embarrassing

5-Other

v. —is for procreation
    was only for the purposes of having a family

w. —should be discussed openly (6q)
    a topic that can be spoken about

x. —should be taken seriously, not misused (6m)
    is not always used as it should be
    not to be joked about

had been trivialized

y. Frequency
    should be something one gets every day
    was missing from my life
    was hard to get
    was a twice a month thing

z. —was underestimated, neglected
    often got a bum rap

E6 Conscientious

6-Favorable

*a. —was satisfying, fulfilling (5d, 5k)
    was both fun and affirming
    is one of the greatest experiences in living
    was very rewarding

*b. —was an expression of love (5h, 7a)
    was solely for love
    was expression of closeness
    is a natural joining of two lovers
    was the greatest form of emotional expression

*c. —was a natural, normal part of life; necessary to life
    (4c, 4d, 5f)
    was a fascinating part of life
    was vital
    was a basic need
    was a necessity for well-being
    was the spice of life

6-Unfavorable

d. —was exploitive (5n)
    was her way of getting someone to love her
    was just another way of using someone else
    is controlled by men—when, how, & why
    was not a shared, loving act
    should not be a pressure-type situation

6-Contingent

*e. —is good, special for people who love each other
    (3e, 5q)
    was appropriate if you love the person
    *was a special thing, only to be done with someone
        she loves*
    *was wonderful between two people who really love
        each other*
    was nice, if it went along with love & respect
    could be fulfilling with love

f. —requires love, is not the same without love
    *should be an important emotional experience, not
        just a way to have fun*
    was for lovers
    should be romantic
    is no replacement for love

g. —should be shared by both
    was a two-way deal
    was good for both of them

should be a loving and sharing experience
should be done when both parties want it

h. —wonderful, beautiful in marriage, love (5e, 5j)
would be a beautiful experience w/ someone he loved
was a wonderful experience of passion

i. Approval with reservations (5q)
is something I enjoy but don't have to have
was momentarily satisfying
like liquor, leaves a hang-over
was enjoyable but lately a lot of trouble
was fun, but he didn't like to be pushed into it

j. —was not always important; was secondary to other
things (4g)
was just a diversion
was important but not all important
was not as important as a good personal relationship
is not that important; it's the caring and loving
is less important than true friendship
was secondary to achievement
*would be a nice thing to have, but often the need for
sleep is greater*

k. Contrasting attitudes or ideas (7d, 8c)
is vulgar, but sometimes it's beautiful
although not unsatisfying, was a bit of a chore
was scary but exciting!
was right for her, but sometimes it was empty
*is better with someone you love, but sometimes he
had it with women he didn't love*
is not just for procreation but for self-expression
controlled him, rather than vice versa
is dangerous and stupid outside of a love relationship

l. Physical vs. emotional aspects
was only a physical component of love
*was better when between the ears rather than be-
tween the legs*
*fell into 2 categories: physical, and meaningful and
romantic*
was physical, not emotional

m. Concern with meaning (5x)
has a meaning other than two teenagers making love
meant commitment
*was only a good thing if it had deep meaning for
each partner*
was meaningless

n. —depends on the person (5q)
is good for some people
*was alright depending on who she is. If she's me,
forget it*
depends on who he is

6-Private

*o. —was a private matter (2b, 5t)
*was something 2 people shared intimately & pri-
vately*
was a very personal thing
was an invasion of her privacy

6-Other

p. Sex as subject matter (7c)
*was something that should be discovered about w/
her mate*
was something I would learn about later
was something to be taught in the home
was very confusing

q. Denial of negative feelings (5w)
was nothing to be ashamed of

E7 Individualistic

7-Favorable

a. An expression of love (elaborated) (6b)
was a special way to show she loves him
*was an expression of one's true emotions in that
relationship*
was an enjoyable way to tell his wife he loved her

b. —brings a couple closer (8b)
makes a relationship as intimate as it can be
was a deep connecting time to come together

c. —was mysterious (6p)
was a pleasure, a mystery, and a marvelous joke
is a special and miraculous thing
was a form of magic
was a wonderful thing—beautiful and mysterious

7-Contingent

d. Feelings change with time and experience (6k)
was overemphasized and not critical in later life
was once a real pain, but now enjoyable
*was a lot of work; now he finally realized it didn't
have to be*
was a relationship; now he knows it was only a part

7-Other

e. Evaluation of others' opinions
*is great when she's in love—awful without a love—
begging for closeness*
*is the most important aspect of life. I don't feel that
way*
*[Usually I felt that sex] was too much of a preoc-
cupation with my friends*
*was a forbidden word in the vocabulary of "good"
people*
was something that others enjoyed more than she

f. Gentle, nonhostile humor
*was like puppies playing—fun and warm and gentle
and tender*
*was something he could take or leave—until there
was an opportunity to take*

g. Unclassified
was enjoyable and was a means to share self
*is an important part of being human and a need that
most people have*
is an integral and meaningful part of a relationship

is too complex a subject to deal with in one sentence

was a source of mixed feeling and reactions

was not going to be the deciding factor in my pursuit of happiness

is agreeable, a necessary part of any final relationship with one's wife, but spoiled by S. Freud

was a terrific, exciting, & too rare occurrence

for the sake of sex only was not enough without affection

was extremely important, but that too much tended to drain one's personality somewhat

was a delicious experience and an indispensable outlet

E8 Autonomous

a. —was a means of discovering self, others

was simply & naturally a good way to know himself and others

was a way to identify who she was

was a place she was learning a lot about herself and her husband in

b. —strengthens the bonds of a relationship (7b)

helped to make a stronger bond in her relationship

was exhilarating & good clean fun—and the best cement for marital relations

c. Complexity: 3 elements, one E6 (6k)

was a confusing thing. It was seen as a very strong drive that he knew very little about

was of secondary importance in marriage to a solid friendship and tolerant understanding

was fun and enjoyable, and too intimate of an experience to [be] shared with anyone but a woman he cared for

E9 Integrated

Unclassified

had been removed from its relation to love and to life, & used as a medium to promote sales, & he felt deeply resentful of it & its contribution to dehumanization of people

was both mysteriously exciting in itself, yet more significant because of its context and for what it expressed (or failed to express) than as an immediate experience

For a Woman a Career Is . . .

The term *career* rather than *job* in this stem produces a middle-class bias, and the content of some low-level responses reflects realities of life in lower socioeconomic classes. A secretary may be a career girl, but a cleaning woman has a job.

There is little if any relation between ego level and approval or disapproval of a career for women. Unequivocally disapproving statements are not frequent at any level, and they are rarer in the 1980s samples than in the 1960s samples. The largest group of responses comprises stereotyped expressions of approval and is rated E4. The difficulties that a career poses for women, particularly in relation to marriage, are stressed at E6. Above E6, many responses concern problems and advantages of combining career and marriage. Criticisms at higher levels are more like reservations than outright criticism.

Four views about a woman's career were frequently expressed by women tested in the 1960s. First, a career is a job to be given up at marriage; second, being a wife, mother, and homemaker is a woman's career; third, a career is a kind of self-indulgence, hence secondary to a woman's duty to her family; fourth, a career is viewed as a means of self-expression, whether a job or at home. Those themes are present in women and men tested in the 1980s, but the first two are no longer prominent. New themes are that a career is important or necessary, it is the woman's option or choice, and it is as important as a man's career. In addition, the belief that a career enhances a woman's self-esteem is now a popular category; no such remark appears in the old manual.

Some of the responses classed at E2 may indicate a poor understanding of the stem. At E4, a career is a thing you have, whereas, at E5, it tends to be seen more often as a goal or process. Choices and contingencies, particularly marriage, enter at E5. At E6, some subjects see career in relation to inner needs rather than only the outside situation. A few responses beginning at E5 and increasingly at higher levels put a career in a wider social context than simply self and family. At E8, more responses concern integration of career and marriage than at lower levels; some also state or imply that the obstacles to a career result from the woman's own conflicts.

The theme "tied to family" does not refer to the woman being tied to her family but to the response having reference to family.

Themes:

Criticism (E2–E7): nothing; hard work; unimportant; demanding; important if it's what she wants; it depends on the woman.

Approval (E2–E7): nice; a good thing; important; an important part of life today; rewarding; an outlet for self-expression.

Purpose (E3–E7): money; a source of security; necessary for independence; a dream to be realized; a means of achieving identity.

Tied to family (E3–E8): being a housewife; good but marriage is better; fine until children come along; important but family is first; whatever she wants to do, being a housewife or having a job; in conflict with desire to be a good mother.

Other (E2–E7): be good; typing; as important as a man's; getting to be a necessary evil; good if it is her OWN ambition.

ITEM 34: FOR A WOMAN A CAREER IS . . .

E2 Impulsive

2-Criticism

  a. —nothing

2-Approval

  b. —nice (3c, 4e, 4f)
  c. —having a good job
    a career
    a job

2-Other

  d. Unclassified: inappropriate responses
    sleeping all day
    that she don't mess with dope [sic]
    be good
    be clean

E3 Self-Protective

3-Criticism

  a. —hard work (5a)
    lots of work
    very hard for her
  b. —not good (4b)

3-Approval

  c. —good (2b, 4e. 4f)
    a good thing
  d. —great; special (4e)
  e. —everything
    sometimes everything

3-Purpose

  f. A way to get money (5l)
    money

3-Tied to Family

  g. —being a wife, mother (4i)
    stay home and take care of the children
    having kids and cleaning house
    in the kitchen

3-Other

  h. Specific occupations
    nurse
    going to school
    typing

E4 Conformist

4-Criticism

  a. —secondary, unimportant [unelaborated] (5f)
    not as essential
    not that important

  b. —not satisfactory; not enough (3b)
    limited

4-Approval

  **c. —important, necessary [unelaborated] (5d, 5f)
    kind of important
    essential
    a must!
  d. —valuable
    a reward
    considered a gift
    something desired and worth having
  e. —fine; wonderful; OK (2b, 3c, 3d)
    pleasure
    happiness
  f. —good (nice) to have (2b, 3c)
    the best thing for her
    positive
  g. —sometimes good (5c, 6d)
    good for a while

4-Tied to Family

  h. Value compared with that of marriage (unelaborated) (6p, 6s)
    anything but motherhood
    as important as a family
    good but marriage is better
  i. —raising a family (3g)

E5 Self-Aware

5-Criticism

  a. —difficult; demanding; time-consuming (3a, 6o)
    the result of hard work
    too consuming
    possible, but difficult—
    something she works hard to get and keep
  b. —hard to attain
  c. —somewhat debatable (4g, 6c)
    unsure
    not always the best thing

5-Approval

  *d. —an important part of life (today) (4c, 6b, 6t)
    or should be, an important part of her life
    as important as anything else
    a key element of life
    her number one thing in life for herself
  *e. —challenging, satisfying (6e)
    something she should enjoy
    a good stimulus
    motivating
    a life time of happiness if she enjoys what she does
  f. —good but not necessary (4a, 4c)

important but not necessarily vital

5-Purpose

*g. —a goal (6g, 7d)
   the most important goal in her life
   her dream
*h. —a source of security (independence, freedom)
   [unelaborated] (6m)
   stability
   her only hope
   making her an independent person
   an insurance policy that will provide for her future
  i. —an opportunity; a stepping stone (6g)
   very important to success
   a chance in life
   a chance to move up in the world
  j. —an outlet; a way out (6i)
   *usually taken up to satisfy the need to be more than
      a housewife*
   an escape
  k. —a side-line
   not that important but something on the side
   something for her to busy herself
  l. —a way to make a living, help family's financial
      needs (3f)
   pay bills, support kids' needs

5-Tied to Family

  m. Importance, value contingent on marital status (6n,
      6p, 6q, 6s)
   *important, because it helps her take care of her
      family*
   most important if she's single & has children
   fine until children came along

5-Other

**n. Comparison with a man's career (unqualified)
   not as important as a man's career
   harder than for a man
   probably no less satisfying than it is for a man
*o. —anything she wants to do, likes to do (6a, 6d, 7f,
      7i)
   what she wants to do with herself
   whatever she chooses
   doing what makes her happy
  p. —what she makes of it (6d)
   as important as she wants it to be
   anything that makes her feel that she is doing a job
  q. —her life (6b)
   the main point in her life
   a way of life
  r. Society's views (unelaborated) (6t)
   getting easier
   becoming a necessity
   more of an option in today's society
   in vogue
   more important now than it was for my mother

E6 Conscientious

6-Criticism

*a. —good (important) if it's what she wants to do (5o,
      7f, 7i)
   *very important, if she so chooses to pursue one
      whole-heartedly*
   wonderful, if she finds the right one
  b. —(only) part of her life (5d, 5q)
   not the most important thing in life
   part of her lifestyle
   important, not her life
  c. —sometimes important and sometimes not (4g, 5c,
      7b)
   important for some and not for others
   sometimes meaningful, sometimes not desirable

6-Approval

*d. —an option; her choice (5o, 5p, 7f)
   up to her
   as impt. as she feels it is
   should be available if she wants it
*e. —rewarding, fulfilling (5e, 7c)
   a fulfillment of herself
   a difficult but satisfying achievement
   gratifying
*f. —important for self-esteem (7c, 8a)
   *important to many because it is makes them feel
      important*
   part of her self
   very prestigious to her
   a personality statement
  g. —an achievement, accomplishment (5g, 5i, 7d)
   very important. Gives her a sense of accomplishment
   an important part of her successfulness
   what she spent all that time preparing for
  h. —a way to express herself, show her abilities (7c)
   helping her prove a point in many cases
   a way of testing her limitations
  i. —emancipation from the home (5j)
   an escape from the tediousness of being a housewife
   an outlet where she can conform in a new direction
   escape from her first responsibility to a family
  j. —(good, important if it is) something she can do
      well, suited to her abilities
   anything she has the drive to be qualified for
   sometimes suited to her calling
  k. —important for her growth, development [unelabo-
      rated] (7c, 8a)
   something to well-round her as a person
   a growing experience
  l. —important for her well-being (7g)
   needed for mental health
   very important so that she won't get bored with life
   vital if she is the type who needs that to remain sane

6-Purpose

*m. —necessary for (feeling of) independence (5h)
very important to show her independence and worthiness
necessary, for her to be able to depend on someone, knowing that she doesn't have to
very important, especially to support herself and not depend in nobody [sic]

6-Tied to Family

*n. —secondary to marriage, her family, her home (5m)
not always [as] important as the family
secondary and distracting
an option but not priority to family
either first or second in her life
very important, but her family is first

o. —difficult to mix with raising a family; should not interfere with marriage (5a)
hampered by the role of mother, housekeeper, etc.
frequently going to take or demand priority over family issues
tough if she has a family
a difficult path if you are involved with a successful or demanding man

p. Compared with family (elaborated) (4h, 5m)
essential—it is half of her life, the other half being love
a right, but she can't really expect to be a man's equal while she's having children
important, but no more important than being a mother
very important and a top priority, second is raising a family

q. —good if she considers her husband and family first (5m)
a fine opportunity as long as the children are not sacrificed

r. —either marriage or a profession
essential, even if the career is motherhood
whatever she plans to do, be it raise a family or work

s. (Not) An alternative to or substitute for marriage and family (4h, 5m)
a challenge—and sometimes a substitute for not enough love in her life
sometimes more attractive than being a mother & wife

6-Other

t. Society's views (elaborated) (5r)
usually considered secondary, but it shouldn't be getting to be a necessary evil in the U.S.A.
difficult in a male-oriented and -dominated society
now becoming first compared to a family
now possible without guilt
difficult to manage in our culture

enjoyable but not compensated accordingly or equally

E7 Individualistic

7-Criticism

a. Personal or inner reservations
very competitive
for me it's important
being independent but there is a price to pay
often overemphasized—the same for a man
good, but it's not for me

b. —it depends on the woman (6c)
important, depending on her needs and wants
either important or not, depending on the woman

7-Approval

*c. Means of self-expression, self-fulfillment, self-development (6e, 6f, 6h, 6k, 8a)
important to develop as a whole human being
one important aspect of personal development
a great opportunity to round out her life and enhance her as a total person

7-Purpose

d. —a dream to be realized (5g, 6g)
a dream that one has worked to get for long and hard working years
a dream, a goal to be brought to reality

7-Tied to Family

e. Relation to marriage, complex or original contingencies
second to her family but an important expanding resource as well
important only if it is not at the expense of her family. In some situations it contributes to the emotional stability of a family
possible in conjunction with marriage and family rearing and can be kept along with marriage
secondary to a happy home life, if she is wise

f. —whatever she wants to do: whether being a housewife or having an outside job (5o, 6a, 6d)
whatever it is that truly makes her happy, whether working in the job force or staying home being a full-time wife & mother
something she has to really want

g. —a conflict, balance [unelaborated] (6l, 8b)
what balances out her life
the basis for her equilibrium with others

7-Other

h. Evaluation in context of identity or of role as a woman (8a)

another part of her self aside from her family that is necessary to her for her own personal development

an estrangement from the usual role a woman has been subjected to

sometimes important to make her feel she is someone, but she should not have to feel ashamed of being "just" a wife & mother

another identity, another part of a multi-faceted self

i. Individual choice in social context (5o, 6a)

good if that is her OWN ambition, not society's

of her making, but restricted somewhat by societal constraints

a matter of choice with respect to her assessment of her self in terms of the world in which she lives

j. Unclassified

not only her security blanket, but also a positive self-esteem builder

another alternative lifestyle, a way to assert, a way to get a more comfortable standard of living

a means to (and expression of) independence

E8 Autonomous

a. —a means of achieving identity (6f, 6k, 7c, 7h)

sometimes very important because they can identify themselves by it and sometimes sacrifice a family for it

a way of developing an independent identity

an expression of who she is in the world

b. Conflict, balance of own needs, goals, and family's (7g)

her choice alone, until a family and/or are involved, then both husband & wife's choice [sic]

a means of fulfillment, helping make her an intellectual, interesting person, so that she may be a better wife-companion

tolerated, until she finds an inner security for herself and her children

frequently in conflict with her desires to be a good mother

hazardous if married. I feel it would probably conflict with the husband's sense of importance

My Conscience Bothers Me if . . .

Although this stem has one of the hardest words in the test form, most subjects give clear, pertinent replies.

Responses are not interpreted as the kind of transgression the subject is likely to commit, but rather as what she would consider a transgression: What value system would lead to this response? Because the stem is a potentially embarrassing one, some disguise can be expected; so some inferences about what is meant may be needed. In general, progress is from actions classed as bad per se, to disobeying external rules, to bad consequences for others, to breaking the social compact or violating internal standards. Acts of commission are recognized at an earlier stage than corresponding acts of omission.

Theoretically, the E2 subject lacks an adult conscience. The distinctive responses at this level just say bad behavior, but other likely responses, also found at E3 and E4, name more or less taboo acts (often sexual ones). Any implication of violation of general rules, loss of attempted control, or concern for interpersonal consequences would raise the rating to a higher level than E2.

At E3, the most frequent response is just doing something wrong, a response that does not discriminate well between levels. Other characteristic E3 responses indicate callousness or getting caught. Some categories at this level would be classed as irrelevant by a person with a more mature conscience. The one category that refers to violation of a rule mentions stealing, a concrete transgression.

At E4, responses refer chiefly to infractions of specific, concrete, externally imposed rules. Awareness of inner life, one's own or that of others, is characteristic of E5. Thus, hurting someone's feelings or knowing that one has done wrong are typical E5 answers.

At E6, intentions and purposes are prominent. Thus "do something I feel is wrong," compared with knowing I have done something wrong, implies that I have chosen the standards by which I call something wrong. Not only will a subject at this level say her conscience bothers her when she has intentionally done something wrong, but paradoxically, some will say their conscience bothers them when they have unintentionally done so. Prohibitions decline in importance and are replaced by obligations and responsibilities.

At E7 and E8, there is further internalization of standards, sometimes expressed as failing to meet one's own or others' expectations. Another aspect of the highest levels is criticism of one's own conscience; it may be bothered even for trivial things, like lying or scolding, the person may say. The implication is self-examination not only of behavior but of conscience, thus criticism of excessive self-criticism.

Themes:

I behave badly (E2–E6): am bad; do something wrong; lie; do something I know is wrong; not sincere.

I fail standards (E3–E7): can't have my way; don't do the right thing; not doing my work; go against what I believe in; not done my best.

I harm someone (E4–E7): scold my child; hurt someone's feelings; have been unfair; break a trust; did not help for selfish reasons.

Other (E2–E7): get caught; don't have a conscience; don't say what I feel.

ITEM 35: MY CONSCIENCE BOTHERS ME IF . . .

E2 Impulsive

2-I Behave Badly

   a. —I am bad (4d)
     I am unpure

2-Other

   b. Repetition of stem (3i)
     my conscience bothers me

E3 Self-Protective

3-I Behave Badly

**a. —I do something wrong (4b, 4h, 5b, 5c)
     I do something that is not right
     I do something
     I do wrong to anything
   b. —I steal (4a)
     I lyed or stole [sic]
   c. —I get mad (5m)
     I'm angry

3-I Fail Standards

   d. —I don't do what I want to do
     I don't buy something that I want
     I can't have my own way

3-Other

   e. —I let it (4l)
     I do it anyway
   f. Stem read as "I feel bad when"
     I don't have a boyfriend
     my sister do something wrong
     people hurt me
     someone dies in the family
     people are abused
   g. —I get caught; I am under suspicion (4e)
     I get in trouble
   h. —I worry
     I worry about something for a long time
     I have nothing to worry about
   i. Evasion (2b)
     I don't talk about
     don't no

E4 Conformist

4-I Behave Badly

**a. —I lie, cheat [unelaborated] (3b, 5a, 5c, 6a)
     I tell someone a lie
     I am not telling the truth
   b. —I make a foolish mistake (3a, 5l, 5x)
     I make the wrong decision
     I've acted like a fool with a guy

   c. —I spend too much money (5i)
     I waste money
     I don't pay a bill on time
   d. Sexual acts (no implication of standards) (2a, 5n)
     I screwed around
     stay out late at night
     I miss a period
   e. —I think of bad things, my past (3g, 6q)
     people talk about things in my past
     I think about my past which is a sad one
   f. —I break a rule (5g)
     I speed too much
     I drink too much
   g. —I say the wrong thing (5f, 5w)
     I use bad language
     I say something that maybe I shouldn't have
     I say something really mean

4-I Fail Standards

   h. —I do not do the right thing (3a, 5b, 5c, 5q, 6f)
     I don't do something right

4-I Harm Someone

   i. —I fight, argue, nag
     I get in a fight with my boyfriend
     talk back to my mother
     I have an argument with a girl
     I scold people
   j. —I am hard on my kids [vague] (5h, 5v)
     I scold my child
   k. —I don't help people [unelaborated] (5u)

4-Other

   l. —I don't have a conscience; my conscience never
     bothers me (3e)
     I tell it to shut up
   m. —I do certain things [vague]
     I forget things
     I let something go on
   n. —my children misbehave
     my son acts up in public or in school

E5 Self-Aware

5-I Behave Badly

**a. —I lie [elaborated]; I am dishonest [trait, not behavior] (4a, 6a)
     I'm not truthful
     I am false
     I am not completely honest and straight forward
     I say one thing to a person, then something else to
     another
     I don't tell the whole truth
     I tell a lie to someone I care about

I lie about something important
I lie unnecessarily
I tell a white lie

*b. —I do something I know is wrong (3a, 4h, 6d, 6h, 8b)

I know or do something that shouldn't be done
I do something I know was wrong so as to benefit me

c. —I do something I shouldn't (3a, 4h)

I am doing something that I shouldn't be doing

d. —I do something (wrong) without admitting it (6o)

I didn't tell my wife where I was going
I do something wrong behind someone's back
I do something wrong to someone and then deny it later

e. —I have to lie to someone (4a)

I have to keep something from a close friend
I can't tell the truth about something
I have to lie to spare someone's feelings

f. —I talk about someone (4g)

I talk behind someone's back

g. —I disobey my parents (4f)

I do something that would embarrass my mom
I do something I have been taught against

h. Inappropriate discipline (4j)

I am too critical of my child or husband
I shouted at my child and he did not deserve it

i. —I buy something I don't need, can't afford (4c)

I spend money on things I want and not on what I need

5-I Fail Standards

*j. —I have sinned; I disobey God (6c)

I don't pray often enough
I do something against my religion
I have not read the Bible that day
I go against G-d's conscience

*k. —I am not doing my work; I waste time (6e)

I am not studying and I should be
I've left work early
I don't get something done on time
I don't get things accomplished

l. —I don't do a task well [unelaborated] (4b, 6p)

I fail a class
I don't feel I have put in a good day's work for my pay

m. Lack of self-discipline, self-restraint (3c)

I don't get something done because of being lazy
I cheat on my diet
I give in to myself too much
I procrastinate
I lose my temper

n. Sexual transgressions (implied standards) (4d)

I were to cheat on my husband
I lie, cheat, steal, and sometimes have indiscriminate sex

I go & "make out" more than I should
I don't take a pill and I have sex

o. Differentiated emotions, self-critical

I am guilty
I don't feel guilty when I should
I mistrust people
I don't feel grateful

p. Petty transgressions

I kill an insect
I don't work out
I litter

q. —I don't do what I think is right (4h, 6f)

5-I Harm Someone

**r. —I hurt someone's feelings [unelaborated] (6i, 6k, 7c)

I offend others
I make anyone feel bad
hurt people

*s. —I mistreat someone; I do wrong to others [vague or unspecified] (6l, 8b)

I am unkind
I am rude to someone
I am cruel
I don't put others first
I forget how to be nice to people

*t. —I break a promise, let someone down (6e, 6m, 7d)

I make plans with friends, then don't follow through
I don't keep my word
I forget an obligation

u. —I don't help people when they need it, when asked, if I could (4k, 7e)

I ignore the downtrodden
I pass by a beggar
I turned down a request to help someone
I don't help someone, especially someone I know

v. —I neglect my family (4j)

I don't keep in touch with my family as often as I should
I can't spend time with my daughter
my child is sick and I can't be with him

5-Other

w. —I don't say what's on my mind (4g)

I am dishonest or non-communicative
I don't say what I feel I should say

x. —I can't figure something out; I make a bad decision (4b)

can't explain to myself why I made that decision
I have a problem and don't know what to do about it

E6 Conscientious

6-I Behave Badly

a. —I am dishonest [elaborated] [trait, not just behavior] (4a, 5a)

I lie to someone I like, regardless of the situation

I am less than honest w/ those I care about

b. —I misrepresent something (5a)

I have intentionally misstated the facts or have not shared all the facts

I feel I may have misstated someone's else's position

I tell big lies to people or deliberately mislead them

6-I Fail Standards

c. —I act contrary to my principles [unelaborated] (5j, 5q, 8a)

I go against what I believe in to conform with others

I stray from my morals

I go against my honor

I don't listen to it

I am forced to do something I don't believe in

I preach one thing and do the opposite

d. —I am not true to myself (5b)

I do something that I feel is wrong—not what others feel

I am not honest with myself

I am not sincere in what I say

I believe that I have been hypocritical

e. —I don't fulfill my responsibilities (5k, 5t, 5v)

I ignore an obligation

I don't live up to the expectations set for me

f. —I don't do something I should (4h, 5c, 5q)

g. —I have not done my best [unelaborated] (7a)

I don't live up to my expectations

I know I could do better

I haven't "given it my all"

h. —I do something I feel is wrong [elaborated] (5b, 5o)

I go along with something I think is wrong because I was too scared to speak out

I do something I know I should not have done, and I begin to feel guilty

6-I Harm Someone

i. —I intentionally (unintentionally) hurt someone (5r, 7b, 7c)

I have hurt someone with a joke, or unintentionally

I have unwittingly injured someone

I lie—or am intentionally cruel to anyone

I deliberately do something against my parents' wills

j. —I have been selfish, inconsiderate (8c)

I put what I want before the wants of my family

I don't consider someone else's feelings

I have spoken thoughtlessly

k. —I feel that I have hurt someone (5r)

I have caused mental or physical anguish to another individual

I am the cause of hurt and anguish to another person

l. —I have been unfair, unjust (5s)

I feel that I'm not being fair to my child

I see an injustice occurring

I become angry at my 3-year-old daughter because of some of my internal [illegible] rather than anything she did

m. —I deceive others (5t, 7d)

I have betrayed someone

I dissemble

I am dishonest to my parents, friends, myself

I give people the wrong impression and don't straighten them out

I pretend to like a guy who likes me just because I don't want to hurt his feelings

I put someone off and have made up a "white lie"

n. —I take advantage of others

o. —I do wrong without atoning, making amends (5d)

I do something that I know is wrong and don't do anything to change it

I don't finish with interpersonal conflicts

I have unconfessed sin

I do something I shouldn't and I haven't been punished

6-Other

p. —I don't correct my errors (5l)

I don't do anything when I have a problem

q. Taboo thoughts (4e)

I think too much about sex

I think of other men

I think bad things about other people

E7 Individualistic

7-I Fail Standards

a. —I have not done my best [elaborated] (5l, 6g)

I am not able to do a good complete job at what I am working on

I don't do what I am suppose to do or if I see wrong & don't do anything about it

I feel that I haven't put enough work into an assignment or a particular task or goal

b. Even if action is unintentional, insignificant, unavoidable (6i)

I act in ways that aren't my value system or if others are hurt by my actions even if I believe in my actions

I tell even the whitest lie or gossip

I do the littlest thing wrong

I cheat 10 cents on my taxes

I either intentionally or unintentionally hurt someone

7-I Harm Someone

c. —I hurt others' feelings [elaborated, differentiated] (5r, 6i)

I lie about something that will come out later on & will hurt my loved ones

I get close to a guy too quickly and then realise I've made a mistake and have to back off

I do not really listen to a person

d. —I break a trust (5t, 6m)
   I lie to a person who relies on my truthfulness
   I don't carry through with a commitment to myself or others

e. —I have failed to help [elaborated] (5u, 8c)
   do something for somebody and I know that I am not helping them in the long-run
   I have refused help to someone who needed it (whether asked or not)
   I reject an honest plea for help (whether it's direct or hidden)

E8 Autonomous

a. —I act contrary to my principles [elaborated or unique expression] (6c)
   I do something that my inner guide says not to do & I do it anyway
   I violate the values and principles that are me—it is always with me
   I do something I consider is seriously wrong—integrity is important

I hold back my feelings, tell a lie, or don't live up to my expectations
   and that is very often, I don't live anywhere up to my expectations of myself

b. —I deliberately harm someone [elaborated] (5b. 5s)
   say something stupid or demeaning—especially if I cannot correct the situation
   I have done something for my benefit but at someone else's expense
   I feel I could have been more honest but was afraid of the potential criticism or rejection that would result

c. —I did not help others for selfish reasons (6j, 7e)
   I do not do the extra thoughtful or ethical acts I have no excuse for not doing
   I nag my husband or have selfish motives for what I do

d. Unclassified
   I lie—but I don't know if it bothers me because I'm sorry or because I'm afraid I'll be caught
   I scold my children over minor faults, then later realize how trivial it was

A Woman (Man) Should Always . . .

This stem invites response in terms of rules and social norms. The rules may be cautionary ones, typical at E3; conventional social norms, typical at E4; or duties and obligations, typical at E6. There is another major theme, prominent at E5 and E6, that includes rights, hopes, and aspirations for the self. At the highest levels, E7 and E8, the surest clue is cognitive complexity. However, miscellaneous responses grouped as unclassified at E8 illustrate a variety of themes found at that level for other items. Subjects who object to the imperative "should always" are likely to be at high levels. The rare responses that express concern for social issues also come from high levels.

This stem was included in the original women's form, and the main part of this manual is based on their responses. Male responses are given as a supplement; however, the male manual is richer in illustrations of the highest levels. Corresponding categories for the two parts are given the same E-level and letter, even when they are worded slightly differently. Responses included in the women's manual are not repeated for men. Categories omitted in the male version did not appear in the responses from men; if such responses occur, as they probably will, they should be rated according to the women's version.

There do not seem to be categories that are clearly at different ego levels for men and women. The closest were "be faithful, honest, truthful" (E4h), and "be himself, be true to himself" (E5j). Both are marginally higher for male subjects.

Although levels do not differ for men and women, the frequency of certain topics is different. Remarks about being faithful and taking care of the family are more frequent among men, whereas remarks about keeping up appearance are more frequent among women.

Responses concerned with the woman's role—particularly clichés like "be feminine" or "act like a woman"—come from subjects at all levels, but are relatively more frequent at E5 and higher. The expressions "be, talk like, remain, or act like a lady or woman," although in principle not identical, seem to be used interchangeably and are classed E5. However, to feel like a lady or to remember that one is a lady or woman, classed at E6, is different from being or acting like one. At E8, the response may be to look, feel, *and* act like a lady or woman; the distinctions are within the intellectual capacity of lower levels, but they are rarely made at lower levels, particularly below E5.

Thoughtful consideration of the roles that society assigns to men and women, more or less in those terms, characterizes high levels. Men's concerns are often expressed in relation to playing a macho role.

The popular (for women) category, "be attractive, well groomed" (E4), discriminates poorly, but there are small variations on that topic at neighboring levels, including actions to improve appearance (E3), looking as attractive as possible (E5), and feelings about appearance (E6).

Themes:

Caution (E3–E6): be careful; work out; think before she speaks; use protection.

Norm (E2–E5): stay home; be clean; be attractive; be feminine.

Obligation (E2–E7): be nice; have a job; take care of his family; be responsible; do her best; be aware of the outside world.

Self (E2–E7): have money; be happy; be herself; be proud to be a woman; be human first.

Other (E4–E7): I don't know; breathe; nothing is that absolute.

ITEM 36: A WOMAN SHOULD ALWAYS...

E2 Impulsive

2-Norm

   a. —stay home, in a woman's place (4j)
     be at home

2-Obligation

   b. —be nice (4e)

2-Self

   c. —get what she wants; have things (5p)
     have money

E3 Self-Protective

3-Caution

   *a. —take care of herself (4a, 5o)
     care for herself
     look after herself first
   b. —be careful, watchful (5a, 6a)
     keep a good head on her shoulder
     look out for herself
     watch her enemy
     be on guard
   c. —be careful (in control) with men (6a)
     carry a contraceptive with her
     be cautious as to who she goes out with
     stay one step ahead of a man

3-Norm

   d. —be clean (4b)
     wash up
     clean up

3-Obligation

   e. —work

3-Self

   f. —be happy (5r)

E4 Conformist

4-Caution

   a. —keep herself in good health (3a, 6i)
     take care of her body
     be active
     give herself 5 minutes quiet time per day

4-Norm

   *b. —be neat, well-groomed, attractive (3d, 5c)
     be clean & neat
     be beautiful
   c. —look, dress nice (5c)
   d. Concrete actions related to appearance

     wear dresses
     wash her hair
   e. —be friendly, pleasant, polite (2b, 5e)
     have good manners
   f. —be respectable; keep a good reputation (6a)
     be decent
     keep herself virtuous
     protect herself and reputation
   g. —get married
     have a boyfriend

4-Obligation

   h. —be honest, truthful (5j, 6d, 6k)
     tell the truth
     be sincere
   i. —love (please, obey) her husband; be loving (5e, 5m)
     love her family
     be loving and thoughtful
   j. —be a good wife and mother (2a, 5f)
     take care of her children

4-Other

   k. —I don't know

E5 Self-Aware

5-Caution

   a. —think before she speaks (acts); be careful of what she says (does) (3b)

5-Norm

   **b. —be feminine, a lady, a woman; act feminine, like a lady, like a woman (6g)
     be a woman, dress right, talk right, walk right, and take care of herself
     present herself as a woman
     try to behave in a ladylike manner
     be a woman and in total control
     remember she's a lady
   *c. —look her best, as attractive as possible (4b, 4c, 6n)
     wear make-up & look the best she can!
     take proper care of herself—especially her skin and hair because her hair is her beauty
     keep her head up tall; be neat and smell good
   d. —be calm; maintain her dignity
     keep her composure
     be modest

5-Obligation

   e. —be kind, understanding (2b, 4e, 4i, 6e)
     be loving, caring and honest
     be caring
     be gracious
     listen
     be loving, kind, thoughtful, considerate

f. —keep her family happy; think of her family first; cater to her husband (4j)

make sure her children are taken well care of
let a man think he is the leader
be submissive to her husband/boyfriend
be there if her children need her

g. —do the right thing; be responsible (6c, 6d)

stand up for what's right

h. —be a good example; be a credit to her sex (6l)

be a good representative of God

i. —have outside interests; help others (7a)

have a career and be independent in case she gets divorced
get a good education

5-Self

**j. —be herself; be true to herself (4h, 6k, 7c)

be her own person
be true to what she feels inside

*k. —respect herself; be respected (6e, 7f)

be treated with respect
carry herself with respect

*l. —feel good about herself, confident (6j, 6n)

be positive about herself
think very well of herself, even if she has a child
do things that make her feel good

m. —love herself; be loved (4i)

feel like she is loved

*n. —stick up for her rights; have a mind of her own (6h, 6i)

remain strong
stand up for her career
stand her ground
be assertive
learn how to be aggressive
hold her own, and not be a follower
go her own way
say what is on her mind

*o. —strive for independence (3a)

be able to support herself
be able to care for herself financially as long as she is healthy
have their own bank account and their own job
feel self-sufficient
be able to take care of herself

p. —stand on her own; do what she wants to do (2c)

work to get what she wants
be in control of her own life
have complete control of herself

q. —be an individual; keep her identity (after marriage)

keep her self-identity in a relationship

r. —be optimistic; enjoy life; get the best out of life (3f, 6g)

have a good way of thinking about life
be able to relax around others
try to enjoy life to the fullest

feel comfortable in any situation

s. —express her emotions; say what she feels

be honest about her feelings
say what she really feels

E6 Conscientious

6-Caution

a. —protect herself from unwanted pregnancy, sexual assault (3b, 3c, 4f)

beware of rapists
use protection
be alert or at least look alert when walking among strangers at night or on bad streets

b. —be realistic, adaptable [unelaborated] (8a, 8b)

be ready to face any situation
be aware of how the world works and take care of herself
be her own self, not letting everything get to her, when problems arise

6-Obligation

*c. —do, be her best (5g)

try to do her best at whatever she's doing
strive for the best

d. —follow her conscience (4h, 5g)

respect herself and hold on to her values no matter what
live by her values she sets for herself
be able to stand up for what she believes in
take a stand for truth

e. —respect, show consideration for others (5e, 5k, 7f)

try to understand how others feel
love and respect her mate for what he is

f. —put God first

obey God
point others to Christ

6-Self

*g. —be proud to be a woman; enjoy being a woman (5b, 5r)

be proud of who she is
carry herself as a woman at all times no matter what
honor the feminine, remain in touch with the earth

*h. —try to be (feel) equal to men (5n)

have the same rights as a man
think like a man!
remember that she is not inferior to anyone
be able to get whatever a man gets

i. —consider her own needs, too (4a, 5n, 7a)

think of herself as being a person and take care of herself
take some time for herself
care about herself also and not just her family
be good to herself

j. —believe in herself; have self-esteem (5l)

keep her self up
keep her head up and her name clean
keep and guard her pride

k. —understand, be honest with herself (4h, 5j, 7b, 7c, 7d)
know what she wants in life
know her position in life
let her position be understood & know where she stands

*l. —set high goals; try to succeed (5h)
reach for the stars
be herself, an achiever
look for opportunities to learn anything
go for it all!
try to accomplish the most that she can, and set an example to others

m. —fulfill her potential; develop her abilities (7d)
feel she can achieve anything at any level
try to grow beyond what she is
push herself to her limits
become the best well-rounded person she possibly can

n. Feelings about appearance (5c, 5l)
walk with pride
be aware that her body is a powerful machine
protect herself, and care about her appearance

o. Balancing of opposites, one E5
be versatile: feminine at one time, yet aggressive and masculine at another time
be strong but retain femininity

p. Three different traits, one E5 (8c)
be herself, be clean, look her best, be independent and be happy
carry herself as a lady. Independent, courteous, kind, groom properly, & self-opinionated
look gorgeous, be well educated and have a lot of common sense
be clean, neat, think with her mind, have her eyes open & have a career & be independent

q. Contrast of physical and mental (emotional) (8c)
take care of herself in all ways—emotionally, physically, spiritually, & financially

6-Other

r. Humor (not hostile)
flush the toilet, finish tests—what?
keep her legs closed if she falls down

E7 Individualistic

7-Obligation

a. —be aware of (concerned about) the outside world [elaborated] (5i, 6i)
take into consideration the needs of others, but remember herself, because a woman cannot make others happy if she isn't happy

7-Self

b. —accept her limitations (6k, 8a)
know her limitations and not be afraid to ask for help

c. Overcome role stereotypes (5j, 6d, 6k)
stand up for what she believes and show society that she is not inferior and weak
be true to herself, not what society tells her she should be
go out and do what she must, even if others don't agree
be herself & don't try to be someone people want you to be
challenge herself to break out of traditional gender roles

d. Self-fulfillment (6k, 6m)
try to stay in touch with herself—her dreams, needs, wants
try her best to be the most true to her self-image
believe that her potential is achievable and strive for that
work on becoming a full human being
realize that she is what she wants to be
remember what makes her a special human being and celebrate it!

e. Share human qualities with men
be human first

f. —respect herself as well as respecting men (5k, 6e)

7-Other

g. —nothing is that absolute and universal
too absolute
feel that she doesn't ALWAYS have to do anything
try her best to get rid of words like "should" in her life

E8 Autonomous

a. Accept herself or others as they are (6b, 7b)
try to respect others and not be judgmental
choose roles that she believes are reflective of her true feelings of self
respect herself and love herself, and if she needs to improve, then work
be conscious of herself as a woman, for if she forgets, she will be shocked by both herself and responses she may elicit

b. —be able to adjust to life [elaborated]; strive for inner happiness and harmony (6b)
strive for balance in her life

c. Unclassified
have trust in relationship. Also be able to take care of herself alone in society
hunt for possibilities in improbable times and then take a risk
strive to be the most she can be for herself first and then her loved ones

ITEM 36: A MAN SHOULD ALWAYS . . .

E2 Impulsive

2-Obligation

b. —be nice (4e)

2-Self

c. —get what he wants; have things (5p)
make good money than women [sic]

E3 Self-Protective

3-Caution

a. —take care of himself (4a)
b. —be careful; watchful (5a)
be alert of everything
c. —be in control with women
be on top

3-Norm

d. —be clean (4b)
button his fly

3-Obligation

e. —work
keep a job
have a good job

3-Self

f. —be happy (5r)

E4 Conformist

4-Caution

a. —keep himself in good health (3a)
take time off
work out (exercise)

4-Norm

b. —be neat, well-groomed (3d)
c. —look, dress nice
d. Concrete actions related to appearance
walk erect
e. —be friendly, pleasant, polite (2b, 5e)
be on his best behavior
present himself in a good way
be a gentleman
have courtesy

4-Obligation

h. —be faithful, honest, truthful (5j, 6k)
be honest & loyal to his loved ones
i. —love his wife; be loving (5e)
love his family
*j. —take care of his family (5f)

protect his family
care for his family
support his wife

4-Other

k. —I don't know

E5 Self-Aware

5-Caution

a. —think before he speaks (acts); be careful of what
he says (does) (3b)
look at what he is doing
think twice

5-Norm

**b. —be a man; act like a man (6g)
be strong
d. —be calm; maintain his dignity
keep the stiff upper lip

5-Obligation

e. —be kind, understanding (4e, 4i)
care
be fair
help others
f. —keep his family happy (4j)
be supportive of his family
provide & take care of his family
be alert in protecting his family
*g. —do the right thing; be responsible (6c, 6d)
be honorable
practice what is good & right
live by priorities
remain solvent
i. —have outside interests; help others (7a)
take care of the weak

5-Self

**j. —be himself; be true to himself (4h, 6k)
be true to thine own self
be true to his feelings
k. —respect himself; be respected (6e, 7f)
l. —feel good about himself, confident (6j)
be comfortable with himself
feel special and loved by his mate
p. —stand on his own; do what he wants to do (2c)
stand tall
r. —be optimistic; enjoy life; get the best out of life
(3f, 6g)
take life with a smile and try harder
s. —express emotions; say what he feels

E6 Conscientious

6-Caution

  b. —be realistic, adaptable [unelaborated] (8a, 8b)
  have an open mind
  try to be objective
  strive to be open
  keep proper perspective

6-Obligation

  *c. —do, be his best (5g)
  try as hard as he can to become a better person for himself and family
  d. —follow his conscience (5g)
  stick by his virtues
  keep his integrity
  fight for what he believes in
  be accountable for his own actions
  e. —respect, show consideration for others (5k, 7f)
  respect himself and others
  treat women right (with respect)
  try not to purposely hurt someone else
  consider others' opinions
  f. —love God
  walk with the Lord
  rely on God's strength for a full life

6-Self

  g. —enjoy being a man (5b, 5r)
  enjoy his manhood
  j. —believe in himself; have self-esteem (5l)
  seek self-love and acceptance
  k. —understand, be honest with himself (4h, 5j, 7b)
  be honest with himself and others
  be in touch with his emotions
  l. —set high goals; try to succeed
  want to achieve goals
  m. —fulfill his potential; develop his abilities (7d)
  try his hardest to be a good person
  be no more and no less than what he is capable of being
  o. Balancing of opposites, one E5
  lead & give
  be strong, but also be able to show his emotions
  be firm yet considerate
  p. Three different traits, one E5 (8c)
  be honest, fair, and considerate of other
  be honest, brave, & beautiful
  be open, honest, and communicative
  q. Contrast of physical and mental (emotional) (8c)
  be physically & mentally balanced

6-Other

  r. Humor (not hostile)
  put the toilet seat down when finished!
  take care not to burp in public
  keep breathing if he wishes to live

E7 Individualistic

7-Obligation

  a. —be aware of (concerned about) the outside world [elaborated] (5i)
  be aware of the feelings and rights of others until they prove unworthy of that treatment
  strive for personal happiness while giving back something good to society
  consider himself in relation to others
  be ready to serve his town, his state, and his country in time of need

7-Self

  b. —accept his limitations (6k, 8a)
  be aware of his limitations and seek counsel from others in matters that he is weak
  be aware of how fallible he is
  c. Overcome role sterotypes
  be compassionate, considerate, and just a person instead of a "macho stud"
  be conscious of not over womanizing or over-powering his woman/wife
  d. Self-fulfillment (6m)
  set virtues and the pursuit thereof as one of the highest goals in his life and try to never waver from this attempt
  e. Share human qualities with women
  f. —respect men as well as respecting women (5k, 6e)
  respect others including: women, his fellowman, family, other families and most importantly God
  be honest and straightforward in all his relationships, family, business, social, etc.

7-Other

  g. —nothing is that absolute and universal
  ["always" crossed out] never be an always nothing—I don't like the word "should"

E8 Autonomous

  a. Accept himself or others as they are (6b, 7b)
  recognize his limitations, striving to improve where it's possible, but not wearing himself out trying to change
  b. —be able to adjust to life [elaborated] (6b)
  be adaptable and not let a single conviction rule his other thoughts
  weigh all the possible consequences of his actions & choose the one he thinks best for all . . .
  c. Unclassified (6p, 6q)
  be gentle and strong, commanding and understanding, practical and wishful, predictable and paradoxical
  be honest, open, and receptive to constructive criticism
  try to keep learning about himself and to be aware of how he thinks and feels

*be caring & considerate of the world's problems &
especially avoid to use his animal-like actions of
war to [illegible word]*

*try to keep in the back of his mind that each day
happens only once*

*try to be reasonably creative. Creativity is a major
human need*

*try to keep the big picture in mind when he does
things & not try too hard to justify himself by
making money*

Author and Subject Index